The
Southern Baptist
Mission in Japan,
1889-1989

F. Calvin Parker

UNIVERSITY
PRESS OF
AMERICA

Lanham • New York • London

Copyright © 1991 by
University Press of America®, Inc.
4720 Boston Way
Lanham, Maryland 20706

3 Henrietta Street
London WC2E 8LU England

ISBN 0–8191–8107–2 (cloth)
ISBN 0–8191–8108–0 (paper)

Acknowledgments

This book could not have been written without the encouragement and support of fellow missionaries and other friends. Hazel Watson suggested the project and insisted that I undertake it. She even xeroxed for my use a six-inch stack of materials left by missionary-historian Edwin Dozier.

Long before the word *xerox* was coined, Dozier spent many days at the Southern Baptist Foreign Mission Board copying reports and correspondence by hand in his tiny, tidy script. I found his papers invaluable, for they include detailed notes on the Japan Mission and its work for each year beginning in 1889 and continuing through 1963. These notes greatly enhance the value of his formal writings.

Other Doziers also contributed to the making of this book. Edwin's father Kelsey filled 17 diaries with thoughtful observations. His mother Maude wrote a history of Baptist women's work in Japan and a brief biography of her husband. More recently, Edwin's widow Mary Ellen recorded several audiocassettes for the Foreign Mission Board's oral history project.

Also useful were an insightful biography of Edwin Dozier by Lois Whaley; autobiographies by George Bouldin, Bob Culpepper, Bill Emanuel, Worth Grant, Cecile Lancaster, and Elizabeth Watkins; oral history recordings by Max Garrott, Dorothy Garrott, and Lucy Smith; and materials collected by Tom Masaki and the Christian History Project he launched in 1961. Details on these items can be found in the footnotes and bibliography.

I am further indebted to Frank K. Means, who retired from the Foreign Mission Board staff in 1977 but contributed his skills for many years as a research scholar. After conducting a pilot study on China in 1983, Means devoted 1984 to a "Japan Project," compiling summaries of a large quantity of material as background information for the Office of Communications to use in missions education and "as possible aid for person chosen to write the centennial history of Southern Baptist mission work in Japan." I profited greatly from these summaries and from conversations with their compiler.

Other personnel at the Board, especially in Jenkins Library and the archives, cheerfully gave assistance during my many visits to do research. Archivist Edie

Jeter pulled out numerous storage boxes and microfilms without complaint. The area director for East Asia, George Hays, followed by Sam James, granted permission for me to unseal bulging envelopes of restricted correspondence. Other persons kindly answered queries for information.

Fred S. Rolater, professor of history in Middle Tennessee State University and sometime exchange professor in Japan, read the first draft of my manuscript critically and prepared several pages of suggestions for improving it. Hap Bryant, Matsumi Takeshi, Johnni Johnson Scofield, and several members of the Mission read much of the manuscript and made helpful comments.

Harriett Parker prepared the rosters of missionaries and journeymen, and Barbara Darley typed the rosters. Victoria Bleick supplied photographs from Foreign Mission Board files and granted permission for their use. Norman F. Williamson, Jr., provided additional illustrations. Credit lines are given following the captions.

Several missionaries who read the original edition of this work (see Preface) took the trouble to point out errors that otherwise might have been carried into this revision. Luther Copeland, Glenn Gano, George Hays, and June Seat were especially helpful in this regard. Gene Hines kindly proofread the revised manuscript.

To all the above and others who have helped with this project, I am deeply grateful. I alone am to blame for any errors or deficiencies that remain.

Contents

List of Illustrations

Preface

This book was written originally for the Southern Baptist Mission in Japan, of which I was a member from 1951 to 1989. It was first published in Tokyo under the title, *Southern Baptist Missions in Japan: A Centennial History*. Intended primarily for current and former members of the Mission, the work was rushed into print prior to centennial celebrations held in August 1989. So auspicious an anniversary was deemed an appropriate time to review the history of this Christian enterprise so that the lessons of the past might be applied to the challenge of a new century.

The present work, issued under a different title, corrects the known errors in the original edition, includes new material in several chapters, and updates the story to the end of 1989. I have endeavored to make the work intelligible and interesting to the larger community of persons who have an interest in Christian missions in Japan. True, the foreign mission work done in one country by one denomination within the span of one century may seem unimportant against the backdrop of that enormous missionary enterprise of 20 centuries by which Christianity became the world's most influential religious faith. But of such parts the whole is formed, and to some degree each part encapsulates the whole. In today's world, moreover, Southern Baptists and the Japanese people both enjoy a prominence that has heightened the significance of the ties between the two.

The 14.9-million-member Southern Baptist Convention, America's largest Protestant body, has been called "the most successful missionary-minded Protestant denomination in the world."[1] In recent years it has been the most publicized denomination in the United States, though not because of its missionary work. The SBC has been embroiled in a power struggle, with "fundamentalists" consistently defeating "moderates" for control of its many institutions, boards, and commissions. This "uncivil war," so conspicuous in the media, has begun to rob

---

[1]Joe Edward Barnhart, *The Southern Baptist Holy War* (Austin: Texas Monthly Press, 1986), 163.

the denomination of its enormous strength.[2] In 1989, nevertheless, the SBC's Foreign Mission Board, with revenues of $179 million, supported 3,780 missionaries in 116 countries and sponsored more than 10,000 volunteers who served largely at their own expense.[3]

In Japan, the Southern Baptist Mission is the largest missionary body of any single Protestant denomination. In 1989 its 180 members (volunteers are not included in the count) were deployed on the four main islands and in Okinawa. They were engaged in virtually every type of missionary activity: church planting, pastoral leadership, education, music, medicine, social work, mass media, and other specialized ministries. The missionaries served in churches, schools, and medical institutions related to the 29,000-member Japan Baptist Convention and the 2,000-member Okinawa Baptist Convention. They also staffed Mission-sponsored institutions such as "friendship houses" and a modern communications center.

As for Japan itself, this economic superpower is a modern-day miracle, a marvel of productivity and prosperity. In land area it ranks 55th among the nations of the world, being roughly equal to the state of California or to Florida, Georgia, and South Carolina combined. Its population of 123.9 million is the seventh largest in the world, after China, India, the Soviet Union, the United States, Indonesia, and Brazil. Yet Japan is the fierce and feared economic archrival of the United States, which has twice the population, 25 times the land area, and incalculably more natural resources. It has replaced the United States as the world's largest donor of aid and supplier of capital. Japanese dollars even fund about 30 percent of the U.S. budget deficit.[4]

In 1988-89 Japanese interests gained control of such notable companies as Columbia Pictures, CBS Records, Firestone Tire & Rubber, Intercontinental Hotels, and the Rockefeller Group. Such acquisitions prompted a widespread outcry that Japan was "buying up America." To some alarmists it had replaced the Soviet Union as "the enemy." Yet the U.S. government and many business leaders urged even closer cooperation with the Japanese.

In 1989 Japan's per capita GNP (gross national product) exceeded that of the United States by $22,879 to $20,920. This gap is not reflected in living standards, however, because of higher prices and a severe shortage of land in Japan. Even so, Japan has the world's longest life expectancy--79.1 years--and the lowest rate

---

[2]*Wall Street Journal*, 25 Apr. 1990; Bill J. Leonard, *God's Last and Only Hope: The Fragmentation of the Southern Baptist Convention* (Grand Rapids: William B. Eerdmans Publishing Co., 1990), 4-9, 131-72.

[3]*Quarterly Review* 50, no. 4 (July Aug. Sept. 1990): 7, 51; Foreign Mission Board, SBC, "1989 Annual Report," supplement to the *Commission*, Mar. 1990.

[4]*Business Week*, 23 Apr. 1990, 46.

in infant mortality--5.5 per 1,000.[5] Crime is relatively scarce and illiteracy virtually unknown.

Japan has the advantage of a highly intelligent and educated population. Its advanced technology was well demonstrated in 1988 with the completion of the world's longest undersea tunnel (33.5 miles) and longest motorcar-train bridge system (5.8 miles).[6] Neither of these mammoth projects was undertaken, however, without the traditional religious ceremonies to placate any gods that might be disturbed by the construction. Religion is alive and well in Japan. Assorted new religions thrive alongside the ancient faiths of Buddhism and Shinto. But according to the 1990 *Kirisutokyō nenkan* (Japan Christian yearbook), the total membership of Roman Catholic, Orthodox, and Protestant churches is only 1,074,676, less than 1 percent of the population.[7] The larger Christian community is estimated at 3 percent.

Either way, the percentage is low, considering the heavy investment in efforts to convert the people. Since the introduction of Roman Catholicism in the mid-16th century and of Orthodoxy and Protestantism in the mid-19th century, many thousands of missionaries from Europe and North America have spent themselves in preaching the gospel. Converts have suffered persecution and repression from time to time, but full freedom of religion has prevailed since the end of World War II. Over the past four decades foreign missionaries have legally been permitted to enter in unlimited numbers, to stay a lifetime if they wish, and to spread their faith without hindrance. Japanese citizens are free to be baptized at any age, and the Christian faith seems to be no barrier to advancement in business or politics. Indeed, four of the postwar prime ministers--Yoshida, Katayama, Hatoyama, and Ōhira--have been Christians. Still, the ratio of believers to the population has remained flat over the last 20 years. Probably no other country so openly tolerant of Christian evangelism has been so resistant to conversion. It remains to be seen whether the death of Emperor Hirohito in January 1989 and the inauguration of a new era, Heisei, will result in more openness to the Christian way of life.

I suggested above that the prominence and peculiarity of Japan as a mission field, coupled with the prominence and peculiarity of Southern Baptists as missioners, endows this history with a significance greater than its narrow confines would indicate. Be that as it may, this work clearly fills a void. No other history of the Southern Baptist mission in Japan has appeared since the semicentennial volume by Edwin Dozier, *A Golden Milestone in Japan.*[8] Much has transpired

---

[5]*Asiaweek,* 5 Jan. 1990, 6, 13; *New York Times,* 7 Apr. 1990; *Asheville Citizen,* 6 Apr. 1990.
[6]*Japan Times,* 9 Apr. 1988.
[7]*Kirisutokyō nenkan, 1990,* 512-15. The total includes 92,267 Mormons.
[8]Edwin B. Dozier, *A Golden Milestone in Japan* (Nashville: Broadman Press, 1940). Dozier is cited hereafter as EBD.

since its publication in 1940, prior to Pearl Harbor and the Pacific War, and the 50 years that it covered need to be examined afresh from the vantage point of another half-century.

At this distance in time we can treat the early missionaries as historical figures whose lives are open to critical inspection. We need not gloss over their character flaws or errors of judgment. This realistic approach was unfeasible when Dozier wrote his history, for the pioneers or their children were still alive, and missionary hagiography was still in vogue. Among contemporary writers, it is generally agreed that only by dealing candidly with the human frailties and failures of the missionaries can the full scope of their commitment and achievements be rightly understood.

I have explored the lives of the Mission's forebears with the same curiosity that I would research my family's genealogy. I have tried to include enough biographical data to form a balanced picture of each subject, keeping in mind that details which fascinate one reader may seem tedious or even trite to another. However deficient the result, surely the heart of the Mission's history is the story of its missionaries.

The reader will notice that the second half of the book is far less biographical than the first half. Like Edwin Dozier a half-century ago, I respect the right to privacy of missionaries still living or recently died. Where they have chosen to disclose their feats and failures in autobiographies or other public communications, I have felt free to draw on this intelligence. I have tried scrupulously not to divulge any information, however savory or titillating, that might embarrass anyone. If I have portrayed some missionaries in glowing terms only, the reader is free to assume that a more objective treatment at a later date would depict them as no less fallible than their predecessors. We are all of the same clay.

Another reason for the shift away from biography in the latter part of the book is the growing number of persons involved in the action. Space limitations make it impractical to introduce those who came to Japan after the early 1950s, when the number of missionaries passed the 100 mark. I have made exceptions for singular achievement or death while in service, but the chapters on the last three decades deal mainly with group activities, movements, and events. In A.D. 2039, perhaps, a sesquicentennial history may do justice to the more prominent missionaries of the present generation.

One may get the impression that this book slights Japanese Baptists, so limited is the space devoted to them. Admittedly, it contrasts sharply with Dozier's *Golden Milestone*, which is adorned with inspiring life sketches of their prominent leaders. One should bear in mind that Dozier's book is the English version of a history prepared for Japanese Baptists as well as Southern Baptists. The present work, aimed at a wider readership, focuses on the Mission and its members-- their characteristics, accomplishments, and interpersonal relationships.

From the outset, of course, the missionaries had frequent contacts with Japanese people, with whom they formed close and meaningful bonds. They freely acknowledged that their Japanese coworkers contributed more to the evangelization of Japan than they themselves. This is all the more true today. The Baptist witness in Japan is primarily and overwhelmingly the witness of Japanese Baptists, not of missionaries from abroad. But it lies beyond the scope of the present work to demonstrate this truth. The history of Japanese Baptists requires separate treatment, however intertwined it may be with the history of the Mission.

A brief explanation of some textual matters may be helpful. To conserve space, the familiar abbreviation SBC is used for Southern Baptist Convention. Several oft-used terms are capitalized to convey a particular meaning. Unless the context indicates otherwise, "Board" refers to the Foreign Mission Board of the SBC, "Mission" refers to the organization of Southern Baptist missionaries in Japan, and "Convention" refers to the Japan Baptist Convention or its prewar antecedents. The word "convention" is not capitalized when it indicates a general meeting of delegates (or "messengers") rather than the Convention as an organization.

In the main text, Japanese personal names are given in the Japanese order of surname first. In the footnotes, the names are given as they appear in the works cited.

Japanese vowels and diphthongs are pronounced approximately as follows:

a as in father
e as in red
i as in machine
o as in bone
u as in rule
ai as in aisle
ei as in eight

A macron over an *ō* or *ū* indicates that the pronunciation is prolonged. I have omitted the macrons from place names that occur frequently in the text: the islands of Honshū, Hokkaidō, and Kyūshū; and the cities of Tōkyō, Kyōto, Ōsaka, and Kōbe. The macrons on these names are retained in the index and when the name occurs as part of a Japanese title.

Consonants in Japanese terms are generally pronounced as in English. The doubling of a consonant indicates a protraction of its sound.

To reduce the number of footnotes, all the citations within a paragraph are normally grouped in a single note. Direct quotations are cited first, in the order of their appearance in the paragraph. In preparing the manuscript I generally have followed *The Chicago Manual of Style*, 13th edition (1982). A notable exception is my use of numerals for numbers over nine, as recommended by *The MLA Style Manual* (1985).

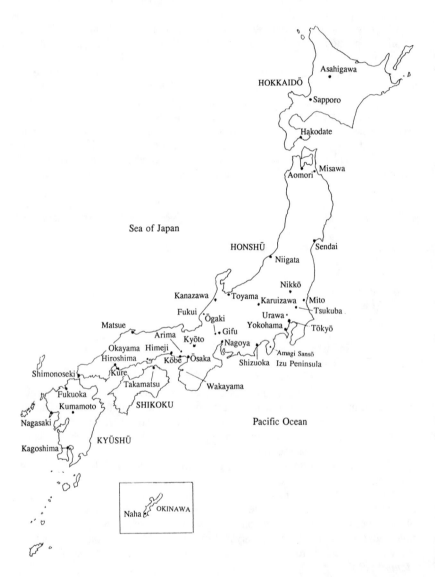

Map of Japan, showing places mentioned in text. See page 36 for Kyūshū in greater detail.

1

Introduction: Sitting Out an Era

The Southern Baptist Convention was organized in 1845 at Augusta, Georgia, for the purpose of conducting missionary work and other benevolent enterprises at home and abroad. Previously, Baptists in both the South and the North had conducted such enterprises through voluntary participation in national societies, most notably the Triennial Convention. By 1845 a number of sectional differences among Baptists had raised insuperable barriers to North-South cooperation. The most serious difference lay in clashing attitudes toward slavery, an institution peculiar to the South and deeply entrenched in its economy and mores.[1]

The SBC was organized as a centralized, exclusive denomination with "separate and distinct Boards, for each object of benevolent enterprise." Unlike the autonomous societies, these boards were made accountable to the convention rather than to individuals who contributed to their support. Established in 1845 were the Board of Domestic Missions in Marion, Alabama, site of two Baptist schools; and the Foreign Mission Board in Richmond, Virginia, an older bastion of Baptist influence.[2]

The Foreign Mission Board adopted China as its first mission field. Baptist missionaries from the South were already at work in that country under the Triennial Convention, and China's huge population (350 million), ancient culture, and religious variety continued to pose an irresistible challenge. In the following years the Board also gave attention to Africa, establishing missions in Liberia,

[1]Robert A. Baker, *The Southern Baptist Convention and Its People* (Nashville: Broadman Press, 1974), 161-76. "Triennial Convention" is shorthand for the General Missionary Convention of the Baptist Denomination in the United States of America for Foreign Missions.

[2]William B. Johnson, quoted in Robert A. Baker, *A Baptist Source Book* (Nashville: Broadman Press, 1966), 114; William Wright Barnes, *The Southern Baptist Convention 1845-1953* (Nashville: Broadman Press, 1954), 31-32. The schools in Marion were Howard College and Judson Female Institute.

Nigeria, and Sierra Leone. Then, in the second half of the 1850s, it took steps to enter Japan.[3]

Most of Japan's 30 million people lived by two dominant religions: Shinto, the primitive "way of the gods," and Mahayana Buddhism, introduced in the sixth century A.D. with a superior Chinese civilization. By a gradual process Buddhism had been accommodated to the indigenous Shinto faith. Chinese Taoism and Confucianism also exerted widespread influence.[4]

An intriguing legend persists that Jesus Christ made his way to Japan in the first century after a look-alike brother died in his place on the cross, and evidence has been cited of a Nestorian presence in the eighth century. But most scholars ignore these claims as without substance. They agree that Christianity was introduced in 1549 by Francis Xavier, the fiery Basque Jesuit who was later canonized and named patron of all missions.[5]

The mid-16th century was a propitious time for Xavier to offer a new faith to the Japanese. The nation had been devastated by more than 80 years of peasant uprisings, samurai revolts, and incessant warfare among the clans. Buddhism was in decline. Moreover, the welcome mat was out for Europeans, since they could supply the armaments then in demand. During his one-time stay of 27 months, Xavier made a thousand converts and inaugurated "the Christian century in Japan." So fruitful were the ministries of the Jesuits, and of the friars who joined them in the 1590s, that the number of converts rose to 300,000, or 1.5 percent of the population (estimated at 20 million).[6]

This phenomenal success bred suspicion. By 1600, when the country had been pacified and unified by a succession of able generals, the Christian faith had come to be viewed as politically subversive. In 1614 the ruling Tokugawa clan began to expel missionaries and force Japanese converts to recant. Over 2,100 believers chose martyrdom, while thousands more recanted outwardly but preserved their faith in secret.[7] So determined was the government to rid Japan of this "evil religion" and prevent reinfection in the future, that it adopted a strict policy of

---

[3]*Encyclopedia of Southern Baptists*, vol. 2, s.v. "Foreign Mission Board" (hereafter cited as *ESB*).

[4]A helpful treatment of each of these religions is found in *Kodansha Encyclopedia of Japan* (Tokyo: Kodansha, 1983).

[5]*Kodansha Encyclopedia of Japan*, s.v. "Christianity." The Jesus-in-Japan legend has been discussed in many periodicals, among them *Nippon Times*, 24 Dec. 1952; *Times* (London), 28 Dec. 1970; *Chicago Daily News*, 2 Aug. 1971; and *Tokyo*, 1 Sept. 1977, 38-39. The Nestorian evidence is summarized in John M. L. Young, *By Foot to China* (Tokyo, 1984), 18-20.

[6]C. R. Boxer, *The Christian Century in Japan* (Berkeley: University of California Press, 1951), 39, 320-21. On the number of converts, see also Joseph Jennes, *A History of the Catholic Church in Japan* (Tokyo: Oriens Institute, 1973), 240-41.

[7]Boxer (*Christian Century in Japan*, 448) gives 2,128 as the total number of martyrs, and Jennes (*Catholic Church*, 245) gives 2,126. Apparently there were "many others" not included in these counts.

national seclusion, permitting no contacts with the outside world except for tightly controlled trade with Dutch and Chinese merchants at Nagasaki. For more than two centuries the shores of the 1,500-mile-long archipelago were virtually sealed.

The first Protestant overtures to Japan of lasting import were made in 1837. An American merchant and three missionaries assigned to China attempted to open a breach in the wall of seclusion by returning seven Japanese castaways to their homeland. The party sailed into Tokyo Bay aboard the unarmed *Morrison*, a smelly merchant brig named after Robert Morrison, the first Protestant missionary to China. Despite the humanitarian aspect of their mission, the intruders were fired upon by shore batteries and chased away by gunboats, barely escaping destruction. The *Morrison* made a second attempt to return the homesick castaways at Kagoshima, the southern port where Xavier had entered Japan. There the ship was furnished with fresh water but again bombarded without warning. Frightened and disappointed, the *Morrison* party returned to Macao.[8]

Yet all was not lost. Two of the missionaries, Karl Gützlaff and S. Wells Williams, learned a smattering of Japanese from the castaways and led some of them to faith in Christ. With the assistance of these castaways, Gützlaff translated and published the Gospel and the Epistles of John--the oldest extant Scripture portions printed in the Japanese language. Williams translated the Gospel of Matthew, and his manuscript was later made available to Protestant pioneers in Japan. The third missionary, Dr. Peter Parker, and the expedition's leader, Charles W. King, each wrote a book about the thwarted attempt to return the seven castaways. These books proved influential in arousing among Protestants a deep concern for evangelizing Japan.[9]

Protestant mission leaders were joined by politicians, traders, whalers, scientists, adventurers, and others in calling for the opening of Japan. Further attempts were made to bring it about, though without success. It remained for Commodore Matthew C. Perry's carefully planned expedition of 1853-54 to pry open "that double-bolted land," as Herman Melville described Japan in *Moby Dick*. Commodore Perry, an Episcopalian said to read through the Bible on every cruise, forced the Tokugawa regime--without bloodshed--to sign a treaty of

---

[8]C. W. King and G. T. Lay, *The Claims of Japan and Malaysia upon Christendom* (New York, 1839), xx, 126-29, 153-57; P. Parker, *Journal of an Expedition from Singapore to Japan* (London, 1838), 1-2, 41, 50, 57, 73; S. Wells Williams, "Narrative of a voyage of the ship Morrison," *Chinese Repository* 6 (1837): 209-29.

[9]The books by Parker and King are given in note 8 above. On the translation work of Gützlaff and Williams, see *Bible Society Record* 25 (1880): 81-82; and Bernardin Schneider, "Japan's Encounter with the Bible," *Japan Christian Quarterly* 48 (1982): 69-71 (hereafter cited as *JCQ*).

friendship that American evangelicals hailed as the work of Providence, the first step toward opening the country to the gospel.[10]

Jonathan Goble, afterwards the first Baptist missionary sent to Japan, accompanied the expedition as "a guardsman to Commodore Perry."[11] His stated intention was to spy out the land for evangelistic work. Both during and after the treaty negotiations, the pious marine from upstate New York went ashore and fraternized with the Japanese. "The time is near at hand," he wrote in his journal, "when they shall open their arms to receive the savior of the world."[12] Goble's confident hope was rekindled a few years later when Townsend Harris negotiated a commercial treaty that permitted Americans to reside in designated Japanese ports beginning in July 1859. The treaty specified that Americans could erect church buildings and enjoy freedom of worship.[13] After two centuries of self-imposed isolation to keep out the hated foreign faith, the Japanese would have to tolerate the presence of Christian propagandists on their sacred soil.

Southern Baptists Are Drawn to Japan

Since Japan lay off the coast of China and had been strongly influenced by its culture and religion, Christian missionaries in China naturally followed with deep interest the unfolding drama of the island nation's opening to the West. One Southern Baptist missionary was so desirous of starting a mission in Japan that "he offered, should the Board deem it advisable, and if no suitable man could be found to commence, to go himself and make a beginning."[14]

In 1855 the Foreign Mission Board reported to the biannual meeting of the SBC that "enquiries have been made about entering Japan." At the 1857 convention the Committee on New Foreign Fields offered a resolution directing the Board to enlarge the scope of its work and to "watch the providence of God,

---

[10]The official record of the Perry Expedition is Francis L. Hawks, *Narrative of the Expedition of an American Squadron to the China Seas and Japan* (Washington, 1856). On Perry as a Bible reader, see William Elliot Griffis, *Matthew Calbraith Perry: A Typical American Naval Officer* (Boston, 1887), 404.

[11]Goble to S. Wells Williams, quoted in F. Calvin Parker, *Jonathan Goble of Japan: Marine, Missionary, Maverick* (Lanham, Md.: University Press of America, 1990), 31.

[12]Keith Seat, ed., "Jonathan Goble's Book," in *Transactions of the Asiatic Society of Japan*, 3d ser., vol. 16 (Tokyo, 1981), 130. Goble's journal entry is dated 18 Apr. 1854.

[13]Article 8 of the treaty, which deals with religious freedom, is cited in Otis Cary, *A History of Christianity in Japan* (1909; reprint, 2 vols. in 1, Tokyo: Charles E. Tuttle Co., 1976), 2:39.

[14]*Commission* 3 (Jan. 1859): 219. In references to this and other periodicals of the Foreign Mission Board, SBC, I generally have omitted the authors and titles of short pieces, many of which are unsigned editorials. The China missionary quoted is unnamed but was probably Matthew T. Yates.

as it now points to Japan and South America, as important and prominent fields of missionary labor." The resolution was adopted.[15]

The 1859 convention, held in the Board's own city of Richmond, drew an attendance of 580 delegates, the highest number on record prior to 1883. On foreign missions night, stirring addresses were given by Matthew T. Yates of China and W. H. Clarke of Central Africa. Who could have foreseen that Yates would advocate a mission in Japan as long as he lived or that Clarke would give a son and a grandson as missionaries to Japan? At this convention the Committee on New Foreign Fields specifically recommended the opening of work in Japan and Brazil and supported its recommendations with a lengthy report on each country. The report on Japan offered three "facts" that urged the start of a mission there.[16]

First, said the committee, "Japan seems to be thrown particularly on the hands of American Christians." British Christians showed little interest, for they were preoccupied with the evangelization of peoples within the widespread British Empire, particularly in Africa and India. The Protestant societies of other European countries likewise had no immediate plans to enter Japan. As the committee pointed out, an American naval mission had opened the locked doors of Japan, and an American diplomat had wrung from Japanese negotiators the first commercial treaty with a Western country. Great Britain, France, the Netherlands, Germany, and Russia had followed suit and concluded their own treaties with Japan, but America had taken the lead and forged a unique relationship with its Pacific neighbor. It turned out, in fact, that during the first 10 years of Protestant missions in Japan, American boards and societies had the field to themselves.[17]

Second, said the committee, "the way is now fairly open." No longer was that nation of 30 million people "the impenetrable, the hopeless Japan." Not only were missionaries guaranteed protection in the treaty ports, but those who had visited the port of Nagasaki prior to its formal opening had been warmly received by local officials. An Episcopal bishop from China had stated in a Richmond lecture that a missionary of his denomination, E. W. Syle, during a brief call at Nagasaki in 1858, was invited by the vice governor to return to the city and teach English under government auspices. Syle was promised a house and the freedom to teach Christianity to his students.[18]

---

[15]*Proceedings* (or *Annual*) *of the Southern Baptist Convention, 1855*, 41 (hereafter cited as *ASBC*); *ASBC, 1857*, 15 .

[16]*ESB*, vol. 1, 1258; *ASBC, 1859*, 48, 51-53. Yates's life-long support for Japan is described in the next chapter. Clarke's son Harvey served in Japan 1898-1936, and his grandson Coleman served 1948-76.

[17]*ASBC, 1859*, 51-52. The Church Missionary Society of England broke the American monopoly when it sent George Ensor to Nagasaki in 1869.

[18]*ASBC, 1859*, 52. Cf. O. Cary, *History*, 2:40-41. The bishop was William J. Boone.

In early 1859 a Northern Baptist missionary-physician, D. J. Macgowan, spent five weeks in Nagasaki while en route from Ningpo, China, to the United States for furlough. He was permitted this extended residence prior to the port's formal opening in July in return for his temporary services as an English teacher. His students, members of the Chinese interpreters' guild, were allowed to keep a few religious books and papers in Chinese that Macgowan gave them, though not the English-Chinese New Testaments he offered.[19] The hospitality shown to Syle and Macgowan in Nagasaki suggested that mature and discreet workers sent to Japan would be able to overcome the dreadful bias against Christianity, a bias stemming from early Roman Catholic involvement in Japanese politics and reinforced by Protestant misdeeds in the China opium wars.

The Committee on New Fields offered one more "fact" about Japan: "Other Mission Boards have seen the importance of such a field, and are pressing forward with praiseworthy alacrity to enter it." The Episcopal board voted to transfer to Japan two of its most promising single men in China, John Liggins and Channing Moore Williams. Both were graduates of the Episcopal Theological Seminary in Virginia. The Presbyterian board reappointed James C. Hepburn, a New York physician who earlier had served in a mission hospital in Amoy, China. The American Dutch Reformed board, which had a unique interest in Japan because of that nation's long-time commercial ties with Holland, appointed three men: Samuel Robbins Brown, a Yale-trained educator and pastor who had taught school in Macao; Duane B. Simmons, a physician with literary talent; and Guido F. Verbeck, a Dutch-born engineer-turned-minister who spoke four European languages. The Methodists made no appointments to Japan in 1859 but were raising money for a mission there.[20]

Since the evangelization of Japan was primarily an American responsibility, the country was fairly open to missionary efforts, and the mission boards of other denominations were responding quickly to the long-awaited opportunity, the challenge confronting Southern Baptists, said the committee report, was to match the other denominations in sending out highly qualified missionaries without delay. The report was adopted.

Soon after the 1859 convention, the Board received a long and eloquent call for prompt action from A. B. Cabaniss, a missionary in Shanghai. Cabaniss pointed out that many preparatory years would be required for learning the Japanese language, translating the scriptures, and adapting to the culture. "Such is the embarrassed state of the Missionary Union at the North," he added, "they can scarcely support the missions they already have. The Baptists of England seem to have so much to do in other quarters, they are not turning their attention in this direction. Thus Providence seems to devolve it upon the Southern Baptist

---

[19]Macgowan letter in *Baptist Missionary Magazine* 39 (Sept. 1859): 331-36.
[20]*ASBC, 1859*, 52-53; O. Cary, *History*, 2:45-50. Methodists did not enter Japan until 1874.

Convention to start a mission in Japan, if we think they ought to have Baptist as well as Pedo-baptist preaching."[21]

Cabaniss was correct in his assessment. The American Baptist Missionary Union, organized in 1845 as successor to the Triennial Convention, was hard pressed to sustain its missionaries in Burma, India, China, and other fields. For several years it had been embroiled in disputes over slavery and mission polity at home and abroad, disputes that had caused income to fall and debts to mount. The Baptist Missionary Society of London was also in financial straits. In response to an inquiry from Jonathan Goble, its officers reported that "their present responsibilities, and the state of the Society's funds, utterly preclude any attempt to undertake a mission to Japan."[22]

Likewise, the American Baptist Free Mission Society, an organization not mentioned by Cabaniss, lacked the means to enter Japan. This "little society," widely despised because it was stridently abolitionist, was struggling to sustain a few workers in Burma and to reopen work in Haiti that had been discontinued. To enter Japan at this time, its executive board reported, would be "rash and improvident."[23]

Though strapped for funds, the Free Mission Society was confronted with an irresistible candidate, Jonathan Goble. He had won acclaim for bringing to the States a Japanese castaway nicknamed Sam Patch. Both men had enrolled in the academy at Madison (now Colgate) University in Hamilton, New York. There Sam had been converted and baptized, becoming the first known Japanese Baptist and a potential missionary as Goble's assistant. Even Commodore Perry, before his death in 1858, had encouraged Goble's return to Japan for religious work.[24]

"Certainly the Board," said the Free Mission Society's 1859 report, "would not themselves have sought out that hitherto most inaccessible island of the farthest East, as a field of labor at the present time."[25] Providence, it seemed, had thrust an obligation upon them. So Goble was appointed in May 1859 and sent out among the widely-scattered Free Mission churches with his wife Eliza to raise their own support.

In sharp contrast to these other Baptist organizations, the Foreign Mission Board of the SBC recruited volunteers for Japan with unbridled enthusiasm. This board alone had the resources to meet the challenge. SBC membership had grown from 404,600 in 1849 to 639,240 in 1859, and the Board's receipts had increased from $16,727 to $39,823 in the same period. Obviously, the antimissionary

---

[21]Cabiness letter of 26 Apr. 1859 in *Commission* 4 (Aug. 1859): 42-43.

[22]Baptist Missionary Society, Minutes, 1 Nov. 1864, Baptist Missionary Society Archives, London (microfilm, reel 3, vol. 19, SBC Historical Commission, Nashville); Robert G. Torbet, *Venture of Faith* (Philadelphia: Judson Press, 1955), 124-45; *American Baptist*, 31 May 1859.

[23]*American Baptist*, 7 June 1859, 16 Mar. 1858.

[24]Parker, *Jonathan Goble of Japan*, 1, 76-78.

[25]*American Baptist*, 7 June 1859.

sentiment fostered by hyper-Calvinism and Campbellism was losing ground. Southern Baptists were giving far more generously to missions than before the separation from Northern Baptists in 1845.[26]

The First Appointees

In April 1859, John Q. A. Rohrer, a native of Maryland, stood before the Board as a candidate for appointment. His gentle and polished manner impressed the examiners, as did his religious and academic credentials. Formerly a member of the Winebrennarian Church of God, Rohrer had joined a Baptist church and volunteered for foreign missions while studying medicine at Lewisburg (now Bucknell) University in Pennsylvania. The Board voted unanimously to appoint him with "his field to be determined hereafter." Later he was assigned to Japan "at his own request."[27]

In May, Crawford H. Toy contacted the Board. "I desire to devote my life to preaching the gospel to the Japanese," he wrote. While a student in the University of Virginia, Toy had been baptized by John A. Broadus, eminent pastor of the Charlottesville Baptist Church, and inspired by a Broadus sermon to serve overseas. After receiving his M.A. degree, he had taught at the Baptist-sponsored Albemarle Female Institute, where his star pupil was Lottie Moon, future patron saint of Southern Baptist foreign missions.[28]

Crawford Toy met the highest expectations of the Board. He was brilliant, humble, pious, and--like Adoniram Judson, the first American Baptist missionary to serve overseas--committed to "mission for life." Toy was appointed to Japan in July 1859 with the understanding that he would delay his sailing one year, in order to attend the newly founded Southern Baptist Theological Seminary in Greenville, South Carolina. He wished to acquire more Hebrew and engage in other biblical and theological studies that would enhance his qualifications for translating the Bible into Japanese.[29]

After entering the seminary in Greenville, Toy informed the Board that he still hoped to sail for Japan in the fall of 1860 but preferred to have a companion to go with him. The prospects of finding a "proper wife" were slim, Toy admitted. So he suggested that John L. Johnson, a candidate for appointment to Canton,

---

[26]Barnes, *Southern Baptist Convention*, 41-42, 306.

[27]Foreign Mission Board, SBC, minutes, 4 June 1859 (hereafter cited as FMB minutes), Foreign Mission Board Archives, Richmond, Va. (hereafter, FMBA); H. A. Tupper, *Foreign Missions of the Southern Baptist Convention* (Philadelphia, 1880), 247-48.

[28]Toy to J. B. Taylor, 18 May 1859, FMBA; Billy Grey Hurt, "Crawford Howell Toy: Interpreter of the Old Testament" (Ph.D. diss., Southern Baptist Theological Seminary, 1965), 15-16. Unless otherwise indicated, correspondence between a missionary and a Board official is found in FMBA under the missionary's name.

[29]FMB minutes, 15 July 1859.

China, be assigned to Japan instead. Johnson was a fellow Virginian and college friend who, like Toy, had volunteered for foreign missions under Broadus's ministry. Wrote Toy to the Board: "It is true you have few laborers at Canton-- but there are still fewer in Japan. [Johnson] will draw me out to visit, to mingle with the people. I will keep him down to books. We will correct each the other's wrong tendencies, and so make the best substitute, each to the other, for a wife."[30]

Toy got his wish. When Johnson was appointed in December, "Japan was agreed upon as his field of labor, & the time of his embarkation to be next fall."[31] Thus by the end of 1859 the Board had matched the Dutch Reformed record of three appointments to Japan. There was a significant difference, however. The Reformed appointees, already married and ready to sail, arrived in Japan with their families within the year. The Baptist appointees were single and unordained, and none was expected to sail before the summer or fall of 1860.

Rohrer was the first of the trio to gain a wife. In April 1860 he married Sarah Robinson, a well-educated Pennsylvanian who had taken advanced musical training in New England. Sarah was reviewing her French and German for possible use in Japan, and she planned to take her piano and guitar in hopes that they would "win the Japanese females to civilization and religion, and also be a source of living, if anything should deprive them of support."[32]

Ironically, Sarah had been baptized by A. L. Post, president of the American Baptist Free Mission Society. This abolitionist society often attacked the Board on grounds that it dispatched "Pro-slavery missionaries" and paid them from its "Robbery" funds contributed by "Christian merchants in the souls of men." Post must have been appalled that Sarah would marry a man whose roots were in Maryland, a slave state, and who, though bearing the full name of an antislavery president (John Quincy Adams), had accepted appointment from a slavery-tainted board. John and Sarah both joined the SBC-related First Baptist Church of Baltimore, where John was ordained to the ministry.[33]

While the Rohrers were preparing for service overseas, John Johnson fell prey to typhoid and measles. At the May 1860 Board meeting it was reported that "the condition of his health has raised anew the question of expediency as to his going abroad next fall." The Board agreed to leave the decision to Johnson himself. On June 10 he was sufficiently recovered to be ordained together with Crawford Toy in the Charlottesville church. One month later he married Toy's sister Julia. The

[30]Toy to A. M. Poindexter, 4 Oct., 12 Dec. 1859, FMBA.
[31]FMB minutes, 6 Dec. 1859.
[32]Tupper, *Foreign Missions*, 247-48.
[33]Ibid., 249; *American Baptist*, 28 May 1857, 1, 22 May 1860; *Commission* 4 (Oct. 1859): 120.

groom was 24, the bride was 17. Their marriage had been planned with a view to their departure for Japan in autumn.[34]

On August 3 John and Sarah Rohrer sailed from New York on the *Edwin Forrest*, a small ship named for the successful but beleaguered actor. The vessel was bound for Hong Kong; the Rohrers' ultimate destination was Kanagawa, the treaty port near Edo (Tokyo). Among the well-wishers who boarded the vessel before its departure was Sarah's mother, who dreaded the separation from her only child. "Mother," Sarah told her, "with the exception of parting with you, this is the happiest day of my life. If we are lost at sea, death will find us in the path of duty."[35]

During that August, Jesse and Eliza Hartwell, Southern Baptist missionaries in Shanghai, were visiting Jonathan and Eliza Goble in Kanagawa. The Gobles had arrived in April and obtained a house in the same Buddhist temple compound as the Presbyterian Hepburns and the Dutch Reformed Browns. Jesse asked Jonathan to find a house for the Rohrers. The abolitionist was flustered enough at having to entertain the Hartwells, for he believed it a sin to fellowship with Christians who compromised on slavery. Yet he agreed "out of kindness" to assist the Rohrers, "though resolved to have no connection with them."[36]

This dilemma Goble never had to face. The Rohrers died "in the path of duty" when the *Edwin Forrest* was lost at sea without a trace. Said a China missionary: "I hear their ship was carrying coal. It often catches fire at sea and probably did so."[37]

Crawford Toy spent much of the summer and early fall of 1860 promoting the cause of missions in his home association at Portsmouth, Virginia, which had voted to adopt him as its missionary and raise $1,000 annually for his support. Meanwhile, John Johnson's health continued delicate, and it was decided that he and Julia should remain at least a year in America. He accepted positions as a pastor and school teacher. Toy resigned himself to sailing for Japan alone.[38]

Unfortunately, the lower South was resolved to secede from the Union if a "black Republican"--Abraham Lincoln--was elected president in the November election. Lincoln's subsequent victory cast a pall over the December 3 meeting of the Foreign Mission Board. The Board expressed concern that its income would

---

[34]FMB minutes, 7 May 1860; Catherine B. Allen, *The New Lottie Moon Story* (Nashville: Broadman Press, 1980), 37; Hurt, "Toy," 31; L. S. Foster, *Mississippi Baptist Preachers* (St. Louis, 1895), 398.

[35]Tupper, *Foreign Missions*, 249-50; *Commission* 5 (Aug. 1860): 77; *New York Times*, 2, 3 Aug. 1860. The Rohrers were accompanied by Alfred and Helena Bond, Southern Baptist appointees to Shanghai. The only other passengers reported aboard were Mrs. B. W. Crocker with child and servant, and Mr. and Mrs. J. E. Watkins.

[36]Goble letter in *American Baptist*, 8 Jan. 1861; Jesse Hartwell letter in *Commission* 5 (Feb. 1861): 233-34.

[37]T. P. Crawford to J. B. Taylor, 3 Oct. 1861, FMBA.

[38]Hurt, "Toy," 32-33; Foster, *Mississippi Preachers*, 400.

be affected by the "political distractions and commercial pressures now prevailing." It also noted that contributions were being withheld because of "a very general failure of crops" and divisions in the denomination such as those stemming from the Landmark controversy.[39]

One week later, on December 10, Toy wrote to the Board from his home in Norfolk: "I am anxious to start as soon as possible, and can be ready by the first of January." Since the Portsmouth Association had agreed to provide his support, Toy argued, "I would entail on the Board no new expense besides the passage money." On December 13, however, the Board, fearing economic disruption, voted "to decline for the present sending out more missionaries." On January 1, 1861, Toy wrote again, urging the Board "to engage passage immediately." But the Board held firm to its decision and allowed no exception, not even for Crawford Toy.[40]

If the Rohrers, the Johnsons, and Toy had made it to Japan in 1860 or 1861, they would have been kindly received and aided by the Presbyterian, Reformed, and Episcopal missionaries on the field. Only Goble the Baptist would have snubbed them for their cultural and denominational ties to slavery. Among those at Kanagawa, Clara Hepburn, a gracious and hospitable North Carolinian, was being supported by Southern Presbyterians, who separated from Northern Presbyterians in 1860. Her husband James, though an antislavery Pennsylvanian, had no objection to this arrangement. Clara showed her loyalty to the Confederacy throughout the war by attending British church services in the foreigners' settlement while James attended the American services. Robbins Brown also had intimate ties with the "rebels," having attended seminary in South Carolina for two years. So did James and Margaret Ballagh, Reformed missionaries sent to the same temple compound in 1861. Margaret was a Virginian, raised in a home attended by slaves. Had the Southern Baptists gone to Nagasaki, they would have been welcomed by Virginian C. M. Williams, afterwards Episcopal bishop of Japan, and polyglot Guido Verbeck, who would have found much in common with Toy.[41]

Brown, Hepburn, and Verbeck ranked among the best educated and most gifted missionaries to be found anywhere in the world. All three were musicians, and each was a competent Bible translator, educator, and evangelist. Yet Johnson, Toy, and Rohrer were roughly their equals, even if bound to the narrower cultural

---

[39]FMB minutes, 3 Dec. 1860.

[40]Toy to Taylor, 10 Dec. 1860, 1 Jan. 1861; FMB minutes, 13 Dec. 1860.

[41]On the Hepburns: J. C. Hepburn to W. Lowrie, 23 Apr. 1862, Japan letters, Presbyterian Historical Society, Philadelphia; Edwin B. Lee, "Robert H. Pruyn in Japan, 1862-1865," *New York History* 66 (1985): 136. On S. R. Brown: William Elliot Griffis, *A Maker of the New Orient* (New York: Fleming H. Revell, 1902), 51. On Margaret Ballagh: Lyle Kinnear to author, 7 Nov. 1984. On Verbeck and Williams: Frank Cary, *History of Christianity in Japan* (Tokyo: Kyo Bun Kwan, 1959), 172-80, 184-87.

strictures of the South. For the Board to recruit men of this caliber was no small achievement. When Johnson and Toy were enrolled in the University of Virginia, the school had less than 500 students and yet was the largest university in America. The total enrollment of all colleges and universities in the United States was only 12,000.[42] Among this student elite Johnson and Toy stood high, as their subsequent careers indicate.

After the Civil War erupted in April 1861, Johnson served as a cavalry chaplain in the Confederate army. In the postwar years he was pastor of strong churches in Portsmouth and Norfolk. Later he was professor of English in the University of Mississippi and president of two colleges, simultaneously serving as pastor of small, hard-pressed churches. He also was president of the Mississippi Baptist Mission Board and editor of the *Baptist Layman*. Appropriately, he was awarded honorary degrees by state universities as well as Baptist colleges. Throughout his life, whatever his position, Johnson did the work of an evangelist; his eloquence and ardor led to numerous baptisms in many churches. Despite the health problems that plagued him in 1860, his was a long life of 79 years that could have been highly productive in Japan.[43]

Julia Johnson, mother of five children, reached the age of 91. A gifted teacher of French and Greek, she doubtless could have learned Japanese better than any of the early missionary wives in Japan. Julia is remembered as the foremost advocate of missionary support among the Baptist women of Mississippi. She helped to organize the Woman's Missionary Union of that state and served as president of its central committee for eight years.[44]

Julia's brother Crawford, like her husband, joined the Confederate army upon the outbreak of war. Rising from private in artillery to chaplain in the infantry, Toy was captured in the Battle of Gettysburg but released in a prisoner exchange. After the war, when he was teaching Greek in the University of Virginia, the Board offered to send him to China, which needed reinforcements, but not to Japan. It was the Board's opinion that the depressed economy of the times precluded the establishment of a new mission. With service in Japan not an option, Toy decided to follow through on plans he had made for two years of study at the University of Berlin. There he imbibed the critical approach to Scripture that eventually led to his separation from Southern Baptists.[45]

When Toy returned from Germany in 1868, cotton and tobacco were again producing hard money in the South, and the Board's income was beginning to recover from the lean war years. Japan, however, lacked its former appeal as a mission field. It had suffered a civil war of its own, with government forces and rebellious clans fighting off and on since 1863. In 1868, when the feudal

[42]*American Baptist*, 4 Oct. 1855.
[43]Foster, *Mississippi Preachers*, 404-6.
[44]*ESB*, vol. 1, s.v. "Johnson, Julia Anna (Toy)."
[45]Toy to J. B. Taylor, 3 Feb. 1866; Hurt, "Toy," 34-67.

Tokugawa shogunate was overthrown and replaced by a coalition of imperialists, the new Meiji regime reaffirmed the ban on Christianity and stepped up the persecution of Christians. No new mission had been opened since Goble's arrival in 1860, and the total Protestant missionary force had only increased from seven to eight.[46]

The Board's attention was drawn instead to Europe, where anti-Catholic movements and a trend toward Protestantism were opening new doors for evangelical missions. In 1869 Toy suggested to the Board that "a good man" be sent to Germany to open a mission in cooperation with German Baptist leaders. Having recently joined the faculty of Southern Baptist Theological Seminary, Toy did not feel that he himself should go. Nor would the seminary have been willing to give up its "shining pearl of learning," as Broadus called him. Toy also declined an appointment to Italy--his language repertoire included Italian--urged by the Board in 1872. "I feel myself obliged," he wrote, "to remain in my present position."[47]

Only one mission field appealed to Toy. He still harbored the call to Japan that had come to him under Broadus's ministry in Charlottesville. Toy proposed marriage to Lottie Moon, suggesting mission work together in Japan. Though seriously interested, Lottie was troubled by Toy's controversial views on Darwinism and biblical inspiration that led to his forced resignation from Southern Baptist Theological Seminary in 1879. However sincere his proposal, his doctrinal position clearly disqualified him with the Foreign Mission Board. Two appointees for China, whom the Board's corresponding secretary, H. A. Tupper, called "the noblest among the noble," had their appointments withdrawn when they admitted holding views on Scripture similar to Toy's position.[48]

In 1880 Toy went to Harvard University as Hancock Professor of Hebrew and Other Oriental Languages, and the next year Lottie Moon broke off their relationship to remain at her post in China. In 1888 he married a minister's daughter from Virginia. Though widely respected as the first non-Unitarian professor in Harvard's Divinity School (founded 1816), Toy then withdrew his membership from the Old Cambridge Baptist Church and cast his lot with the Unitarians. For many Southern Baptists, Toy's experience demonstrated that

[46]G. F. Verbeck, "History of Protestant Missions in Japan," in *Proceedings of the General Conference of Protestant Missionaries in Japan, 1900* (Tokyo: Methodist Publishing House, 1901), 742-44.

[47]Toy to J. B. Taylor, 6 Sept. 1869; Toy to H. A. Tupper, 2 Nov. 1872; A. T. Robertson, *Life and Letters of John Albert Broadus* (Philadelphia: American Baptist Publication Society, 1901), 313.

[48]Allen, *Lottie Moon*, 112, 136-39; Irwin T. Hyatt, Jr., *Our Ordered Lives Confess* (Cambridge: Harvard University Press, 1976), 98-99. See also John Powell Clayton, "Crawford Howell Toy of Virginia," *Baptist Quarterly* 24 (1971): 53-56.

bibilical criticism could be a dangerous "slippery slope."[49] One can only speculate on what his life might have been had the way opened for Toy to go to Japan instead of Germany.

In 1880, when the Toy-Moon romance was still in bloom, and Secretary Tupper was privy to it, Tupper published his *Foreign Missions of the Southern Baptist Convention*. In a chapter entitled "Japan Mission and Our Lost Missionaries," he devoted three pages to a general description of Japan--its climate, government, language, and religion. A foldout map of Japan was bound into the volume at this place. Apparently Tupper nourished the hope of a new start in Japan. But in 1880 the Board entered Mexico, whose proximity to Southern Baptists enhanced its appeal, and the next year it entered Brazil, which had been recommended in 1859 along with Japan. In both Mexico and Brazil the Board assumed responsibility for Baptist work already in progress. A mission in Japan, it seems, depended on the shattered dream of Crawford Toy, at least until the debut of a new generation of volunteers.[50]

The Christian Movement in Japan

For three decades, a full generation, Christian missions were conducted in Japan without Southern Baptist involvement. During this momentous era of rapid development and modernization, representatives of the Roman Catholic Church, the Russian Orthodox Church, and many Protestant denominations made their distinctive contributions to the religious life of the nation. The Protestants, especially America's Northern Baptists, laid the foundations on which Southern Baptists would build.

Little progress was made in the earlier years, 1859-72, with the centuries-old ban on Christianity still in effect. The missionaries were mostly confined to the foreign settlements in Nagasaki, Kanagawa, and Yokohama (by 1863 Yokohama had replaced the adjacent town of Kanagawa as a treaty port). They devoted themselves to language study, Scripture translation, English teaching, medical work, and discreet evangelism among the educated samurai with the aid of Chinese Bibles and tracts. By 1871, despite the risks, they had privately baptized about 10 converts. A major breakthrough occurred in the spring of 1872, when rising criticism from the Western powers had forced Japanese officials to display a more tolerant attitude toward Christianity. On March 10, James Ballagh and Robbins Brown baptized nine young men in Yokohama and organized the first Japanese Protestant church.[51]

---

[49]Hurt, "Toy," 70-82.
[50]Tupper, *Foreign Missions*, 244-47, 9; H. A. Tupper, *A Decade of Foreign Missions, 1880-1890* (Richmond, Va.: Foreign Mission Board, SBC, 1891), 159-68.
[51]Verbeck, "History," 764-65.

The only Baptist missionary in Japan prior to 1873 was Jonathan Goble, pitied by his Protestant colleagues as uncouth, sectarian, and deprived. His salary from the Free Mission Society depended on special gifts, which were sparse and sporadic. To make ends meet, Eliza Goble took in sewing and taught English, while Jonathan mended shoes, imported merchandise for sale, and supervised construction projects. Despite his excessive moonlighting, Jonathan found time to translate more than half the New Testament into Japanese. His Gospel of Matthew, secretly printed just before his furlough in 1871, is the oldest extant Bible portion published inside Japan.[52]

In February 1873 the anti-Christian signboards throughout the land were removed under pressure from Western governments. This signaled that the legal ban, though unrevoked, would no longer be enforced. During this one year, 29 new Protestant missionaries arrived in Japan, more than the total on the field at the end of 1872. The American Baptist Missionary Union, accepting the transfer of the Japan field from the Free Mission Society, sent out Goble and Nathan Brown with their families. Brown, a former missionary to Assam, was 65 years old. With his bent frame, high-piled white hair, and snowy beard, he clearly looked his years, especially when accompanied by his recently acquired wife Lottie, who was 33. Yet his extraordinary mind still had the capacity to absorb a new language.[53]

The Gobles and Browns organized the first Baptist church in Japan at Yokohama on March 2, 1873. The two couples were the only charter members. In December, Jonathan was forced to withdraw from the church after striking a Japanese assistant repeatedly. He was also dismissed by the Missionary Union on charges of slander against its leaders and violence against his own wife and workmen. Despite his soiled reputation, Goble remained in Japan as a free-lance missionary until after his wife's death in 1882. Nathan Brown, himself a strong-willed individualist, came to be revered as the true founder of the Baptist denomination in Japan. Brown's integrity and brilliance contrasted sharply with the cruder traits of Goble.[54]

Baptist missionaries came to Japan not only from the United States but also from Australia, Scotland, and England. In 1874 Wilton Hack, a well-born Baptist minister from Australia, arrived as a self-supporting missionary accompanied by several lay associates. After founding a mission press in Nagasaki and a secular paper, the *Rising Sun*, he taught English at a government school in Hiroshima. There he baptized 16 Japanese converts and organized a Baptist church, apparently

---

[52]F. Calvin Parker, "Jonathan Goble, Missionary Extraordinary," in *Transactions of the Asiatic Society of Japan*, 3d series, vol. 16 (Tokyo, 1981), 77-107.

[53]Verbeck, "History," 768; Albert Arnold Bennett, "Rev. Nathan Brown, D.D.," *Japan Evangelist* 2 (1895): 318-20.

[54]Parker, "Jonathan Goble," 88-89; William Wynd, *Seventy Years in Japan: A Saga of Northern Baptists* (ca. 1943), 3-5, 36.

the first Protestant church started outside the foreign settlements. But while Hack toured England and Australia to raise support for his work, the Hiroshima church was oppressed by local authorities and forced to disband. Moreover, his lay workers in Nagasaki fell into poverty and dissension among themselves. So Hack nobly informed his scattered supporters that his attempt to establish an independent Baptist mission had failed. He and his family withdrew from Japan in 1877, after the British consul in Nagasaki had opened a subscription list to pay for their passage home.[55]

A Scottish Baptist, Theobald A. Palm, came to Japan with his wife in 1874 under the Edinburgh Medical Missionary Society. He did extensive medical and evangelistic work amid the heavy snows of Niigata Prefecture. Palm antagonized the American Baptist missionaries by employing a Reformed Church evangelist and permitting him to sprinkle converts rather than immerse them. Upon concluding 10 years of fruitful service in Japan, moreover, Palm left his church of 60 members in the hands of the Congregationalists.[56]

In 1878 the Baptist Missionary Society of London sent out William J. White, the first of its two missionaries to Japan. White had been a teacher and merchant in Tokyo and Yokohama before returning to England to study at Spurgeon's College and launch a new career in missions. After 12 years the London society, beset with economic difficulties, relinquished its Japan work to the American Baptist Missionary Union.[57]

By the 1880s Western culture had gained widespread approval, and the more progressive Japanese were making feverish efforts to acquire it. This "Western intoxication" greatly enhanced the appeal of the Christian faith, which offered a social ethic--monogamy, temperance, and concern for every individual--on which to build a new society. Gospel preaching drew large crowds, conversions increased dramatically, many new churches were born, and the English word *revival* found a permanent place in the Japanese vocabulary. Excited at the long-awaited breakthrough, some of the veteran missionaries stated in 1883 that Japan would become a Christian nation before the end of the century. James Hepburn thought the transformation would take 15 years; Guido Verbeck expected it within a decade. Indeed, the next few years seemed to justify their rosy predictions. Protestant church membership rose from 5,092 in 1882 to 23,026 in 1888, more than a fourfold increase. By 1890, however, the upward surge had been checked by a conservative reaction that Hepburn and Verbeck had not

---

[55]*Baptist Magazine* 68 (Jan. 1876): 22-28; *Freeman*, 24 Sept., 17 Dec. 1875, 25 May 1877; Harold S. Williams, *Foreigners in Mikadoland* (Tokyo: Charles E. Tuttle Co., 1963), 182-83.

[56]F. Cary, *History*, 203.

[57]A. S. Clement, "The Baptist Missionary Society in Japan," *Baptist Quarterly* 26 (Apr. 1975): 68-73.

anticipated. Protestant growth leveled off with only 30,000 believers in a population of 40 million--less than 0.1 percent.[58]

Though Baptists had been at work in Japan since Goble's arrival in 1860, they lagged behind the other four major denominations and were known as the smallest of the "Big Five." In 1888, when Baptists reported 900 members, the Episcopalians, Congregationalists, Presbyterians, and Methodists claimed several thousand each. The most conspicuous reason for the poor showing of Baptists was fewer personnel--only 12 missionaries in 1885 out of a total of 172, excluding wives. Neither American nor British Baptists gave high priority to the work in Japan. The corresponding secretary of the Missionary Union frankly acknowledged that his board would not have opened a mission in Japan in 1873 had it known that a generous legacy left to the Free Mission Society would not pass under its control. Relatively few missionaries were sent, and several resigned early because of illness. One died on the field after four and a half months of service.[59]

Furthermore, as suggested above, three of the most aggressive Baptist evangelists made little or no permanent contribution to Baptist advance. Goble sold his Yokohama chapel to the Methodist Episcopal mission for personal profit, and the converts he had baptized were said to disappear.[60] Hack saw his work collapse because he lacked a supporting board to provide stability and continuity. Palm, sponsored by a non-Baptist society, chose to ignore denominational lines.

Such losses were somewhat offset by the addition to Baptist ranks of both missionaries and Japanese believers from other denominations. It is well known that Adoniram Judson was sent to India as a Congregationalist and immersed there by an associate of William Carey, the pioneer English Baptist. Judson was not the only missionary to be convinced from a study of the New Testament that immersion was the proper mode of baptism. Among the American Baptist missionaries in Japan prior to 1889, at least three men and two wives had served previously under Episcopal, Presbyterian, or Methodist boards. Among the Japanese converts, Kawakatsu Tetsuya, who assisted Nathan Brown in Scripture translation and later worked with Southern Baptist missionaries, was first baptized by the Reformed Church's Ballagh. Some of the other national workers served previously in the Russian Orthodox Church. Two Baptist churches in northern

---

[58]O. Cary, *History*, 2:164-72. Hepburn and Verbeck are quoted indirectly in J. Merle Davis, *Davis, Soldier Missionary: A Biography of Rev. Jerome D. Davis* (Boston: Pilgrim Press, 1916), 199. Statistics are found in *Proceedings, 1900*, 988-89.

[59]Charles W. Iglehart, *A Century of Protestant Christianity in Japan* (Tokyo: Charles E. Tuttle Co., 1959), 80; J. N. Murdock to N. Brown, 8 Oct. 1878, quoted in N. Brown to Murdock, 9 Jan. 1879, American Baptist Historical Society, Rochester, N.Y.; Wynd, *Seventy Years*, 57; C. K. Harrington, "Baptist Work in Japan, the Past," in *Minutes of the Japan Mission of the American Baptist Foreign Mission Society, 1910*, 114-15. The missionary who died on the field was C. H. Carpenter.

[60]J. N. Murdock to E. Judson, 16 Mar. 1888, American Baptist Historical Society; N. Brown to J. N. Murdock, 16 Feb. 1875, American Baptist Historical Society.

Japan were organized from former Orthodox believers who had been swayed by the proselytizing zeal of Thomas Poate, an Englishman under appointment of the Missionary Union.[61]

Baptist missionaries could have done worse, considering the amount of energy expended on internal disputes. After his dismissal by the Missionary Union, Goble harassed Nathan Brown for many years with critical and accusatory letters sent to the local English press and to pastors and mission leaders in America. Brown wasted precious time defending himself against false charges ranging from drunkenness to incompetence in the language. Not only Goble and Brown, but all the Baptist missionaries were involved in disputes over evangelistic strategy and church polity. They split most sharply on the issue of close (or closed) communion, advocated by most of the Americans, versus open communion, practiced by the Australians and British. Brown, a rigorous close communionist, called Poate a "dangerous man." He sent Kawakatsu to preach in the Tokyo church for the avowed purpose of checking Poate's influence there.[62]

In their approach to evangelism, Baptist missionaries gave priority to Bible translation and literature distribution. Goble published not only his Matthew but an attractive pamphlet entitled *Tendō annai* (Guide to the heavenly way). As chief colporteur for the American Bible Society, he distributed thousands of scriptures and tracts from the northern end of Kantō Plain to the southern tip of Kyushu. Nathan Brown established the Yokohama Bible Press and devoted most of his dozen years in Japan to the production of scriptures, tracts, and a 300-page hymnal that included some of his own compositions. In 1879 he published the first Japanese translation of the entire New Testament. This work preceded by one year the translation of a joint committee representing several denominations. Later, the Englishman White, another devotee of literature evangelism, revised Brown's New Testament and translated *Pilgrim's Progress*. After British Baptists closed their mission and cut off White's support, he remained in Japan and served effectively as agent for the American Tract Society.[63]

The chief reason for the Baptist preoccupation with Scripture translation was the conviction that the Greek word for baptism should be rendered by a term clearly denoting immersion. The time and resources devoted to this effort could have been more fruitfully invested in churches or schools, for Japanese Baptists eventually adopted the interdenominational translation of the Bible in preference

[61]Wynd, *Seventy Years*, 10-11, 16, 34-35, 71.

[62]N. Brown to J. N. Murdock, 23 Apr. 1874, 9 Sep., 15 Dec. 1884, 16 Feb. 1875, 12, 21 Apr. 1877, American Baptist Historical Society.

[63]Parker, *Jonathan Goble of Japan*, 198-99, 229-42; E. W. Brown, *The Whole World Kin: A Pioneer Experience among remote tribes and other labors of Nathan Brown* (Philadelphia, 1890), 545-60; Clement, "Baptist Missionary Society," 72-73.

to the immersionist version.[64] It was this interdenominational translation that Goble distributed as a colporteur, not his own or Nathan Brown's.

Unlike the other denominations, Baptists were reluctant to utilize Christian education as a means of evangelism, for they sought more immediate results through direct means. True, most Baptist missionaries taught pupils informally, and by 1888 four schools had been started for girls. But no school was established for boys until 1895, when Duncan Academy opened in Tokyo. The delay was costly, for Christian schools--34 were reported in 1882 and 72 in 1888--produced the majority of converts in the 1880s.[65] At a time when churches bore the onus of foreign colonies, the schools, being compatible with the traditional value system, served as a spearhead for the gospel and the "birthplace of the church." It has even been argued that "the Christian school was the only field of Christian evangelism that could be called successful."[66]

Lacking a boys' school, Baptists failed to attract and develop strong Japanese leaders--with two exceptions. One was Kawakatsu, a proselyte from Ballagh's group of converts. The other was Chiba Yūgorō, who was sent to America for college and seminary training. Baptists had no seedbed of leadership like the Yokohama schools conducted by Hepburn, Ballagh, and Robbins Brown. There was no Baptist equivalent of the Kumamoto Band, converts of Leroy Janes in Kyushu, nor of the Sapporo Band, followers of William Clark in Hokkaido. From such dynamic teachers came the early giants of Protestantism in Japan.[67]

Baptists also trailed the other denominations in opening a theological school, established at Yokohama in 1884. Even then the Missionary Union refused to provide financial support, on grounds that the work had not developed sufficiently to require a seminary. Two years later the Missionary Union permitted a vacant mission house to be used for this purpose, but only because the house was too dilapidated for use as a residence. Then for many years the seminary was crippled for want of qualified students, since Baptists lacked a preparatory school. In 1888, when Protestant theological schools had an enrollment of 233, the lone Baptist seminary had fewer than 10 students.[68]

Whatever their shortcomings, the early Baptist missionaries deserve recognition for their interest in the common people. D. A. Macgowan had come

---

[64]Wynd, *Seventy Years*, 8-9; Harrington, "Baptist Work," 120.

[65]C. B. Tenny, "Baptist Beginnings in Japan," *Japan Evangelist* 31 (June 1924): 11-12; *Proceedings, 1900*, 994-97. The figures include both boarding and day schools.

[66]Takaaki Aikawa and Lynn Leavenworth, *The Mind of Japan* (Valley Forge: Judson Press, 1967), 110-11. See also James E. Wood, Jr., "The Teaching of English as a Missionary Method" (Th.D. diss., Southern Baptist Theological Seminary, 1957), 276.

[67]A helpful introduction to the several "bands" is given in Richard H. Drummond, *A History of Christianity in Japan* (Grand Rapids: William B. Eerdmans, 1971), 166-73.

[68]C. K. Harrington, "Historical Sketch of the Theological School," in *Minutes of the American Baptist Missionary Union in Japan, 1893*, 52-55 (hereafter cited as *ABMU Minutes*).

away from Nagasaki in 1859 convinced that Baptists in Japan should begin "by commending themselves to the governing classes through whom alone the people can be reached. The usual process must be reversed. You must work from above downward."[69] Goble rejected this approach as the same crucial error made by the early Jesuits, whose success in converting powerful daimyo had triggered the ban on Christianity as politically subversive. Goble dared to preach in outcaste villages. He rendered Scripture in a colloquial style understandable to the masses, not in the literary style favored by the samurai, a mere 5 percent of the population.[70] Nathan Brown likewise aimed his translations at the common people.

The same concern motivated Anna H. Kidder, a New Englander who had taught in the black schools of the South and taken charge of the "Shelter for Colored Orphans" in Providence, Rhode Island. The first single woman to serve as a Baptist missionary in Japan, she politely but firmly declined to teach the children of nobility apart from commoners.[71] In like spirit, the W. H. Whites conducted a school for the poor in Tokyo, while other Baptist missionaries traveled in the rural districts and opened up Sunday schools for the children of farmers.[72] This type of evangelism gave expression to one of the noblest ideals of the Baptist tradition. Unlike evangelism among the urban middle class and intellectuals, however, it failed to produce self-supporting churches. In the 1890s, congregations in rural areas sharply declined in number and strength.

Their relative weakness notwithstanding, Baptists laid a broad and durable foundation during the first three decades of Protestant missions in Japan. In 1888 they were a recognized segment of the growing Christian community. The American Baptist Missionary Union was prepared both to enlarge its forces and to welcome the cooperation of Southern Baptists for a more effective witness throughout the nation. This cooperation was needed more than anyone could foresee, for the next decade was to be a trying time for Christian missions in the "land of the gods."

---

[69]Macgowan letter in *Baptist Missionary Magazine* 39 (Sept. 1859): 334.

[70]Parker, *Jonathan Goble of Japan*, 176-77.

[71]Clara Arthur Mason, *Etchings from Two Lands* (Boston, 1886), 146-47; Katakosawa Chiyomatsu, "Nihon Baputesuto kyōkai no dendō hōshin" (Evangelistic strategy of the Japan Baptist church), *Kirisutokyō shigaku* 15 (1965): 20.

[72]H. Ritter, *A History of Protestant Missions in Japan*, trans. George E. Albrecht (Tokyo, 1898), 382; Wynd, *Seventy Years*, 13. The Whites' school, Seikei Shōgakkō, had 125 pupils.

2

Joining in a Movement (1889-1891)

In the 1880s a number of formerly hesitant mission boards responded positively to the explosive church growth that raised hopes for the speedy conversion of Japan. Among them, the Southern Presbyterian board opened work in 1885, and the Southern Methodist, in 1886. The latter, like the Southern Baptist board, had appointed its first missionary before the Civil War but had suspended the enterprise. So promising was the field in the mid-1880s that within a period of 10 years Southern Methodists placed 21 missionaries in Japan, not counting wives.[1]

For Southern Baptists, the death of Matthew T. Yates at Shanghai in March 1888, following two paralytic strokes, reinforced the challenge. This prominent missionary had urged a mission in Japan throughout his long career in China. He had even offered to pay a missionary's salary (Yates enjoyed income from investments and moonlighting, which the Board winked at in early years). As Secretary Tupper wrote, Yates "did not appreciate the wisdom of our being so shocked by the loss at sea of our missionaries to Japan . . . as to paralyze all further efforts in that direction. . . . There was something noble in his appeal for a field not his own; and peculiarly touching when that appeal failed." Tupper called on Southern Baptists to "make the death of our Brother Yates the occasion of our heeding his voice, now hushed, which we failed to do when he was living."[2]

A committee report adopted at the 1888 meeting of the SBC commended "the establishment of a mission in the long-neglected but progressive empire of Japan." By coincidence, the meeting was held in Richmond, the same location as

---

[1]Lois Johnson Erickson, *The White Fields of Japan* (Richmond, Va.: Presbyterian Committee of Publication, 1923), 71-72; S. H. Wainright, *The Methodist Mission in Japan* (Nashville: Board of Missions, Methodist Episcopal Church, South, 1935), 21.

[2]Tupper, *Decade*, 594-98; Charles E. Taylor, *The Story of Yates the Missionary* (Nashville: Sunday School Board, SBC, 1898), 279-98.

the 1859 convention, which had endorsed a mission to Japan. The committee offered two reasons for its recommendation.[3]

First, "the commercial relations of this people with the United States are of such a nature as greatly to favor the success of the enterprise." As a direct result of its participation in the New Orleans Industrial and Cotton Exposition in 1884, for example, Japan began to produce chemical fertilizer in 1888, using machinery and phosphate imported from the United States. America was becoming Japan's chief customer for raw silk.[4] The growing dependence of Japan's economy on that of its Pacific neighbor was to give rise to the saying, "When America sneezes, Japan comes down with the flu."

Second, said the committee, Japan was "so situated geographically as to afford a most valuable strategic territory for the capture of the boundless regions beyond." The situation in Asia had changed dramatically since the 16th century, when Francis Xavier concluded that the conversion of China was the key to winning Japan. Japan had far surpassed the other Asian countries in modernizing its industries and institutions. Now it was the key to China, and the surrounding lands as well.

The committee report further asked, "Shall our brethren of the North and English Baptists be permitted to toil there with no help from their Southern brethren?" Secretary Tupper felt this obligation most keenly after attending the historic London Missionary Conference of June 1888, where he learned more about the flourishing Christian movement in Japan and the trend toward church union. "Other evangelical denominations are banding together in Japan," Tupper said, "and the feeble Baptist force there stands at fearful odds." He warned that the shrinking percentage of Baptists in the growing Protestant community would "give a vast preponderance against views and doctrines of inestimable importance." This threat to the survival of Baptist influence was reason enough, he urged, to go to the help of Northern and English Baptists in Japan.[5]

In November 1888 a Japan missionary of the American Baptist Missionary Union was invited before the Board to give firsthand information about his field of service. He was George H. Appleton, who had first gone to China as an Episcopal missionary but had been baptized by Yates in Shanghai. He had served one term as a Baptist missionary in Japan, opening new work in several towns, but was unable to return because of failing health. A keen observer with deep insight, Appleton shared with the Board a wealth of information about traveling to Japan and succeeding at the work there. He insisted that "Japan, as a point for missionary radiation, has no superior," that it was indeed the key to China and Korea. And unabashedly he revealed the potential for proselytism: "Of seven

[3]*ASBC, 1888,* 22.
[4]Robert S. Schwantes, *Japanese and Americans* (New York: Harper & Brothers, 1955), 51-52.
[5]Tupper, *Decade,* 597-98.

Japanese Christians of from three to five years' standing, who came to ask why I left the Paedo-baptist ranks after more than twenty-five years' connection therewith, I baptized six." Later, Tupper cited "the seemingly providential presence of Brother Appleton" as a factor in the Board's decision to enter Japan.[6]

One hurdle yet remained: a clear understanding with the Missionary Union. J. N. Murdock, a lawyer and licensed Methodist preacher before turning Baptist, had been the Union's secretary for more than 20 years. It was Murdock who fired Jonathan Goble in 1873, an act for which Goble was still threatening to sue the Missionary Union, though quite in vain. During a visit to Richmond in December 1888, the powerful secretary gave his assurance that a Southern Baptist presence in Japan would be "entirely agreeable to the Missionary Union." With this crucial matter settled, in January 1889 the Board voted unanimously to establish a mission in Japan. Tupper was elated. He described Japan as "probably the most promising missionary field now open to Christ's messengers."[7]

One peculiar and attractive feature of Japan was that it had never been apportioned among the different denominations by comity agreements. Most other fields, excepting major cities, had been divided among Protestant mission agencies in order to stretch available resources and assure the evangelization of every region. A secondary purpose of comity was to avoid the confusion and strife of overlapping programs. Baptists, both Northern and Southern, had respected such agreements. In the case of Japan, however, they were free to divide the entire country between themselves.[8] In mutual consultations it was agreed that Southern Baptists would work to the south and west of Kobe, a treaty port in western Honshu. This was the same territory where Southern Methodists were concentrating their work.

The Missionary Pioneers

In May 1889 the Board appointed J. W. McCollum to Japan and reassigned J. A. Brunson to that field. Brunson had been appointed to North China in June 1888. Both men were single but engaged to be married. Tupper praised them as "first-class young men."[9]

John Alexander Brunson was born in 1862 in Darlington, South Carolina, the youngest of three children. When he was four months old his father, a Confederate soldier, died in the second battle of Bull Run (won by the Confeder-

---

[6]Ibid., 786-801; R. Austin Thompson, "Historical Sketch of the South-West Japan Mission," in *ABMU Minutes, 1901*, 83-84.

[7]Tupper, *Decade*, 785-86. On Murdock see *New York Baptist Annual, 1898*, 72; Torbet, *Venture of Faith*, 146-47.

[8]*Encyclopædia Britannica*, 1968 ed., s.v. "missions"; R. Pierce Beaver, "The History of Mission Strategy," *Southwestern Journal of Theology*, 12 (spring 1970): 25-26.

[9]Tupper, *Decade*, 629, 619.

ates). John, or Jack as he was often called, was converted in boyhood at the Ebenezer church, which dated back to the Revolutionary War. He left school at 11, worked on the farm steadily till he was 18, then entered the normal school in nearby Florence. A half-year later the tall and brilliant youth, despite the paucity of his early education, passed an examination in Darlington that qualified him to teach in the public schools of the county. After two years of teaching he entered Furman University to prepare for the gospel ministry, to which he was ordained in his senior year. He graduated in 1887 with an A.M. degree and proceeded to Southern Baptist Theological Seminary in Louisville. Richly endowed with an assimilative mind, a powerful voice, and a commanding presence, Brunson showed promise of becoming one of the strongest preachers in the denomination.[10]

John William McCollum, born two years after Brunson, was reared on an Alabama farm. He joined a Baptist church at the age of 13 (his father was baptized with him) and left school at 16 for full-time farming. Four years later, convinced that God had called him to preach, the sturdy youth enrolled at Howard College in nearby Marion. Mac, as he was often called, impressed his fellow students with his healthy frame, steady nerves, and unfailing courtesy. Though a good mixer with a jolly disposition, he was remembered best for his high virtue. His closest friend later said that he never heard Mac utter a word "under any conditions, at work or at play, that his mother might not have repeated with unblushing cheeks." Graduating fourth in a class of 14, Mac entered seminary in 1886, one year ahead of Brunson.[11]

Southern Seminary at the time had no building of its own, though one was under construction at its campus site in downtown Louisville. Classes met in the Public Library Hall, and students lived in a hotel. So it was a memorable day in March 1888 when Jack Brunson and J. W. McCollum with their fellow seminarians moved into a new five-story building--New York Hall--with dormitory space for 200 students as well as classrooms, offices, and a dining room served by black waiters. The elegant structure was heated by steam, but at night the occupants studied by kerosene lamp.[12]

What the seminary lacked in physical facilities when Brunson and McCollum first enrolled, it compensated for with a strong academic program. Of the original stellar faculty of four when the school was founded in 1859, three were still

[10]Ibid., 807.

[11]L. O. Dawson, "Pioneer of the Japan Mission, S.B.C.," typescript, Edwin B. Dozier papers (hereafter cited as EBD papers), Japan Baptist Mission, Tokyo (hereafter, JBM); Tupper, *Decade*, 806.

[12]John R. Sampey, *Memoirs of John R. Sampey* (Nashville: Broadman Press, 1947), 49; Everett Gill, *A. T. Robertson: A Biography* (New York: MacMillan Co., 1943), 57; William A. Mueller, *A History of Southern Baptist Theological Seminary* (Nashville: Broadman Press, 1959), 49; George W. Bouldin, "Autobiography" (George W. Bouldin papers, Historical Commission, SBC, ca. 1960), 48; Southern Baptist Theological Seminary, *Catalogue, 1904-5*, 40.

lecturing: James P. Boyce, John A. Broadus, and Basil Manley, Jr. Boyce died in 1888, but A. T. Robertson began teaching Greek that year, joining other younger faculty members such as William H. Whitsitt (church history) and John R. Sampey (Old Testament).[13] Thus surrounded by brilliant teachers of both the passing and rising generations, Brunson and McCollum had their minds nourished by the best of Southern Baptist scholarship.

Moreover, the spirit of evangelism and missions pervaded the life of the seminary. In January and February of 1888, evangelist D. L. Moody conducted a six-week campaign in a 5,000-seat tabernacle erected on the campus. Faculty and students gave the effort their full support. Interest in missions was kept at a high pitch through regular meetings of the Society of Missionary Inquiry and the seminary-wide celebration of Missionary Day at the beginning of each month. On that day all classes were suspended and a mass meeting held in chapel for the consideration of missions at home and abroad. Visiting missionaries and mission board representatives reported on the needs of the fields and sounded urgent calls for volunteers.[14]

Brunson applied to the Foreign Mission Board for appointment before completing his first year of study. His home-church pastor had urged upon him the claims of foreign fields, and the appeals he heard on Missionary Day convinced him that he lacked sufficient reason for staying at home. "I haven't a consuming desire to go to foreign fields," he wrote to Secretary Tupper, "nor have I received any Macedonian call to any particular place. I am much in love with my own native land. [But] if the Holy Spirit and my brethren say that I must go, Here am I send me." However praiseworthy Brunson's attitude, it had an ominous ring--more the attitude of a draftee than a volunteer. His sincerity of heart was offset by misgivings of mind.[15]

Tupper considered Brunson a fit candidate for China and obtained the customary recommendations from his acquaintances. The president and several professors at Furman testified to his "excellent character" and "many admirable qualities" but thought it would be a "great mistake" for him to cut short his seminary course to enter the foreign field. They insisted that the Board allow him to finish his training. A South Carolina pastor urged a permanent postponement. "My judgment," the pastor wrote, "is that Brunson will be worth more to the Master in America than in China . . . . leave him alone and take in his place the brother of equal promise for missionary work who has less preaching ability." Brunson himself prayerfully reached the conclusion that it was his duty to return to seminary for another session. Upon weighing all the factors, the Board

[13]Sampey, *Memoirs*, 28; Mueller, *History*, 234.

[14]Sampey, *Memoirs*, 48; Gill, *A. T. Robertson*, 55; Mueller, *History*, 123.

[15]Brunson to Tupper, 22 May 1888; Brunson to T. P. Bell, 23 May 1892, FMBA; George R. Pettigrew, "John A. Brunson, D.D., the Man and the Preacher," *Baptist Courier*, 30 Dec. 1943, 9.

promptly appointed Brunson to North China with the stipulation that he would complete another year of study before sailing.[16]

In April 1889 Brunson learned through McCollum that the Board wanted to change him from China to Japan. "I am your servant for Christ's sake," he wrote Tupper. So when McCollum was appointed in May, Brunson was formally transferred and designated "Sallie R. Brown Missionary to Japan." The title indicated that Brunson's support was provided by the family of the deceased Sallie Brown in her memory.[17]

In June, Brunson married Sophia Boatwright, a quick-minded woman who had been educated by governesses and at private schools in South Carolina. She was a future physician of "exceptional skill."[18] Unfortunately, information about Sophia and other missionary wives of the time is sparse, because they were not appointed by the Board and hence did not submit the biographical sketch and references required of appointees. Under Board rules, wives were regarded as "assistant missionaries" and were expected, "as far as their domestic duties allow, . . . to contribute especially by instructing natives of their sex to the advancement of the work and interests of the mission."[19]

McCollum graduated from the three-year seminary course soon after his missionary appointment and took a temporary pastorate. In September he married Drucilla Franklin Collins, daughter of a farmer-merchant. Five years younger than Mac, Dru had attended Judson Institute, the Baptist girls' school in Marion near Howard College. She was to accomplish far more in Japan than instructing "natives" of her own sex.[20]

In October, after crossing the continent by train, the Brunsons and McCollums boarded the SS *Belgic* at San Francisco in company with six new missionaries of the American Baptist Missionary Union. The leisurely 17-day voyage across the Pacific spawned a number of enduring friendships. On November 5, 1889, the party arrived in Yokohama in mist, wind, and rain. The gloomy weather, said McCollum, "only enhanced the more than generous welcome" extended by Baptist missionaries awaiting their arrival. "One could see no difference," he added, "in our reception and that of the missionaries sent out by the Northern Board."[21]

---

[16]Charles Manley to T. P. Bell, 29 May 1888, Brunson file, FMBA; John S. Fout to Bell, 27 Mar. 1888, Brunson file, FMBA; Tupper, *Decade*, 807-8.

[17]Brunson to Tupper, 22 Apr. 1889; Tupper, *Decade*, 807.

[18]Pettigrew, "John A. Brunson," 9; undated news clipping furnished by the late Jesse Myers, Sumter, S.C.

[19]Tupper, *Decade*, 70.

[20]Ibid., 807; McCollum file, FMBA.

[21]J. W. McCollum, "A Historical Sketch of Southern Baptist Missions to Japan," in *ABMU Minutes, 1899*, 99; Tupper, *Decade*, 805-6. McCollum identifies the ship as the *Belgic*; Tupper, less reliably, calls it the *Baltic*.

After completing the usual immigration procedures at the customhouse wharf, the party climbed into waiting rickshaws. The rickshaw, or jinrikisha (literally, "man-power-vehicle"), often attributed to Jonathan Goble (its origin is disputed), was a two-wheeled carriage pulled by a man running between two shafts protruding from the front. Some models carried two passengers, others only one. The new arrivals were whisked by their human horses through the streets of Yokohama and up the hill to the missionary boardinghouse at Bluff No. 2. During the next few days Brunson and Mac attended conferences with the Northern Baptist men while the women did sightseeing and visited the fascinating shops that sold embroideries, hand-painted china, sandalwood fans, cloisonné, damascene, lacquerware, and tortoise shell. Dru McCollum, aged 20, took in the unfamiliar sights, sounds, and smells with the curiosity and wonder of a child.[22]

Among the sounds were the distinctive calls of peddlers, such as the sellers of tofu (bean curd), whose plaintive horns made the sweetest of music; the pleasant clatter of geta (wooden clogs) on the pavement, a clatter that could become a deafening roar on a crowded street; and in the nighttime quiet, the sharp clapping of two sticks together by a watchman who moved about the neighborhood to urge caution with fires. The smells emanating from cafes and food carts could be enticing or repulsive, while the stench of "honey buckets" carrying human waste used for fertilizer was well-nigh unbearable.

To Jack Brunson, "the sensation of novelty was overwhelming." What impressed him most strongly was the smallness of everything, from stunted trees to "pigmy-like" people. This miniature world reminded him of "a gigantic play-house." As a man who stood head and shoulders above even his fellow missionaries--he often said he was "5 feet, 18 inches"--Brunson must have felt like Gulliver among the Lilliputians. It is not surprising that he took a low--and mistaken--view of Japan's potential. "Japan is not and can not become a truly great nation," he wrote. "Both the features of the country and the quality and character of the people forbid it."[23]

Two Years of Language Study and Other Trials

Brunson and McCollum made a tour of southwestern Japan, the territory assigned to them by comity agreement with Northern Baptists. Traveling by jinrikisha, they inspected Shimonoseki, Nagasaki, and other cities. Then in consultation with missionary colleagues, they decided to begin their language study in Kobe rather than Tokyo or Yokohama, "as that is adjacent to our work." The two couples rented a spacious two-story house on Kobe's Bluff, where

---

[22]Parker, *Jonathan Goble of Japan*, 218-27; Foy Johnson Farmer, *At the Gate of Asia* (Nashville: Sunday School Board, 1934), 50.

[23]J. A. Brunson, "My First Impressions of Japan," in Tupper, *Decade*, 808-11; Pettigrew, "John A. Brunson," 9.

foreigners were clustered as on the Yokohama Bluff. Experienced tutors, all male, were available for about ¥10 ($5) per month.[24]

It was desirable that the men learn Japanese from male teachers, because the language spoken by women was vastly different. For the same reason the wives were put at a disadvantage. Like Margaret Ballagh before them, Sophia and Dru had to reconcile what they learned from a male teacher with the flowery utterances from members of their own sex. It was also necessary for both husbands and wives to avoid talking like their servants, for the proper language to use on any occasion depended further on the social status of the speaker and of the one spoken to.

So difficult is the Japanese language for foreigners that it has been called the devil's tongue. Not only is it complicated by class and gender distinctions, but it is heavily burdened with the thousands of complex kanji (Chinese characters) used to write it. The Japanese had no system of writing until they began using the Chinese system around the fourth century A.D. One might say that Mr. Japanese took a picture bride, Miss Chinese. He was polysyllabic and inflected; she was monosyllabic and uninflected. So mismatched were the two that their marriage was perhaps the most tragic in linguistic history. Still, the incompatible union has persisted so long that modern efforts to untie the knot have all failed.

To read and write Japanese, one had to learn from 3,000 to 5,000 kanji, many of which had both a native Japanese reading and several Chinese readings. One also had to master two different syllabaries, each with 73 characters known as kana. Even after the written language was simplified somewhat in the mid-20th century, one study indicated that American students require six times more contact hours to learn Japanese than to learn French.[25]

Brunson quickly sensed that "the study of Japanese is a lifetime business." Commented Mac: "The only definite thing about the language is its indefiniteness."[26]

Indeed, Japanese did and still does strike a Westerner as vague and ambiguous. It is wholly unlike English in construction. It lacks the distinctions between singular and plural and between *a* and *the* as well as gender. Often it fails to specify the subject of a sentence. Japanese speakers tend to avoid clear, concise, and logical statements, relying instead on nonverbal communication known as *haragei* ("belly talk"). In the face of such formidable barriers, the Brunsons and McCollums could at least give thanks that all Japanese spoke the same language, making it unnecessary to learn several vernaculars or to print the Bible in different dialects, as required in many mission fields. It was also in their favor that

[24]McCollum to Tupper, Nov. 1889, in Tupper, *Decade*, 805-6; Tupper, *Decade*, 787, 838; Wainright, *Methodist Mission*, 23-24; *ASBC, 1891* , xiv; *ABMU Minutes, 1891*, 12. See *ABMU Minutes, 1899*, 72-85, for details on language learning.

[25]*Japan Times*, 17 Apr. 1970.

[26]Quoted in Farmer, *Gate of Asia*, 50-51.

Japanese is not a tonal language but fairly easy to pronounce, though the crucial distinction between short and long vowel sounds often trips up Southerners who speak with a drawl.

Brunson seemed to have a knack for reading and writing the Chinese characters, while McCollum showed unusual aptitude for spoken Japanese. Their wives too, whose limited tutoring was partly compensated by limitless curiosity, soon picked up the rudiments of the language. On one occasion Mac was surprised to find Dru speaking to a small child with ease. "What were you saying?" he asked her. "I don't know," Dru replied, "but that's what the mothers say to their little children."[27]

The spiritual needs confronting the missionaries had the double effect of spurring their language efforts while making the long hours of study a grind. Brunson and Mac were impatient to get on with the work of evangelism. For every church, there were hundreds of Buddhist temples and Shinto shrines. In 1890, as noted already, Japan had only 30,000 Protestants (1,000 were Baptists) in a population of 40 million. Some 300 evangelical missionaries were at work, but because of the demands of schools and other institutions, only a minority of these were engaged full time in direct evangelism.

The Southern Baptist missionaries asked the Board for "a school, with lady teachers, as indispensable to the highest success." Their main reason was that a Japanese passport for residence in the interior was usually granted to foreigners on the condition that they conduct a school. Brunson emphasized, however, that "Japan's greatest need is preachers." Concurring, McCollum requested "fifty men for Japan this fall!" Then bowing to reality, he asked for six men. Baptist male missionaries--Northern, Southern, English--totaled only 16.[28]

The Board planned to send reinforcements in modest numbers but found it difficult to recruit them. "Do you know two first rate men who wish to join you?" Tupper queried Mac. Tupper also wanted to send "two young ladies of strong health and thorough education, and consecrated spirit." The southwide Woman's Missionary Union, organized in 1888, had taken its first Christmas offering that year--at Lottie Moon's urging--to send women missionaries to China. In 1890 the WMU was promoting Japan as a new mission field, raising hopes that some women could be found to join the Brunsons and McCollums. "We have a number of applications from both sexes," wrote Tupper, "but when they are sifted . . . the number is much reduced."[29]

While awaiting reinforcements, Mac was drawn to the 400,000 people of Osaka, the nation's commercial center and second largest city. It was only 20 miles east of Kobe, and train service between the two cities was frequent. Osaka

[27]Ibid., 51.

[28]*ASBC, 1890*, xxxv; Brunson in *Foreign Mission Journal*, 22 (July 1891): 363 (hereafter cited as *FMJ*); McCollum in ibid., 22 (Aug. 1890): 16; Wynd, *Seventy Years*, 86.

[29]Tupper to McCollum, 25 July 1890, FMBA; Tupper, *Decade*, 822.

at the time was embarking on a course of modernization that would widen the narrow, rickshaw-clogged streets, deepen the junk-crowded harbors to accommodate ocean liners, and replace many of the hand looms with giant spinning mills. Such a course would enlarge the minds of the people to make room for new ideas, including Christian beliefs.[30]

Congregationalists and Episcopalians had established schools in Osaka as early as 1872, and Presbyterians also were at work in the city. The Baptist witness dated from 1888, when R. Austin Thompson, a Scotch Presbyterian before joining the Northern Baptists, started services in a rented room near Umeda Station in the heart of the city. He conducted his first baptismal service in a nearby river under the gaze of hundreds of spectators who lined the bridge above. Even after obtaining the services of a Japanese evangelist, Austin and his wife Gazelle went up to Osaka from their Kobe home three times a week for Bible work and evening classes. They saw the mission grow to 17 members.[31]

In the fall of 1889 Kobe's senior missionary, Henry H. Rhees, left for furlough. His heavy work load fell on the shoulders of Thompson, who soon felt compelled to relinquish his own ministry in Osaka. The McCollums, now close friends of the Thompsons, volunteered to fill the gap. Subsequently, the Northern Baptist missionaries in Japan agreed to a Southern Baptist ministry in Osaka, and both Tupper and the Missionary Union's secretary-elect, Henry C. Mabie, gave their consent. It was understood that the Kobe field would be left entirely to the Northern Baptists and that the Brunsons would be free to work in Kyushu, the southernmost of Japan's four main islands. In the same year Northern Presbyterians, by contrast, turned over Kobe to Southern Presbyterians in order to concentrate on Osaka.[32]

The McCollums inspected the various wards of sprawling Osaka with a view to beginning work in the district most neglected by Christian evangelists. They settled on Kogawa-chō in East Ward, some three miles distant from the work at Umeda, rented a house, and moved there at once. The movers wrapped the McCollums' furniture with matting and rope made from rice straw and delivered it safely to their new residence. With the indispensable aid of a Japanese evangelist and the transfer of a number of converts from Umeda, where services were discontinued, Mac organized the Kogawa-chō Baptist Church on March 5, 1891, with 15 charter members. The McCollums also started a day school to fulfill the requirements for government permission to reside in that part of Osaka. This

---

[30]Wynd, *Seventy Years*, 80-81.

[31]O. Cary, *History*, 2:78; Thompson, "Historical Sketch," 84-85; Wynd, *Seventy Years*, 80-81.

[32]Wynd, *Seventy Years*, 80-81; Tupper to McCollum, 15 Oct. 1890; McCollum to Tupper, 31 Oct. 1890, in *FMJ* 22 (Feb. 1891): 213; Erickson, *White Fields*, 82.

school, which had 45 enrolled and an average attendance of 15, produced several candidates for baptism.[33]

The Board reported to the 1891 session of the SBC that by agreement with the Missionary Union, Osaka was the "permanent location" of the Brunsons and McCollums. The Brunsons planned to move there as soon as Jack had fulfilled his contract as an English teacher in a government school in Kobe. Both couples were full of hope, and the new field was full of promise. A friendly Buddhist built a residence for the McCollums close to his own so that "the two families could exchange greetings, and study each others' habits without the necessity of formal visits." The McCollums occupied the new home in June. Bursting with optimism, Mac asked the Board for $1,000 for a church lot and building.[34]

Then the sky fell in. The Rheeses returned from furlough. Henry Rhees had started the Kobe work in 1882 and supervised the whole western mission until his furlough. He was outraged that Southern Baptists had invaded Osaka without his consent. Rhees "had been brought up in the old school," said a colleague, "where rivalry was more conspicuous than cooperation." His wife Hester, by contrast, was dominated by love, and he had mellowed somewhat under her influence. But the old legalism in Henry, a former lawyer and judge, sternly insisted that Southern Baptists should adhere to the original agreement of working to the west and south of Kobe. And "Kobe" he understood as the entire "Kobe field," which extended to the far end of Honshu and over to Shikoku. This meant that Southern Baptists, in his view, belonged on the island of Kyushu. Whether or not Rhees was trying to protect his own turf, his argument was sound, however cold. His colleagues agreed to his demands, and the two home boards ratified the decision.[35]

Their hearts broken, their hopes dashed to the ground, the McCollums moved back to Kobe after a mere six months in Osaka. The effect on the Osaka church was "disastrous," said William Wynd, the Northern Baptist missionary who succeeded Mac as pastor. The Southern grace and courtesy of Mac and Dru, augmented by his phenomenal fluency in the language, had endeared them to the congregation and won the respect of the neighborhood. Following their untimely departure, Wynd explained, the sheep were scattered, and a new beginning had to be made.[36]

Prior to the return of the Rheeses from furlough, the Southern Baptist missionaries enjoyed blissful fellowship with their Northern counterparts. At the annual Missionary Union conference held in Kobe in December 1890, the Brunsons and McCollums joined with the Thompsons in entertaining the missionaries from out of town. On that occasion a union conference of Baptist missionaries in Japan was formally inaugurated to be held each year in connection

---

[33]Wynd, *Seventy Years*, 81; *ASBC, 1891*, xvi.
[34]*ASBC, 1891*, xiii-xiv; Wynd, *Seventy Years*, 81.
[35]Wynd, *Seventy Years*, 68, 80-81.
[36]Ibid., 82; *ABMU Minutes, 1893*, 72.

with the conference of missionaries of the Missionary Union. The Southern Baptists attended the Northern Baptist sessions as non-voters, but they participated fully in the union conference. McCollum was elected president of the union conference, and Brunson was named associate editor of *Karashi dane* (Mustard seed), which was made the organ of the Baptist denomination in Japan.[37]

The 1891 sessions were held in Yokohama in September, after the McCollums had been forced to withdraw from Osaka. Henry Rhees took center stage. He was elected president of the Missionary Union conference, succeeding Thompson, and he prepared a statement for publication in the minutes affirming the inerrancy and infallibility of the Bible. J. W. McCollum, the offended party, was conspicuous by his absence. During the union conference Jack Brunson, the only Southern Baptist present, was elected vice president (a Northern Baptist succeeded Mac as president) and chairman of the publications committee. He also read a paper, "An Exalted Apostleship," that is notable for its clarity, logic, and dogmatism.[38]

In this paper Brunson stated his philosophy of missions as two basic principles. First, direct preaching alone is the divinely ordained method of evangelism. This principle is clearly seen, he argued, in the ministry and writings of the apostle Paul. Accordingly, Brunson drew a sharp contrast between preaching and education. "Are we not spending too much time, money and talent in the humdrum work of schoolteaching?" he asked. "It will be poor consolation in eternity to reflect that the mighty ocean was crossed in order to teach heathen boys and girls--*Barnes' Readers*." The former schoolteacher further urged that money given by American Christians, some of them too poor to educate their own children, should not be used to educate Japanese children. Apparently he was influenced by the Gospel Mission movement recently launched by T. P. Crawford of China. Crawford opposed the conducting of mission schools.[39]

Brunson's second principle was no less relevant: missionaries should avoid materialism and luxuries. In this section of his paper he renewed his attack on the "material means" of school work and also called on the missionaries to "live as nearly like the natives as possible."[40] This too was a Gospel Mission emphasis, which urged the adoption of native housing, dress, and food. Did Brunson feel a twinge of conscience for his own lifestyle in Kobe's foreign enclave? Most other missionaries in Japan looked upon "going native" as a health-impairing course to endure when unavoidable, not an ideal to be striven for. The Southern Baptists who were sent to Japan after Brunson and McCollum likewise adopted Western housing and diets as their standard.

---

[37]*ABMU Minutes, 1890*, 11-13.

[38]*ABMU Minutes, 1891*, 1, 17, 19. Brunson's paper, "An Exalted Apostleship," was published with the 1891 minutes as an eight-page pamphlet with its own pagination. He expressed the same sentiments in "The Great Need in Japan and All Mission Fields," *FMJ* 22 (July 1891), 363.

[39]Brunson, "An Exalted Apostleship," 4-5; *ESB*, vol. 1, s.v. "gospel missions."

[40]Brunson, "An Exalted Apostleship," 5-8.

Brunson was heard with respect, and the body voted unanimously to have his paper printed with the minutes. As the Northern Baptists had gone on record as giving priority to preaching and direct evangelism over everything else, no doubt they agreed with much of what Brunson said. But as he surely knew, they had started four girls' schools and were looking at possible sites for their boys' school that opened in 1895. The lone Southern Baptist could have been heard as a courageous reformer promoting an unpopular cause or as an arrogant upstart telling a score of veterans how to do their work.

The rules of the Foreign Mission Board at the time defined the "chief business" of its missionaries as "the oral communication of the gospel, the formation of churches, the training and ordination of a native ministry, the translation and circulation of the scriptures and the extension of missionary work by the aid of native laborers, supported, as far as practicable, by the natives themselves."[41] Brunson and McCollum were expected to carry out these tasks except for Scripture translation, which had been well accomplished by others. One should note that the statement affirms ministerial training but says nothing about general school work.

The Board took a neutral stance on this issue, for there was a wide variety of opinions among its missionaries. Its policy was to leave the matter of schools, "both as to kind and number, largely to the judgment of the several missions, approving and aiding schools when established by the missions; and not disapproving when they have been abandoned." The Board wisely recognized that "different countries and conditions may require different practices."[42]

Admittedly, it was a difficult time for mission schools in Japan. The 1890 Imperial Rescript on Education, rooted in Shinto tradition and Confucian ethics, seemed to be directed against Christianity. Government opposition to religious instruction was a growing problem. Still, education was so fruitful for evangelism that in later years Southern Baptist missionaries demanded and established mission schools of their own. No less devoted to the authority of Scripture, they found in Paul's own methods a flexibility that somehow eluded Brunson.[43]

The growing hostility toward mission schools in the early 1890s was part of a larger pattern of anti-Christian sentiment. Openness to Western values, a major characteristic of the "joyful '80s," had given way to resurgent nationalism, represented by the slogan, "Preserve our national values." An emperor-centered constitution had been promulgated in 1889, and a national parliament, called the Diet, established in 1890. Political rallies and elections distracted many from Christian meetings, which were increasingly subject to disturbances. Buddhists and Shintoists opposed Christianity with renewed vigor, and advocates of a strong

[41]Tupper, *Decade*, 69.
[42]Ibid., 814.
[43]See chapter 4 for Southern Baptist arguments in favor of mission schools.

emperor system accused Christians of disloyalty. Consequently, dozens of Protestant pastors, even the famous Paul Kanamori, defected from the faith, and the number of theological students declined from 316 in 1891 to 98 in 1900. Many lay persons quietly "graduated" from their churches. One missionary described the situation as "complete stagnation." The 1890s have since been called the period of "retarded" or "inward" church growth. Protestant membership increased less than 50 percent, in marked contrast to the 10-fold increase of the previous decade.[44]

An underlying motivation for the Western craze of the 1880s was the desire for revision of the degrading unequal treaties, by which extraterritoriality and customs restraints were maintained. The fervid acquisition of Western culture was promoted by the government itself in order to prove that Japan was sufficiently "civilized" to try foreign offenders in its own courts and handle its own commercial affairs. But an all-out effort to obtain treaty revision in 1889 ended in failure. As a result, Japanese in the early '90s were highly resentful of Westerners, and officials were more reluctant to grant passports for travel or residence outside the foreign settlements. "We are very much hampered by this rigid system of passports," complained Brunson, "which will be abolished only when treaty revision has been affected."[45] This was not accomplished until 1899.

In October 1891 the Southern Baptist missionaries were introduced to the fury of a major earthquake, one of about 25 that have struck Japan during the past hundred years. Sophia Brunson was bathing her baby, Sophia, Jr., when "I suddenly felt myself rocking to and fro, and saw the walls dancing about as if intoxicated." Kobe suffered little damage, but in some of the cities farther east, especially Gifu and Ōgaki, rows of buildings collapsed with great loss of life. Fires broke out, and many towns and villages were left a mass of smoldering ruins. As many as 8,000 people were killed and 15,000 injured, and 100,000 homes were partially or totally destroyed. The Brunsons and McCollums, after hearing eyewitness accounts of the horrible destruction, gave of their means to alleviate the suffering.[46]

In November 1891 the missionaries completed two years in Japan, the usual period for language study and cultural adaptation before engagement in permanent work. During that time the Brunsons gained their only child, Sophia, while the McCollums had their first, Joseph, and prepared for the birth of Catherine in December 1891. The two years were fruitful in other ways also, and not without

[44]Iglehart, *Century*, 92; O. Cary, *History*, 2:212-20; *Japan Christian Yearbook, 1910*, 72 (hereafter cited as *JCY*); E. Luther Copeland, "The Crisis of Protestant Missions to Japan 1889-1900," (Ph.D. diss., Yale University, 1949), iii. Kanamori's Japanese name was Tsūrin or Michitomo.

[45]Brunson letter in *FMJ* 22 (July 1891): 363-64.

[46]Sophia Brunson letter in *FMJ* 23 (Jan. 1892): 175-76; O. Cary, *History*, 2:236-37.

travail. The McCollums led in establishing a church outside a treaty port but were forced to abandon it. Brunson gained experience teaching in a government school but failed to grasp the value of English instruction as a mode of evangelism. Both couples were initiated into the workings of an organized mission, that of Northern Baptists. They also learned something of the complications that arise in missionary interpersonal relationships--complications that can be more unnerving than an earthquake. The two years in Kobe and Osaka were needed preparation for the challenges awaiting them in the distant world of Kyushu.

Map of Kyūshū, with inset showing cities that merged in 1963 to form Kita Kyūshū

3

Breaking New Ground (1892-1899)

Kyushu, literally "nine provinces," is the third largest of Japan's four main islands and about half the size of South Carolina. It lies in the same latitude as the state of Georgia. Renowned for its scenic mountains and lovely seascapes, Kyushu has at its center Mount Aso, a still-active volcano whose crater is 50 miles in circumference--the world's largest--and whose lava flow in years past has covered most of the island. Although Kyushu has only one-tenth of Japan's total land area, its 1892 population of nine million made up one-fifth of the nation's people. These "suffering millions" stirred the hearts of the Southern Baptist pioneers.[1]

Kyushu is the cradle of Japanese civilization. Due to its proximity to the Asian mainland, this island was the first to be touched by continental culture. It is also the cradle of Japanese Christianity. As noted earlier, the Jesuit pioneer Francis Xavier first introduced the gospel to Japan at Kagoshima in southern Kyushu. During the "Christian century" that followed, Kyushu remained the heart of missionary activity. The bustling port of Nagasaki became the "little Rome" of Japan; most of its 40,000 inhabitants were baptized Catholics.[2]

Then came the dreadful ban, two and a half centuries of cruel and persistent government efforts to destroy all trace of the foreign religion. Yet when Japan was opened to the West in the mid-19th century, there emerged in the Nagasaki area a community of 20,000 Christians who had preserved their faith in secret. This revelation brought a new wave of persecution; several thousand were sent into exile, and hundreds died a martyr's death.[3] If the survival of so large a community of believers testified to the success of early Catholic missions in Kyushu, it also renewed the legacy of revulsion to the "evil religion." As Guido Verbeck pointed

---

[1]Tupper, *Decade*, 788; *ASBC, 1892*, xxxv.
[2]Jennes, *History*, 105.
[3]Ibid., 216-18, 223-29. The total number of "hidden Christians" is estimated at about 60,000, only about half of whom chose to return to the Roman Catholic Church (*Kodansha Encylopedia of Japan*, s.v. "Christianity").

out, if Christianity were mentioned in the presence of a Japanese, "his hand would, almost involuntarily, be applied to his throat, to indicate the extreme perilousness of such a topic."[4]

Not only was Christianity greatly feared in Kyushu, but Buddhism was deeply entrenched. Merely by posing as a monk, it was said, a man could travel for days on the island with only one *rin*, the smallest of coins. The traveler had only to wear pilgrim's garb, make the local temple in each town his first stop, and have the *rin* visible between the tips of his hands extended in prayer. This would convince the Buddhist faithful that he was a holy man, and they would provide his food and lodging.[5]

Protestantism in Kyushu, as indicated before, had its start in 1859 at Nagasaki through the witness of Verbeck and others. In 1874 there emerged from central Kyushu the highly influential Kumamoto Band, some 40 converts of Leroy Janes, a Presbyterian. Confronted by persecution, many of the converts left Kyushu for further training at Dōshisha, the Congregational school in Kyoto. Some of these returned to convert family members and start Congregational churches. Methodists also entered the island and established churches and schools in a number of towns, with the work in Ōita showing unusual success. In northern Kyushu, where Baptists were to gain a foothold, Protestant work dates from 1879 in Fukuoka and 1880 in Kokura. Both of these cities were old castle towns and sites of early Jesuit mission residences.[6]

In 1889, when Brunson and McCollum made their first rickshaw tour of northern and western Kyushu, the Board suggested Nagasaki as "a good place" to locate. But during a second survey trip after the McCollums' expulsion from Osaka, the missionaries made arrangements to live in Kokura, "a town of about 15,000 inhabitants, with good facilities for travelling." It was conveniently located at a railroad junction and only 10 miles from the newly developed port of Moji on Kammon Strait, the mile-wide swirl of eddies and current that separates Kyushu from Honshu. In January 1892 the Brunsons moved into a rented house large enough for two families, and the McCollums, who tarried to fulfill their evangelistic commitments in the Kobe area, joined them in March.[7]

Kokura lay at the heart of the pioneer work in Kyushu to which Southern Baptists fell heir. Northern Baptists maintained one of their best-staffed and -equipped stations in Yamaguchi Prefecture, just across the strait at the western

[4]Verbeck, "History," 746.

[5]Lloyd R. Neve, *Japan: God's Door to the Far East* (Minneapolis: Augsburg Publishing House, 1973), 38.

[6]F. G. Notehelfer, *American Samurai: Captain L. L. Janes and Japan* (Princeton: Princeton University Press, 1985), 179-209, 229, 234; *Proceedings, 1900*, 917; *Nihon Kirisutokyō rekishi daijiten* (Dictionary of Japanese Christian history), s.v. "Kumamoto-ken," "Fukuoka-ken"; Iglehart, *Century*, 73.

[7]Tupper to McCollum, 5 May 1890; *ASBC, 1892*, xxxv-xxxvii; Tupper, *Decade*, 806.

tip of Honshu. It was here that G. H. Appleton had evangelized so successfully before his visit to the Board in Richmond. The Kyushu work was launched on November 3, 1890, in the town of Wakamatsu, four miles from Kokura. On that date Gotō Mutsuo, an evangelist under the supervision of Yamaguchi's R. L. Halsey, began to conduct meetings in the home of Tsuruhara Gorō, a druggist and fervent Baptist layman. In 1891 Gotō opened additional preaching stations, called *kōgisho*, in Kokura, Moji, and Ashiya. As generously proposed by Halsey, the zealous but tactful Gotō was transferred to the Southern Baptist mission.[8]

When Brunson moved to Kokura, Gotō had seven converts ready to be baptized at Wakamatsu. Those seven had the courage to wade into the chilling sea and yield themselves to the big hands of a newly come foreigner, one whose strange face was half concealed by a long black beard. With these additions to the Wakamatsu fellowship, a total of 13 believers received communion at the house used as a chapel. "This forms the nucleus of our work in Kyushu," Brunson reported.[9] Gotō's most outstanding convert was a primary school principal, Sugano Hanji, who was to serve in the Baptist ministry for 38 years. Sugano's refreshing frankness and affability were exceeded only by his evangelistic ardor. Several of his daughters became Christian teachers, and one son, Kyūji, walked in his father's footsteps as a minister. The honor of baptizing Sugano Hanji fell to Jack Brunson.[10]

After the McCollums had moved to Kyushu in March 1892, the missionaries reported 25 church members and 20 inquirers. In Kokura they had four Sunday schools in different parts of the city. At first the work went smoothly. "But soon came troublesome and vexatious experiences," said McCollum. "The men who had secured passports for the Missionaries [to live in the interior] proved false to their profession as Christians and shrewdly deceiving the too-trusting Missionaries, succeeded in misappropriating over a hundred dollars." The money had been paid to these men for rents. Wiser for the experience, the pioneer missionaries were never again defrauded by the Japanese in whom they confided.[11]

Their letters to the Board asked repeatedly for additional workers to be sent to Japan. The Board itself supported "all possible progressive movement in Japan, owing to the great interest manifested there on the part of the government in the

---

[8]*ASBC, 1892*, xxxiv; Wynd, *Seventy Years*, 123; Thompson, "Historical Sketch," 85; McCollum, "Historical Sketch," 101.

[9]*ASBC, 1892*, xxxv. A bearded Brunson is pictured with Japanese converts in Egasaki Kiyomi, ed., *Baputesuto senkyō hachijūnen no ayumi* (Eighty years of Baptist evangelism) (Tokyo: Nihon Baputesuto Remmei, 1969), 10.

[10]EBD, *Golden Milestone*, 54-58.

[11]McCollum, "Historical Sketch," 99; *ASBC, 1892*, xxxvi; J. F. Love, *Southern Baptists and Their Far Eastern Missions* (Richmond, Va: FMB, 1922), 271-72. Love says the fraud occurred soon after the arrival of the Walnes in Nov. 1892, but McCollum implies that it occurred earlier.

educational development and elevation of that people."[12] Sophia Brunson called attention to the numerous obstacles to the gospel, including the negative example of so-called Christians from Europe and America. "A lady asked her interpreter how many wives the Japanese had," she related. "He innocently replied, 'Two or three, just as the foreigners in Yokohama do.'" Sophia pled for two single ladies and four families to join them in the fall and help them overcome such obstacles.[13]

Resignation and Replacement of the Brunsons

Less than a month after Sophia sent her stirring appeal from Kokura, Jack sent a shocking letter of resignation. Her letter appeared in the July 1892 issue of the *Foreign Mission Journal*, his in the August issue. "God has never called me to the work," he wrote. "I am a Board-called missionary and not a God-called one." He had been misled, Jack claimed, by the "specious argument that in the absence of sufficient reason why one should remain at home, duty called him to foreign fields." Yet he wished to blame no one but himself: "I alone am culpable in that I responded without definite and decided convictions."[14]

Scores of his successors have resigned for one reason or another, usually disappointing their colleagues and sometimes shocking them. One appointee in the 1980s who was unsure of God's call stayed in Japan only three weeks, making Brunson's three years seem like a very long time to resolve the problem. But of the approximately 200 resignations in the history of the Mission, Brunson's is the most dramatic and intriguing if not the saddest.

What prompted his disclosure that God had never called him overseas? It is not entirely facetious to suggest that he grew tired of bumping his head on the door lintels in Japanese "doll houses," as tall foreigners still do today. Clearly he disliked being cramped in the rickshaws that carried him from place to place. Once on a trip with McCollum, it is related, Brunson reached the limit of endurance. "Well Scotch," he said, "you may go ahead this way if you wish, but from here and now on I walk." They both walked for the rest of the trip.[15]

We may also surmise that Brunson was weary of Lilliputian stares and scornful glances. It was but natural that the Japanese regarded themselves as normal people and the foreigners--extremely rare in northern Kyushu--as oddities to be scrutinized. One sophisticated prince had told Jonathan Goble that he formerly thought foreigners were "but so many different kinds of monkeys, and that the Japanese only were truly human beings." A Japanese pastor, only half in jest, said that white Americans had been undercooked in God's oven, black

---

[12]*ASBC, 1892*, cited in EBD notes, 11.
[13]Sophia Brunson letter, 28 Apr. 1892, in *FMJ* 23 (July 1892), 368.
[14]Brunson to Bell, 23 May 1892, in *FMJ* 24 (Aug. 1892), 12.
[15]Pettigrew, "John A. Brunson," 9.

Africans had been burnt, and the Japanese had been baked just right to a beautiful golden brown.[16]

We may further assume that Brunson was dismayed by the contrast between Mac's growing fluency in the spoken language and his own faltering efforts. He was a logical thinker, as his sermons clearly show, but to speak Japanese, "one had to think backwards, inside out, and upside down."[17] A man of his intellect and ability must have agonized over his language handicap and his childlike dependence on Japanese helpers.

Perhaps Brunson was also troubled by the incompatibility of his missionary ideals, enunciated so ably at the Baptist missionary conference of 1891, with the realities of Japan. He may have realized that even apostolic preaching would never get the results one could expect in America. And it probably disturbed him that the McCollums planned to start a day school in Kyushu and have single women sent out as teachers.

Whatever pressures weighed upon Brunson, the root of his agony was lack of a clear call from God. He was haunted by this lack before he came to Japan and throughout his stay. Tupper had warned him in 1891: "Do not give way to Doubts! That is one of Satan's strongest weapons." But it was Brunson's honest conviction that God had never called him overseas and that he was a misfit in Japan. "McCollum, I can't stand it," he often told his colleague. "The Lord does not want me here. I'm a square pin in a round hole."[18]

Would Brunson have suffered the same frustration had he gone to China, to which he was first appointed? Probably so. His philosophy of missions suggests that he would have joined the Gospel Mission movement there, which spawned 10 or more resignations.

How Sophia felt is veiled in obscurity. Though not an appointed missionary, this highly gifted woman seems to have been committed to a lifetime of service in Japan. She, along with her husband, won McCollum's praise as "a tower of strength, grace and consecration."[19] The loss of Jack Brunson to the work meant, of course, the loss of Sophia too.

Brunson thoughtfully refrained from submitting his resignation until he had learned that new missionaries would be sent out. "I am unwilling to leave McCollum alone," he wrote. "He is brave, noble, and efficient, and is capable of bearing the burden, but my presence will be helpful till others come to share the responsibility." He postponed his departure until fall, when his replacement was en route to Japan. In September he lectured on "Baptist Distinctives" at a four-day retreat for missionaries and evangelists, and in other ways also he continued to

---

[16]J. Goble to N. Brown, 12 Mar. 1871, in *American Baptist*, 11 May 1871; Farmer, *Gate of Asia*, 23.

[17]Cecile Lancaster, "My Life on the Mission Field" (typescript; n.d., FMBA), 21.

[18]Tupper to Brunson, 9 Mar. 1891; McCollum, "Historical Sketch," 99.

[19]McCollum, "Historical Survey," 99-100.

contribute to the work. Yet he offered to refund to the Board every dollar expended on his support.[20]

The Board accepted Brunson's resignation "with deep regret" and "with no diminished regard for our faithful and conscientious co-worker." It sadly noted that "he did not appreciate his own successes." McCollum described his own sorrow as "akin to that of seeing buried the friend and brother of one's bosom."[21]

During the next several years Brunson was pastor of small Baptist churches in his native South Carolina. Then for reasons unknown he joined the Seventh-day Adventists and served as a chaplain at their sanatorium in Battle Creek, Michigan. "Elder Brunson" rose to such prominence among Seventh-day Adventists that in 1899 he preached on the second coming of Christ at a worldwide meeting of that denomination. Sophia Brunson demonstrated her abiding interest in missions by attending the 1900 Ecumenical Conference on Foreign Missions as an honorary delegate. She became a physician in 1902, when she was 37, upon graduation from Ohio State Medical College.[22]

In 1905 the Brunsons returned to South Carolina and the fellowship of Southern Baptists. Jack was elected moderator of his association. He was often called on for revivals, widely used as a lecturer on prohibition, and well received as convention preacher at the annual meeting of South Carolina Baptists. He served his last pastorate--25 years long--at the 600-member Grace Baptist Church in Sumter. During those years "Doctor Sophia" had a large medical practice that included many patients unable to pay for her services, and she was elected president of the Sumter Medical Association. Jack and Sophia both died in their 80s.[23]

The ship bearing the Brunsons back to America passed in mid-ocean the ship bringing to Japan a third missionary couple, Ernest and Claudia Walne. In sharp contrast to the Brunsons, who had served three years, the Walnes were to serve 43 years, an all-time record for the Japan Mission.

Ernest Nathan Walne was born in Mississippi, where his mother served with Julia Toy Johnson on the central committee for organizing missionary societies.

---

[20]Brunson to Bell, 23 May 1892; *Nihon Baputesuto Remmei shi (1889-1959)* (History of the Japan Baptist Convention, 1889-1959) (Tokyo: Nihon Baputesuto Remmei, 1959), 35-36 (hereafter cited as *NBRS*).

[21]*ASBC, 1893*, xxvii; McCollum, "Historical Sketch," 100.

[22]Welsh Neck (S.C.) Baptist Association, *Minutes*, 1892-97; Orangeburg (S.C.) Baptist Association, *Minutes*, 1910-15; Santee (S.C.) Baptist Association, *Minutes*, 1916-41; Pettigrew, "John A. Brunson," 9; John S. Ramond, comp., *Among Southern Baptists*, vol. 1 (Shreveport, La., 1936), 67; *Ecumenical Missionary Conference*, vol. 2 (New York: American Tract Society, 1900), 397; Jesse Myers, telephone conversation with author, 28 Jan. 1989. Sermons by Brunson were published in *General Conference Daily Bulletin* (1899, 39-40), and *Advent Review and Sabbath Herald* (1 Apr. 1902), 194.

[23]*Baptist Courier*, 30 Dec. 1943, 12; ibid., 13 Jan. 1944, 15; undated news clippings furnished by the late Jesse Myers.

His father, a pastor and Sunday school promoter, served on the SBC's Foreign Missions Committee. Baptized at the age of 13 by J. B. Gambrell, who later served four terms as SBC president, Ernest was inspired by the life of Adoniram Judson to devote himself to foreign missions. After attending Mississippi College and Southern Baptist Seminary, he moved to Ghent, Kentucky, as pastor for one year. Claudia McCann, a graduate of the Cincinnati Conservatory of Music who had grown up in that church, quickly caught his attention. Ernest was struck by "her beautiful brown eyes" and the "magnificent way" she sang "The Holy City." He decided that "here was the one thing needed for a successful missionary career." Claudia, his junior by one year, was equally attracted to the brilliant young minister with close-set eyes, protruding ears, neatly trimmed mustache, and a heart on fire for missions. In May 1892 they were married at Boscobel College, a short-lived Baptist girls' school in Nashville, where she was teaching music.[24]

Three months later the Walnes took a train to Toronto and across the Canadian Rockies to Vancouver, where they boarded the swift white steamer *Empress of China*. After a stormy passage they arrived at Yokohama November 13, on a bright Sunday morning. They attended English-language worship at the Union Church, then steamed on to Kobe. There Walne "saw my old friend McCollum advancing, his face split with a grin from ear to ear. Regardless of spectators we leaped into each other's arms and had a genuine old 'hug.'" Brunson's departure had made Mac's heart "bleed with sadness"; Walne's arrival made it "leap for joy." After the customary shopping spree, the two couples traveled by steamer through the scenic Inland Sea to Moji, then took a launch on to Kokura.[25]

Pushing Back the Frontiers

For the next several months the two families lived together in Kokura, enduring the icy winds that assail the western shores of Japan. Kokura was not only a chilly place, Walne discovered, but "a Buddhist stronghold" where "anti-Christian and anti-foreign feeling is very strong and bitter." In 1893, in order to oversee the preaching stations "more advantageously and economically," the McCollums moved to Moji, and the Walnes moved in the opposite direction to Fukuoka, the prefectural capital with a population of 100,000. Moji and Fukuoka, 45 miles apart, were conveniently linked by rail, and third-class fares were less than one cent per mile. Regular church services were conducted in these two cities and three towns in between: Kokura, Wakamatsu, and Ashiya. Most of

---

[24]*Home and Foreign Fields* 16 (Apr. 1932), 14-15 (hereafter cited as *HFF*); Richard A. McLemore, *A History of Mississippi Baptists, 1780-1970* (Jackson: Mississippi Baptist Convention Board, 1971), 224-25.

[25]*HFF* 12 (July 1928), 7-8; McCollum to Bell, 14 Nov. 1892, in *FMJ* 24 (Jan. 1893), 175; Farmer, *Gate of Asia*, 56-57.

the preaching was done by Gotō and Sugano, both of whom had the full confidence of the missionaries.[26]

In early 1893, to the delight of Kyushu Baptists, Kawakatsu Tetsuya, Japan's first ordained Baptist minister, came to Kokura from Yokohama on "temporary loan" from the Missionary Union. Born a samurai in Ōmura near Nagasaki in 1850, Kawakatsu had been wounded in the Battle of Ueno in the civil war that overthrew the shogunate. Subsequently he had proved an able and fearless soldier for Christ, first as Nathan Brown's language assistant and then as a pioneer evangelist. "I desired to work in Kyushu, my native country, very much," he wrote, "and prayed for it many years so that the gate may be opened for me." Kawakatsu agreed to join Ernest Walne in Fukuoka as interpreter and evangelist for six months. Not only did the two men forge an enduring bond, but Kawakatsu chose to work in his native Kyushu with Southern Baptists until his death in 1915.[27]

The McCollums found Moji an exciting port that handled ocean-going vessels and did a brisk trade in coal and rice. An unforgettable sight was the coaling of steamers by scores of men, women, and children, who would stand on tiers of hanging platforms on each side of the ship from stem to stern and pass up hundreds of tons of coal by hand. Though the raw, new town was a dangerous place with more than its share of ruffians, McCollum preached with the fearless zeal of the early Jesuits.[28]

Under the impetus of Mac's ministry, Moji Baptist Church (Moji Baputesuma Kyōkai), the first Baptist church in Kyushu, was organized on October 4, 1893. The festive occasion drew an attendance of 55, including Northern Baptist delegates from Kobe, Osaka, and Shimonoseki. Kawakatsu delivered the sermon, and Gorō Tsuruhara, in whose Moji home the church met for many years, spoke in behalf of the 30 charter members. These members--all the Baptists in Kyushu-- were scattered over an area 50 miles long and 10 or 15 miles wide. Previously they were counted as members of the church in Shimonoseki, just across the strait. So the organization of the Moji church in effect completed the transfer of the Kyushu field to Southern Baptists. With McCollum as temporary pastor, the church gained 11 new members the first year.[29]

The McCollums opened a day school, Kiyotaki Gakuen, that attracted children from the better families of the town. Under the immediate supervision of Dru McCollum, the school was conducted by a young woman who also served as her language teacher. They were assisted by volunteers from the church.[30]

[26]Walne letter, 30 Dec. 1892, cited in *HFF* 12 (July 1928), 6; McCollum, "Historical Sketch," 100; *FMJ* 24 (May 1893): 296.

[27]Kawakatsu to FMB, 17 Jan. 1896, in EBD papers; *HFF* 12 (July 1928), 9.

[28]Farmer, *Gate of Asia*, 56-57; *NBRS*, 56-57.

[29]*ASBC, 1894*, xx; *NBRS*, 53-54, 56-57.

[30]*ASBC, 1894*, xx; *NBRS*, 55.

Soon tragedy struck the McCollums: in April 1894 two-year-old Catherine died of cholera. Earlier, the Jonathan Gobles, the G. H. Appletons, and other missionaries had lost children to this dreaded disease, as had countless thousands of Japanese parents. "The native Christians came from distant places to offer their sympathy," reported Walne. Catherine was buried on the mountainside overlooking Kammon Strait, and in 1911 her remains were moved to the Moji church's burial ground on another mountain with a lovely view. The gravestone has since fallen over, but the inscription can still be read.[31]

In the same year that Catherine died, Mac suffered from catarrh, an inflammation of the mucous membranes in the nose and throat. By autumn his condition had so worsened that the family returned to the States on medical leave. Satō Kitarō, an evangelist of the Dutch Reformed mission who had turned Baptist under Walne's instruction and had worked for McCollum as language teacher, succeeded the missionary as pastor of the Moji church. Satō also took charge of Kiyotaki Gakuen, but it was soon discontinued when a public school was established in the town.[32]

In Fukuoka, meanwhile, Walne preached and taught Bible to young Japanese evangelists, with Kawakatsu serving as interpreter. In a July 1894 letter to the Board, he pleaded for a missionary "to organize and teach a training school for native evangelists." Southern Baptists needed their own training school, Walne argued, because it was impractical to send students to the Northern Baptist seminary in distant Yokohama. Japanese workers were so few that their services were badly needed in Kyushu while they pursued their studies. Furthermore, a local school would serve to insulate them from the theological unrest then plaguing Japanese Protestants. "You know of course," said Walne, "how fond the Japanese are of new ideas. . . . Any new departure in theology, no matter how absurd, will find zealous and loud advocates here before it is two months old in Europe or America."[33]

"Such a school as I have indicated," continued Walne, "will involve little or no cost beyond the salary of the missionary. There will be no need for buildings until the native Christians are able to pay for them." Even so, the Board offered no encouragement, and more than a decade was to pass before Southern Baptists established a formal school in Japan. Walne was to lament "our mistake in failing to continue educational work in those early days."[34]

As the loss of the Brunsons in 1892 had been compensated by the timely arrival of the Walnes, the departure of the McCollums in the fall of 1894 was counterbalanced by the coming of Nathan and Bessie Maynard from the pastorate

---

[31]Walne to FMB, 19 Apr. 1894; *NBRS*, 55-56; EBD notes, 1911. The author visited the grave in 1988.
[32]*NBRS*, 55; EBD notes, 1895; Love, *Far Eastern Missions*, 277.
[33]Walne to R. J. Willingham, 7 July 1894; *ASBC, 1894*, xxi.
[34]Ibid.; Love, *Far Eastern Missions*, 272.

of the Baptist church in Covington, Tennessee. They arrived in Japan on
December 1. The Walnes had lived with the McCollums in Kokura, and now the
Maynards lived with the Walnes at Fukuoka. After a year of language study, the
promising new couple moved to Kokura for permanent work. "Thus the station
which became the first residence of Southern Baptists on Kyushu," said
McCollum, "has become the residence of the best Missionaries of Southern
Baptists in Japan."[35]

The "best Missionaries" were also the oldest. Nathan Maynard was born on
a Maryland farm in 1858, five years before McCollum. Converted while
employed by the Western Maryland Railroad, he was 34 when he graduated from
Southern Seminary. His fellow students called him Deacon Maynard, a title that
persisted even in Japan. Nathan was 35 when he married Bessie Harlowe, two
years his junior. The dainty, frail daughter of a Baptist pastor in Salem, Virginia,
"Miss Bessie" was organist for her home church, music teacher in a private
school, and leader of the "infant class" in Sunday school--roles that were excellent
preparation for her oft-praised children's work in Japan. After three years on the
field Bessie wrote: "There has never been aught but joy and thankfulness that God
let me come; never a moment when I have wished to return." The Maynards
endeared themselves to the Japanese with their warm hospitality and aptness for
personal work.[36]

When the McCollums returned to Japan in the fall of 1895, soon after the
Maynards' move to Kokura, they located in Fukuoka rather than Moji. A few
months later the Walnes moved to Nagasaki, where they savored the rich and
distinctive old culture that blended Chinese and European influences. In the
heyday of Roman Catholicism, this "little Rome" belonged to the Jesuits for a
decade, a gift to them from the first Christian daimyo. Then during the two and
a half centuries of national seclusion, a small Dutch trading post in the harbor
served as Japan's only window to the West. This left a strong Dutch flavor to the
city. The Chinese trading post there also remained active during this period. But
the Walnes went to Nagasaki, not to enjoy the culture and beauty of this historic
port, but to preach the gospel to a resistant population of 70,000. With Sugano as
coworker, Walne inaugurated services in March 1896 and soon opened three
outstations, including Sasebo, a new naval port 60 miles to the north. Several
years were to pass before the first baptism.[37]

The difficult start in Nagasaki was explained in part by the Sino-Japanese
War of 1894-95, which left the Japanese elated with their victory over China.
Consequently, wrote McCollum in 1896, the people were "more bitterly opposed
than ever to the propagation of the truth." But after a year or two it became

---

[35]McCollum, "Historical Survey," 100; *ASBC, 1895*, xxii.
[36]*FMJ*, Sept. 1898, 126-27; EBD, *Golden Milestone*, 60-61.
[37]Jennes, "History," 34; *ASBC, 1897*, lxii; *ASBC, 1899*, lxiv.

evident that this imperialist war, unjust though it was, had served to break down some of the prejudice against the Christian faith. Three reasons may be cited. Several Christian ministers were allowed to serve as chaplains--called "comforters"--to the troops, Christian soldiers on the battlefield proved their loyalty to the emperor, and the highly admired work of the Red Cross Society weakened the taboo against the symbol of the cross. During hostilities, Southern Baptist and other missionaries were allowed to visit the military hospital at Kokura and distribute literature among troops en route to the seat of war--ministries formerly prohibited. From time to time detachments of soldiers were quartered in the Baptist preaching places. Said Walne: "We have taken advantage of the exceptional opportunities afforded for personal work."[38]

Walne and Sugano were especially pleased with the response in the naval town of Sasebo. They found that sailors who had visited foreign countries were less prejudiced against Christianity than most other Japanese, and that young men from the seamen's training school were quite willing to listen to the gospel. Walne and Sugano conducted open chapel services that frequently drew as many as 300 listeners.[39]

The Mission gained its first real estate in 1896 when McCollum purchased 800 tsubo of land, nearly two-thirds of an acre (one tsubo is about 36 square feet), in Daimyō-machi, Fukuoka. The cost was $900. The next year Mac built a $600 Western-style house on a portion of the land and proudly moved in with his family. "A Japanese house is fairly comfortable during spring and autumn," Mac explained, "but during the coldest months it is simply a question of how much cold one can endure."[40] The new residence had a foundation of granite, and most of the lumber used in the construction was cedar. It was a box-like frame dwelling with eight large rooms, four up and four down, and kitchen, bath and servant's room. Like Japanese houses, even many built today, it had no closets. The Fukuoka residence served as home, office, and meeting place for a succession of missionaries.[41]

The Maynards wanted a Mission residence no less than the McCollums. Their native house in Kokura was open not only to the gentle neighbors but to the unfriendly elements. In March 1897 Nathan wrote: "We both have contracted catarrh and neuralgia since we came here and it is so serious in the case of my wife that we dread a change in the weather." In June he wrote that they had just come home from Kobe, where Bessie had undergone three weeks of medical treatment, when "a storm melted the mud from the East end of our house & left us instead of a wall a bamboo frame such as they plaster against, along the entire side

---

[38]McCollum in *ASBC, 1896*, xlix; Walne in *ASBC, 1895*, xxi; O. Cary, *History*, 2:249-52.
[39]*ASBC, 1899*, lxiii-lxiv.
[40]W. Thorburn Clark, *Outriders for the King* (Nashville: Broadman Press, 1931) 110-11; Maynard to R. J. Willingham, 18 Jan. 1899, FMBA.
[41]Maude B. Dozier, *Charles Kelsey Dozier of Japan* (Nashville: Broadman Press, 1953), 11.

of our bed-room. Of course when the wall fell it woke us up and as the rain was driving entirely through the room we had to seek other quarters." Rugs, furniture, and books throughout the house were damaged by the rain.[42]

The house was repaired and the furnishings were dried out, but still the place left much to be desired. The Maynards had to use a 9-by-12-foot study for preaching services, with an attendance of 12 to 20, and for Sunday school, with an average attendance of 40. On one occasion more than 60 children were crowded into that little room. So Nathan kept appealing to the Board for a new house. At length, Secretary R. J. Willingham, who had succeeded Tupper in 1893, told him he was suffering from the "blues." Not so, Nathan replied. "My wife thinks my 'blues' are the sky-blues." He still insisted that "I want a home with all my heart. . . . We have both suffered."[43]

The touching story of "dear Mrs. Maynard's house" in Southern Baptist publications brought forth a flood of nickels and dimes, mostly from children. The offerings enabled the Maynards to build a Kokura residence in 1899. It was erected on a 308-tsubo (one-fourth acre) lot purchased in 1897 for $924 and registered in Kawakatsu's name. Painted a somber brown, the residence had "lovely verandahs, upstairs and down, on the east and on the south." On one side of the house were the study, dining room, kitchen, pantry, and laundry room with a well. On the other side were a large Japanese-style meeting room and smaller rooms for a Bible woman and servants. Upstairs were a sitting room, guest room, and master bedroom. Each room in the house had a fireplace. The total cost of land, walls, and house was $2,500, a princely sum at the time.[44]

From his own comfortable home in Fukuoka, McCollum sallied forth with his customary zeal, preaching indoors and out, pleading for conversions and urging believers to tithe and attain self-support. His stress on stewardship was pertinent, for in 1897 only 70 of the 375 organized Protestant churches in Japan were self-supporting. Mac also devoted himself to the training of Japanese workers. During the summer of 1897 he helped conduct a Bible school for five evangelists at the Northern Baptist station in Chōfu. In January and February 1899 he instructed two evangelists at his home four hours a day, concentrating on theology and New Testament interpretation.[45]

Overcoming Obstacles

Disappointments were many. In 1898 the son of Pastor Gotō was jailed for theft, bringing shame on his father. "Here where Christianity is on trial," said

[42]Maynard to Willingham, 19 Mar. 1897, 6 June 1897.

[43]Maynard to Willingham, 18 Mar. 1898; *ASBC, 1899*, lxv.

[44]Foy Johnson Farmer, *Mrs. Maynard's House* (Nashville: Broadman Press, 1940), 24-25; Maynard to Willingham, 18 Jan. 1899.

[45]*ASBC, 1896*, xlix; *Proceedings, 1900*, 990-93; *ASBC, 1899*, lxii-lxvii.

McCollum, "the people gloat over his shame. Two of the most influential newspapers have published sensational accounts of the occurrence, and the people in Fukuoka and Hakata are only too glad to use the misdemeanor of the son in order to disgrace the father." Consequently, Gotō was removed from northern Kyushu to Kumamoto, where he opened a new station and did his customary good work.[46]

A more serious crisis struck in Moji. It involved Tsuruhara, the church's most prominent layman and the owner of the house used for services. Tsuruhara "got into trouble over borrowed money," reported Maynard, "and finally was imprisoned for a year on the charge of embezzlement. The newspapers took up the case and used it in a vigorous campaign against Christianity." This had a serious effect on the church. Some of the members refused to attend services at Tsuruhara's house, and no other meeting place could be obtained. "The scandalous reports of our enemies have hung like a pall over our work there," Maynard said. As for the "brother in distress," Maynard reported that "he did not get the consideration he deserved from the court, although we admit that his conduct was not consistent with his religious beliefs."[47]

Maynard's next report likewise had a gloomy cast. At the poorly attended services in Moji, he wrote, "some scoff, and on rare occasions we are abused by some evil character." He told of adults standing around the room during Sunday school "who ridicule the teacher, and often say shameful things to the pupils during the lesson." The situation was no better at the preaching place in Kokura, which suffered "a great deal of rowdyism." "Often stones were thrown against the sides of the house," said Maynard. "Youths and children, with horns and drums, made hideous noises while we attempted to hold preaching services."[48]

Maynard had the joy of baptizing a city official, who subsequently was promoted to a higher position, but he also had the sorrow of losing several members. "We were compelled to expel two of our female members," he said, "because one, the mother, gave the other, her daughter, as a concubine to an officer." There were, however, many seekers and many opportunities to share the gospel. Wrote Maynard: "We were not compelled to preach behind closed doors at Kokura during this winter as was the case in many other places."[49]

The situation in Fukuoka was bleak. "As yet," wrote Mac in 1899, "no one reared in the town has been added to our little band of believers." The five who had been baptized were immigrants from other places in Japan. The most hostile part of Fukuoka was Hakata, the section east of the Naka River with a population of 60,000. The work there had to be suspended when a place used by Gotō for

---

[46]McCollum to FMB, 20 Aug. 1898.
[47]*ASBC, 1899*, lxvi.
[48]*ASBC, 1900*, 113.
[49]Ibid., 114.

four years could no longer be obtained.[50] A separate town until early in the decade, Hakata retained its prestige as the commercial center of northern Kyushu, and to this day Fukuoka's main depot is called Hakata Station.

"Here in Fukuoka," wrote McCollum, "we are having a peculiarly trying time, as all open-air meetings have been forbidden, and the doors of our rented chapels (on the streets) ordered closed while holding service." Such restrictions were hard on McCollum. He had to see progress in the work. He demanded rapid church growth. He yearned for an end to the "stolid indifference" that greeted his earnest preaching. "Look a hundred years ahead," Secretary Tupper had advised him. "Be content to make haste slowly." Townsend Harris had given similar advice to the first Protestant missionaries at Kanagawa, but in Latin: *festina lente* (hasten slowly). McCollum's Japanese colleagues also urged patience. The seasoning of wood, they knew, results in a better building. But the anxious and restless missionary showed signs of discouragement.[51]

"The progress has been painfully slow," wrote McCollum again. "For years the other missions have had comfortable homes for the missionaries and in many places permanent and rather well-appointed preaching places. Up to three years ago, we were at the orders of heathen landlords who suffered us to occupy only so long as was convenient and profitable to them. Consequently the history of our work here might be written with the one word - *move*."[52]

The missionaries and their Japanese coworkers all knew the sad consequences of being "thrown out of a place to preach," as Maynard put it. "In one of our stations," reported Walne, "we were forced to change the location of our chapel five times within six years. Each move involves a loss in the results of the work that it would be difficult to calculate. In each new place we have to go through the successive stages of opposition, idle curiosity, indifference, and then a slowly developed interest." It is no wonder that Walne and his associates came to believe that "a well located chapel for each of our stations and out stations is a *sine qua non*."[53]

In 1898 Walne fell into ill-health and returned to the States with his family. But the reassuring pattern of welcoming a new missionary during the absence of an older one remained intact. W. Harvey Clarke, whose father had pioneered in Nigeria in the 1850s, was appointed in 1898 and sent to Japan with the financial backing of First Baptist Church, Atlanta, Georgia. He arrived in January 1899, after his steamer had been delayed five days by a storm at sea. Harvey--also called Billy--lived with the McCollums while studying the language. His thoughts would

[50]*ASBC, 1899*, lxiii, lxvi.

[51]*ASBC, 1900*, 112; H. A. Tupper as quoted in McCollum to FMB, 21 Feb. 1898; Clark, *Outriders for the King*, 107; Townsend Harris as quoted in J. C. Hepburn to W. Lowrie, 10 Jan. 1860, Presbyterian Historical Society, Philadelphia.

[52]McCollum to FMB, 6 July 1900.

[53]Maynard in *ASBC, 1899*, lxvi; Walne in *ASBC, 1902*, 103.

drift back to his fiancée, Lucile Daniel, a "Georgia beauty" and "accomplished musician" who planned to join him in the fall of 1899. Naturally anxious about her travel--Lucile was nine years younger than Harvey--he wrote to Secretary Willingham: "I shall trust you to see that she is treated just as your own sister would be."[54]

Lucile was sent out in the best of company--with the returning Walnes--and she reached Yokohama in time for a Thanksgiving Day wedding at the home of W. B. Parshley, a Northern Baptist missionary. Harvey had plenty of help from Northern Baptist friends in making it a perfect day. They remembered "the carefulness with which he superintended all preparations even to the baking of the cake."[55] The handsome couple took their honeymoon in Nikkō, a tourist town 75 miles north of Tokyo renowned for its beautiful temples and picturesque scenery. Then they went to live with the McCollums in Fukuoka. Harvey lamented his inability to tell the Japanese "of Jesus and his love for them." The two million people of Georgia had an abundance of Christian preaching, he pointed out, while the nine million people of Kyushu had but little.[56]

The 1890s came to a close with four Southern Baptist couples--McCollums, Walnes, Maynards, Clarkes--assigned to Japan and all of them present on the field. Only the Brunsons had resigned. After eight years of work in Kyushu, the Southern Baptists had one organized church, Moji, with a membership of 75. This number included the believers not only at Moji but at nine preaching stations: Kokura, Wakamatsu, Ashiya, Fukuoka, Hakata, Kurume, Kumamoto, Nagasaki, and Sasebo. As late-comers confined to a difficult area, Southern Baptists lagged far behind most other Protestant groups. Northern Baptists reported 1,885 members; Congregationalists, 10,214; and all Protestants together, 37,968.[57]

On the brighter side, Southern Baptists enjoyed cordial and harmonious relations with Northern Baptists, their forerunners and guides. True, the Southern Baptist presence in Osaka had precipitated a crisis in 1891, and the Brunsons and McCollums had removed to Kyushu "under stress of circumstances."[58] But in Kyushu they had been given complete charge of the believers and workers awaiting them, and they had enjoyed the full support of the Northern missionaries just across the strait. Southern Baptists continued to attend Northern Baptist mission meetings as observers and to participate in the Union Conference of Baptist Missionaries in Japan.

The Union Conference was held annually until 1897, when it was decided to hold the next meeting in 1899. Maynard was elected president, succeeding

---

[54]Clarke to Willingham, 10 Nov. 1898, 31 Jan. 1899; *HFF* 16 (Apr. 1932), 15; *ASBC, 1899*, ii.

[55]*HFF*, April 1932, 15; *ASBC, 1900*, 112; Clarke to Willingham, 19 Dec. 1899.

[56]Harvey Clarke to Willingham, 7 Mar. 1899; Lucile Clarke to Willingham, 22 Dec. 1899.

[57]*Proceedings, 1900*, 988-89.

[58]*ASBC, 1902*, 103.

McCollum. At the 1899 meeting, in which newly arrived Clarke was elected vice president, the name was changed to the Triennial Conference of Baptist Missionaries in Japan, with the next meeting set for 1902. The conference sponsored a Japanese monthly paper, *Kyōhō* (Church record), and an English paper, *Gleanings*. A publications committee examined and recommended tracts and other literature published by the Tract Society (headed by English Baptist W. J. White) and other agencies.[59]

Not least among the gains from the earlier work of Baptists and other Protestants were the evangelists who served with the Southern Baptist missionaries. The revered Kawakatsu, originally a Reformed Church convert, now led the congregation in Wakamatsu. Gotō Mutsuo, trained by Northern Baptists, was developing a strong station in Kumamoto. Sugano Hanji, a Gotō convert, was working hard at Nagasaki. Satō Kitarō, the former Reformed-Presbyterian evangelist, was serving well in Fukuoka. One other, Nozaki Kisaburō, a former Congregational evangelist, was proving valuable to Maynard. Nozaki had studied Baptist polity under the pastor at Kobe before coming to Kokura, where he was baptized and licensed to the ministry. All these evangelists sacrificed much to serve their Lord, and they remained on the skirmish line without respite. Without the aid of these men, McCollum acknowledged, "but a tithe of the little which has been accomplished, could have been done."[60]

However the credit should be divided, Southern Baptist missionaries and their dedicated coworkers had broken new ground in Kyushu and sowed the good seed of the gospel. The soil was dry and rocky, but the sowers were confident that God would give the increase.

[59]*ABMU Minutes, 1897*, 35; *ABMU Minutes, 1899*, 58.
[60]McCollum, "Historical Survey," 101-2.

4

Organizing for Growth (1900-1909)

The pivotal year 1900 marked the start of a bright and promising era for the Christian movement in Japan. The era of reaction and resentment had reached its limit in 1899 with the recognition of reciprocal treaty rights by the Western powers and the abolition of extraterritorial courts. Forty years of discriminatory treatment had come to an end; Japan now enjoyed equal status with the advanced nations of the world. With full jurisdiction over foreigners within its shores, the government removed all restrictions on travel and residence in the interior and recognized the right of aliens to own property in their own name. These changes greatly facilitated the work of Christian missions, especially in conservative areas like Kyushu.[1]

On the evening of June 27, 1900, the four men comprising the Southern Baptist mission in Japan--J. W. McCollum, Ernest Walne, Nathan Maynard, Harvey Clarke--gathered in Fukuoka and organized themselves into an "association." This was the first step toward incorporating the Mission in accordance with the new Civil Code of Japan and gaining the legal status required for owning property. It also marked the beginning of the Mission as a formally organized body. On a motion by McCollum, Maynard was elected chairman. McCollum was elected secretary. Walne moved that a committee be named to draft a constitution and bylaws. The chairman appointed Walne to prepare the draft. The group also discussed possible locations for Clarke, who was still in language study at Fukuoka. They decided to postpone a decision until fall (he was then assigned to Kumamoto to work with Gotō Mutsuo). The body further took action to return two students to the Baptist seminary in Yokohama for the next school term.[2]

---

[1]James E. Hoare, "Extraterritoriality in Japan, 1859-1899," in *Transactions of the Asiatic Society of Japan*, 3d ser., vol. 18 (1983), 96-97; O. Cary, *History*, 2:244, 284-85.
[2]EBD notes, 1900.

Missionaries in 1900. *Left to right:* J. W. and Drucilla McCollum, Claudia and Ernest Walne, Nathan and Bessie Maynard, Lucile and Harvey Clarke (*W. H. Clarke Collection, Foreign Mission Board, SBC*)

The next day, June 28, the Mission recommended to the Board that the following budget be granted for 1901:[3]

W. H. Clarke and wife	$1,200
N. Maynard and wife	1,200
E. N. Walne and wife, 3 children	1,500
J. W. McCollum and wife, 4 children	1,650
Evangelists	1,200
25 yen for single man	
30 yen for couple	
Rents	600
Chapels	700
Teachers and Bible women	500
Travel	250
	$8,800

Missionary salaries and child allowances, fixed by the Board, were the same as in 1889 when McCollum was appointed. The salary was $600 per year for a single missionary and $1,200 for a married missionary. An allowance of $100 per year was provided for each child up to 10 years old and $150 for each child from 10 to 16 years old. The other budget items were set by the Mission. The ¥25 or ¥30 paid to evangelists was described as a monthly "subsistence allowance" (the exchange rate was two yen to the dollar).[4]

In October 1900 McCollum attended the historic conference of Protestant missionaries in Japan held at the Tokyo YMCA. More than 400 delegates from 42 missions and agencies gathered to celebrate the opening of the new century and to seek new strategies for evangelizing the nation's 40 million people. This was the third and largest such conference; the earlier ones were held at Yokohama in 1872 and at Osaka in 1883. The only Southern Baptist present, Mac had been asked to make a formal response to another missionary's paper on methods of evangelistic work. "Until recently," said McCollum in his response, "the teaching of English was a necessary condition of our entering the interior. But the time has come when this can and should be dropped." He urged his colleagues to preach the gospel of repentance in the language of the people "in spite of our lisping tongues." He called for the upbuilding of Christian character by three proven methods: "Preach in an expository way. . . . Come in close touch with the people. . . . Live the Gospel."[5]

---

[3]Ibid.

[4]Tupper, *Decade*, 70. Some average wages earned by Japanese workmen in 1900: carpenter or plasterer, $0.270 per day; stonemason, $0.365 per day; dyer, $0.145 per day; employee in sake brewery, $5.456 per month; male servant, $1.36 per month (Ernest W. Clement, *A Handbook of Modern Japan* [Chicago: A. C. McClurg & Co., 1910], 346).

[5]*Proceedings, 1900*, 182-84; Iglehart, *Century*, 89.

No one took issue with McCollum's emphases, but others added balance to the program with their testimonies about the value of teaching English.[6] It is strange that Mac failed to appreciate an approach so strategic for Japan. Others less fluent in Japanese than he, as well as some equally at home in the language, found that they could get close to the people and lead them to repentance and faith by meeting their need for English instruction. William Wynd, Mac's successor in Osaka, stated that half the believers gained during his six years of work there had been won through the teaching of English, and that "they have a better knowledge of the word of God, and are better fitted to do church work than the average Christian reached by other methods."[7] Even Mac's colleagues in Kyushu never dropped this method of evangelism. They knew that all members of the Kumamoto Band and many other Christian leaders had been converted through English.

Emboldened by the growing acceptance of Christianity and the challenge of a new era, Protestants throughout Japan joined forces to promote the Twentieth Century Forward Evangelistic Campaign of 1901-4, an extended series of rallies and revivals buttressed by fervent prayer meetings, personal witnessing, the use of decision cards, and the systematic follow-up of converts and seekers. The campaign motto was "Our Country for Christ." It was the most ambitious joint effort yet attempted, and over 1,000 baptisms were reported. Some missionaries called it "Pentecost in Japan."[8]

Ernest Walne took the lead in bringing the Forward Campaign to Nagasaki in 1901. Two lecture meetings in a theater building drew 1,200 people the first night and 1,500 the second night. "For three hours each evening the crowds listened quietly and respectfully to the preaching of the Gospel," reported Walne, typing while "nearly blind" from a sty on each eye. So successful were these meetings that four denominational missions agreed to cooperate in an extended campaign. "The city was divided into six districts," Walne continued, "one for each church or chapel, and all united in working through each district in turn. Tracts were distributed by the carload. We tried to put one in every house in the city. We had street preaching during the day, and in the evening, just before service, bands of Christians walked the streets carrying lighted paper lanterns, singing as they went and inviting the people to come and hear 'The Better Way.'"[9]

Services were conducted nearly every night for three months. Attendance was good even during the rainy season (June-July), which had 32 days of continuous rain. The Baptist chapel, the only church or chapel in Nagasaki without a building

[6]*Proceedings, 1900*, 132, 344-47.

[7]Wynd in *ABMU Minutes, 1898*, 65-66.

[8]J. Edwin Orr, *The Flaming Tongue*, 2d ed. (Chicago: Moody Press, 1975), 172-76; Iglehart, *Century*, 119.

[9]Walne to R. J. Willingham, 17 Sept. 1901.

of its own, was small and poorly located, but it too had crowded services and some long-awaited conversions.[10]

In Fukuoka only one convert was baptized in 1900, despite the earnest efforts of McCollum and Satō in conducting Sunday services in the McCollum house and frequent evening services in a rented chapel. The next year there were five baptisms: three Japanese and the two older McCollum boys, Joseph and J. W., Jr. Early that year the Mission paid $600 for a 50-tsubo lot (1,800 square feet) with two houses, one of which served as a home for the Satōs and the other, after renovation, as a chapel. In that chapel Fukuoka Baptist Church (Fukuoka Shinrei Kyōkai) was organized in October 1901, with Satō as pastor. The result of eight years of evangelistic effort, this was the second Baptist church in Kyushu (after Moji) and the first to be developed entirely under Southern Baptist auspices.[11]

From July 1900 until April 1901, Lottie Moon and a coworker, Mattie Dutton, lived in Fukuoka as refugees from the Boxer Rebellion in China, a holocaust in which 135 Protestant missionaries, 53 missionary children, and countless numbers of Chinese Christians were murdered. After a short stay with the McCollums, the two women moved into a rented Japanese house. Lottie Moon taught English in a commercial school, using the Bible as textbook, and took private students in her home. Through her influence three young men became Christians. A photograph of Lottie with the three converts shows her in Chinese dress. Lottie also tutored Joseph and J. W. So fulfilling was her nine-month stint in Fukuoka that she left with reluctance. Japan had been her first choice as a mission field, and it had loomed large during the years Crawford Toy had sought her hand in marriage. This Southern Baptist saint even died in Japan--in Kobe harbor in 1912.[12]

While Lottie Moon was staying with the McCollum family, one of the boys got a reprimand from his father for loudly commenting on her strange custom of daily cold baths. But both Joseph and J. W. learned much from their brilliant teacher, and they got high marks from their parents for conducting a Sunday school attended each week by more than 25 Japanese children. The budding teachers used large picture rolls sent out each quarter by the Sunday School Board in Nashville.[13]

Lottie Moon's temporary service as tutor of the McCollum boys freed Drucilla for a wider ministry among the Japanese. "In the house-to-house visiting," Dru wrote, ". . . our babies have been a great help. People who do not care to see us are anxious to see a 'white child' who can talk in two languages."[14] Many Japanese

---

[10]Ibid.

[11]*ASBC, 1901*, 119-20; *ASBC, 1902*, 101; *NBRS*, 67-68.

[12]Allen, *Lottie Moon*, 224-27, 287. The death figures are taken from Stephen Neil, *A History of Christian Missions* (Harmondsworth, Middlesex: Penguin Books, 1964), 339-40.

[13]Allen, *Lottie Moon*, 227; *ASBC, 1901*, 120.

[14]*ASBC, 1901*, 122.

women were said to be "shut up in their houses" or "spending their time, while their husbands are away from home, in playing cards and gambling at each other's houses." Such women were prime targets of Christian visitation. But going from house to house was not without danger, for small boys sometimes threw stones at Drucilla or sicked the dogs on her.[15]

Bessie Maynard also visited women in their homes, accompanied by a helper. At first she would wait patiently for an opportunity to speak about Christianity or to read the Bible, but as she grew more confident she changed her approach. "Now as soon as possible after the *aisatsu* [greeting]," Bessie wrote, "I . . . ask the privilege of reading some passages to them, and am rarely ever denied and often invited to come and read again. My helper shrank from what she considered rather a bold way." Bessie found the homes of the wealthy or very poor more accessible than those of the working class.[16]

All the missionary wives made opportunities for sharing their faith through classes in English, singing, cooking, crochet, or other handwork. Dru McCollum, for example, had a regular knitting class for young girls, who were given Bible instruction after each lesson. Bessie Maynard reported 20 girls in her knitting class at Kokura and another 16 at Moji. The wives also assumed much of the responsibility for entertaining and orienting new Southern Baptist missionaries sent to the field. In addition, a few held positions in cooperation with Northern Baptists. Dru McCollum was elected to the Missionary Union's committee on Sunday school work and Claudia Walne to the committee on Bible Woman's work.[17]

The 1901 arrival of newly-weds George and Elizabeth Hambleton increased the Mission to five couples. A Th.D. graduate of Southern Seminary, George was the first "doctor' appointed to Japan. The Hambletons resided in Kokura for a year of language study--both systematic study and "talking to the people"--while the Maynards were on furlough. Then in the fall of 1902, after the Maynards had returned to Kokura, they moved to Kagoshima by ship and opened a new station. This city of 56,000 inhabitants had six churches of other denominations. Happily, the Hambletons found two Baptists there with whom to make a start. Jonathan Goble had sold scriptures here in 1881 but had not attempted to start a church.[18]

The Kagoshima region, somewhat isolated by mountain barriers from the rest of Kyushu, had a peculiar dialect and some strange customs. It was not a backward region, however. Kagoshima was the home of the Satsuma clan, which had taken the lead in overthrowing the Tokugawa regime and had filled many of the top positions in the Meiji government. Kagoshima City ranked second in

[15]*Ecumenical Missionary Conference*, 2:70; Clark, *Outriders for the King*, 120.

[16]*ABMU Minutes, 1901*, 16.

[17]*ASBC, 1901*, 121-22, 124-25; *ABMU Minutes, 1901*, 16, 6.

[18]*ASBC, 1902*, 106; ibid., 1903, 147-48; Hambleton file, FMBA; Parker, *Jonathan Goble of Japan*, 240-41.

Kyushu, after Kumamoto, as an educational center. In 1901 its higher school had been designated the Seventh Higher School (grades 12-14), one of seven government schools that prepared students for the imperial universities at Tokyo and Kyoto. The prestigious seven--Tokyo, Sendai, Osaka-Kyoto, Kanazawa, Kumamoto, Okayama, Kagoshima--had a total enrollment of only 5,300, at a time when primary schools had an enrollment of 5.3 million. The Scotch educator James Murdoch taught in Kagoshima's new Seventh Higher School from 1901 to 1908. It was here that he began to write his monumental, three-volume *History of Japan*.[19]

The Naples of Japan, Kagoshima is dominated by an ever-smoking volcano, Sakurajima, that rises 3,700 feet above the bay and frequently spews ashes over the city. It was an ironic setting for George Hambleton, who, like Goble, had a volcanic temper. He also matched Goble in language aptitude, and within months the scholarly George preached in Japanese without notes. Such diligence "almost cost him his health," a colleague said.[20]

In March 1902, for the first time, the Board appointed a woman to Japan, Bessie Bell Hardy. For several years she had taught Latin and German in the high school at Salem, Virginia. Unlike male candidates, single women like Bessie were appointed solely on the basis of recommendations, since it was thought improper for a lone woman to be interviewed by a panel of men. Only after a policy change in 1904 were single women expected to come to Richmond and appear before the Board. Wives of male appointees were still not invited, for until the next decade they were not appointed and did not need to stand examinations with their husbands.[21]

Bessie Hardy's full missionary status lasted only four months. In July 1902 she married Calder T. Willingham, who had been appointed in May. By marrying, she demoted herself to "assistant missionary." And since Calder was a son of the Board's corresponding secretary, Bessie found herself overshadowed by her husband more than other wives did. At the 1902 session of the SBC, Calder spoke as a new appointee while his father was sitting on the platform. A dramatic scene followed, in which the two "clasped hands and gazed into each other's tear-stained faces."[22]

Soon after his son's departure, Secretary Willingham "felt as if he had received a blow, or as if a part of his heart had been torn out." He better

[19]Donald Roden, *Schooldays in Imperial Japan* (Berkeley: University of California Press, 1980), 64-65, 97, 256; D. C. S. Sissons, "James Murdoch (1856-1921)," in *Transactions of the Asiatic Society of Japan*, 4th ser., vol. 2 (1987), 35-36.

[20]Calder Willingham to R. J. Willingham, 9 Mar. 1903.

[21]*ASBC, 1903*, 60; *FMJ* 52 (Feb. 1902): 346; Catherine B. Allen, *A Century to Celebrate: History of Woman's Missionary Union* (Birmingham: Woman's Missionary Union, 1987), 177-78.

[22]Elizabeth Walton Willingham, *Life of Robert Josiah Willingham* (Nashville: Sunday School Board, 1917), 226; *ASBC, 1903*, 60.

understood the feelings of parents whose children go to the foreign field. As both parent and Board secretary he sent words of advice to Calder and Bessie that remain sound to this day: "When you first get to Japan it will be well to be slow to speak and swift to hear. It is impossible for new missionaries to give wise counsel on problems when the conditions are unknown to them and entirely different from anything they have ever known."[23]

The Willinghams arrived in Fukuoka in the fall of 1902. Like his distinguished father, Calder proved to be methodical and efficient, neat and courteous, given to hospitality. His friends were legion. He seemed to live up to his middle name, Trueheart, and to the title of his childhood keepsake book, *Little Merryheart*. During his first year of language study he taught English to a class of boys four nights a week. Former schoolteacher Bessie conducted a weekly singing class.[24]

The course of Japanese study that Calder followed was prepared by McCollum and Walne, the Mission's language committee. Formally adopted by the Mission in 1903, the course covered a period of three years, with examinations every six months. "The schedule was made retroactive," said McCollum, "so that I and all others must take the course and pass the examinations. In case after a fair trial a man fails (after the 3rd attempt) he will be expected to resign and return to America." By 1904 all the men had passed the first year's course, though not all with flying colors. Walne advised the Board "to inquire into the linguistic ability of applicants to this field before making appointments." He did not indicate whose lackluster performance prompted this advise. Both McCollum and Walne, models of fluency in Japanese, underestimated the potential of Clarke and others less competent in the language.[25]

Failures and Successes

McCollum's conviction that a mastery of the language was essential to effective evangelism must have been tempered by the realization that it was no guarantee of effective evangelism. The Fukuoka church was growing--it had 15 members in 1903--but the preaching stations in the area that he served, including adjacent Hakata, still showed little or no response. "Suspicions and doubt transmitted for many generations have crystallized into stubborn prejudice," McCollum said of Hakata. "All our work here is regarded as a wily scheme of the 'hairy barbarian' to entrap the people and ultimately to destroy the nation." By 1903 a few people there were willing to listen to Christian preaching, but "not even one has evinced a desire for salvation."[26]

[23]Willingham, *Life of Willingham*, 226-27.
[24]EBD, *Golden Milestone*, 108; *ASBC, 1903*, 148.
[25]McCollum to FMB, 20 Aug. 1903; Walne to FMB, 9 Aug. 1904; EBD notes, 1904, 1905.
[26]*ASBC, 1902*, 101; *ASBC, 1903*, 141-42.

Kurume, 25 miles southwest of Fukuoka, also seemed resistant to the gospel. It was a prosperous city of 30,000. The area was known as the breadbasket or "rice storehouse" of the Buddhist Shinshū sect, so generously did the farmers support that sect with their rice. McCollum described Kurume as "overgrown with briars, brambles, and thorns of prejudice, superstition, and the love of money." Even though preaching was done once or twice a week in a well-located house, the response was virtually nil. An evangelist and his family were placed there in 1906, but at length the work was abandoned, not to be renewed until after World War II. The Lutherans fared much better. The famed J. M. T. Winther, whose ministry in Japan spanned 72 years (he died in Kobe at 95), became Kurume's first resident missionary in 1901. He succeeded in renting a house at that early date because it was thought to be haunted. Winther was joined by an able Japanese, and a strong church was developed that produced many Lutheran pastors.[27]

Some of the other Baptist stations in Kyushu showed great promise. The Kumamoto work started by Gotō was strengthened by the coming of the Clarkes in 1901. A prefectural capital with a population of 80,000, Kumamoto had many schools, including the Fifth Higher School, and a large military garrison. "The students and soldiers are about 20,000 in number," said Harvey, "and are splendid material for our work." The Clarkes opened their home to the young people and endeared themselves to many. "There is only one other foreign child in Kumamoto," wrote Lucile, "so our baby [Harvey, Jr.] is quite an attraction." A year later, in May 1902, the "First Baptist Church of Kumamoto" was formally organized. Reported Harvey: "Bible classes, especially for the students, have been one of the best ways of reaching young men and women who do not attend the regular services, and through these private studies some have been led to Christ."[28]

Two months later, in July 1902, a church was organized at Sasebo, where seamen away from home sought the warm fellowship of Christians. Ozaki Genroku, a Kyushu native trained in the Baptist seminary at Yokohama, came from Osaka to be installed as "resident evangelist."[29] Ozaki became an outstanding pastor, and later his son Shuichi rose to prominence as seminary professor, preacher, and interpreter to Billy Graham.

In October the church at Nagasaki was organized in a two-story building newly purchased with $2,500 appropriated by the Board. The building was ideally located on the main thoroughfare in the heart of the city. The congregation, consisting mainly of young men, some of them volunteers for the ministry, voted to pay a portion of Pastor Sugano's salary in addition to all the incidental expenses

---

[27]*ASBC, 1901*, 120; *ASBC, 1902*, 102; *ASBC, 1903*, 142; EBD, "Lantern Lights of Baptist Work in South-western Japan" (Fukuoka: JBM, 1935; mimeographed), 7; Neve, *Japan*, 38-40. On Lutheran work, see also *JCQ* 51 (1985): 208.

[28]*ASBC, 1901*, 126; *FMJ* 51(1901): 385; *ASBC, 1902*, 104.

[29]*ASBC, 1903*, 143-44.

of the church. The members further showed their zeal by gathering in front of the church before services to invite passers-by to drop in. Walne attributed the success at Nagasaki to two persons in particular. One was Sugano, tireless soul-winner and generous contributor from his meager salary. The other was Claudia Walne. "She can sing the Gospel effectively," Ernest said, "and her services are constantly in demand. Though her home duties are exacting, she rarely misses a meeting."[30]

With the organization of three churches in 1902, the Mission could proudly report five churches and five preaching stations. Yet the achievements of 1903, when the nationwide Forward Evangelistic Campaign was in high gear, far outshone those of 1902. Protestants in central Japan took advantage of a National Exhibition held in Osaka from March 1 to July 31. The exhibition featured a vast array of Japanese and foreign products, including Canadian furniture and American automobiles. The Protestants rented a building that was located on the open square before the main entrance to the exhibition. With catchy signs and stirring music, especially the tune of "Marching through Georgia," they drew crowds into the "Gospel Hall" daily from 9 A.M. to 10 P.M. So effective was this approach that out of the four million who attended the exhibition, an estimated 246,000 heard the gospel proclaimed. The responsibility for conducting services and distributing literature was divided among the various denominations. During Baptist week, McCollum and two Japanese preachers registered 391 inquirers. That Mac was chosen for such a ministry testified afresh to his skill and power as a preacher in the Japanese language, with the result that the churches of Kyushu clamored for his services as evangelist. Despite serious throat trouble, he held revivals in nearly all the churches.[31]

The banner year 1903 was also a year of organization. In April, representatives of the five churches in Kyushu and two of the missions met in the Fukuoka church with representatives of three Northern Baptist-related congregations in Yamaguchi Prefecture. Together they formed the Southwestern Association (Seibu Bukai). Ozaki Genroku of Sasebo was elected moderator. The association was the outgrowth of the annual meeting (*nenkai*) of Japanese Baptists first held in 1901 in Tokyo, and of earlier meetings of Japanese workers and joint conferences of missionaries and nationals. It was a fraternal, consultative body with no administrative functions, since the Northern and Southern missionary organizations assumed full responsibility for operations.[32]

Two years later, however, the Southern Mission began to shift that responsibility to the Japanese. At the suggestion of the Mission, the churches "assumed control of their own affairs" and agreed to defray their own expenses except for annually reduced subsidies on the pastors' salaries. This freed the Mission to "give

---

[30]Ibid.

[31]EBD, *Golden Milestone*, 73; O. Cary, *History*, 2:302-5; Clement, *Handbook*, 342-44.

[32]*NBRS*, 73-74; EBD, "The Mission and the Convention" (1963, mimeographed), 4, 29.

more attention to pioneer work in undeveloped fields." Then in 1905 the Mission set up a Standing Advisory Committee of three missionaries and three Japanese to deal with problems involving nationals, the churches, and cooperative work through the association.[33]

The missionaries often praised their Japanese colleagues in glowing terms. Maynard, for instance, bore testimony to "the faithfulness and efficiency of our fellow workers, the native preachers." An evangelist who nearly split the Moji church because of "lack of tact and some serious blunders" was regarded as an exception. In Kagoshima, Hambleton praised his evangelist as "a live worker, who keeps God's work in view as his chief business, and makes everything contribute to that." As proof, the Kagoshima station had 16 baptisms in 1903 and was organized into a church in November of that year.[34]

We have noted that in 1900 the Mission set out to obtain government recognition as a juridical association. During the first year, McCollum negotiated with local officials in Fukuoka but got nowhere. Then Walne continued negotiations in Nagasaki while making several trips to Tokyo to consult with the nation's Department of Home Affairs. Under the department's guidance, Walne drafted a 16-article constitution for the Association of Southern Baptist Mission- aries in Japan. "The object of the Association," said Article 5, "shall be to hold and manage land, buildings and other property, for the extension of Christianity, the carrying on of Christian education, and the performance of works of charity and benevolence." A supplementary statement following the 16 articles described the organization and work of the SBC and its Foreign Mission Board, which provided funds and personnel for the Mission.[35]

Walne spent months trying to convince the local officials in Nagasaki that "the law granted to foreigners the right to own a little of the sacred soil of Japan." Some of the officials argued that "the Government had no authority to grant such a right!" But the matter was settled in December 1903, when the Japanese government formally approved the Mission's constitution and granted legal status. This recognition meant that the Mission could begin transferring its property from the names of Japanese individuals to the names of the Southern Baptist mission- aries who had signed the application to become a property-holding body. The process went smoothly. In 1905 the Mission legally owned five chapels and three residences. At least two other missions suffered heavy losses from the refusal of Japanese holders to transfer property registered in their names. In some cases the holders mortgaged or sold the property and retained the money. The victimized aliens had no legal redress.[36]

[33]*ASBC, 1906*, 160; EBD, "Mission and Convention," 4-5.
[34]*ASBC, 1907*, 170; *ASBC, 1906*, 161; *ASBC, 1903*, 148.
[35]Walne to FMB, 19 Jan. 1904. A copy of the constitution is attached to EBD notes, 1903.
[36]Walne to FMB, 19 Jan. 1904; *ASBC, 1905*, 118; O. Cary, *History*, 2:244.

Yet another far-reaching event took place in the memorable year of 1903. Using a portion of the centrally located church building in Nagasaki, Walne established the Gospel Book Store (Fukuin Shokwan). The new enterprise was made possible by a $500 gift from the Sunday School Board in Nashville for a "Bible and Book Depository." The Sunday School Board had made the gift at the suggestion of Joshua Levering, who visited Japan in 1903. A prominent layman and Maryland's representative on the Foreign Mission Board, Levering afterwards served as SBC president. The timely $500 gift enabled Walne to purchase and distribute a large quantity of the newly published *Union Hymnal*, which replaced the denominational hymnbooks used by Baptists and most other Protestants. Baptists in Japan have used interdenominational hymnals ever since.[37]

The establishment of the Gospel Book Store marked the beginning of a highly successful ministry of book distribution and publishing to which Walne devoted the major part of his missionary career. This ministry was especially appropriate among a people mostly literate. By 1905 more than 95 percent of children of statutory school age attended primary school, and in the next decade the number reached 99 percent. Even rickshaw pullers read books while awaiting their fares.[38]

Walne was innovative and resourceful. He promoted small circulating libraries in the churches. In 1905 he started a monthly paper for the Southwestern Association called *Seikō*, meaning "starlight." Walne succeeded in getting Chiba Yūgorō to move to Nagasaki from Kyoto in order to serve as editor of the paper and as general evangelist for Southern Baptists. Chiba's contribution was enormous. A graduate of Colby College and Rochester Theological Seminary, he was a needed bridge between nationals and missionaries and between the vastly different cultures they represented.[39]

The Russo-Japanese War of 1904-5, even more than the Sino-Japanese War of the previous decade, opened new doors for Christian witness in Japan. Prime Minister Katsura Tarō, whose first wife was a Christian, went out of his way to assure missionaries and pastors that Japan's war against a so-called Christian nation in no way implied an anti-Christian stance on the part of the government. The YMCA was permitted to minister to soldiers at the front, and churches were given access to military hospitals where the wounded were cared for. A few Christians, notably Uchimura Kanzō, opposed the war as unjust, but the vast majority supported it with enthusiasm, thereby demonstrating their loyalty as Japanese subjects.[40]

---

[37]Walne to FMB, 23 Nov. 1903; *ASBC, 1904*, 136-37. The hymnal used by most churches of the Japan Baptist Convention in Sunday morning worship services is *Sambika*, published by the United Church of Christ. Some churches use *Seika*, published by Word of Life Press. These are supplemented with a small Baptist hymnal published by the JBC in 1989.

[38]*JCY, 1907*, 76; *Kodansha Encyclopedia of Japan*, s.v. "education."

[39]EBD notes, 1905.

[40]O. Cary, *History*, 2:316-31; Drummond, *History*, 205.

The effects the war had on Southern Baptist work were mixed. At Moji, from which the majority of men and munitions were sent to the front on the Asian mainland, and to which many sick and wounded were evacuated, the war had "a decidedly demoralizing effect," reported Maynard, "causing many to neglect their church duties." At Sasebo, headquarters of Admiral Tōgō's fleet (which won the war for Japan by destroying the Russian fleet sent from the Baltic Sea), the congregation virtually disappeared, for nearly all the men were connected with the navy. The church's rented quarters had to be returned to the landlord. Security in the town was so tight that no missionary was allowed to enter, though Pastor Ozaki was able to minister in homes and hospitals. The work at Nagasaki was similarly hampered. Among those drafted into service were the Sunday school superintendent and Pastor Sugano's wife, a Red Cross nurse who served aboard an army hospital ship. Without a tear, it was reported, Mrs. Sugano left her two-year-old daughter in the care of the sick father and a feeble grandmother.[41]

In Kokura, where the Mission now had a new chapel seating 125, a gift from Maryland Baptists, the war gave a boost to the work. "The physician in charge of the three military hospitals at this place," said Maynard, "being a devoted Christian, gave us every facility for reaching the sick and the wounded." The physician even preached in the Baptist church several times. Tens of thousands of Scripture portions and tracts were distributed, and a number of conversions were reported. Afterwards the Baptist Sunday school received a lacquer cup and a letter of thanks from military headquarters in Tokyo.[42]

In Kumamoto the story was much the same. "The war has in no way retarded the progress of our work," wrote Harvey Clarke, "but our sympathy for those in distress seems to draw us closer to the people." The missionaries were permitted to conduct services in the military hospitals and to deal personally with the soldiers. For this ministry each was given a bronze medal. Lucile Clarke ministered so effectively through her singing and her genuine interest in the soldiers that she received from the emperor a silver cup bearing the imperial crest. She treasured the award as long as she lived.[43] It can be seen in retrospect, however, that such actions on the part of the government helped to blind the missionaries to the injustices and ultimate consequences of Japan's growing involvement in Korea and China. This "first victory of yellow armies over white," followed by dissatisfaction with the spoils of war, paved the way for Japanese imperialists to "restore Asia to the Asiatics."

The Mission meanwhile increased in numbers. J. Franklin Ray and Daisy Pettus Ray arrived in 1904 and plunged into language study at Fukuoka. Both had been appointed by the Board in May, he to Persia and she to Mexico. Subsequent-

[41]*ASBC, 1906*, 161-63; *ASBC, 1905*, 119-21.
[42]*ASBC, 1906*, 161-62.
[43]*ASBC, 1905*, 122; W. H. Clarke to Inabelle Coleman, 20 Dec. 1939, FMBA.

ly they had married and changed their fields to Japan. Franklin, a former pastor and school teacher, was a quiet but influential leader who guided many young men into the ministry. Daisy had taught mathematics for several years before attending Southern Seminary. She had a quick mind and facile tongue that made her a great conversationalist--witty, at times acerbic, always stimulating. Husband and wife complemented one another notably.[44]

Relations between George and Elizabeth Hambleton, however, had become scandalous, according to reports from other missionaries in Kagoshima. Elizabeth, eight years his junior, told tales of abuse that "freeze the blood," and the hot-tempered George acknowledged "that on several different occasions he has (repeatedly) struck his wife." The Mission put him on probation, for he was an effective evangelist with many Japanese friends. Sadly, the outrages recurred, and in 1906, said a Board report, the Hambletons "retired from the work." Walne called this episode "the greatest of all the sorrows which have come to us as a mission." It was a replay of wife-beater Goble's dismissal from the Missionary Union a generation before. But unlike Goble, who defiantly remained in Japan, Hambleton pursued his ministry in the homeland as pastor of Northern Baptist churches.[45]

It was a time when the Mission had to bear many sorrows. The Willinghams went on medical furlough in 1905 after Bessie had spent several months in the Tokyo Sanitarium critically ill. She had incurable tuberculosis. The Rays went on medical leave in 1906 because of Daisy's nervous breakdown following childbirth complications. That summer Claudia Walne was so ill with meningitis that for six weeks she seemed unlikely to recover, and her son Herbert was incapacitated for months by a fall from a tree. Ernest Walne was worn out from overwork. McCollum, who suffered paralysis of some of his vocal chords from constant speaking in open chapels, was again forced to take a medical leave before the end of the year. His doctor had warned him, Mac said, that he was in danger of losing the power of speech--"truly a fearsome diagnosis for one who likes to talk as well as I do." Bessie Maynard had heart trouble that took the Maynards back to the States a few months later and permanently blocked their return to Japan. Had it not been for the faithful Japanese pastors and evangelists, the work would have been seriously impaired, so crippled was the missionary force.[46]

---

[44]*ASBC, 1904*, 60; *Southern Baptist Foreign Missionaries* (Richmond: FMB, 1936), 104; Max Garrott, taped interview by Tom Masaki, 10 Mar. 1971, JBM.

[45]Walne to R. J. Willingham, 2 May, 16 July 1906; portion of McCollum letter, no date or salutation, in Hambleton file, FMBA; *ASBC, 1907*, 73.

[46]McCollum as quoted in Clark, *Outriders for the King*, 121; EBD notes, 1905, 1906; *ASBC, 1906*, 163.

The Dozier-Rowe-Bouldin Connection

It was a cause of great rejoicing, therefore, that in 1906 three young and healthy couples were sent to Japan, a new record for a single year. They were the Kelsey Doziers, John Rowes, and George Bouldins. The nonalphabetical Dozier-Rowe-Bouldin order of listing derives solely from the affectionate term used by the Japanese of the three men: *do-ro-bō*, literally "mud-stick," meaning burglar or thief. All three men were appointed by the Board in April and presented to the SBC's annual meeting at Chattanooga in May. Later that month all three were among the 25 students who graduated from Southern Seminary with the Th.M. degree, which meant that they had read part of the Old Testament in Hebrew and all of the New Testament in Greek (the other 100 members of their class had dropped out or settled for a Th.B.). All three men married their sweethearts in June and traveled to Japan on the SS *Korea* in September, disembarking at Nagasaki after sightseeing stops in Yokohama and Kobe. These three musketeers were also to pass their final, third-year language exams together at the Mission meeting in December 1909.[47]

Upon arrival in Nagasaki the three couples were warmly greeted by McCollum and Walne, who clambered up the side of the ship from a sampan. After half a day in the second-class car of a smoky, poky train to Fukuoka--most Japanese rode third-class--the party joined Dru McCollum, Claudia Walne, the Maynards, the Clarkes, and all the children for a full Mission meeting. "For one happy week," wrote Maude Dozier, "work, play and introductions to missionary life filled the Fukuoka missionary residence--a square, eight-room, two-story structure with thin walls and floors that gave little chance for secrets or quiet." As if they had not been together enough, the three new couples lived in this "Doves' Nest" for the next five months (the McCollums had moved to Kumamoto). Fortunately there was a small tennis court on the grounds where the three men worked off their frustrations after language study each day.[48]

Charles Kelsey Dozier was the youngest of three sons of a Presbyterian elder who ran a hardware store in Gainesville, Georgia. His Huguenot great-grandparents had fled from persecution in France. Converted at the First Baptist Church in Gainesville, Kelsey attended Mercer University as a ministerial student. At Southern Seminary he met Maude Burke, a North Carolinian descended from the Irish statesman Edmund Burke.[49]

Maude was a product of one of the earliest Sunbeam Bands and a graduate of the Baptist Female University, now Meredith College. She had served as a summer volunteer teacher in the North Carolina mountains. At seminary she had

---

[47]*ASBC, 1907*, 73; Bouldin, "Autobiography," 47, 64; *ASBC, 1910*, 209.

[48]M. B. Dozier, *Dozier of Japan*, 11; Bouldin, "Autobiography," 72-73.

[49]M. B. Dozier, *Dozier of Japan*, 5-9.

the distinction of being one of the first women to take the regular course. For some years the wives of married students and sometimes other women had attended classes as visitors. Between 1903 and 1906 a few like Maude did all the class work and had their papers graded. Still, they were not granted degrees or formal credit. Not until 1907, after Maude's departure, was the education of women formalized with the founding of the Woman's Missionary Union Training School.[50]

Kelsey and Maude both were foreign mission volunteers, but he planned to serve in South America and she in China. Kelsey preferred a Spanish-speaking country because he feared that an Oriental language might prove beyond his grasp. But at a Student Volunteer Conference in Asheville, North Carolina, Kelsey heard J. W. McCollum and Calder Willingham plead for workers in Japan. He talked with Calder till two o'clock one morning, and afterwards he and Maude agreed that God was leading them to Japan, not South America or China. They never doubted this sense of leading, even during their first four years on the field, when the strain of adjustment was aggravated by their having to move 11 times.[51]

John Hansford Rowe was the oldest of eight children of a Virginia farmer. A lover of sports, he played varsity football at Richmond University and made good use of Levering Gymnasium while attending seminary. He and Bouldin first met on an athletic field in Louisville, where both were practicing the high jump.[52] John also studied hard and served as a pastor. After graduation he married Sarah Margaret Cobb, a student from Texas who had served two years in New Mexico as a missionary teacher to the Navajo Indians. Margaret, like Maude Burke, completed seminary training at the same time as her fiancé. Ominously, one of her referents in New Mexico stated that Margaret's "physical health disqualified her from foreign service." Indeed, she was to suffer much illness in the years ahead and die at the age of 36.[53]

George Washington Bouldin was a handsome Alabamian with 13 brothers and sisters. He was as tall as Jack Brunson and no less self-conscious of his height, especially while in Japan. After attending Winchester (Tennessee) Normal College, where it was customary for every student to memorize the last five chapters of Paul's Epistle to the Romans, George entered the University of Alabama with the intention of becoming a lawyer like his brother Virgil. But under the powerful preaching of L. O. Dawson in the Baptist church at Tusca-

---

[50]Foy Johnson Farmer, *Hitherto: History of North Carolina Woman's Missionary Union* (Raleigh: Woman's Missionary Union of North Carolina, 1952), 25-26, 92; Southern Baptist Theological Seminary, *Catalogue, 1905-6*, 38-39; *ESB*, vol. 1, 237.

[51]M. B. Dozier, *Dozier of Japan*, 9; *Seinan Gakuin nanajūnen shi* (Seventy-year history of Seinan Gakuin), 2 vols. (Fukuoka: Seinan Gakuin, 1986), 1:159-60; Lois Whaley, *Edwin Dozier of Japan* (Birmingham: Woman's Missionary Union, 1983), 21.

[52]Matsuta Hara, ed., *Rev. John Hansford Rowe* (Kokura: Seinan Jo Gakuin, 1930), 12, 30.

[53]Rowe file, FMBA; *JCY, 1921*, 309.

loosa, he felt called to the ministry. He quit the university and entered seminary at Louisville, where he also worked as a street-car conductor and taught Sunday school classes for orphans and slum children. George volunteered for mission work in Argentina but switched to Japan at the request of Secretary Willingham. His graduation thesis was entitled "Verbeck of Japan."[54]

One of the questions asked by the Board concerning candidates for appointment was, "Is he in any respect peculiar or eccentric?" Concerning Bouldin, Professor W. O. Carver replied, "Yes - thoroughly unprofessional in the right sense. A little too careless of making friends. More man than minister." Carver rated him "above the average as a prospective missionary."[55]

After seminary graduation Bouldin went to Winchester, Tennessee, to marry Margaret Lee, a public school teacher. They had met years before when both were enrolled at the college there. Maggie, brought up in the Cumberland Presbyterian Church, joined a Baptist church by immersion in the Tennessee River less than two weeks before she married George. Acquaintances described her as a "self-made" and "high toned" lady of "sterling character" who "has the blues sometimes."[56]

The Doziers, Rowes, and Bouldins had five months of language study in Fukuoka with a former Buddhist priest. Then the Rowes replaced the Maynards in Kokura, and the Bouldins replaced the Hambletons at Kagoshima. The Doziers remained in Fukuoka until the fall of 1907, when they rented a house in Sasebo and became the only resident missionaries of any denomination in that thriving city of 70,000. The Doziers faced the challenge of a church with 31 members-- only 9 of them resident--in a newly built Grecian-style chapel that seated 200 people. The chapel had been made spacious in hopes of reaching many lonely seamen and some of the hundreds of workers who passed the church daily on their way to and from the navy yards.[57]

People and Events

In 1907 Paul and Lenna Medling, both Tennesseans, were sent to Japan with their baby Julia. They began their language study in Nagasaki and continued it in Kokura. Paul was a quiet man of great confidence and determination, who was said to look on the bright side of every question and never get discouraged. It was his good fortune to marry Lenna Rushing, an "elegant and splendid" woman from a good family. She had told the Board that she was ready and anxious to

[54]Bouldin, "Autobiography," 1-63.
[55]Confidential form submitted by Carver, Bouldin file, FMBA.
[56]Bouldin file, FMBA; Bouldin, "Autobiography," 65.
[57]*ASBC, 1908*, 192, 197-98.

accompany Paul to Japan because "I married Mr. Medling with the expectation and desire of helping him in his life."[58]

Without Lenna, Paul might not have been appointed. He was said to be "slightly peculiar socially" and to have "bad habits" (smoking cigarettes and chewing tobacco). M. E. Dodd, his roommate for four years at Union University, declined to recommend him because Paul smoked "incessantly" and attended meetings of the Missionary Society as little as possible. But under prodding from the Board, Dodd, later president of the SBC, allowed that Paul was "decidedly original" and probably fit for the mission field. Paul smoked cigars while in Japan, though usually in private, often on a mountainside near his home.[59]

The most exciting event of 1907 for the Japan mission was the fall visit of Secretary Willingham and his wife Corneille. Never before had a secretary of the Foreign Mission Board visited a mission field overseas. The Willinghams had a special affection for Japan as the field of their son Calder, and they in turn were highly regarded by the missionaries. Kelsey Dozier, for one, loved the secretary as a father, for he had influenced Kelsey to give his life to foreign missions. So spirits soared when the distinguished couple arrived in Fukuoka and attended Mission meeting at the Dozier residence. It was the same house where Calder and Bessie had lived before their sad return to the States, and flowers they had planted still bloomed in the yard.[60]

After listening to passionate pleas for more workers, more money, and more buildings, the Willinghams toured Kyushu with the Clarkes as their guides. The secretary later spoke of Harvey as "the best man on the field." In Kumamoto, Willingham spoke to an overflow crowd in the commodious chapel provided by the Stone Mountain Baptist Association in Georgia. Pressing on to Kagoshima, a two-day journey in a one-horse wagon, the visitors watched George Bouldin baptize four converts in the sea. At Sasebo they participated in the dedication of the new chapel, and at Nagasaki, despite a late-night arrival, they were greeted by a large number of church members with Ernest Walne. In Fukuoka again, Willingham gave a memorable address at the formal opening of Fukuoka Baptist Seminary on October 17. This service, held at the Reception Hall in West Park, was the most auspicious occasion of his visit.[61]

McCollum and Walne had tutored Japanese workers off and on since 1893, and Pastor Satō had taught in a semiformal course of study offered in 1902-3. Maynard and Kawakatsu also had helped to train evangelists. In 1906 the Mission agreed that the time had come to establish a full-fledged seminary, and it asked

[58]Appointment documents in P. P. Medling file, FMBA.

[59]Ibid.; M. E. Dodd to Willingham, 18 Aug. 1904; W. R. Medling, interview with author, Nashville, 19 Feb. 1987.

[60]Willingham, *Life of Willingham*, 167, 224.

[61]R. J. Willingham as quoted by Lucile Clarke, 14 Mar. 1909, in Josephine Eden ms., Seinan Jo Gakuin; Willingham, *Life of Willingham*, 167-69; *FMJ* 39 (Dec. 1907), 179.

(**Upper**) Young men's Bible class taught by Harvey Clarke, Kumamoto, 1902 *(W. H. Clarke Collection, Foreign Mission Board, SBC)*. (**Lower**) New missionaries in 1906. *Left to right:* Kelsey and Maude Dozier, George and Maggie Bouldin, John and Margaret Rowe *(Courtesy of Publicity Department, Seinan Gakuin)*

the Board to provide $15,000 for a building. No grant was made until 1908, but the seminary opened in rented quarters on October 1, 1907. Chiba Yūgorō, who was named president of the school, taught systematic theology. "His influence over young men is remarkable," wrote Maynard, "and our Mission has never had a man with whom it was a greater pleasure to work." Satō, trained at Meiji Gakuin, resigned as pastor of the Fukuoka church to teach Old Testament. McCollum taught New Testament and homiletics, and Walne taught church history. "Dr. Mac," as he was affectionately called, had been granted a doctor of divinity degree by his alma mater, Howard College. Walne was honored with the same degree by his alma mater, Mississippi College.[62]

This faculty of four taught seven students the first year. Three students were enrolled in the regular course and two each in the partial and preparatory courses. The regular students, who could read English "tolerably well," used John A. Broadus's *Treatise on the Preparation and Delivery of Sermons* and other basic texts in English (Broadus's work was not available in Japanese translation until 1915). All the students did practical work. They conducted four Sunday schools scattered about the city, and four of the older ones took turns preaching at a local mission. One married student led the work in Kurume, where his family lived.[63]

The seminary building erected in 1908 was situated on a two-acre lot near the site of Fukuoka Castle, where 2,000 soldiers were garrisoned. It was a wooden structure, attractive and quite substantial, being built almost entirely of cedar. It contained four recitation rooms, a small library, reception room, business office, and 16 dormitory rooms with space for two students each. For lack of funds, however, the furnishings were spartan, and a detached Japanese house on the property served as kitchen and dining room.[64]

Prior to the school's opening in 1907, the McCollums moved to Fukuoka from Kumamoto, where they had lived temporarily, and the Walnes moved up from Nagasaki. The Rowes were transferred from Kokura to Nagasaki to oversee that field and continue the bookstore and literature ministry started by Walne. Missionaries were shuffled again in 1908 when Mac quit the seminary under pressure because of poor health, both mental and physical. George Bouldin was then elected to the seminary faculty by secret ballot. The Bouldins left Kagoshima and occupied a house in Fukuoka rented from the Methodist mission. George, who felt "very much unprepared," later wondered "if Dr. McCollum was treated right when he was pushed out and I was pushed in." The Medlings replaced the Bouldins in Kagoshima after attending language school in Tokyo during the winter

---

[62]*ASBC, 1907*, 166; *ASBC, 1908*, 193-94; Clark, *Outriders for the King*, 118; *JCY, 1912*, 502.

[63]*ASBC, 1908*, 194.

[64]*ASBC, 1909*, 189.

of 1908-9. Another move in 1908 was that of the Doziers, who reluctantly left Sasebo for Shimonoseki.[65]

The Dozier move was prompted by a redrawing of the boundary line between Northern and Southern Baptist territory. The Northerners had suffered heavy personnel losses in Yamaguchi Prefecture due mainly to illness. Their girls' school in Chōfu had been discontinued in 1901, when fire destroyed the school building. Furthermore, the few missionaries who remained in Chōfu and Shimonoseki were separated by 250 miles from the nearest member of their mission, while just across the strait--only 10 minutes by ferry--the Southern Baptist missionaries were growing in number and coveting a larger field of operations. As Walne pointed out, among the 25 cities of Japan with a population of more than 50,000, 10 had no Baptist work, but none of these unoccupied cities lay in Kyushu.[66]

Negotiations between the two missions in 1907-8 resulted in the transfer of work in southwestern Honshu to Southern Baptists. It was understood that Hiroshima and Kure would mark the northern limit of their work on Honshu and that they would be at liberty to open work in Shikoku, leaving to Northern Baptists the work among the islands of the Inland Sea. Secretary Willingham approved this plan during his visit to Japan in 1907, and his Northern counterpart ratified it during a visit in 1908. The Board paid $16,535 for the church buildings and missionary residences in Shimonoseki and Chōfu. What for Northern Baptists was a "strategic retreat" was for Southern Baptists a timely advance. The agreement virtually tripled the Southern Baptist field, for southwestern Honshu had a population of 10 million and Shikoku, 4 million.[67] Work was not begun in Hiroshima and Kure, however, until the end of the next decade, and for lack of personnel Shikoku was not entered until after World War II.

The moving of the geographical boundary between Northern and Southern Baptists seemed to enhance cooperation between them. At a joint mission meeting held in July 1909 at Arima, a mountain resort near Kobe blessed with azaleas and mineral springs, the two groups voted to combine their respective magazines into one. It was named *Kirisuto kyōhō* (Christian church record). More significantly, they voted to establish a seminary in Tokyo that would replace the separate schools at Yokohama and Fukuoka. For several years prior to the opening of the Fukuoka seminary, negotiations had been conducted between the two missions and their home boards for a union seminary, but a satisfactory agreement had not been reached. The renewed effort, as related in the next chapter, would prove successful, though not for long.[68]

---

[65]Bouldin to T. B. Ray, 16 Sept. 1932; Bouldin, "Autobiography," 51-53; *ASBC, 1909*, 188, 193.

[66]*ASBC, 1909*, 193-94; Wynd, *Seventy Years*, 123-28; Walne to J. H. Scott, 6 June 1908.

[67]Wynd, *Seventy Years*, 128; EBD, *Golden Milestone*, 77.

[68]EBD notes, 1909; W. Harvey Clarke, "Statement made before the Trustees of the Baptist Union Theo. Seminary," 5 Aug. 1913, Clarke file, FMBA.

More about the Missionaries

The year 1909 was one the Bouldins never forgot. In March, Maggie Lee gave birth to their only child, Mary Janette, at Shimonoseki. An English-speaking doctor was available there, and one of the two missionary residences was open for the Bouldins' use. Then the family moved into a new house they had built at Fujiidana (Wisteria shelf), a small mountain on the south side of Fukuoka. Hardly were they settled when the summer heat drove them off to higher mountains. After attending the joint mission meeting at Arima, they relaxed in their summer cottage at Ninooka in Gotemba, at the base of Mount Fuji. They had purchased the cedar house for $112.50 and added a room for guests, who happened to be the Rowes that summer. The Doziers also bought a house in Gotemba, but the Bouldins seem to have been the first among the scores of Southern Baptist missionaries who have owned a vacation house in Japan.[69]

In August, tragedy struck the Bouldins. Mary Janette developed digestion problems and died in a Yokohama hospital. She was buried in Yokohama Foreigners' Cemetery, where the Gobles had laid their firstborn a half century before. The Bouldins were the second Southern Baptist couple--the McCollums were the first--to lose a child. In that same year Franklin and Daisy Ray almost lost their son Hermon, a future missionary. Hermon contracted meningitis and lay unconscious for a whole week.[70]

In America, meanwhile, the Maynards were passing through a nettlesome trial that may be cited for both its humor and its pathos. "While in Japan," wrote Secretary Willingham to McCollum, "I several times heard the reports that Sister Maynard had caused feelings on the part of some missionaries by advising young missionary wives against bearing children when they first go out to the work in Japan. Have you not heard these reports?" Replied Mac: "I have heard such reports."[71]

When Willingham saw Nathan Maynard briefly in Portsmouth, Virginia, he referred to the charges against Bessie "in a grave manner." Nathan denied them categorically. He discounted Mac's testimony as "worthless" on grounds that his sanity was in question. Maynard further queried the members of the Mission in an attempt to learn the original source, but each correspondent claimed innocence. All that Maynard himself would admit to was "a single incident when, while it did concern the most intimate affairs of a husband and wife, was intended as an act of affectionate interest." Apparently this was a letter from Bessie Maynard to Bessie Willingham.[72]

[69]Bouldin, "Autobiography," 93-98.

[70]Ibid., 98-99; *ASBC, 1909*, 210, 218.

[71]Willingham to McCollum, 12 Oct. 1908. McCollum's reply is written in the margin of this letter.

[72]Maynard to Willingham, 7, 10, 17 Dec. 1908.

Despite their consternation over this matter, the Maynards pled for medical clearance to return to the field. Wrote Nathan: "I do feel that I am both equipped for the work and adapted to it. . . . [Bessie] had her heart set on returning to Japan." Bessie was determined to return despite the strain of leaving her 88-year-old father, who was recovering from a heart attack. As a girl she had been influenced by reading and rereading the life of Ann Hasseltine Judson, and she felt that her commitment to her husband and to their work in a difficult field was no less firm than Ann's. She herself had a "bad lesion of the heart," but her doctors suggested that she would probably live longer in Japan than in the United States. Since the Board thought otherwise, the Maynards resigned in April 1910. They spent their remaining years of service in pastorates and on the staff of the Virginia Baptist orphanage at Salem. Tiny, frail Bessie--"dear Mrs. Maynard"-- lived to celebrate her 72nd birthday.[73]

The end of the second decade of Southern Baptist work in Japan marked the end of the fruitful ministry of J. W. McCollum. Though briefly a professor in the Fukuoka seminary, his first love was preaching, and for many years he was deluged with invitations to speak in churches from Kagoshima to Tokyo. None of his colleagues could match his power in the pulpit. Always his preaching was fervent and animated. On one occasion, to stress a point he struck his left hand so forcefully with his right hand that it became red and swollen.[74]

Mac pushed himself too hard, to the detriment of his health. He was compared to a spirited race horse straining at the bit. When urged to slow down, he would say, "I'd rather burn out than rust out"--words attributed to the great Welsh Baptist evangelist, Christmas Evans. In the damp and unfriendly climate of Japan, as noted earlier, Mac developed catarrh during his first term. Thereafter he was harassed by sore throats that often limited his preaching to one time a day. Though he prayed that he might work for 50 years in Japan, his body was worn down in 20.[75] His mind too, his colleagues believed, had gone awry.

"We believe very strongly," the Mission informed Secretary Willingham, "that his reckless use of money, which has become a source of so much embarrassment to the Mission and which is becoming more and more a demoralizing influence among the native workers, is not due solely to his natural free-heartedness, but is traceable to the same thing that has caused his present physical and nervous condition." The root cause of the trouble was identified as "the habitual use of Cocaine." The Mission reaffirmed Mac's integrity and assured Willingham that he could resume his work in Japan if this impediment were removed. Mac had begun to use cocaine for his chronic throat trouble at a time when the drug was widely touted as an elixir. Free of legal restrictions, it was readily available in

[73]Maynard to Willingham, 25 Mar., 6 Apr. 1910; EBD, *Golden Milestone*, 62; Operation Baptist Biography, Bessie Harlowe Maynard, SBC Historical Commission, Nashville.

[74]*NBRS*, 125.

[75]EBD, *Golden Milestone*, 78; Clark, *Outriders for the King*, 120-21.

numerous forms and products, even in Coca-Cola and other soda drinks. Since it was used to treat ailments such as asthma and hay fever, Mac's plight was well understood. He was pitied, not censured, for his addiction.[76]

Mac reported to Willingham that he got tired and was "unable to conceal it." He complained that he was heavily in debt. "The continual moving, in obedience to Mission action," Mac wrote, "is indirectly the partial cause of the continual deficit." His salary of $1,850 was $650 short of the minimum he required. "I must have $2,500 from the Board," he concluded, "or I must resign."[77]

The McCollums returned to the United States in 1909 and lived in Seattle. Mac resigned from the Board September 1 and took a secular job. On January 23, 1910, at 45 years of age, he died of pneumonia. Dru and the children returned to Marion, Alabama, where friends built and furnished them a home as a memorial to the deceased husband and father. Dru served as dean of women at her alma mater, Judson College, until retirement years. She lived more than twice as long as Mac, dying in 1963 at 94 years of age.[78]

The pioneer missionary wife in Japan was herself fluent in Japanese, and no less than her husband, she endeared herself to many by her Southern charm and hospitality. She gave birth to six children and played a major role in educating the five who survived. Even so, she conducted day schools and Sunday schools for Japanese children and often visited in the homes of the poor and unlearned. "Besides this," wrote Mac, "she has taken a large, if quiet, part in all that I have undertaken." In another of his many tributes, Mac confessed "that I should be worth but little . . . without the continued help of my wife."[79]

---

[76]G. W. Bouldin and C. K. Dozier to Willingham, 5 Mar. 1909; David F. Musto, "America's Forgotten Drug War," *Reader's Digest* 136 (Apr. 1990): 147-50.

[77]McCollum to Willingham, [spring 1909].

[78]Dawson, "Pioneer of the Japan Mission."

[79]*ASBC, 1904*, 139.

5

Training Leadership (1910-1919)

Southern Baptist missionaries entered their third decade of witness in Japan with 10 churches, 11 outstations, 504 church members, and 13 Sunday schools with 617 pupils. Doubtless the statistics would have been more impressive had not so many failures in health reduced the missionary ranks. Following the death of J. W. McCollum, Bessie Willingham succumbed in March 1910 at Battle Creek, Michigan, ending a five-year bout with tuberculosis.[1]

Paul and Lenna Medling were still at work in Kagoshima, Harvey and Lucile Clarke in Kumamoto, John and Margaret Rowe in Nagasaki, and George and Maggie Bouldin in Fukuoka. Kelsey and Maude Dozier had moved to Fukuoka for seminary teaching, and Franklin and Daisy Ray had replaced them in Shimonoseki. Ernest and Claudia Walne were on furlough. The seven couples yearned for reinforcements on the field.

John Moncure, a Virginia pastor's son and Southern Seminary graduate, had arrived in November 1909. He was the first single missionary sent to Japan with no prospect of marriage. Slender and of intellectual cast like Bouldin, but neither as tall nor as domineering, Moncure was patently thoughtful of others. He served in Fukuoka with distinction until 1913, when he wrote a shocking letter of resignation. "I have felt a growing inability," he explained, "to reconcile my plans and ideas with the policies of the Mission as an organization." He thought he could "work to better advantage as an independent worker." Like many first termers after him, Moncure respected his seniors as individuals but abhorred the web of regulations they had woven through the years to keep one another in check.[2]

Walne explained to Secretary Ray that Moncure was unable to live on the salary of a single person--$600--and that he developed "eccentricities" during his

[1]*ASBC, 1910*, 220, 89; *JCY, 1911*, 349.

[2]Moncure to Willingham, 8 Feb. 1913; Moncure to Willingham, n.d.; George Braxton Taylor, *Virginia Baptist Ministers*, 6th ser., 1914-1934 (Lynchburg, Va.: J. P. Bell Co., 1935), 353-54.

last months in Japan. More specifically, Moncure owed the Mission "quite a bit of money" and wanted to marry a certain Japanese girl, of whom he was said to be jealous. Walne rated Moncure highly, nevertheless, and expressed the hope that he would find a wife in the States who met Board requirements and would return to Japan. Willingham agreed. In 1915, when newly married Moncure reapplied to the Board with his wife Grace, the Mission--save for one couple--heartily approved their coming. The one couple's dissent, however, constituted a veto, for it was Board policy to reappoint a resigned missionary only with the unanimous approval of the mission concerned. Thus rejected, Moncure ably served churches in Virginia and Maryland until his death from a surgical operation at the age of 50.[3]

The Mission welcomed another single male in 1910 when Ernest Oscar Mills of Wisconsin was appointed on the field. Mills was 37, the oldest appointee to Japan thus far. He was one of some 200 men sent to Japan by the YMCA under a two-year contract to teach English in government schools and to contribute to the evangelization of the nation. During the two years prior to his Board appointment, he taught at the middle school in Chōfu, Yamaguchi Prefecture, and won the confidence of Southern Baptist missionaries. Then two years after his appointment, he added a valuable worker to the Mission by marrying Grace Anne Hughes, a Northern Baptist missionary from Missouri who had served in Osaka and Sendai since 1900.[4]

In 1911 Calder Willingham returned to Japan with a new wife, Elisabeth Foy. Her father was Livingston Johnson, corresponding secretary of the North Carolina Baptist State Convention. It is reported that "when Mrs. Johnson questioned her daughter as to whether she felt definitely called of God to go as a missionary, Foy answered that she felt called to marry Mr. Willingham!" Indeed, in her application to the Board, Foy wrote frankly that she wanted to be a missionary "because my fiancé is a missionary," and she preferred Japan "because that is my fiancé's field."[5] The Willinghams settled in Kokura in "Mrs. Maynard's House," later the title to one of Foy's many books.

A Foothold in Tokyo

The most heralded event of the year 1910 was the October opening of the Japan Baptist Seminary in Tokyo, a union of the Yokohama and Fukuoka seminaries.[6] Though bathed in sunny publicity, the union took shape under a

---

[3]Walne to T. B. Ray, 17 Feb. 1916; Calder Willingham to Ray, 18 Feb. 1916; Taylor, *Virginia Baptist Ministers*, 353-54.

[4]*ASBC, 1911*, 85, 217; Wood, "Teaching of English," 152-53; *JCY, 1911*, 198; Iglehart, *Century*, 160.

[5]Farmer, *Hitherto*, xii; C. T. Willingham file, FMBA.

[6]*ASBC, 1911*, 217; *FMJ* 44 (Jan. 1912): 210.

cloud, beginning with a resolution to merge the two schools that was passed in May 1909 at the 10th annual convention of Japanese Baptist churches. Since the convention was held in Tokyo, of the 52 messengers present, only 8 represented churches in the Southwestern Association. These included two missionaries, George Bouldin and Kelsey Dozier, and six Japanese, among them Chiba Yūgorō, president of the Fukuoka seminary. Chiba was chosen moderator of the convention. Himself a product of Northern Baptist work, Chiba strongly favored the union seminary. Under his gavel the proposed merger was approved.[7]

The next month, as related above, a joint mission meeting of Northern and Southern Baptists was held in Arima. After extensive discussion the missionaries, who in fact controlled the seminaries, decided in favor of the union by a "hearty and unanimous vote." They also asked their respective boards to provide $50,000 on a 50-50 basis for land and buildings. "Missionaries and natives agreed to union," reported Bouldin, "believing it would be for the best interest of the work in Japan, and expecting that seminary union would only be a step toward the larger cooperation in Baptist work in Japan." It was hoped, added Harvey Clarke, "that the union seminary might become a stronger institution than either Mission could afford to support separately, a great center of influence from which New Testament principles as taught and practiced by Baptists might be propagated throughout Japan."[8]

Bouldin's statement that "missionaries and natives agreed to union" obscures the fact that a significant minority dissented. This minority was a majority of the "natives" who worked with Southern Baptist missionaries. When the Southwestern Association met in May 1910 at Fukuoka Church, some of the delegates voiced strong opposition to the merger on grounds that it would deprive them of the growing Fukuoka seminary and remove the students--15 in number--to distant Tokyo. Discussion of this problem had to be postponed until the second day, however, for the evening was given over to the seminary's first graduation ceremony. Three men received diplomas, which were presented by Satō Kitarō in the absence of Chiba, who unexpectedly had been called to attend the world missionary conference in Edinburgh, Scotland. When business was resumed the next day, a motion to postpone the seminary merger indefinitely was passed by an impressive margin of 19 to 3. The result was telegraphed to Chiba.[9]

The Mission, anxious to be fair in the matter, voted to pay the expenses of pastors to the 1910 convention held at Arima in June, so that the Southwestern Association would be well represented. A record 12 messengers were sent. The atmosphere was tense when the motion to postpone the seminary merger indefinitely came before the assembly. Arase Tsuruki, spokesman for the

[7]*NBRS*, 114.
[8]*JCY, 1910*, 433; Bouldin in *ASBC, 1910*, 211; Clarke, "Statement," 2-3.
[9]*NBRS*, 114-16; *Seinan Gakuin nanajūnen shi*, 1:95-96; Clarke, "Statement," 3.

southwestern bloc, argued that the previous year's action had been taken in haste without due consideration of the difficulties in carrying it out. But despite his eloquent plea, the motion to postpone failed by a vote of 27 nays against 18 ayes. "The strong ought to show compassion toward the weak," commented one pastor. "The defeat of this motion left a heavy stain on the history of Japanese Baptist annual meetings." It also seems to have affected the three men who had just graduated from the Fukuoka seminary. All three eventually left the ministry.[10]

Nevertheless, the annual convention had expressed its support two years in a row, and the two boards in America had ratified the decision of the two missions on the field. Moreover, a board of nine trustees had been elected, three each by the Japanese convention, the Northern mission, and the Southern mission (these were Harvey Clarke, Franklin Ray, and John Rowe). Then the trustees had elected a faculty of four missionaries and four Japanese and had recommended that the academic year be nine months, from October to June. So the school opened as scheduled in October 1910, using leased quarters in Koishikawa, Tokyo. Fifteen students transferred from the Yokohama seminary and seven from the Fukuoka seminary. Three new students were admitted, making a total enrollment of 25.[11]

Southern Baptists were represented on the faculty by Bouldin, Chiba, and Satō. Chiba was named dean, or head teacher. The former president of the Yokohama seminary, W. B. Parshley, assumed the same position in the new school. It is worth noting that the teacher of church history, Takahashi Tateo, though related to Northern Baptists, had graduated from Southern Seminary in Louisville with Dozier, Rowe, and Bouldin. The first of nine or more Japanese trained at Southern Seminary before World War II, Takahashi later worked in the Southwestern Association as teacher and pastor.[12]

Bouldin taught New Testament history and interpretation. He and Maggie Lee endeared themselves to the Northern Baptists by keeping open house, often entertaining all the missionaries in the station. "Their little Japanese house," said William Wynd, "seemed to have expanding walls and was seldom without visitors." The Bouldins also boarded the Walnes' son Ratliff, who was attending high school. In consultation with the Northern Baptists, who had six churches in Tokyo, Bouldin selected two areas in the northern part of the city as evangelistic fields for himself and the students from Kyushu. One of these students, Amano Eizō, who was older and more experienced than Bouldin, worked as his assistant and then stayed on after graduation as evangelist at the two chapels. Maggie

[10]*Seinan Gakuin nanajūnen shi*, 1:196; *NBRS*, 116-19; Clarke, "Statement," 3. The pastor quoted was Aoyagi Shigeru.

[11]"Minutes of the First Meeting of the Board of Trustees of the Japan Baptist Theological Seminary," 12 Nov. 1909, in *Minutes of the Japan Mission of the American Baptist Foreign Mission Society, 1910*, 102-3; *Seinan Gakuin nanajūnen shi*, 1:200; *NBRS*, 118-19; Wynd, *Seventy Years*, 158; *FMJ* 44 (Jan. 1912): 210.

[12]*JCY, 1911*, 305; *ASBC, 1912*, 243; Bouldin, "Autobiography," 48-49.

Bouldin meanwhile started two kindergartens, and she conducted night classes that resulted in several baptisms. Thus the Southern Baptists, hitherto restricted to southwestern Japan, gained a foothold in the nation's capital.[13]

In 1912 a five-acre campus was purchased for the seminary in Shinjuku, then on the outskirts of Tokyo. The two mission boards provided $12,500 each for the purchase. Additional funds were to be provided for buildings, but due to serious problems that developed, the campus was never developed. The joint seminary that was designed to foster Baptist unity became a house divided against itself, a house that could not stand.[14]

The root cause of the disunity was opposing attitudes toward the accelerating drive for Christian unity known as the ecumenical movement. The Northern Baptist Convention (organized 1907), a charter member of the Federal Council of Churches of Christ in America (founded 1908), played an active role in the movement. So did the American Baptist Foreign Mission Society (successor to the American Baptist Missionary Union), which advocated interdenominational cooperation in educational work abroad. In 1912 its foreign secretary, James H. Franklin, visited Japan and encouraged the Northern and Southern Baptist missions to join with the Presbyterian and Dutch Reformed missions in conducting a union Christian college on the campus of Meiji Gakuin. As a result, beginning in 1914 this college served as a preparatory school for men who took the full course in the Baptist seminary. This arrangement gave promise of raising the seminary's academic level by attracting better students and preparing them more thoroughly for theological studies.[15]

The SBC meanwhile looked askance at such interdenominational cooperation. In 1914 it adopted a statement on Christian unity, written by Edgar Young Mullins of Southern Seminary, that said "yes" to the ecumenical movement, but it also adopted a statement on denominational efficiency, written by James B. Gambrell of Southwestern Seminary, that said "no" more emphatically. Reflecting this ambivalent attitude, the Foreign Mission Board permitted the cooperative arrangement in Tokyo with great reluctance.[16]

At the union conference of Japan Baptist missionaries held in 1914, Walne urged the building of a strong seminary "without relying on a co-operating school." Northern Baptist C. B. Tenny urged the building of a strong seminary "by co-operating with other denominational schools." For the sake of harmony, the divisive issue was not brought to a vote.[17]

---

[13]Wynd, *Seventy Years*, 166; Walne to Bouldin, 21 Sept. 1911; *JCY, 1912*, 245; Bouldin, "Autobiography," 106.

[14]*HFF* 1 (Dec. 1916): 6.

[15]Wynd, *Seventy Years*, 160.

[16]James Leo Garrett, ed., *Baptist Relations with Other Christians* (Valley Forge: Judson Press, 1974), 70-73; Clarke, "Statement," 9; *ASBC, 1914*, 104-6.

[17]Mission meeting minutes, 1914 (hereafter cited as MM minutes).

Annual meeting of Southwestern Baptist Association (Seinan bukai), Kumamoto, 1917. Missionaries, *left to right:* Kelsey Dozier, Calder Willingham, Ernest Walne, Harvey and Lucile Clarke, George Bouldin, Paul Medling (*W. H. Clarke Collection, Foreign Mission Board, SBC*)

To the consternation of its advocates, the cooperative arrangement so nobly conceived was burdened with insurmountable problems. The Baptist seminary and Meiji Gakuin happened to lie at opposite ends of sprawling Tokyo, and the teachers and students wore themselves out shuttling back and forth in crowded cars. Chiba, who taught on both campuses, suffered a breakdown and had to leave the seminary for a number of years. The situation was eased somewhat in 1916 when the seminary acquired the buildings of Duncan Academy, located near the center of Tokyo and closer to Meiji Gakuin. But as far as Kyushu Baptists were concerned, nothing could save the union seminary. They were highly dissatisfied with sending their ministerial students to a school 800 miles away. And the Southern Baptist missionaries, though less concerned about geography, were increasingly worried that through the ties with Meiji Gakuin, Baptist policy was being overly influenced by Presbyterian and Reformed views.[18]

It remained for the Foreign Mission Board to settle the matter. Influenced by the mounting popularity of J. B. Gambrell's hostile stand against the ecumenical movement, the Board promised the SBC that it would "pursue an unentangled course in educational and other mission work." It voted "not to co-operate with other denominations in Theological Education on the foreign field." Since Northern Baptists were firmly committed to this kind of cooperation, Southern Baptists in Japan withdrew from the Tokyo seminary in 1918. The five-acre campus purchased by the two boards was sold and the proceeds divided between the two missions. The Bouldins moved back to Fukuoka.[19]

Seinan Gakuin is Born

During the eight years that the Bouldins lived in Tokyo, their colleagues in southwestern Japan gave top priority to educational work in Fukuoka. In 1909 the Mission had voted to ask the Board for permission to open a boys' school in the fall of 1910, when the Fukuoka seminary building was to become available. Fukuoka had a Methodist girls' school, established in 1885, but the only Protestant boys' schools in all of Kyushu were located in Nagasaki and Kumamoto. "If Southern Baptists ever expect to begin education of boys," the Mission's resolution said, "now is the time."[20]

The spring of 1910 brought a disappointing reply from the Board: "We do not think it best to take up Academic or Collegiate work in Japan." Secretary Willingham suspected that a school in Japan would require a heavy outlay of funds

[18]Wynd, *Seventy Years*, 160-62; *ASBC, 1917*, 255-56.

[19]William R. Estep, *Baptists and Christian Unity* (Nashville: Broadman Press, 1966), 151; *ASBC, 1916*, 120-22; EBD, "Mission and Convention," 8.

[20]EBD notes, 1909-10; *JCY, 1909*, 587; C. K. Dozier to FMB, 1 Jan. 1910.

for an indefinite period, and Chiba, who happened to be in the United States at the time, confirmed his suspicion.[21]

Its aims thwarted, the Mission found another way to utilize the vacated seminary building. On February 1, 1911, it opened a night school--Fukuoka Yagakkai--that was mainly an English school, though Chinese was offered, for young men from the offices, banks, and schools of the city. Kelsey Dozier served as principal. He called the new enterprise "a means of getting hold of men and bringing them in personal touch with the missionaries and under the influence of our work" (today it would be called an "encounter ministry"). Classes were held every night except Saturday and Sunday. Tuition charges were small, and enrollment grew rapidly to more than 100, making this night school the largest in Japan conducted under missionary auspices.[22]

The faculty consisted of four missionaries (Dozier, Moncure, Mills, Claudia Walne) and three Japanese. Two of the Japanese were already employed by the Mission, one as an evangelist and the other as a language teacher. Only the instructor in Chinese had to be specially employed. The school's main attraction was English, but Christianity aroused more interest than the missionaries had anticipated. A wall had to be torn out between two rooms to accommodate the students at the daily chapel exercises, 25-minute periods of Scripture reading, prayer, singing, and addresses by members of the faculty or invited speakers.[23]

The flourishing night school soon added afternoon classes for women and girls, while the Mission continued to plead with the Board for a full-fledged institution for boys. "We need a school," wrote Moncure, "in which our Christian young men and the sons of Christians may be shielded from the non-Christian and often atheistic influences that surround them in the government schools and where sturdy Christian character may be built up." Clarke emphasized the need for training church leaders. "Our dependence upon other denominations to do this training for us," he wrote, "has kept us in an embarrassing position too long. It has classed us among the weaker denominations in Japan, while we are second to none in ability in America."[24]

Confident that Board approval was forthcoming, the Mission asked John Rowe to assume responsibility for establishing the school. But in 1913, when Margaret's illness raised doubts about the Rowes' returning from furlough, the responsibility was shifted to Kelsey Dozier. It was Kelsey's conviction that a school for boys was "absolutely essential." He had come to Japan for evangelistic work but had become convinced that he could best evangelize through education. His joy was

---

[21]EBD notes, 1910.

[22]*ASBC, 1912*, 244-45; C. K. Dozier to FMB, 26 Sept. 1911.

[23]*ASBC, 1912*, 244-45.

[24]Ibid., 248; W. Harvey Clarke, *Boys' School for Fukuoka, Japan*, pamphlet (Richmond: FMB, n.d.), 4.

unbounded when, in January 1915, the Mission received from the Board permission to establish a school and the promise of $30,000 for buildings.[25]

Churches and individuals were asked to suggest names for the school. Rowe proposed Seinan Gakuin (Southwestern Academy), "as there was Tohoku Gakuin in Sendai and Kansei Gakuin in Kobe and so Seinan would finish the chain of Christian schools from northeast to southwest Japan." Tōhoku (northeastern) Gakuin had been established by Reformed Church missionaries, and Kansei ("west of the barrier") Gakuin by Southern Methodists. Rowe's sensible proposal was adopted.[26]

The Mission named Dozier as missionary administrator of the school and elected Jō Inohiko, a Baptist layman, as principal. A native of Kumamoto Prefecture, Jō had taught in middle schools since his graduation from Kyoto Imperial University in 1910. He accepted the principalship at a salary of ¥100 per month, about twice the salary of a full-time teacher.[27]

Dozier and Jō were named ex officio members of the board of trustees. The other trustees, elected by the Mission, were Rowe (chairman), Ray, Willingham, Ozaki Genroku (then pastor at Wakamatsu), and Saitō Saiichi. Saitō, a graduate of Tokyo Imperial University, was teaching English literature at the Fifth Higher School in Kumamoto where he had once been a student. He was also a deacon and Sunday school superintendent at the Baptist church, and later he was executive secretary of the national YMCA. Saitō devoted much time and effort to helping the Baptist school get started. It was on his recommendation that Jō had been chosen as principal.[28]

No sooner had Jō assumed the position than he was hospitalized with tuberculosis. Dozier called on him often for consultation, especially in the delicate matter of selecting teachers. But the herculean task of starting the school fell almost entirely on Dozier's own shoulders. Accompanied by Rowe or Willingham, he visited Christian boys' schools in several cities to observe their facilities and operations. He talked with educational authorities, real estate agents, architects, prospective teachers. The classroom building formerly used by the seminary had to be modified, and a gymnasium-chapel had to be constructed on a shoestring budget. A dormitory had to be provided, and when a Japanese house was rented for this purpose, rules for its use had to be drawn up. Desks had to be built. The *Encyclopædia Britannica*, a globe, and many other items had to be purchased. The style and color of spring and winter uniforms had to be selected, and a monogram

---

[25]Maude B. Dozier, "Seinan Gakuin" (typescript, Seinan Gakuin University), 10; C. K. Dozier address delivered at the 15th anniversary of Seinan Gakuin, in EBD notes, 1931.

[26]C. K. Dozier address, 1931.

[27]Ibid.; *Seinan Gakuin shi shiryō* (Seinan Gakuin historical materials), 2 vols. (Fukuoka: Seinan Gakuin, 1980), 1:8. Jō was elected *inchō*, or "school head." As the school developed, the term was successively translated "principal," "president," and "chancellor."

[28]*Seinan Gakuin nanajūnen shi*, 1:261-70.

had to be designed for the buttons. Dozier personally drew the model for the S.W.A. monogram. With indispensable help from Pastor Kawakatsu's son, who joined the faculty, he completed the tedious procedures required for getting the school approved by the authorities and properly registered. Without a doubt Kelsey Dozier earned the fame that is his as founder of what is now one of Japan's prestigious universities (though Maude was said to be the brains behind the enterprise). Yet had it not been for Margaret Rowe's untimely illness, the fame would belong to John Rowe, a fact that Kelsey generously and publicly acknowledged.[29]

Seinan Gakuin was established as a middle school, a five-year school equivalent to grades 7 through 11 in the American system. All Japanese children were provided a six-year elementary education in free public schools that were coeducational and, since 1907, compulsory. But only the elite gained entrance to the public middle schools--separate for boys and girls--for they were limited in number and necessarily selective. The boys' school in Fukuoka, for instance, was accepting about 190 first-year students each year out of some 600 applicants. This situation created a strong public demand for a private school of any kind, even one that was avowedly Christian. Children who were denied entrance to a middle school were cut off permanently from higher education; they either started working or attended specialized schools. Boys (not girls) who completed middle school could take entrance exams for three-year higher schools, which were preparatory schools for the imperial universities. No private schools were accorded university status until 1918.[30]

Seinan Gakuin gave entrance exams to 118 applicants. Many others had applied but had been rejected because they were over 15 years of age or obviously unfit. Of the 118 examinees, only 13 failed. The school's opening ceremony was held on April 11, 1916, attended by the first class of 105 boys, the faculty of 12 teachers, and more than 100 guests. So auspicious was the occasion that Principal Jō left his sick bed to take part. "The purpose of this school," he told the audience, "is to build strong character, and to do that we believe Christianity is necessary. . . . We shall not force the boys to be Christians, but we hope all of them will become followers of the Christ." His consumption growing worse, Jō came to the school only three times before resigning as principal in July. He died 11 years later, at the age of 46.[31]

As business manager and teacher of English Bible, Kelsey Dozier was anxious to be relieved of his additional duties as acting principal. The trustees worked diligently to find a Japanese successor to Jō. They approached four different men,

[29]C. K. Dozier report, 17 March 1916, in EBD notes, 1916; C. K. Dozier address, 1931; M. B. Dozier, "Seinan Gakuin," 20; Operation Baptist Biography, Maude B. Dozier.
[30]C. K. Dozier to FMB, 9 Mar. 1914; HFF 5 (Oct. 1921): 311; Kodansha Encyclopedia of Japan, s.v. "education."
[31]Seinan News, 25 June 1935.

all graduates of Tokyo Imperial University, but each one declined the position. Unable to find a qualified Japanese willing to serve, in February 1917 the trustees elected Dozier as principal, a position he held until July 1929.[32]

Dozier saw to it that the students were introduced to Christianity through daily chapel services, weekly Bible classes, and the classes he himself taught in morals (*shūshin*) and English. Japanese teachers also gave instruction in morals and English, as well as Japanese language, mathematics, history, geography, science, art, gymnastics, fencing, and judo.[33]

"Southern Baptists have one baby born with fine prospects," said Calder Willingham of the new school, "and if they fail to give it nourishment it will be a shame." Yet for a while it appeared that the baby would starve. The prefectural authorities had given permission for the school to operate in the temporary buildings the first year only. A new campus had to be provided to accommodate the second class of students in 1917 and succeeding classes until the school had the full five-year program of studies. On February 13, 1917, after a sleepless night, Principal Dozier wrote a prayer in his diary: "If Seinan Gakuin is not of thy planting, speedily open our eyes that we may close it. If it is of thy planting, water it."[34]

April came, and the school entered its second year on the same substandard campus. "It was hard to get the people of the city to believe that we meant business," Dozier later recalled. A letter from the Board stated unequivocally that no money was in sight. If he had revealed this letter to the Japanese, said Dozier, it "would have caused a panic in the school, and we would not have gotten the 75 new boys we did get." About a third of the students in the first class had dropped out for various reasons, so the 75 additions increased the enrollment to 143.[35]

Dozier had written to Franklin Ray, then on furlough, to explain the school's predicament and solicit his help in obtaining the needed funds. Ray responded by making a stirring appeal at the Southern Baptist convention in New Orleans. Subsequently, Baptist laymen raised $6,000 to save the floundering school. This amount added to the $18,843 gained from the sale of the school's property enabled Seinan Gakuin to move to a five-acre site on Hakata Bay, just outside the city limits in Nishijin ("new west"). The land was purchased from Hakata Electric Company for $18,000. Under Rowe's supervision, the two existing buildings were moved to Nishijin, and a new eight-classroom building was constructed. The old classroom building was turned into a dormitory. Classes met on the new campus from January 1918.[36]

[32]C. K. Dozier address, 1931.
[33]*Seinan Gakuin nanajūnen shi*, 1:279.
[34]M. B. Dozier, "Seinan Gakuin," 23; C. K. Dozier diary, 1917, FMBA.
[35]*ASBC, 1918*, 311-12,
[36]C. K. Dozier address, 1931; *ASBC, 1918*, 174.

love   The new site was adorned with famous old pine trees that had been planted along the shore as a windbreak. Later it was discovered that a massive earth-and-stone wall lay buried under the sand of the campus. This was a part of the wall built around Hakata Bay after the foiled Mongol invasion of 1274. Upon the Mongols' return in 1281, with their forces increased from 40,000 to 140,000 men, the wall had enabled the Japanese defenders to withstand the enemy for nearly two months, until a typhoon--called *kamikaze* ("divine wind")--destroyed much of the Mongol fleet and forced the survivors to sail for home.[37]

"A heavy burden has been lifted from my shoulders," said Dozier. "The school is now assured of success." His hearty laugh could often be heard in the halls of the new classroom building.[38] He could not have foreseen that 70 years later, his little school that nearly folded for lack of $6,000 would have an annual budget in excess of $25 million.

The first year on the new campus--1918--was filled with optimism. World War I came to a close, a war in which Japan, allied with Britain and America, had taken over valuable German possessions in Asia and the Pacific and gained new prestige as a world power. Seinan boys and their families shared in their nation's pride, and the missionaries from America enjoyed their respect. The missionaries exulted most in the signs of spiritual awakening seen among the students. Famed evangelists Yamamuro Gumpei, a Salvation Army leader, and Kimura Seimatsu, a Congregationalist trained at Moody Bible Institute, preached on campus and inspired 70 of the boys to express a desire to follow Christ. Some of the Christian students formed a Gethsemane Band to pray for unbelieving students and teachers. Another highlight of the year was the October visit of J. F. Love, the Board's corresponding secretary, and Mrs. Love. Upon inspecting Seinan Gakuin's cheaply constructed facilities, Secretary Love said to Dozier, "Do not build any more buildings like these." He foresaw that the school would play a permanent role in the Baptist witness in Japan.[39]

In 1919 the Education Ministry in Tokyo granted formal recognition to Seinan Gakuin. This assured its students of exemption from military service. The school spirit soared yet higher, and plans proceeded for opening a college department in 1921 to accommodate the first graduates of the five-year course.[40]

Unavoidably, the campus move produced a negative side-effect: the five-year-old night school was discontinued. The new site was too isolated for night classes, and no funds were available for renting a downtown building or employing teachers. During its five years of operation, the night school had served to introduce the gospel to hundreds of young men from the influential classes, one

---

[37]*Kodansha Encyclopedia of Japan*, s.v. "history of Japan (Kamakura history)." An excavated portion of the wall may be seen today in a small park adjacent to the campus.

[38]M. B. Dozier, "Seinan Gakuin," 30, 33.

[39]Ibid., 35.

[40]Ibid., 39; *ASBC, 1920*, 331.

of whom later became a principal at Seinan Gakuin. The void left by the Baptists was filled by Lutheran missionaries, who in 1920 opened a night school in Hakata that enrolled 75 students.[41]

Other Efforts at Christian Education

For a dozen years and more there had been frequent discussion of opening a school for girls in Kumamoto. The school was the grand dream of Lucile Clarke, who liked to quote Itō Hirobumi, Japan's preeminent Meiji-era statesman. Said Ito: "Educate a boy and you make a good citizen; educate a girl and you bring enlightenment to a whole family." Both the Clarkes promoted the enterprise with a torrent of words, and the Board's foreign secretary, T. B. Ray, a chummy friend of Harvey's (they addressed one another as "Dear Bronson" and "Dear Billy"), lent his support. For instance, Ray added his endorsement to Lucile's pamphlet entitled *Girls' School Kumamoto Japan*, urging the women of the South to give $30,000 to this project as part of the Judson Centennial campaign.[42]

The Clarkes also won the support of most of their colleagues. "We are almost devoid of women workers," said Moncure, "good, bad or indifferent." He pointed out "the great preponderance of men over women" in all the congregations, since "the position of women in the East makes them much harder to reach by evangelistic methods than men." In 1914 the Mission voted to request the Board for two single ladies to serve as teachers in the proposed girls' school. But turning Lucile's dream into reality consumed more years than anyone expected. Available funds were insufficient even for the boys' school that opened in 1916, and Ernest Walne, who brandished considerable clout as the senior missionary, insisted that the girls' school should be located, not in Kumamoto, but in Fukuoka or another city in thickly populated northern Kyushu.[43]

Lucile meanwhile concentrated her appeals on the Baptist women in her native Georgia. "I have had more than 50 girls in my classes in my home, many of whom have become earnest Christians," she wrote. "How much greater would have been the result if there had been 500 girls instead of 50." She emphasized that "this is not primarily an educational work, but an evangelistic work using education as a means." In response, the Georgia WMU gave top priority to this project and made an initial gift of $6,000 in 1918. Then in 1919 the Board

---

[41]*ASBC, 1918*, 312-13; *ASBC, 1919*, 325; *JCY, 1921*, xxxii.

[42]EBD, *Golden Milestone*, 123-24; Mrs. W. Harvey Clarke, *Girls' School Kumamoto Japan*, leaflet (Richmond: FMB, 1912). For examples of chummy salutations, see Ray to Clarke, 29 Jan. 1915, and Clarke to Ray, 2 Feb. 1915. According to the Georgia WMU's *Mission Messenger*, Feb. 1918, the Clarkes had "begged for this school seventeen years."

[43]*ASBC, 1912*, 241-42; Lucile Clarke in Eden ms., 190-91.

designated $15,000 for the "Kumamoto Girls' School." The appropriation set the Mission to wrangling anew over where the school should be located.[44]

At the 10-day Mission meeting held at Gotemba in July 1919, six missionaries voted for Kumamoto and nine for reconsideration. After a moving appeal by Harvey Clarke, a new vote was taken, and the result was 12 to 4 in favor of Kumamoto. Those opposed were the Walnes, George Bouldin, and John Rowe (who previously supported Kumamoto). Ernest Walne was said to be "hopping mad"; he never again spoke to the Clarkes during that Mission meeting. Lucile was "disgusted with two or three men trying to run the whole mission." Her daughter Josephine, appalled at the fracas, said that she would never be a missionary. And despite the impressive 12-to-4 vote in favor of Kumamoto, the Mission was to reverse itself again in 1920 and eventually locate the school in northern Kyushu.[45]

Another facet of education that engaged Southern Baptist missionaries in this decade was the kindergarten. A German specialist invited by the Japanese government introduced the kindergarten into the educational system as early as 1876, and a Presbyterian missionary started the first Christian kindergarten in 1884. Northern Baptists got involved in 1894, when Gazelle Thompson founded the Zenrin Kindergarten in a Kobe slum. By 1911 there were nearly 100 Christian kindergartens among the total of 443 reported in government statistics.[46]

In 1912 the Southern Baptist mission opened its first kindergarten in connection with its Sunday school in Chiyomachi, a commercial area in East Fukuoka where the prefectural government offices are now located. The venture was entrusted to Grace Mills, who had worked with kindergartens during her years with Northern Baptists. In the summer of 1913, however, when it became apparent that a large outlay of funds would be required for facilities in Chiyomachi, the Mission decided to close the kindergarten and start anew elsewhere. "After much good advice from our Japanese friends," said Grace, "we located in the residence part of our city, at the foot of our beautiful West Park. Here we were able to rent a temporary building that would do for both home and kindergarten."[47]

The new location was within walking distance for 1,000 children of kindergarten age. Only 16 enrolled on the first day, but in one year the number increased to 44, with an average attendance of 32. They came "from the best families of the city," in sharp contrast to the pupils at Zenrin Kindergarten, which intentionally drew the unregistered children of Kobe's poorest families. Tuition was set at 50 sen (25 cents) per month. Three Japanese women, two of whom held diplomas in kindergarten work, served with Grace as teachers. Thus was born the

[44]Eden ms., 183-84; EBD, "Mission and Convention," 8-9.
[45]Lucile Clarke in Eden ms., 192-93.
[46]*JCY, 1914*, 265-71.
[47]*ASBC, 1914*, 168.

Maizuru Kindergarten that thrives to this day. The name Maizuru, literally "dancing crane," was taken from that of the old Fukuoka castle whose ruins lie nearby.[48]

"From the beginning," the Mission reported, "the children were taught, through the morning story and opening prayer, to know of the one true God as their Creator and loving Protector." They learned Bible verses and Sunday school songs with ease, as only children can. The well-attended meetings for mothers, which opened with prayer and hymns, added to the Christian witness carried into homes through the children.[49]

When the Millses went on furlough in 1916, the kindergarten was turned over to Maude Dozier and then to Carrie Hooker Chiles, a 1915 appointee who was a specialist in children's work. The first unengaged single woman to join the Mission, Hooker had been highly popular at the Louisville Training School despite "frequent attacks of Quinsy [inflammation of the throat]."[50] Under her supervision Maizuru Kindergarten continued to grow in numbers and in reputation. "Go to the Baptist Maizuru Kindergarten," city officials often said, "if you wish to observe the best methods for training little children." By 1919 the Mission was operating four kindergartens with 107 pupils. The children were highly privileged, for in Japan as a whole only one in 80 of that age group attended kindergarten.[51]

Though heavily involved in new educational ventures during this decade, the Mission by no means neglected the Sunday schools, "the hope of the churches of the future." Japanese children showed a "remarkable readiness" to attend despite the poor quality of instruction usually offered. Still, their attendance was quite irregular, because their weekday schools often used Sundays for excursions and other special activities--as is the case today. In 1911 the Mission employed a seminary graduate, Matsushima Takaaki, "to give his time to building up the Sunday Schools in our churches and putting them on an up-to-date basis." As a boy Matsushima had been caught by Ernest Walne throwing rocks at the rear windows of a Mission residence. As Sunday school promoter, he trained teachers, increased attendance, and started several new schools. Total enrollment climbed from 617 in 1910 to 1,527 in 1919. Interestingly, the number of male teachers was twice that of female teachers (in 1919 about 55 percent of elementary school teachers were male), but the attendance of girls was much greater than that of boys.[52]

---

[48]Ibid., 168-69; Charlotte B. DeForest, *The Woman and the Leaven in Japan* (West Medford, Mass.: Central Committee, 1923), 176-77.

[49]*ASBC, 1915*, 245.

[50]Chiles appointment file, FMBA; J. F. Love to J. H. Rowe, 10 Feb. 1922.

[51]*ASBC, 1923*, 131; DeForest, *Woman and the Leaven*, 68

[52]*ASBC, 1912*, 242-43; *ASBC, 1910*, 220; *ASBC, 1919*, 361; EBD notes, 1911; DeForest, *Woman and the Leaven*, 68.

The employment of Matsushima as Sunday school evangelist was in accord with the Mission's practice of hiring pastors and other workers. As an employer the Mission sometimes had to "use the pruning knife," as Dozier put it, on those who proved unfit for the work. It also shuffled pastors when this was thought best for the work. In 1915, after a church union movement in the city of Moji caused the Baptist church to split, even the highly esteemed Pastor Arase had to be replaced. Though the Moji church was the oldest Baptist church in Kyushu and the only one that was self-supporting (since 1912), it reverted to the status of *kōgisho*, or preaching place. This episode contributed to the increasingly negative attitude of the missionaries toward the ecumenical movement.[53]

Outside Relationships

Though opposed to church union, the Mission did not isolate itself from the larger Christian community. It was a full member of the Conference of Federated Missions in Japan, and it cooperated with other denominations in evangelism so long as there was no threat to the unity and Baptist identity of local churches. The Mission joined enthusiastically in the nationwide Cooperative Campaign of Evangelism conducted from 1914 to 1916. An outgrowth of the Edinburgh Missionary Conference and the subsequent visit to Japan of John R. Mott, the campaign drew the active participation of an estimated 90 percent of the entire Protestant movement. Thousands of special meetings were held, and millions of pieces of literature were distributed. In Kagoshima, Medling and his associates gave out 60,000 tracts and testaments in one year. Other Southern Baptist missionaries preached in special meetings and started new missions.[54]

Ernest Mills discovered that he was especially apt at railway evangelism, in which the YMCA (his former employer) and several other missions had pioneered. A number of missionaries and evangelists were traveling about the country with free passes from the railway authorities, preaching and distributing Bibles without hindrance. Mills got involved in 1913 through an English class he was teaching for clerks at Hakata Station. "At first these men were rather shy," Mills said, "but gradually became personal friends, and finally asked for Bible lessons. . . . They seemed quite proud to show me the fine New Testament which the Railway Mission of Tokyo presented to this station." Afterwards Mills obtained a pass from the Kyushu Railway superintendent, himself an earnest Christian, and began a half-time ministry of witnessing in coaches and at stations. In a single month 880 trainmen and passengers listened to his presentation of the gospel.[55]

[53]*JCY, 1912*, 246; MM minutes, 1916.
[54]*JCY, 1912*, 433; Iglehart, *Century*, 151; *ASBC, 1914*, 163-64; *ASBC, 1915*, 246.
[55]*ASBC, 1914*, 168; *ASBC, 1915*, 246; *JCY, 1913*, 48-49; *JCY, 1915*, 117.

Another new program of evangelism launched by the Mission was the publishing of Christian books. In 1912 the Gospel Book Store that Ernest Walne had started in Nagasaki was moved to Fukuoka and again placed under Walne's supervision. In 1913 the store issued its first book, a highly readable translation of Edward Judson's *Life of Adoniram Judson*. Though it was translated by a professor in the Methodist Kansei Gakuin and published through the interdenominational Christian Literature Society in Tokyo, this well-received book paved the way for many other Baptist works issued directly by the Gospel Book Store.[56]

With Mission approval, though two members were strongly opposed, Walne served briefly but effectively as field secretary of the Christian Literature Society in both Tokyo and Fukuoka. His assignment was "the promotion throughout Japan of the distribution of the Society's publications and other wholesome Christian writings." Walne was praised as a man "raised up and prepared" for this work. While in Tokyo he also took charge of *Kirisuto Kyōhō*, the paper issued jointly by the two Baptist missions and the Baptist convention. Walne upgraded the semimonthly paper to a 12-page weekly. But there was a growing feeling in the understaffed Mission that Walne should give his time to denominational work exclusively. The Board concurred and directed Walne to sever his relationship with the Christian Literature Society.[57]

In 1916, therefore, the Walnes moved to Shimonoseki, and Ernest devoted full time to the book store and its publishing work--almost with a vengeance. In 1917, when the Congregational evangelist Paul Kanamori held a series of meetings in Kyushu, Walne published a series of 10 tracts on the fundamentals of Christianity, which Kanamori wrote at his request. Incredibly, the first printing of one million copies was sold out before the end of the year. The series went through four more editions of one million copies each.[58]

Having prohibited the Mission from cooperating with other denominations in theological education and literature work, the Board now warned against the practice of open communion by some of the Japanese pastors in the Southwestern Association. "The history of Southern Baptists," wrote Corresponding Secretary Love, "proves that Southern Baptist ordinances, consistently held to, promote Baptist growth and influence." Foreign Secretary Ray expressed concern about the attitude of the missionaries themselves. "There would be much disturbance throughout the denomination," he told Calder Willingham, "if it should be learned that the views of the denomination are not being promulgated on every mission field." Whatever the stance of the missionaries, most of whom--especially Dozier--insisted on close (closed) communion, the Japanese pastors in question were also

---

[56]*JCY, 1913*, 124; *JCY, 1914*, 234-35, 243; *ASBC, 1914*, 166-67.

[57]*JCY, 1914*, 203, 241; Walne to T. B. Ray, 22 Mar. 1916; *ASBC, 1915*, 244; EBD notes, 1916.

[58]*ASBC, 1918*, 308; EBD, "Lantern Lights," 12. Kanamori was a member of the Kumamoto Band. His Japanese name was Tsūrin or Michitomo.

influenced by the nationwide convention dominated by Northern Baptists. Open communion became the more widely held pattern in Japanese churches cooperating with Southern Baptists, who themselves grew less disposed to make an issue of the matter.[59]

Given the narrow denominationalism of Southern Baptists at the time, the Board's secretaries were pleased that in 1918 the Southwestern Association reorganized itself into the West Japan Baptist Convention (Nihon Baputesuto Seibu Kumiai). The new constitution, written by a committee that included Rowe and Bouldin, recognized all missionaries--wives included--as voting messengers at the annual conventions. It allowed each church two messengers for the first 10 members and one for each additional 10 members. It further empowered the executive committee to conduct negotiations with the Mission. In the same year churches related to the Northern Baptist mission reorganized themselves into the East Japan Convention. The annual joint convention of the two groups was replaced by a fraternal triennial convention.[60]

The Board's secretaries declared as null and void all previous comity agreements with Northern Baptists on the territorial division of Japan. During an October 1918 visit, Love announced that "Southern Baptists have the right to work anywhere in the Empire." He particularly had in mind Tokyo, where the Mission had gotten its camel's nose in the tent by cooperating in the joint seminary until its closure in June 1918. Although the Bouldins returned to Kyushu at that time, the church they left behind in Tokyo with Amano Eizō as pastor voted to retain its connection with Southern Baptists. The church even petitioned the Mission to strengthen its work in the capital. In January 1919, with full support from the Board and feeble opposition from Northern Baptist missionaries, the Mission voted to transfer Harvey and Lucile Clarke from Kumamoto to Tokyo.[61]

The Clarkes were the logical choice for this assignment for three reasons. First, Harvey strongly advocated a missionary presence in the capital, the head and the heart of Japan. "However much we may increase our force and equipment in Kyushu," he said, "unless we are represented in Tokyo our work will have a provincial coloring, and our denominational influence will be necessarily circumscribed." Second, the Clarkes' highly successful work among the thousands of students in Kumamoto qualified them to work among the tens of thousands of students in Tokyo, including many from Kyushu who would respond to their personal touch. Third, the Clarkes needed a better arrangement for their children's schooling, a major concern that has always been a factor in missionary deployment. As Harvey wrote, "This will enable us to keep our two oldest children, who are now in school at Shanghai, China, at an enormous expense on account of the

---

[59]Love as quoted in EBD notes, 1916; T. B. Ray to Calder Willingham, 11 Dec. 1916; Mizumachi Yoshio, ed., *A Memoir of C. K. Dozier* (Fukuoka: Seinan Gakuin, 1934), 40.
[60]*NBRS*, 211-15.
[61]EBD notes, 1918; EBD, "Mission and Convention," 8; Clarke to Ray, 11 Mar. 1919.

heavy rate of exchange, a while longer in our home. . . . The smaller children could also be kept in school, and the mother would be enabled to give more time directly to the work." No other family had a more urgent need to live where a school was available. The Rays had three children in the Canadian Academy at Kobe, but it was only 200 miles from their home in Hiroshima.[62]

The Clarkes moved to Tokyo in September 1919 and lived in a three-story missionary house on the compound of the Methodist school, Aoyama Gakuin. They boarded T. J. Walne at the request of his parents, who wanted the boy to attend school in Tokyo. "It nearly kills me to have the privacy of our home broken into," said Lucile, "but we just hope and pray that our having T. J. will make Mr. Walne feel less hard toward us and maybe he will stop trying to move the [girls'] school." A year later, when the Mission had voted to locate the school in Kokura, Lucile wrote: "They claim now that we killed the girls' school in Kumamoto when we moved to Tokyo. Mr. Walne was at the bottom of our moving for he wanted the school in Kokura. He has had his way and we are blamed for deserting Kumamoto."[63]

However much the seesaw voting on the girls' school might have been manipulated, one bright feature is that Lucile and the other women were not excluded from the process. The Mission had agreed in 1916 that "as the women are appointees of the Board and full members of the Mission their votes would be required on matters passed by correspondence, and they would be expected to vote on all questions raised at Mission conference." In America, women were not allowed to serve as messengers to the SBC until 1918, nor to serve on its boards until after 1922. Five Southern states, including Lucile's home state of Georgia, rejected the 19th Amendment, which extended to women the right to vote in state and national elections. The amendment was ratified in 1920 despite its failure in those states.[64]

Trials and Sorrows

One of the severest trials faced by missionaries in this decade was financial insecurity. Rampant inflation in Japan since the Russo-Japanese War of 1904-5, especially during and after World War I, strained their budgets to the limits. Between 1914 and 1919 the cost of many commodities increased sixfold--large-scale rice riots had to be suppressed by army troops--and the Mission was forced to raise the salaries of Japanese pastors and other workers by 70 percent. Yet their own salaries remained unchanged, despite repeated pleas to the Board for relief.[65]

[62]Clarke to Love, 4 Mar. 1919; *ASBC, 1920*, 337.

[63]Lucile Clarke letters, 22 Sept. 1919, 22 Nov. 1920, in Eden ms., 194, 205.

[64]MM minutes, 1916; Alma Hunt, *History of Woman's Missionary Union* (Nashville: Convention Press, 1964), 107-8.

[65]Walne to T. B. Ray, 13 Aug. 1919; Daisy Ray to T. B. Ray, 16 Feb. 1917.

Mission meeting, Gotemba, July 1918. Missionaries, *left to right:* George and Maggie Bouldin, Grace and Ernest Mills, Paul Medling, Kelsey and Maude Dozier, Hooker Chiles, Ernest and Claudia Walne, John and Margaret Rowe, Lucile and Harvey Clarke (*W. H. Clarke Collection, Foreign Mission Bd.*)

The Board's annual income had risen from $110,000 in 1893 to $600,000 in 1914, while the number of missionaries had only tripled, increasing from 92 to 298. But the corresponding secretary during this period, R. J. Willingham, had been an avid builder of schools and other institutions, and upon his death in 1914, the Board accounts had been in the red for seven years. So when Love succeeded Willingham in 1915, he came under Convention pressure to make the Board debt-free. This he achieved in 1917, when the Board's total income exceeded $1 million for the first time in its history.[66]

It was in February 1917 that Daisy Ray wrote what was undoubtedly the strongest appeal for a salary raise to come from the Japan Mission. She wrote from her furlough home in Birmingham--"a little bare 5-room cottage, with not a single sq. ft. of floor-covering, nor curtain nor even shade at a window."[67]

Daisy challenged the Board's argument that "salaries on one field could not be raised without raising all." Every other item in the Japan budget, she said, was raised year after year in keeping with inflation; only missionary salaries were frozen. The Northern Baptist board had given a 20-percent increase to its personnel in Japan some three or four years before, but Southern Baptist couples still had to make do with $1,000 per year, a salary fixed a generation earlier. They were unable, said Daisy, "even by the strictest (I had almost said 'soul-degrading') economies, to make personal allowances cover living expenses." As for the Franklin Rays, they had been able to leave Japan debt-free, she explained, only by moonlighting for 18 months, selling their cow and furniture, and borrowing from a relative in America. Even so, they arrived in the States with less than $10 in their possession. In summary, wrote Daisy, "it is absolutely impossible for us to continue HONEST and USEFUL and SANE on our present salaries."[68]

The Walnes found their financial plight aggravated by their daughter's illness. After graduating from Georgetown College, the tall and slender Florence returned to Shimonoseki in the fall of 1916 "with her health broken from hard study." Since her services were badly needed in Fukuoka, she taught four days a week in both the day and the night schools until April, when she suffered a complete breakdown. Her mother took her to Severance Hospital in Seoul, a Protestant missionary institution. There Florence underwent an abdominal operation and for a season hovered between life and death. After five weeks the two women returned to Shimonoseki, though Florence was unable to walk for some time. Ernest Walne referred to this experience as "about the darkest hour of my life" because of the double burden of his daughter's intense suffering and the staggering medical bills he had to pay. The Walnes, Rays, and others in the Mission were relieved in 1917 when the Board increased each missionary's salary by $100,

---

[66]Baker, *Southern Baptist Convention*, 288-89; *ASBC, 1918*, 172.
[67]Daisy Ray to T. B. Ray, 16 Feb. 1917.
[68]Ibid.

effective July 1, and again in 1919 when the Board made a special grant for Japan of $200 per missionary and $50 per child.[69]

In April 1917, the month of Florence's breakdown, the United States entered World War I. Three of her four brothers served in the armed forces--in three different branches. Many of her friends, in both America and Japan, enlisted for some kind of service related to the war effort. "I felt that all of these people had part in something big," Florence later recalled, "and I was left out!" Then she caught a vision of something bigger still and far more compelling, the Christian missionary movement. In response to her new life commitment, the Board in 1919 formally appointed Florence to work with her parents in Shimonoseki and put her on the payroll. Born in Arima in 1895, she was the Mission's first second-generation missionary to serve in Japan.[70]

In 1918, when the Willinghams were on furlough, Calder's closest brother Ben, a doctor, fell victim to influenza in the terrifying epidemic that claimed 548,000 lives in the United States and 20 million worldwide. Calder attended his brother faithfully until Ben's death in a Wilmington, North Carolina, hospital. A few days later Calder returned to the same hospital as a patient, with the dreaded symptoms of high fever, chills, nausea, and cramps. Becoming delirious, he fancied that he was in Japan. He prayed and preached in Japanese; his sermon topic was "Jesus Christ, the Sinner's Friend." He would tip his ice cap and say, "Please come in, the service will soon begin." Within a week he was pronounced dead of influenza pneumonia, at the age of 39. His body was taken to Richmond and buried beside his first wife in Hollywood Cemetery.[71]

A cable announcing Calder's death reached the missionaries in Japan as they were gathering in Fukuoka for the meeting with Secretary Love. "The bereaved Mission entered upon its conference," wrote Walne, "with the hearts of the participants well nigh paralyzed by grief and burdened with the realization of irreparable loss." At a memorial service held in the home of Hooker Chiles, the missionaries and the Loves honored Calder Trueheart by singing "Truehearted, Wholehearted." In 1919 the Mission designated Seinan Gakuin as Willingham Memorial School, the English name used for more than a decade in Mission reports and Board publications, then quietly dropped with the rise of Japanese ultranationalism in the 1930s. Calder had served on the school's first board of trustees but had declined Dozier's request that he join the faculty, stating that he was called to direct evangelism.[72]

[69]Walne to T. B. Ray, 9 July 1917; *ASBC, 1916*, 262; *JCY, 1920*, 305; EBD notes, 1917; T. B. Ray to Clarke, 12 Sept. 1919.

[70]*HFF* 5 (Oct. 1921): 317.

[71]Farmer, *Gate of Asia*, 61-62; *JCY, 1919*, 278; T. B. Ray to Rowe, 16 Oct. 1918; *Encyclopædia Britannica*, 1968 ed., s.v. "influenza."

[72]Walne in *ASBC, 1919*, 317.

A peculiar feature of Calder's missionary career is that he remained a member of the Second Baptist Church in Richmond instead of joining a church in Japan. His second wife Foy kept her membership in the First Baptist Church of Raleigh. The couple sent regular offerings to both churches while giving generously to the work in Japan. After his death, Calder's devotion to missions lived on in Foy and in his look-alike brother Edward, who for 10 years was general secretary of the American Baptist Foreign Mission Society.[73]

At the Fukuoka gathering the Mission also welcomed two single missionaries who had recently begun language study in Tokyo and were on their first visit to Kyushu. They were Sarah Frances Fulghum and Norman F. Williamson, both of Georgia. Fulghum had studied music and kindergarten work at Columbia University in addition to completing a three-year course at the Training School in Louisville. She had taught music for two years at Bessie Tift College, her alma mater, and was highly rated as a soprano vocalist.[74]

Williamson, likewise a musician, played the violin and directed the student chorus at Mercer University. Asked by the Board to state his forte, he set music aside and replied, "I can fail to carry my point and still 'keep sweet.'" Perhaps this applied to his relationship with Frances Fulghum, his fiancée during seminary years. They broke off their engagement prior to missionary appointment. Both were sent to Japan in September 1918--on different ships.[75]

While still a student at Southern Seminary, Williamson had taken a romantic interest in another Tift graduate, Fannie Lee McCall. Though a foreign mission volunteer herself, Fannie had discouraged his interest. She was subject to occasional blackouts, and once it had been her misfortune to faint just outside the door of Maud R. McLure, the Training School principal. Subsequently, a report of Fannie's malady had reached the Foreign Mission Board, with the result that she was redirected into home mission work at a good-will center in Savannah.[76]

When Norman renewed his courtship by mail from Japan, Fannie renewed contact with the Board. She found a sympathetic doctor who was willing to give her medical clearance or to turn her down, depending on how badly she wanted to go abroad. The choice was easy. On August 30, 1919, the day she arrived in Yokohama, Fannie and Norman were married by George Bouldin in the American consulate. After a brief honeymoon in fabulous Nikkō, the Williamsons moved to Kokura--over Fanny's strong objection. Before leaving the States she had insisted on, and been promised, two years of language study in Tokyo. In September, however, the Rowes left Fukuoka on medical furlough, the Clarkes transferred from Kumamoto to Tokyo, and the Kumamoto pastor left for America to study in

[73]EBD, *Golden Milestone*, 108-10; *ESB*, vol. 4, s.v. "Willingham, Edward Bacon."

[74]*ASBC, 1919*, 317; Fulghum appointment records, FMBA.

[75]N. F. Williamson appointment records, FMBA; Williamson to T. B. Ray, 1 June 1918; *ASBC, 1919*, 204.

[76]Fannie Williamson, interview with author, Raleigh, N.C., 6 Jan. 1985.

Southern Seminary. So the Williamsons were urgently needed in Kyushu. For a few months they occupied the termite-ridden Kokura residence, where the impish Fannie set out to learn the language like her husband, even though the senior missionary wife, Claudia Walne, advised her not to try. Fannie became so fluent in Japanese that she could still speak it at the age of 90, after a half-century's absence from Japan.[77]

The most promising event of 1919 was the launching of Southern Baptists' spectacular Seventy-five Million Campaign. This was a five-year program to raise $75 million for missionary, educational, and benevolent work. This amount was to be pledged by the first week in December--Victory Week--and paid in full between 1919 and 1924. The campaign was a highly ambitious undertaking to multiply the level of support for all Southern Baptist causes. An incredible sum of $20 million was earmarked for the Foreign Mission Board, which had received only about $12.5 million in all the 74 years of its history.[78]

Excitement mounted in Japan at the prospect of a greatly expanded program. At the annual Mission meeting it was voted to ask the Board for 50 new missionaries and several school and church buildings. In addition to the regular 1920 budget of $60,878, the Mission asked for a five-year-program budget of $1,443,000, including $217,500 to be used in 1920. After Victory Week a cable arrived from the Board with the magic words, CAMPAIGN VICTORIOUS. Over $92 million had been pledged![79]

The decade of the 1910s would have ended on this single note of jubilant optimism had not Paul Medling died in Kagoshima on December 31, 1919. Like Calder Willingham, he succumbed to influenza, and at the same age of 39. Since Paul died at three o'clock in the morning, it was possible for Walne and Bouldin to come during the day, conduct services, and get him buried before midnight, when all work ceased for extended New Year's celebrations. Grace Mills also came and stayed several days to help Lenna and the five children, none of whom had escaped illness. The Medlings were living in a rented Japanese house. They had received a sum of money from Lenna's family estate that could have been used to provide themselves with a nicer home, but they had chosen instead to construct a handsome church building. Little wonder that they were highly regarded by the local Christians. Paul had requested that he be buried in Kagoshima, among the people he had learned to love and to whom he had given the best 12 years of his life. His grave plot, on a beautiful hillside overlooking the bay, was ceded by the city.[80]

[77]Ibid.; *ASBC, 1920*, 330, 336.

[78]*ESB*, vol. 2, s.v. "Seventy-five Million Campaign."

[79]*ASBC, 1920*, 327-28; Walne to T. B. Ray, 13 Aug. 1919.

[80]Lucile Clarke letter, 1 Jan. 1920, in Eden ms., 198; Farmer, *Gate of Asia*, 62; *JCY, 1920*, 187; Love, *Far Eastern Missions*, 292-93.

6

Dealing with Conflict (1920-1929)

The year 1920 ushered in a decade of liberalism and democracy unprecedented in Japanese history, an era marked by an expanded global awareness and a novel freedom of speech and action. Viewed negatively, it was the era of "*ero, guro, and nansensu*"--the erotic, the grotesque, and the nonsensical. An alarming number of students and workers were attracted to Marxist socialism, which had triumphed in the Russian revolution, but a far greater number were enamored with the three *S*s of sports, screen, and sex. Sharp increases were registered for alcoholism, divorce, crime, and prostitution. The nation's 9,837 registered houses of prostitution reported annual client visits in excess of 24 million (the figures on unlicensed prostitution were anybody's guess). In Fukuoka, George Bouldin reported, the police were spending ¥30,000 a year "to keep the girls in the licensed quarter from running away." Saddest of all, the epicurean and libertarian tendencies of the '20s contributed to the rightist reaction and militarist takeover of the '30s.[1]

The motion-picture screen, with its steady run of lurid films made by unconscionable American producers, was said to "blacken" America's reputation in Japan. Sports, on the other hand, aroused feelings of goodwill. The 1920 visit of major league baseball stars proved so popular that anti-America rallies lost their appeal for a season. In the United States, meanwhile, anti-Japanese sentiment continued to mount, both from revulsion to Japanese imperialism and from bias against Japanese immigration. American military experts were discussing the

---

[1]Bouldin in *JCY, 1924*, 86; Edwin O. Reischauer and Albert M. Craig, *Japan: Tradition and Transformation* (Tokyo: Charles E. Tuttle Co., 1978), 207; DeForest, *Woman and the Leaven*, 192; Drummond, *History*, 246.

possibility of incendiary raids on Japanese cities. On both sides of the Pacific there was frequent talk of war.[2]

"To a great extent," wrote Ernest Walne, "[Japan has] lost America's friendship, incurred the undying hatred of China and Russia and created for herself, by the incorporation of Korea [in 1910] and her subsequent treatment of that unhappy country, a problem of administration as difficult as that with which Great Britain is struggling in Ireland." In 1920 Walne traveled to Shanghai to help start a church for the Japanese community, and earlier he had visited Korea. He was neither blind to Japan's imperialist aggression against its neighbors nor unaware of the effect of national politics and international diplomacy on a people's response to the gospel. Walne was pinning great hopes on the upcoming disarmament conference in Washington and on the growing criticism of the militarists within Japan itself--two dynamics that in fact kept the nation on a fairly sane course during the "international interlude" of the 1920s.[3]

As the senior missionary and the preacher on whom J. W. McCollum's mantle had fallen, Walne delivered the main sermon at the March 1920 annual session of the West Japan Baptist Convention. The sermon drew so emotional a response that some participants likened the meeting to a Pentecost. With rare enthusiasm the Convention voted to launch a five-year fund-raising campaign in response to Southern Baptists' Seventy-five Million Campaign. In the months that followed, said a Board report, "a tidal wave of spiritual zeal swept over the Japanese Baptist churches."[4]

An Historic Mission Meeting

The excitement of this season carried over to the Mission meeting held in July at Gotemba. Many far-reaching decisions were made. In the evangelistic service customarily held in annual Mission meetings, three of the children, Herbert Walne, Edwin Dozier, and Helen Dozier, personally accepted Christ as Savior.[5] In the business sessions, group decisions were made by the adults on some of the most important issues ever faced by the Mission.

The missionaries voted to open Seinan Gakuin's higher school (college) in April 1921 on a five-acre tract immediately west of the middle school. This meant doubling the size of the campus and putting up several new buildings at a time when postwar inflation had raised the prices of daily necessities to the highest level of any country in the world. Construction soon began on a $40,000

---

[2]Kinnosuke Adachi, "The Topknot Nine," *Outlook* 146 (22 June 1927): 250-52; Ronald H. Spector, *Eagle Against the Sun: The American War with Japan* (New York: Free Press, 1985), xvi.

[3]*HFF* 5 (Oct. 1921): 303; *ASBC, 1921*, 366.

[4]*ASBC, 1921*, 215; EBD notes, 1920.

[5]L. Whaley, *Edwin Dozier of Japan*, 32-33.

administration building at the middle school--a three-story brick structure with a chapel accommodating 800 students. The design owed much to William Merrill Vories, a prominent architect who, like Ernest Mills, had first come to Japan as a teacher under YMCA auspices. This structure, the oldest one on campus in use today, answered to Secretary Love's request that the Mission not put up any more cheap buildings. Also erected were a science hall, college classroom building, college dormitory, and several missionary and faculty residences. This costly program of expansion was made possible not only by the Seventy-five Million Campaign but by the disposal of the union seminary campus in Tokyo.[6]

There was strong public support--even an urgent demand--for the college. The middle school had won the respect of the community, exemplified by a grateful father of two students who donated 49 cherry trees to beautify the campus. Now the college was needed to provide higher education for the middle school graduates, beginning with the first class of 28 (out of an original 105) who finished the five-year course in 1921. Permission had been granted for them to take entrance exams at government colleges, but the competition for the limited number of openings was intense. Thirteen of the 28 graduates entered Seinan College as part of the first freshman class of 45.[7]

The Mission approved the opening of two departments in the college: literature and commerce. Each offered a four-year course. A theology department added in 1923 offered a five-year course, with the first two years corresponding to the first two in the literature department. The Mission provided no theological education between 1918 and 1923.[8]

The missionaries assembled at Gotemba in 1920 also resumed debate on the establishment of a girls' school. The issue was timely, for a number of movements for "Woman's Rights" came to the fore that year. For the first time, women were admitted as special students at Tokyo Imperial University. At the middle school level, the object of girls' education was redefined by the Education Ministry to include "the development of womanly character as well as training for wifehood and motherhood."[9] In the United States, ratification of the 19th Amendment extended voting rights to women.

The crucial issue for the Mission, as already noted, was where to establish the long-delayed school for which funds were in hand. The previous year's decision to locate it in Kumamoto had to be reconsidered in view of an offer to transfer to the Mission a private girls' school, Kumamoto Jo Gakkō. The offer was made by Fukuda Yoshinobu, a Christian (Congregationalist) physician who had assumed the principalship in 1905 but had since devoted himself mostly to medical and

[6]*ASBC, 1922*, 316, 322; Bouldin report on Seinan Gakuin, 6 Apr. 1922, G. W. Bouldin Collection, Historical Commission, SBC; MM minutes, 1922; Iglehart, *Century*, 159-60.
[7]M. B. Dozier, "Seinan Gakuin," 43; *ASBC, 1922*, 321.
[8]MM minutes, 1920; *ASBC, 1921*, 361-62.
[9]*JCY, 1921*, 8.

social ministries. Ernest Mills made a motion, seconded by Lucile Clarke, to accept Fukuda's offer. By this time the minority who preferred a location in northern Kyushu had been joined by others who felt that the Mission should not try to salvage a school that was beset with problems. So the vote was evenly split: six in favor and six opposed. Chairman Kelsey Dozier ruled that the motion was lost.[10]

The next day an action was taken to seek out a location in "North Kyushu," a booming industrial area centering in Kokura. It was further resolved to "try to find an English name for the school that will keep alive the memory of what Mr. and Mrs. W. Harvey Clarke and the Baptist women of Georgia have done to promote the establishment of the school." This latter resolution, it appears, was intended to sooth the feelings of the Clarkes, who had pain enough that year in sending off two children, Harvey and Josephine, to school in America. But it proved to be an empty gesture. The name afterwards adopted was Seinan Jo Gakuin, or Southwestern Girls' School. Yuya Kiyoki, a Clarke convert, once commented that he approved the choice of northern Kyushu over Kumamoto but disapproved the manner in which the decision was made. Yuya never forgot the look of anguish in the Clarkes' faces.[11]

Another decision made at the 1920 meeting also bore momentous significance for women. At the request of the Woman's Missionary Society, which had met annually at Mission meeting since its organization in 1915, ¥500 was allocated "to hold a general meeting for women in the fall." From the early years, beginning with the ministry of Dru McCollum, Bible-study meetings had been conducted for Japanese women, and several of the churches boasted strong women's organizations. But these local organizations had no ties with one another for mutual sharing. So the missionary women planned a general meeting to be held at the Fukuoka church November 9-11 for the purpose of launching the West Japan Baptist Woman's Missionary Union. Travel and board were to be provided for each pastor's wife and one representative from each society. The missionary women prudently wrote letters of explanation to the pastors and sent a respected Japanese woman to the Convention's annual meeting in Nagasaki to report on their plans.[12]

Maude Dozier, the central figure in the new endeavor, presided at the opening session in Fukuoka. "Instead of only a few women coming to the meeting," she wrote, "the joy of the missionary women knew no bounds when, as a group of fifty-four, they sat on the floor and ate together and praised God together." Every church was represented. Sermons and Bible studies were given by several invited

---

[10]MM minutes, 1920; *ASBC, 1921*, 363-64.

[11]MM minutes, 1920; *ASBC, 1921*; 363-64; Yuya Kiyoki, taped interview by Tom Masaki, n.d.

[12]MM minutes, 1920; Maude B. Dozier, "Baptist Woman's Work in Japan" (n.p., n.d., mimeographed), 1-7.

pastors (a pattern followed ever since), but devotional messages and other talks were given by women. Special music was provided by Seinan Gakuin students and Maizuru Kindergarten children. Not surprisingly, the West Japan WMU was closely patterned after its American parent. It adopted the same seal (open Bible resting on a world map with a flaming torch above), same watchword ("We are laborers together with God"), and same color (a soft lavender).[13]

The women agreed to promote prayer, soul-winning, Bible and mission study, and systematic giving. They passed resolutions on "standing for patriotism, supporting prohibition, maintaining Sabbath observance, keeping the home inviolate, urging family prayers."[14] Neither missionaries nor nationals could have foreseen that in the next two decades the stress on patriotism would play into the hands of militarists who in the name of patriotism would force Christians to do obeisance at Shinto shrines.

The call for prohibition reflected the triumph of the prohibition movement in America, which had been actively supported by the SBC since 1908. The 18th Amendment had taken effect in early 1920. This contrasted sharply with the situation in Japan. A strong Woman's Christian Temperance Union had developed, with 112 branches, but to most Japanese, prohibition was undesirable and unthinkable. Dr. Hepburn once called this people "a nation of drunkards," and Guido Verbeck commented that most Japanese men went to be bed drunken every night. At the very time Americans were ratifying the 18th Amendment, Japanese were drinking all the more, supplementing their native sake with Western beer and whiskey. So the call of the Baptist women for prohibition had value only as a plea for temperance.[15]

In 1922 the women were encouraged by the passage of a bill in the Diet that restricted the use of intoxicating liquor by minors. In 1928, moreover, it was widely publicized that the emperor (Hirohito) had no use for either tobacco or sake and that he did not touch strong drink in any form. A majority of Japanese, however, continued to imbibe and still do today. A 1987 poll indicated that 78.3 percent of Japanese men and 43.2 percent of women drink alcoholic beverages regularly. Many others, Baptists included, indulge occasionally. Teetotalers are rare.[16]

One more item worth noting in the 1920 Mission meeting minutes is an action to pay the travel expenses of three members to attend the Eighth World Sunday School Convention, which met in Tokyo that fall. The interested missionaries drew lots among themselves, and the winners were Kelsey Dozier, Hooker Chiles,

---

[13]EBD, *Golden Milestone*, 139; M. B. Dozier, "Woman's Work," 7-12.

[14]*ASBC, 1921*, 359-60.

[15]Hepburn as quoted in Helen S. Coan Nevius, *Our Life in China* (New York, 1876), 258; Verbeck in *JCY, 1920*, 164-65; DeForest, *Leaven in Japan*, 189. On the SBC and prohibition, see John Lee Eighmy, *Churches in Cultural Captivity* (Knoxville: University of Tennessee Press, 1987), 80-81.

[16]DeForest, *Leaven in Japan*, 189-90; HFF 13 (Feb. 1929): 4; ibid. 13 (Aug. 1929): 25; *Japan Times*, 31 Jan. 1988.

and Norman Williamson. George Bouldin also attended. The 10-day event drew delegates from 29 countries and as many denominations.[17]

A 2,900-seat convention hall, complete with dining and other auxiliary services, had been erected near Tokyo Central Station, mostly with funds contributed by non-Christian businessmen. Three hours before opening time, however, an electrical fire destroyed the hall. Nothing remained but an outside statue of Christ blessing the children of the world. The convention was hastily moved to the YMCA and then to the elegant Imperial Theater, where overflow crowds thrilled to the singing of a 600-voice chorus, watched spectacular pageants, and listened to a variety of lectures on Christian education. Over 40,000 people visited the Sunday school exhibit.[18]

The privy councilor to the emperor called the convention "the turning point in the history of Christianity in Japan." In a sense it was, for the imperial household contributed ¥50,000, equal to $25,000 or one-sixth of the convention's total cost, and the emperor sent a personal message on the closing day. Such favors were tantamount to the highest official sanction for the churches to give religious training to Japanese children through Sunday schools. Moreover, the dramatic loss of the convention hall served to gain widespread publicity and sympathy for the Christian cause. Indeed, missionaries and their coworkers soon reported a lessening of opposition to their work with the youth of the land. In the words of Baptist spokesman Chiba Yūgorō, "People who formerly despised Christianity are sending their children to the Christian Sunday School."[19]

Special meetings related to the Tokyo convention were held in over 60 cities, including Kumamoto, where Norman and Fannie Williamson had worked since January. Norman, who conducted a Sunday-school orchestra and taught three violin classes, used his expertise to adapt the music and pageantry of the convention to the local scene. In December he helped to produce a union Christmas program featuring pageants. The program drew the largest crowd that had ever gathered in Kumamoto's city hall.[20]

Losses and Unprecedented Gains

However rosy the prospects for evangelism in the 1920s, the outlook for missionary personnel was dismal. The deaths of Calder Willingham and Paul Medling in 1918 and 1919 were followed by the death of Margaret Rowe in the spring of 1920. Margaret had suffered intensely with headaches for several years before entering the sanatorium in Glendale, California. After a number of serious operations she improved enough to raise false hopes that she might return to

[17]MM minutes, 1920; Bouldin, "Autobiography," 162.
[18]*JCY, 1921*, 111-25.
[19]Ibid., 5; *JCY, 1923*, 35.
[20]*JCY, 1921*, 118, 122; *ASBC, 1921*, 370.

Japan. Then suddenly she was ill again, and four days later Margaret died of cerebral meningitis, the same disease that had nearly claimed the life of Claudia Walne. Her death reduced the Mission to 20 members, only 4 more than in 1910.[21]

Then Lenna Medling, following the advice of the Mission, returned home to Tennessee where she could put her five children in a "proper school" (the oldest daughter died a few months later). At the time of her marriage, Lenna's father had taken out a $10,000 insurance policy on Paul's life and had deposited $10,000 in the bank for Lenna, the interest from which paid the insurance premiums. With this $20,000 Lenna bought a house and was able to rear her children in relative comfort until the Depression, when her savings were lost in a bank failure. Then she had a costly bout with cancer that forced her to sell the house. Despite these setbacks, one of her sons, Bill, qualified for missionary appointment to postwar Japan.[22]

Besides the loss of Lenna in 1920, three families--Bouldins, Rays, Walnes-- returned to the States temporarily. Maggie Bouldin, Franklin Ray, and Florence Walne required medical treatment, and Florence's parents were due a regular furlough. The number of missionaries on the field dropped to a low of 12.[23]

Though bereaved of his wife, John Rowe returned to Fukuoka in October. He left his four children with a sister in the States. Rowe was "on the ragged edge," said Kelsey Dozier. Soon he was carrying his usual double load of work, with higher hopes than ever before. He was pleased to find that "the Japanese have a different attitude to Christianity from what they had a few years ago."[24]

In the month that Margaret Rowe died, the Board appointed another Texan, Cecile Lancaster, a graduate of Howard-Payne College. Cecile's father had paid her freshman-year tuition with cotton instead of cash. During her sophomore year she attended the first Student Volunteer Convention at Southwestern Seminary in Fort Worth, where she heard an appeal by the seminary's president, L. R. Scarborough, that confirmed her sense of call to foreign missions. Two years of wartime teaching narrowed her focus to educational missions, and at another Southwestern Seminary missions conference, Secretary T. B. Ray enlisted her as a teacher in the girls' school to be established in Japan. He could not have foreseen the magnitude of her contribution as evangelist, teacher, and vice chancellor at Seinan Jo Gakuin.[25]

Cecile traveled to Japan with Foy Willingham, who had been asked to take charge of the girls' school. She became "Little Sister" to Foy, then "Cile" to the

[21]*ASBC, 1920*, 202; *JCQ, 1921*, 310. The date of Margaret Rowe's death is given as Mar. 29 in the first source and Apr. 5 in the second.

[22]*ASBC, 1920*, 336-37; Bill Medling to author, 26 Jan. 1989.

[23]*ASBC, 1921*, 371.

[24]*HFF*, Oct. 1921, 309; *ASBC, 1922*, 320; *JCY, 1921*, 310.

[25]Lancaster, "My Life," 8-11.

(Upper) Seinan Gakuin middle school, built 1921. **(Lower)** Norman Williamson's church orchestra, ca. 1924 *(Photos courtesy of Norman F. Williamson, Jr.)*

other missionaries who met her at Yokohama when the steamer docked on August 31, 1920. It was a propitious time to arrive, for the summer residents of Gotemba had not yet returned to their work in the sultry Southwest. In the welcome party were the Doziers, the Bouldins, the Rays, and Frances Fulghum. From Tokyo had come the Clarkes and Daisy Imai, an orphan reared by the Millses and a student at Tsuda High School. Also gathered on the pier was a smiling band of Japanese Baptists. Cecile was ecstatic with joy.[26] Only a missionary who has experienced such an overwhelming reception can appreciate its power to nurture one's spirit through the trying years that follow.

After a brief visit to Gotemba, Foy and Cecile went to live in Shimonoseki until the Walnes returned from furlough. Foy worked in the bookstore and Cecile did her language study under the older missionary's supervision. Then Foy began suffering from severe headaches that not only kept her from reading Japanese but interfered with ordinary conversations. Her condition worsened, and on the advice of an American physician in Yokohama, Foy left Japan in April 1921, eight months after arrival. Her loss was a blow to the Mission and to the prospects for Seinan Jo Gakuin. "We are about at the end of the rope," said Rowe, himself beset with chronic illness and burdened with the duties of Mission treasurer.[27]

Back in Raleigh, Foy married James S. Farmer, who later succeeded her father as editor of the *Biblical Recorder*. She served as president of the North Carolina WMU for seven years and as vice president of the Southern Baptist WMU. As her prolific writings--seven books and many articles--eloquently testify, Foy's missionary zeal never flagged.[28]

Shortly before Foy's departure from Japan, John Rowe announced that he and Hooker Chiles would get married May 19. In a playful letter to Secretary Ray, he said they had "decided to live in the same town and use the same mission house" in order to "concentrate" their efforts in mission work. "The Board is most humbly entreated," John continued, "to permit either Miss Chiles to change her name or Mr. Rowe to change his." John's recurring ailments persisted, however, and three days before the wedding date, he entered Severance Hospital in Seoul for extended treatment. Consequently, John and Hooker had a June wedding in Seoul. Afterwards they took over the big Maynard house in Kokura and set about getting the girls' school started. Cecile Lancaster lived with them.[29]

The Mission designated John Rowe as the founder of Seinan Jo Gakuin and Hooker as the first principal. Hara Matsuta, a Seinan Gakuin professor educated at Dōshisha College in Kyoto and Oberlin College in Ohio, was secured as vice principal. John Rowe could not escape the high status accorded the founder of a

[26]Ibid., 14-17.
[27]Rowe to Walne, 29 Apr. 1921; Rowe to T. B. Ray, 14 Apr., 4 May 1921; Foy Willingham to J. F. Love, 14 Apr. 1921.
[28]Farmer, *Hitherto*, xiii-xiv; *ESB*, vol. 4, s.v. "Farmer, Foy Elizabeth Johnson."
[29]Rowe to T. B. Ray, 23, 27 Apr. 1921; Lancaster, "My Life," 22-23.

school any more than he could avoid the heavy toil and anxiety the position entailed, but he did not let it go to his head. Just as Kelsey Dozier acknowledged Rowe's part in starting Seinan Gakuin, Rowe gave due credit to Harvey and Lucile Clarke for their pioneer role in launching the girls' school.[30]

On a clear spring day in 1921 a committee of missionaries climbed a prominent hill in Kokura and approved the site for a campus, which included two adjacent hills. They had to crawl through fences and stumble up narrow and steep paths. "The view was gorgeous in every direction we turned," Lancaster recalled. "The air was pure and we felt at that time that girls from the smoky city of Yahata [adjacent to Kokura] would be grateful to attend a school in such a pure atmosphere; and we believed that many girls from Kokura and the other surrounding cities and towns would come, too." No less than 84 primary schools lay within six or seven miles of the site.[31]

The site measured 12,000 tsubo (9.8 acres) and cost ¥20,000. The three hills had to be leveled to form the campus that came to be known as Mt. Zion. Two dormitories and a gymnasium were built, with one of the dormitories to serve as a temporary classroom building. On April 13, 1922, which Hooker Rowe called "a trying day," the school opened with 96 pupils in the first-year class. Sixty other applicants had to be turned away for lack of space. Not one of the enrollees was a Christian. Yet three years later, when enrollment had climbed to 230, Christians numbered 162. The strong religious program, coupled with excellent instruction in English and music (piano, organ, singing), continued to attract far more applicants than could be accepted. It was Hooker's ideal that "Seinan Jo Gakuin shall not be one school in Japan, but must be the best and highest in the country."[32]

In 1923 the school received a visit from Kathleen Mallory, corresponding secretary of the Southern Baptist WMU. Mallory had long declared, "If I could go as a foreign missionary, my field would be Japan." She had just inspected Seinan Gakuin with eyes of wonder, and now at Seinan Jo Gakuin her heart was stirred even more. The visitor was especially moved by the chapel processional, scores of uniformed girls marching on noiseless straw sandals while singing "O Zion, Haste." The school's facilities, however, she found embarrassingly crude and cramped. Even the living room and study of the missionary residence had been pressed into use. The Rowes sent many letters to Richmond asking for capital funds, only to be reminded again and again that the Board was heavily in debt because of unpaid pledges in the Seventy-five Million Campaign. Due primarily

---

[30]Minezaki Yasutada, ed., *Seinan Jo Gakuin sanjūnen shi* (Thirty-year history of Seinan Jo Gakuin) (Kokura: Seinan Jo Gakuin, 1952), 10.

[31]Lancaster in ibid., 1-2; Rowe to Love, 12 Mar. 1922. On Hara, see *HFF* 21 (May 1937): 1-2, 32.

[32]*HFF* 6 (Aug. 1922): 27; *ASBC, 1923*, 130; *ASBC, 1925*, 278; Executive Committee, JBM, minutes, 29 Oct. 1920 (hereafter cited as EC minutes); Minezaki, *Seinan Jo Gakuin*, 277.

to America's depressed economy, at the end of the campaign in 1924 only $58 million had been collected out of $92 million pledged. In 1925, nevertheless, a special gift of $5,000 and a Board grant of $7,500 made possible the construction of Seinan Jo Gakuin's main building with seven classrooms.[33]

In June 1921, when the Seventy-five Million Campaign still held great promise and the stress on "calling out the called" was drawing a good response, the Board appointed 12 new missionaries to Japan--four couples and four singles. Ernest Mills received the news in a letter from Secretary Ray. "I quickly wired to others in the Mission," Mills later recalled, "and most of the afternoon I found myself repeating, 'Twelve! Twelve!'" He considered that day one of the happiest of his 30 years in Japan.[34]

The new appointees represented a new generation, a new breed, a new optimism. Two of the couples--J. Griffin and Vecie Chapman, and M. A. and Ruth Espy Treadwell--were the first missionaries to Japan trained at Southwestern Seminary. Coming from four different states and colleges, they found their spouses at seminary. Southwestern was then owned by the Baptist General Convention of Texas, but it was fast losing its regional character and would be transferred to the SBC in 1925. Among its distinctive emphases were the fiery evangelism of L. R. Scarborough, the rigorous denominationalism of J. B. Gambrell, and the pioneering courses in religious education taught by J. M. Price.[35]

Griffin Chapman, briefly a soldier during World War I, was the first military veteran appointed to Japan. A strong and popular preacher since his mid teens-- he was ordained at 19--Griffin gave low priority to his academic studies and completed only one year of seminary work. He had organized the Volunteer Band at Carson-Newman College, where one of his professors, John D. Everett, warned ominously that he was short on diplomacy. Vecie Chapman, no less attractive physically than her husband, seems to have been better fitted for the mission field intellectually and temperamentally.[36]

M. A. Treadwell, a balding 30-year-old known among his friends as "Skin" or "Red," earned the Th.M. at Southwestern. He was both a successful pastor and a school teacher with six years' experience. His wife Ruth, herself a former high

---

[33]Annie Wright Ussery, *The Story of Kathleen Mallory* (Nashville: Broadman Press, 1956), 69; *ASBC, 1924*, 287; *ASBC, 1925*, 278; Barnes, *Southern Baptist Convention*, 224. On the failure of the campaign, see also James J. Thompson, *Tried as by Fire* (Macon, Ga.: Mercer University Press, 1982), 195-200.

[34]Ernest O. Mills, *Jottings from Japan* (Nashville: Broadman Press, 1949), 81.

[35]*HFF* 5 (Oct. 1921): 318, 320; *ESB*, vol. 2, s.v. "Southwestern Baptist Theological Seminary."

[36]Chapman appointment records, FMBA; *HFF* 5 (Oct. 1921): 318.

school teacher, was one of nine children from a pastor's home. The plain-looking Treadwells were said to have "serious missionary purposes."[37]

The other two couples came the traditional route through Southern Seminary and the Louisville Training School. They were Willard and Minta Nix, and Roscoe and Sadie Smith. Willard Nix, who earned a Th.B., came from a poor, uneducated mountain home. He was said to sing well and work hard but to lack personality. He asked to serve at an industrial school in Interior China but was redirected by the Board to Japan. Minta Nix buttressed her husband with her bright mind and lovable nature.[38]

Roscoe Smith attended Carson-Newman with Griffin Chapman but volunteered for missions after entering seminary. He was recommended as a man who "never gives up," as a "fine singer and fluent speaker." Sadie Smith, a farm girl, was no less articulate and far more literate. Among the Japan missionaries her command of English was extraordinary and refreshing. The Smiths first sought appointment to Russia. "Until conditions are favorable to their admission to that country," said a Board report, "they will be engaged in Japan." The Board's work in Russia consisted only of financial support for a native worker in Siberia.[39]

The Board-required recommendations on the four couples give the impression that all the wives were better qualified than their husbands. In the case of the Smiths, for example, Kyle M. Yates, a seminary professor, considered Roscoe "above average" in promise of usefulness and Sadie "way above" the average. If the four wives came well recommended, so did the four single women. The two singles from Texas, like Cecile Lancaster, had a good college education and above-average intelligence, though no seminary training. Effie Baker, a classmate and close friend of Cecile's at Howard-Payne, taught high school Latin and music and later earned an M.A. from Columbia University. Florence Conrad, who volunteered for educational work in Japan after hearing Bouldin speak at Baylor University, graduated from that institution with B.A. and M.A. degrees.[40]

The other two singles had attended the Training School in Louisville. Naomi Schell had lost her mother in childhood and her father during college years, but she had gained a strong background in school teaching and church work. Leita Hill had worked seven years as subscription and advertising clerk at the *Christian Index* in Atlanta before responding to the "calling out the called" campaign. While attending the Training School in Louisville, she met Ernest Walne, who enlisted her for secretarial work in the bookstore and publishing house at Shimonoseki.[41]

[37]*HFF* 5 (Oct. 1921): 320; T. B. Ray to Rowe, 30 Jan. 1922.

[38]Nix appointment records, FMBA; *HFF* 5 (Oct. 1921): 318.

[39]Smith appointment records, FMBA; *HFF* 5 (Oct. 1921): 320; *ASBC, 1924*, 296-97. For a sample of Sadie's English, see her letter to T. B. Ray, 4 Feb. 1928.

[40]*HFF* 5 (Oct. 1921): 319; Lancaster, "My Life," 24.

[41]*HFF* 5 (Oct. 1921): 319.

Eleven of the appointees sailed for Japan in August. Leita Hill was asked by T. B. Ray to delay her sailing until September in order to serve as his secretary during his upcoming inspection tour of Japan and China. Joining Ray and his wife in Chicago, she accompanied them by train to Vancouver and by steamer to Japan. Unfortunately, Hill had a history of physical and mental disorders that had been withheld from the Board. She fulfilled her duties for the Japan portion of Ray's journey, but in Shanghai she suffered a mental breakdown. "My Japan happiness left me when we reached China," wrote Hill to Walne, "and I remembered the many doubts in my mind before leaving home." She believed that the devil, not God, had brought her to the Orient, that she had committed the "unpardonable sin," and that even to eat or drink was for her a sin.[42]

Hill was placed in the care of the Rowes at Kokura. Her odd behavior, at times bizarre, so upset the household that after two weeks Hooker got her admitted to St. Luke's Hospital in Tokyo. There Hill was counselled, medicated, and force-fed. Twice she succeeded in slipping out of the hospital at night and entering the cold waters of nearby Tokyo Bay. Both times she was rescued, first by Japanese boatmen and next by hospital personnel, but the exposure led to nephritis and other complications. Hill died in the early morning of March 18, 1922. Harvey Clarke, who had visited her often and was present when she died, had the body cremated and the ashes sent to the family in Atlanta. "She was insane," her physician wrote, "and God is kind to have taken her home."[43]

The other three single women adjusted beautifully. Effie Baker did her language study at Kokura while living with Cecile Lancaster and the Rowes and teaching music in Seinan Jo Gakuin. Because Baker and Lancaster both wore white, fluffy woolen caps in cold weather, Pastor Yuya teasingly called them the "Texas Rabbits." Naomi Schell and Florence Conrad studied Japanese in Fukuoka, where Conrad remained as a full-time teacher in Seinan Gakuin. Schell moved to Seinan Jo Gakuin as teacher of music and English, and Baker transferred to the boys' school. The three women supplemented their school work with Bible classes and other evangelistic ministries in the churches and elsewhere. Each completed her first term of service and returned to Japan for a second term.[44]

How different the fortunes of the four couples sent out in 1921. Not one completed the first term of service. The first casualties were the Treadwells, who returned to the United States after a miserable three months on the field. At the time of their appointment, M. A. was "advised" by the Board's physician to have an operation immediately. He failed to do so, possibly because he and Ruth were to be married within a month. Later that summer, when Secretary Ray learned that

[42]Hill to Walne, 28 Jan., 25 Feb. 1922; Walne to Blanche F. White, 20 Mar. 1922, Leita Hill file, FMBA; Hill to T. B. Ray, 2 Sept. 1921.

[43]Margaret H. Sutley, M.D., to Mr. and Mrs. Hill, 22 Mar. 1922, Leita Hill file, FMBA; Clarke to Love, 10 May 1922; *JCY, 1921*, 392-93.

[44]Lancaster, "My Life," 25; *ASBC, 1924*, 290.

the operation had not been performed, he informed Treadwell that he could not go to Japan without it. M. A. then submitted to the surgeon's knife. Since there was insufficient time for recovery before his sailing date, M. A. was "run-down" when he arrived in Japan, and in the new and strange environment, his strength failed to rally. Rowe took him to Severance Hospital in Seoul, then sadly packed him off to the sanatorium at Battle Creek, Michigan. A lifetime commitment was reduced to a shambles. Treadwell "was not 'cut out of' Japanese missionary material anyhow," said a Board letter to Rowe. If these words allayed Rowe's distress over losing a much needed couple, they also called in question the Board's screening process.[45]

The other three couples experienced more stress than the three single women. Husband and wife would enter language school together, but the wife would fall behind at the birth of a child and grow discouraged. The husband, despite persistent study, would be frustrated at his inability to express himself adequately in Japanese and carry meaningful responsibilities with a sense of authority. Moreover the young couples felt that the older missionaries were domineering and, like the Japanese pastors, complacently satisfied with the status quo. As strongly motivated newcomers, they were impatient to make changes, and the frustration of their efforts fueled a deadly sense of anger. The single women, to the contrary, regarded the older missionaries more like surrogate parents or kindly uncles and aunts, and since they had come to Japan specifically for school work, there was little cause for quarreling over where they should locate or what they should do.[46]

The Nixes did their language study in Fukuoka and the Smiths, in Kokura. The Chapmans began their study in Fukuoka but transferred to Tokyo and attended language school with Collis and Hester Cunningham, a new couple sent out in 1922. Both the Chapmans and the Cunninghams were vacationing in Karuizawa when a massive earthquake struck Tokyo on September 1, 1923, leaving 130,000 dead, most of them victims of the fires that ensued. The Cunninghams lost all their possessions except what they had taken to Karuizawa. The Chapmans' house was damaged but not burned. The Mission compound where the Clarkes lived (they were on furlough) also escaped the fire. On September 2, Sunday services were held in the compound church while much of the city was still in flames.[47]

[45]T. B. Ray's secretary to Rowe, 30 Jan. 1922; MM minutes, 1921; Rowe to Love, 14 Dec. 1921.

[46]Lancaster, "My Life," 19-20.

[47]ASBC, 1924, 283-84, 286, 288.

Crisis in the Mission

Even prior to the Tokyo quake, the new couples sensed with growing alarm the ominous rumblings within the Mission structure, indications of a fault in the substratum. Power was concentrated in the hands of four men. Ernest Walne, with 30 years' experience and mastery of both spoken and written Japanese, was the Mission's *genrō*, or elder statesman. No less demanding than able, he wielded awesome power in the Mission and with the Board. Under him were Dozier, Rowe, and Bouldin, class of 1906, a sort of Russian troika or Roman triumvirate that showed deference only to Walne and the Board. Walne saluted them as "inspiration, staff and wise counsellors."[48] They took turns as Mission treasurer. They built buildings, supervised personnel, negotiated with government officials, worked under pressure of deadlines.

If one triumvir stood out among the others, it was "Dr. Bouldin" (he held a D.D. from Howard College), imperious like his brother Virgil who sat on the bench of the Alabama Supreme Court.[49] As bold as he was tall, George was so aggressive that he could scarcely be restrained by the others, and so clever that he got more done with the limited funds by stretching the rules. The others could not help but respect him for his achievements. Not only did Do-Ro-Bō have the advantage of collegiality and competence, but they were entrenched in the geographical power axis of Fukuoka-Kokura. Walne oversaw the operations from nearby Shimonoseki. There were occasional clashes of opinion among the four leaders that produced friction and irritation, but they were mature enough to compromise for the good of the work.

Why were Harvey Clarke and Franklin Ray, who had seniority over the three musketeers, counted among the manipulated and not the manipulators? Clarke was known as an able promoter of mission causes in the United States. In Japan, however, his kind and gentle pastor's heart restrained his political instincts, and his inability to read Japanese or even to speak it well--he was known to slip unconsciously into English while preaching--limited his sphere of service. He had been permanently shunted off to Tokyo in 1919. Ray, isolated in Hiroshima also since 1919, was virtually a pariah to the four men in power. In 1916 the Mission had asked the Rays to go home for some offense that is shrouded in obscurity, and when it was feared that they might come back, the Mission, at the urging of certain Japanese leaders, had taken further action asking them not to return to Japan. Bouldin was no party to the first action, but at the time of the latter action he was the Mission's secretary who wrote the official "stay-home" letter. Walne had written a personal letter expressing the same sentiments ("you can do us far more good at home than you could out here"). Yet the Rays had returned to a cold

[48]Walne, in Love, *Far Eastern Missions*, 274.
[49]Bouldin, "Autobiography," 159, 178.

reception in 1919. Secretary Love was quoted as having said they could do less harm in Japan than they could in the United States if barred from the field. Quite understandably, feelings between the Rays and the four men in power, particularly Walne and Bouldin, were strained.[50]

Ernest Mills, like his Nagasaki station, also occupied a place in the Mission's outer fringes. He was a Yankee with a Northern Baptist wife, a layman with no seminary training (he was ordained at age 53 while on his next furlough), a small and meek poet who always wore a wig. He had good cause to celebrate the appointment of 12 new missionaries in 1921. As Grace Mills later put it, "We thought they would save our mission for democracy."[51]

The youngest couple apart from the appointees of 1921-22 were the Williamsons in Kumamoto. They were indebted to Bouldin for marrying them and orienting them to Japan. Norman held strong opinions and expressed them boldly, to the detriment of his relationship with Walne. He had little ambition for power, however, and it was with great reluctance that he moved to Fukuoka in 1928 to meet an urgent need at the seminary. All the men, Williamson included, held various offices in the Mission and had charge of geographical stations. But as they well understood, no mere title was synonymous with authority.[52]

The missionary wives served on committees but never held a major office in the Mission organization and never had charge of a station. Each was a supporter of her own husband, and to some extent, as a Japanese would put it, the neck that turned the head. The single women, with one or two exceptions, backed the four men in power. They adored Bouldin somewhat as the Louisville Training School women adored W. O. Carver, after whom the school was later named. Several who had lived in the Bouldin home revered Maggie as a saintly mother and honored George as a gallant Christian gentleman. He in turn praised the single women as "100% true and loyal"--a slight exaggeration.[53]

The new couples were militant. Encouraged by the disaffected element in the Mission, they thought it their divine calling to overthrow the oligarchs. The first skirmish took place at the 1923 Mission meeting in Karuizawa, in the presence of--of all people--W. O. Carver. The missions professor, on a tour of the Orient, had come as visiting speaker. He not only led the Bible studies but also gave "a very helpful talk on the problem of the missionary in his relation to his fellow missionaries and with the native Christians." The Mission elected him an honorary life member but paid scant heed to his practical admonitions. The factions in the

[50]Walne to J. F. Ray, 9 July 1917; Bouldin to Love and Ray, 7 Sept. 1925; J. F. Ray to T. B. Ray, 11 Sept. 1925; Daisy Ray to T. B. Ray, 15 Sept. 1925; Ozaki Shuichi, interview with author, 7 Dec. 1985.

[51]Grace Mills to T. B. Ray, 31 Aug. 1925; MM minutes, 1926; Max Garrott interview.

[52]Fannie Williamson to Bouldins, 14 Oct. 1920; Fannie Williamson to Maddry, 26 July 1941; ASBC, 1929, 241.

[53]Bouldin to Love and Ray, 7 Sept. 1925.

Mission squared off against one another with a vehemence that was possible only because the Chapmans, Smiths, and Cunninghams had joined the band of discontents (the Nixes were kept in Fukuoka by Willard's illness).[54]

In the election of a president, repeated balloting took place before anyone got a simple majority of the votes cast. Roscoe Smith finally won. Norman Williamson was elected vice president. The balloting for chairman of the committee on nominations and locations was more time-consuming still. No one could get a majority vote. At length the venerable Walne moved that the president--Smith-- be elected chairman of the committee. The motion carried. Later, Griffin Chapman offered a resolution, seconded by Daisy Ray and then passed, that the first term of service for unmarried members of the Mission be five years instead of seven. The resolution appeared to be a ploy for winning over the single women. Moreover, Chapman brashly took on Bouldin, then Mission treasurer, accusing him of exceeding his authority in putting up buildings. W. O. Carver came away from the meeting with the impression--not far off the mark--that an old feud between Bouldin (whom he admired) and Franklin Ray had caused the other missionaries to take sides with one or the other. He also dropped a remark to the effect that some members of the Mission were "hopeless."[55]

The 1923 Mission meeting closed on August 3. As noted above, the great earthquake struck Tokyo on September 1. Since the Tokyo language school was destroyed, the two couples who had been attending were asked to move to Kyushu. The Cunninghams went to Kokura, and the Chapmans, after first refusing to leave Tokyo, went to Nagasaki. The Rowes returned from furlough to Kokura, from which the Smiths and Bouldins had moved to Fukuoka. The Nixes left Japan with reluctance so that Willard could be treated at the Southern Baptist Sanatorium then operated by the Home Mission Board in El Paso, Texas. He had a mild case of tuberculosis. After his discharge with a clean bill of health, Willard sought reappointment to Japan but was informed by Secretary Ray that "a man having been affected with tuberculosis is always required to remain in the homeland."[56]

Two new appointees arrived in 1923, but they completed only one term or less. Phoebe Lawton taught at Seinan Jo Gakuin until 1926, when she resigned for personal reasons. Mary Walters, known for her "bright and happy spirit," worked efficiently in the book store at Shimonoseki until illness forced her return to the States in 1927. Both women got married after their separation from the Board.[57]

---

[54]MM minutes, 1923.

[55]Smith to Bouldin, 14 Aug. 1923; MM minutes, 1923; Daisy Ray to T. B. Ray, 8, 15 Sept. 1925.

[56]T. B. Ray to Nix, 24 Feb. 1925; C. K. Dozier to Carver, 4 May 1924; Minta Nix to T. B. Ray, 18 July 1923. The tuberculosis sanatorium was operated by the Home Mission Board from 1920 to 1937 and then closed. The FMB acquired the property and converted it to the Baptist Spanish Publishing House.

[57]*ASBC, 1924*, 182; *ASBC, 1928*, 222; EBD notes, 1927.

George Bouldin served as dean of the new seminary department at Seinan Gakuin, and Roscoe Smith, the most belligerent of the green recruits, taught some classes. The two men disagreed over various matters, especially Bouldin's construction of a school gymnasium--"without authority" in Smith's opinion. "Feeling was so bitter," said Griffin Chapman, "that they were on the point of coming to physical blows many times." At the 1924 Mission meeting in Karuizawa, it was Smith rather than Chapman who spoke out against Bouldin. Chapman kept quiet, he later explained, because the anti-Bouldin faction obviously lacked the votes to pass any action. The Clarkes and Millses were in America, and Franklin Ray was ill with appendicitis. Daisy Ray was present, and according to her account of the meeting, she sought reconciliation with Ernest Walne but was rebuffed. In the election of officers, Rowe was chosen president, and Cunningham, whom Bouldin happened to like, was named vice president.[58]

At their own request the Bouldins were transferred to Tokyo to replace the Clarkes, whose return from furlough was delayed another year. This defused the powder-keg tension at Seinan Gakuin. The Bouldins lived on the half-acre compound in Koishikawa that the Mission had purchased in 1921 for $25,000, enabling it to "drive down our stakes firmly in the capital of the Empire." A missionary residence, church, kindergarten, and pastor's home had since been erected. Funds had also been appropriated for a dormitory that would provide a Christian home for some of the myriads of students who flocked to Tokyo for their higher education, but its construction had been postponed. So get-it-done Bouldin built a dormitory with 22 single rooms and 2 double rooms and had it ready for occupancy on January 1, 1925. Rumors spread that the treasurer had again abused his authority, that he had spent funds urgently needed in Kyushu.[59]

In April 1925 the Rowes decided to take an emergency furlough. John had chronic bronchitis that failed to respond to treatment at Severance Hospital. So grave was his condition that Walne said he "may not live through the trip home." To accompany her husband, Hooker resigned as principal of Seinan Jo Gakuin. She suggested Naomi Schell as her successor, but Vice Principal Hara said he would have to resign if Schell were elected (his reason is not recorded). Hooker then discussed the matter with the Mission's executive committee, which happened to be meeting in Fukuoka at the time. The meeting was chaired by Vice President Cunningham, substituting for President Rowe. Hooker suggested that Cunningham himself take charge of the girls' school. He declined. Walne proposed that the Cunninghams move back to Tokyo so that the Bouldins could move to Kokura, where Maggie could direct the school and George could supervise the evangelistic work. Walne's motion was passed unanimously. Seinan Jo Gakuin's trustees

[58]Chapman to Fulghum, 2 June 1925; Daisy Ray to T. B. Ray, 8 Sept. 1925; MM minutes, 1924.

[59]*ASBC, 1921*, 215, 367; *ASBC, 1925*, 279.

endorsed Maggie Bouldin with enthusiasm, as did Hara. Everybody liked Maggie, whatever they thought of her husband.[60]

But Walne's neat solution to the Kokura dilemma infuriated Smith, who saw it as a ruse to get Bouldin back to Seinan Gakuin and the seminary. Smith accused Walne of "wire-pulling." Meanwhile the Cunninghams decided against moving to Tokyo, which meant that the new dormitory ministry would be deprived of missionary supervision if the Bouldins should move to Kokura. Even the Doziers thought this would be unwise. Smith and Cunningham persuaded the Fukuoka missionaries and two executive committee members to join them in protesting the executive committee action in order to override it. When Cunningham ruled the action null and void, however, Bouldin claimed that it "was not set aside by the method the Mission has fixed." He and Maggie had prepared to move, and move they did.[61]

The Smiths and Cunninghams, joined by the Chapmans, reacted with the furor of a volcano spewing out red-hot lava after seething and rumbling under the surface for years. The eruption broke into the open at the 1925 Mission meeting, which by coincidence was held in Beppu, a hot-springs resort near Oita. Beppu is famous for its geysers and boiling ponds, one of them called Bloody Hell. The meeting opened at the Episcopal church on July 1 with Cunningham in the chair. His first action was to resign as president on the grounds that his ruling on the executive committee action had been "disregarded." In the subsequent balloting for his successor, no one could win a majority. Frustrated, the members named Walne as temporary president.[62]

Then Cunningham read a lengthy statement criticizing the Mission as "hopeless" and revealing that six members--Roscoe and Sadie Smith, Griffin and Vecie Chapman, Collis and Hester Cunningham--had submitted their resignations to the Board. It had been a well-kept secret. Except for the three couples, everyone present was shocked. Questions were raised, but the six adamantly refused to divulge what they had written to the Board, though one spoke of having suffered "horror and hell." Nor would they hear pleas to reconsider. Walne announced the hymn, "From Every Stormy Wind That Blows," and the meeting went on, but everyone knew that the Mission was caught in a maelstrom from which it could extricate itself only by sacrificing some of its members. "The most trying experiences," wrote Dozier in his diary, "are caused by those who will not yield."[63]

[60]Walne to Bouldin, 15 Apr. 1925; EC minutes, 9 Apr. 1925.

[61]Rowe to T. B. Ray, 18 Sept. 1925; Dozier to Bouldin, 28 July 1925; Maude Dozier to Bouldin, 28 July 1925; Bouldin to Love and Ray, 7 Sept. 1925; Cunningham to Bouldin, 20 Apr. 1925; Cunningham to JBM, 20 Apr. 1925.

[62]MM minutes, 1925.

[63]Daisy Ray to T. B. Ray, 8 Sept. 1925; C. K. Dozier diary, 3 July 1925; MM minutes, 1925; Bouldin to Love and Ray, 7 Sept. 1925.

The resignation statement of the three couples had been written on May 27 at the Chapman home in Nagasaki. It protested Bouldin's "flagrant disregard for actions taken by the Mission and also by the Board." It spoke of "bondage and tyranny" from which the couples sought deliverance. "Considering the sorrow and broken lives of some missionaries who have gone before," it said, "we are confident that it is not God's purpose for us to submit our lives to the inveterate will of one man."[64]

Secretaries Ray and Love urged the six to withdraw their resignations and seek an amicable settlement of their difficulties with the Mission. Walne and Dozier led the efforts at reconciliation, but to no avail. Bouldin's offer to resign in order to save the six young people for the work was never acted upon. Walne charged the six with "gross misstatements of facts." "I do not hesitate to affirm," he wrote to the Board, "that there are no two of our number whose loss the Mission would feel more keenly than that of Dr. and Mrs. Bouldin." "Should we sacrifice the Bouldins today," said Naomi Schell, "they would demand the head of some one else."[65]

When the dissidents widened their attack to include Walne, Dozier, and Rowe, their scurrilous language and distasteful tactics alienated them even from their sympathizers. Yet all six continued to move in one direction like lemmings. They packed up and left, convinced that they should appeal their case to Southern Baptists. From their ship at sea Chapman sent a cable to Richmond: "WE PRAY THAT GODS SPIRIT MAY YET TRIUMPTH [*sic*] IN THE BOARD."[66]

The disaffected six expected the Board to recall George Bouldin, reprimand and overhaul the Japan Mission, and then return them to the work to which God had called them. To their bitter consternation, however, their resignations were accepted, and neither the Board nor the Mission asked Bouldin to quit. The Mission's seven-page report for 1925 dismissed the entire matter with one sentence: "We see, to our great sorrow, that six members of our already too small band, have resigned from the Board.[67]

Chapman and Smith feuded with the Board for years, vainly seeking reappointment on their own terms. Chapman lectured widely on the Far East and staunchly defended Japan's 1931-32 takeover of Manchuria, an act of aggression rightly condemned by the League of Nations. For his efforts Chapman received official thanks from both the Japanese government and its puppet regime in Manchuria. Smith came to public notice after World War II when, as a Tennessee pastor, he ceremoniously burned a copy of the newly published Revised Standard

[64]Smiths, Cunninghams, and Chapmans to FMB, 27 May 1925.

[65]Walne to Love and Ray, 9 Sept. 1925; Schell to Love and Ray, 9 Sept. 1925; Ray and Love to Smiths, Cunninghams, and Chapmans, 23 June 1925; T. B. Ray to Smith, 24 June 1925; Bouldin to Walne, 1 Sept. 1925.

[66]Chapman cable to FMB, 23 Dec. 1925; Phoebe Lawton to Love and Ray, 5 Sept. 1925.

[67]*ASBC, 1926*, 241.

Version of the New Testament. Cunningham, more restrained than the others, gave his attention to pastorates in Alabama, though Bouldin urged his return to Japan. As late as 1938 the Mission voted unanimously to ask the Board "to consider seriously the reappointment of Rev. and Mrs. Collis Cunningham." But they too had been lost permanently to the work in Japan.[68]

Shocks and Aftershocks

The Mission was still reeling from the shock of 1925 when Sarah Frances Fulghum dropped a bombshell as unexpected as the resignation of the three couples. On May 29, 1927, her 37th birthday, Fulghum visited the Doziers with Uehara Nobuaki, a 23-year-old medical student. "We are engaged to be married," she announced. The one-time fiancée of Norman Williamson was widely known and highly respected as principal of Maizuru Kindergarten, where she resided, and founder-director of Seinan Gakuin's celebrated glee club. Uehara was a member of an English Bible class that Fulghum taught in her home. He was not a Christian, and his family strongly opposed his marrying the middle-aged foreigner.[69]

Shocked and dismayed, the Doziers thought it their duty to share so consequential a matter with the other members of the Mission. The news triggered a barrage of criticism on Fulghum. Grace Mills, herself a single missionary for 12 years, wrote Frances that her relationship with Uehara embarrassed all single women who taught Japanese men in their homes and that the scandal might lead to the closure of Maizuru Kindergarten (it did not). Florence Walne censured her behavior as "selfish and unworthy beyond words." In rebuttal, Fulghum insisted that she was "not any longer a baby" and "it will all blow over if the Mission will only keep its head." But missionaries and Japanese alike urged her to return home for talks with her distressed mother before entangling herself with a Japanese mother-in-law. The Board offered to pay her travel expenses back to the States and asked her to indicate by telegram whether she would come. Her telegram read: NO.[70]

Fulghum resigned from the Board and took a teaching position in Fukuoka's Kaho Middle School. She moved from her Mission residence to a small private

---

[68]MM minutes, 1938; FMB minutes, 5 Mar. 1926; Smith to T. B. Ray, 2 Aug. 1927, 18 Jan., 23 Jan. 1928; Ray to Smith, 30 Aug. 1927, 20 Jan., 1 Feb. 1928; Chapman to Ray, 22 Feb. 1930; Ramond, *Among Southern Baptists*, 93, 467.

[69]Maude Dozier to Mrs. Fulghum, 26 Sept. 1927; Love, *Far Eastern Missions*, 283; *Maizuru Yōchien rokujūnen no ayumi* (Sixty-year history of Maizuru Kindergarten) (Fukuoka: Seinan Gakuin Maizuru Yōchien, 1973), 12.

[70]F. Walne to Fulghum, 29 Sept. 1927; Fulghum to Grace Mills, 4 Sept. 1927; Grace Mills to Fulghum, 23 July 1927; T. B. Ray to Fulghum, 4 Nov. 1927; Fulghum cable to Ray, 25 Nov. 1927.

house and made preparations for her marriage to Uehara. "They are acting in such a way," Kelsey Dozier told his diary, "as to disgust any sensible people." The wedding took place on June 30, 1928, and the bride took the name Uehara Ranko. "Ran," a component of the name Frances as pronounced in Japanese, was written with a Chinese character meaning Dutch or Western. The "ko," meaning child, is the most common ending for a woman's name.[71]

Uehara Nobuaki finished medical school at Kyushu University in 1929. Later he ran a small hospital in Wakayama, specializing in internal medicine and skin diseases. Though the hospital bore a Christian name, Immanuel, Uehara remained aloof from the church and was never baptized. During the Pacific War, Ranko suffered hardship and discrimination as a spy suspect. After the war, when the Convention opened work in Wakayama, she helped with the Sunday school and worship services as organist, pianist, and soloist, until she was too feeble to attend. Upon her death in 1973 at the age of 82, funeral services were held in the Wakayama church. Ranko was survived by her husband and by two daughters and three grandchildren who were living in California and New Jersey.[72]

Another missionary who drew criticism during the 1920s was Kelsey Dozier. As president of Seinan Gakuin he enforced rules that he thought essential for a Christian school, however unpopular with the students. Chapel attendance was required of all students in all departments. Smoking was prohibited everywhere on campus. Drinking was forbidden to faculty and students alike. Dozier even expected his teachers to police the students at all times. When Yuya Kiyoki objected that policing was the duty of policemen, Dozier grew angry and refused to speak to the upstart teacher. But when another faculty member suggested that Yuya be dismissed for rudeness and insubordination, the president brushed the matter aside. "He loves Seinan," Dozier said. Maude took flowers and cakes to Yuya's wife to make amends. Kelsey and Maude themselves used language that Yuya and others considered rude, but as foreigners they enjoyed a measure of exemption from the canons of Japanese etiquette.[73]

The most controversial of Kelsey's policies, one for which a Fukuoka paper called him a bigot, was his absolute prohibition of athletics and other nonreligious activities on Sunday. Dozier played tennis and encouraged wholesome sports among the students. But it was inconceivable to him and most other members of the Mission that a Christian school would allow its students to play on the Lord's Day. Dozier's policy gave rise to a frustrating dilemma. Intercollegiate tournaments in Japan were routinely scheduled for the finals to be played on Sunday. As

[71]C. K. Dozier diary, 19 May 1928; Williamson to Bouldin, 23 August 1928; *Seinan Gakuin shi shiryō*, 2:21.
[72]Andō Hideo and Satō Tetsutsugu, interviews with author, 1987; JBM mailout, 19 Apr. 1973, 2.
[73]Yuya Kiyoki, taped interview by Tom Masaki; Maude Dozier, "Seinan Gakuin," 70-76

Seinan's enrollment grew, so did the quality of its baseball team. Yet however good the team, it could never compete for the championship.[74]

In the summer of 1925 the baseball team played a match game on Sunday, winning by a large score. The boys were jubilant--until Dozier ordered the team to disband, fomenting a crisis in the school. After many days of negotiations between faculty and student body, the students capitulated and the team members pledged that "they would never again play on the Sabbath day." Then Dozier, "taking the letter of punishment from his pocket, tore it into shreds before them."[75]

In subsequent years, however, the controversy intensified, and in 1928 Dozier not only disbanded the team for willfully breaking the rule but also dismissed two teachers who agitated for Sunday sports. The college students then went on strike and called for Dozier's resignation. In response, the trustees, faculty, and alumni closed ranks and rallied around the president, whose heart was weakening under the strain. The cowed students apologized for their actions. Still, it pleased them greatly that Dozier resigned in 1929 before going on furlough and that Bouldin was elected acting president. Bouldin was esteemed on campus as the only missionary who advocated tolerance and open-mindedness on the issue of Sunday sports. The situation remained tense, nonetheless, for he was elected by the trustees on the strict condition that he enforce the ban.[76]

Though usually contrasted by their opposing views on Sunday sports, Bouldin and Dozier differed from one another in numerous ways. Bouldin was tall (six feet, three inches) and slender; Dozier was of medium height (five feet, nine inches) and somewhat stout. Bouldin was intellectual, scholarly, serious-minded, and rather quiet, though he led singing in chapel with enthusiasm, accompanied by Effie Baker at the piano. Dozier was passionate, emotional, and given to loud outbursts. He got angry and scolded others. Fond of jokes, he often broke into a loud, hearty laugh. When preaching, he would walk about the platform like a lion, gesturing and shouting; yet from time to time he would take off his glasses and wipe tears from his eyes.[77]

Bouldin, moreover, was inscrutable, opaque, unrevealing of his true feelings. Though affable and courteous, he could discuss an issue at length without disclosing where he stood on the matter--if indeed he knew himself. Dozier, by contrast, was transparent and straightforward, with strong convictions plain to all. In summary, Bouldin had many oriental traits, while Dozier typified the Westerner. Both men were respected by the Japanese, but Bouldin was the more admired of the two.[78]

[74]C. K. Dozier diary, 6 Aug., 28 Apr. 1928; Bouldin, "Autobiography," 182-84.

[75]*ASBC, 1926*, 237; Dozier to T. B. Ray, 12 Sept. 1925.

[76]C. K. Dozier diary, 23 July 1928; *Seinan Gakuin nanajūnen shi*, 1:594-612.

[77]Mikushi Kazushi, "Itamashii omoide," 2 parts, in *Seinan Gakuin daigaku kōhō*, 1974, nos. 27 and 28.

[78]Ibid.

In 1929 Seinan Gakuin lost another able teacher, Florence Conrad, one of the 12 appointees of 1921. She resigned for personal reasons. An ardent evangelist, Conrad had used her savings to buy land and build a chapel for the Fujisaki Sunday school, as a place where students could teach. After her return to the States, teachers and students of Seinan Gakuin faithfully carried on this work. Florence Conrad, Effie Baker, and Frances Fulghum are regarded as the founding leaders of the English Speaking Society that flourishes on campus today.[79]

Also in 1929, Elizabeth Taylor Watkins came to Japan by freighter to teach in Seinan Gakuin as a self-supporting missionary. The temperamental redhead, nicknamed Spitfire in childhood, had finished the Training School in Louisville at 22 but had been turned down by the Foreign Mission Board as "suffering the malady of youth." After working temporarily for the Home Mission Board in good will centers, she had equipped herself for overseas teaching by earning an M.A. in English at Columbia University and doing a stint with the International Grenfell Mission in Newfoundland.[80]

Except for her first year's salary paid by Seinan Gakuin, Elizabeth supported herself by teaching in government schools at Moji and Fukuoka. At first she lived with the Bouldins, who had invited her to Japan, then moved into a small cabin behind the seminary dormitory that Maggie had built for poor students who could not afford the dormitory. Though she remained a lifelong friend of the Bouldins, her relations with some of the other missionaries were strained from the outset. "You had every chance to enquire about her poise," wrote Kelsey Dozier to Secretary Ray, who apparently had encouraged her to teach in Japan without being appointed. Watkins "lacks balance in religious matters," Dozier complained. "Indeed another wreck will be registered." To the contrary, despite trachoma and other medical problems, and despite complaints about her tactless zeal and free-wheeling ways, Watkins was to win appointment by the Board in 1948 and serve in Japan until her forced retirement at the age of 70.[81]

One more shock awaited the Mission as it neared the close of the most trying decade it had known. During the first four days of August 1929, John Rowe, as Mission president, attended the Conference of the Federation of Missions at Karuizawa. He heard the inspiring addresses of Kagawa Toyohiko, noted evangelist, and Nitobe Inazō, Quaker statesman whose portrait now adorns Japan's ¥5,000 notes. Beginning on August 6, he presided at the Mission meeting in Gotemba. He also led the opening devotion, using the words of Jesus, "Come ye yourselves apart and rest awhile." Rowe had put off his own needed rest too long. The fine athletic body he had brought to Japan 23 years before was worn out from

---

[79]*ASBC, 1930*, 159, 233; *ASBC, 1933*, 216; *HFF* 16 (May 1932): 9; *Seinan Gakuin nanajūnen shi*, 2:1123.

[80]Elizabeth Taylor Watkins, "How God Kept His Promises to a Teenager: The Autobiography of Elizabeth Taylor Watkins," (typescript, n.d., FMB), 1-73.

[81]Dozier to Ray, 13 June 1932; Watkins, "Autobiography," 44-48.

overwork. On August 8 it was learned that he had pneumonia. A foreign doctor was summoned from Tokyo to work with the local physicians in frantic efforts to save his life. But the antibiotics he needed lay in the future. Rowe died on August 12.[82]

The next day the foreign community gathered in the village church to pay its respects. On August 14 the burial service was conducted by Pastor Katatani of Kokura in the foreigners' cemetery at Yokohama. Rowe was laid to rest beside Mary Janette Bouldin, at whose burial 20 years before he had prayed an unforgettably beautiful prayer. "He was one of the most beloved and appreciated missionaries I have ever known," wrote Cecile Lancaster. Walne called him "John the beloved." Missionaries and Japanese alike have been inspired by his last words: "The evangelistic work!"[83]

Surely the evangelistic work of the Mission was hindered by the strife and discord of the '20s, but this is not apparent from the records. Church membership more than doubled in this decade, rising from 1,084 to 2,525. In 1923 alone, 558 baptisms were reported, far more than in any other year until after World War II. The baptisms came mostly from evangelistic meetings conducted by Paul Kanamori, who preached the same three-hour sermon--"God, Sin, and Salvation"-- to changing audiences night after night. As Dozier reported to W. O. Carver, half of the converts did not last, but the half that remained constituted a significant increase. The Mission also cooperated with the nationwide Kingdom of God Movement, a five-year evangelistic campaign that began in 1929 and centered around Kagawa. The movement was aimed primarily at the 30 million farming people, the 5 million factory workers, and other unreached segments of the population.[84]

New churches were started at Seinan Gakuin in 1922 and at Mt. Zion (Kokura) in 1928. The Woman's Missionary Union matured so rapidly during the first half of the decade that in 1926 the women of the Mission discontinued their own society. A Japanese version of the WMU journal *Royal Service* first appeared in 1923. The first YWA (Young Woman's Auxiliary) was organized at Seinan Jo Gakuin in 1922, and the first of the annual YWA camps was held there in 1926, with 88 in attendance. Naomi Schell and Florence Walne played leading roles in this work. Afterwards, Lolita Hannah, a 1925 appointee who was missionary head of the music department at Seinan Jo Gakuin, helped to direct the YWA camps. A college YMCA was established at Seinan Gakuin in 1922. BYPU (Baptist Young People's Union) organizations, promoted especially by the Doziers, took

---

[82]Hara, *John Hansford Rowe*, 14-17; *JCY, 930*, 304.

[83]Lancaster, "Autobiography," 96, Hara, *John Hansford Rowe*, 18-20, 76-78; *ASBC, 1930*, 229.

[84]*ASBC, 1924*, 314; Dozier to Carver, 13 Jan. 1925, W. O. Carver file, Historical Commission, SBC; *NBRS*, 330-334; *ASBC, 1931*, 249; Iglehart, *Century*, 197-200; *JCY, 1930*, 88, 139-47.

Annual convention of Woman's Missionary Union, Kumamoto, 1921 (*Courtesy of Norman F. Williamson, Jr.*)

root at Seinan Gakuin in 1923 and afterwards spread to a number of churches. Unlike BYPUs in America, these organizations were for boys only. A week-long BYPU assembly held each summer at the beach in Fukuoka drew boys from all over Kyushu. Also in this decade the first daily vacation Bible schools were conducted at the Fukuoka and Seinan Gakuin churches.[85]

In 1925, the Mission's "year of sorrow," the Gospel Book Store under Walne's supervision sold more than 20 million tracts, by far the largest number in its history. It also produced materials of its own totaling 3.8 million pages, all religious works except one. The exception was a translation of *Heidi*, the popular story for children, especially girls, by the Swiss author Johanna Spyri. In 1929 the store published 1,750,000 tracts and 250,000 books, its all-time publishing record. This latter feat was accomplished because the widely read Kagawa had written a book and a series of evangelistic tracts especially for the Baptist publishing house.[86]

In this decade Southern Baptists further expanded their territory, though but slightly. On December 1, 1925, the Mission took over Hirado Island from Northern Baptists. A small island (64 square miles) off the northwestern coast of Kyushu, Hirado was formerly an important trading post. The Baptist church there had 20 members.[87]

The Mission could report considerable progress in the 1920s despite internal conflict, as we have seen, but also despite the Immigration Law passed in May 1924 by the U. S. Congress. The law contained an exclusion clause aimed at the Japanese. So offensive was this clause that the immigration law nullified much of the goodwill shown by Americans the previous year when they generously contributed to the relief of earthquake victims. President Calvin Coolidge, Secretary of State Charles Evans Hughes, and many leading newspapers had urged that Japan be assigned a quota like European nations, which would have allowed the admission of 146 Japanese each year. Congress had refused.[88]

At its July 1924 meeting the Mission, by a rising vote, strongly protested as "discriminatory and unjust" the exclusion clause "which would so deeply wound the sensibilities of a sister nation." The Mission's resolution also noted "the courtesy and kindness accorded us as Americans by the Japanese people in the face of their strong feeling of resentment." In contrast, the 1924 session of the SBC adopted the report of its Social Service Commission that lauded Congress for the new legislation. The Commission regretted that the law had caused friction between the United States and Japan and hoped that "our missionary enterprises

---

[85]EBD, "Mission and Convention," 10-12; Maude Dozier, "Baptist Woman's Work," 17, 25; *ASBC, 1926*, 241; EBD, *Golden Milestone*, 129. The BYPU program in the SBC was superceded, in order, by Baptist Training Union, Church Training, and Discipleship Training.

[86]*ASBC, 1926*, 240; *ASBC, 1930*, 155.

[87]*ASBC, 1926*, 236.

[88]Chitoshi Yanaga, *Japan Since Perry* (New York: McGraw-Hill, 1949), 442-45.

in Japan" would not be barred. But it voiced no opposition to the exclusion clause. Afterwards, however, a special Committee on Modification of Chinese Exclusion Laws expressed "regrets that the recently enacted Immigration Law did not treat the citizens of China and Japan, as they did other nations." From 1924 until the attack on Pearl Harbor in 1941, the exclusion law was cited as proof that America looked on Japan with disdain. It played directly into the hands of the militarists and helped to undergird an imperialist foreign policy.[89]

In November 1929, when rightest activity was still largely covert, 4,000 Christians filled the largest hall in Tokyo to celebrate the 70th anniversary of Protestantism in Japan. The meeting attested to Christian advance, for only 300 had attended the 50th anniversary celebration in 1909. But it could not be overlooked that the decade of the '20s was the first in which there had been no increase in the number of missionaries. The silver lining in this cloud was the growing dependence of the churches on Japanese leadership, a welcome sign of maturity.[90]

What was true of Protestantism as a whole was true of Southern Baptist missionaries and their work, now 40 years old. For the first time in the four decades, the number of missionaries showed no gain. Eighteen had been appointed to the work, and the same number had been lost to the work. The decade of the '20s had begun with 20 missionaries, and it ended with 20. Fortunately, strong Japanese Baptist leadership was emerging.

---

[89]MM minutes, 1924; *ASBC, 1924*, 117; *ASBC, 1925*, 126.
[90]*JCY, 1930*, 63.

7

Yielding the Reins (1930-1939)

In 1930 the Mission owned all the land and buildings used by the churches, including the homes of the pastors. Since 1926 it had offered to sell the property to the churches on liberal terms--at original cost, with six years to pay it out-- but no church as yet had accepted the offer.[1] Each region or station remained under the supervision of a "missionary in charge," virtually a bishop. Seinan Gakuin and Seinan Jo Gakuin each had a missionary as principal and a missionary-dominated board of trustees. It was painfully clear that Southern Baptists lagged behind the older Protestant denominations in transferring responsibility for the work to the nationals. Yet few of the missionaries cherished the role of "colonial administrator." Southern Baptists had come on the scene late and opened schools late. They wanted to be sure that their coworkers were equal to the task before shifting the load to their shoulders. In 1930 no one could foresee the swiftness with which the Mission would yield the reins of power to the West Japan Baptist Convention.

The established order was first threatened in 1931 when a band of "self-commissioned reformers" known as Asakai sowed seeds of discord. Founded by Tanaka Tanesuke, pastor of the Kure church, the Asakai was Pentecostal in tenor and teaching. Its chief aim was the revival of stagnant churches. In Japanese, *asa* means "morning" and *kai* means "meeting," and the term Asakai has often been thought to derive from the practice of holding early morning prayer meetings. But Tanaka wrote the *asa* in katakana, which is used for foreign words, and made it the name of the spirit of Christ. The *asa* was also said to relate to the word "amen" and to the rising sun, a symbol of the dispelling of spiritual darkness.[2]

Pastor Tanaka, reported Franklin Ray, "opposed our organized work, abolished all the church officers and all organizations except the Sunday school

[1]EBD, "Mission and Convention," 11.

[2]*ASBC, 1932*, 247-49; EBD notes, 1931; *NBRS*, 357-63; *Nihon Kirisutokyō rekishi daijiten* (Dictionary of Japanese Christian history), s.v. "Tanaka Tanesuke," "Amen Kyōdan."

and women's society, and thus antagonized many of the members." After the Hiroshima pastor, Tanihiro Torazō, fell under Tanaka's influence, Ray was so frustrated that he asked "to be relieved of all official responsibility for the conduct of the work and problems of the church and the Hiroshima field." The Mission-Convention cooperating committee accepted Ray's resignation as "missionary in charge" but also took action against the two pastors. Tanihiro was transferred to another church, and Tanaka was dismissed from the ministerial ranks. Tanaka then took his followers out with him and founded an independent church in Kure that continues to this day under the name Amen no Tomo ("friends of amen").[3]

Several other pastors were affected. Fujimoto Masataka of Yawata, reported Kelsey Dozier, became "erratic in his teaching and fanatical in his practice." The church was hopelessly divided between those who supported Fujimoto and those who opposed him. At a called meeting presided over by Convention president Shimose Kamori, the church voted to dismiss him, but 14 members were lost as a result. Furthermore, "the pastorium was burned down by some incendiary before the final separation took place," said Dozier, who took over as temporary pastor. A young man was arrested on suspicion of arson but later released for lack of evidence. Some other churches were disturbed by the Asakai movement, and the Chōfu church was so stricken that it was disbanded and its property sold.[4]

The forced resignations of several young Asakai pastors left serious gaps in church leadership. The missionaries fretted over the losses, but a majority of the remaining pastors were confident they could carry on the work without their lost colleagues and even without the missionaries themselves. They expressed themselves frankly in 1932 in response to a letter from Blanche S. White, corresponding secretary of the Woman's Missionary Union of Virginia. The letter asked whether missionaries were still needed in Japan.[5]

There were 23 replies. Though a few were ambiguous--"difficult to say whether needed or not needed; some places need them, some do not need them"--most were clear and pointed, and all were signed. "The present missionaries worked in the kindergarten age of Japanese work," said Amano Eizō, afterwards a missionary to Manchuria. "But Japan has made much progress since then. The present missionaries do not understand the present times, so probably are a hindrance to evangelistic work." Ueyama Akira wrote: "If missionaries do not try to understand, are selfish, poisoned with self-importance, and lazy, living in big houses, we don't need them." Higasa Shinji, later an executive secretary of the postwar Convention, said, "If missionaries have the attitude of some of the present missionaries, we do not need any more." Miyoshi Toshio was more practical minded. "If there is money in America to send missionaries," he wrote, "it would

---

[3]*ASBC, 1932*, 247-79; *NBRS*, 357-63.
[4]*ASBC, 1932*, 246; *NBRS*, 363.
[5]EBD notes, 1932.

be better to send promising young pastors to the USA for special training."
Miyoshi was one of five Japanese sent to Southern Seminary during the 1930s.[6]

An overwhelming majority of the pastors spoke positively of the need for
missionaries but qualified their answers. Only a few are needed, one correspondent said, "and they should be carefully selected." Among the qualifications
specified were noble character, wisdom, understanding, steadfastness, specialized
training, sense of calling, healthy faith, and evangelistic zeal. It was urged that
missionaries were "needed as helpers but not as leaders." Especially desired was
the "gift of grasping the Japanese spirit." Pastor Shimose, who wanted missionaries "not for working in the established churches but for pioneer work," saw hope
for the future in second generation missionaries who "love Japan." Several
correspondents thought missionaries were needed for rural evangelism or pioneer
work, though not for work in the established churches. Ozaki Genroku said there
was "an urgent need for missionaries to cooperate in evangelism." Yet another
pastor thought it "better for missionaries to do educational work rather than
evangelistic work." Still others said they were needed only to teach English.[7]

The 23 answers reveal that Japanese Baptist leaders were in accord on one
vital issue: they had come of age; they *should* do the work and they *could* do the
work. Doubtless their attitudes were influenced in part by the growing nationalism
of the times and by the missionary shortcomings revealed so clearly in the
preceding years, but antagonism toward missionaries on the part of a few has been
in evidence ever since. The answers also reveal the absence of a consensus on the
kind of work missionaries should do in Japan. Among those who expressed a need
for missionaries, opinion was especially divided over whether they were more
effective in pioneer evangelism or school teaching. This issue also has persisted
without resolution in recent decades, and missionaries have been free to respond
to a variety of opportunities for service. Still, the paramount issue was the
question of authority and control.

The Rapid Shift of Power

In 1933 the missionaries made some major concessions to the Japanese. They
agreed that the Mission and the Convention would share in various administrative
functions, and the Convention's constitution was revised accordingly. The
Japanese gained a seven-to-five majority on the cooperating committee, which was
given increased authority over the evangelistic work, including the all-important
management of funds. The key positions on the committee--chairman, secretary,

---

[6]Ibid. Others sent to Southern Seminary: Kawano Sadamoto, Kuriya Hiroji, Ozaki Shuichi,
and Shimose Kiyoko (Training School). Takahashi Tateo, Ono Hyōei, and Yuya Kiyoki had
attended earlier.

[7]Ibid.

treasurer--all went to the Japanese. "We must relinquish the stage. . . ," said one missionary. "It will take a lot of grace to carry on unsung."[8]

This did not mean, explained the Mission's annual report to the Board, "that the Japanese in their own strength can carry on. . . . The fact remains that the missionary behind the scenes as a trusted advisor dreams out what the nationals put into practice. It is a far day before the presence and work of the missionary shall no longer be needed." Kelsey Dozier had warned, "If we leave the churches in their weak condition, they will cease to exist."[9]

In 1934, however, Japanese began to serve jointly with missionaries as trustees of the Mission's legal person, with its considerable property holdings stretching from Kagoshima to Tokyo. The boards of trustees of Seinan Gakuin and Seinan Jo Gakuin were reorganized to consist of three missionaries and three Japanese for each school. The Mission informed Hooker Rowe, then on furlough, that "in view of the rapidly changing conditions, it is deemed inadvisable to wait longer to elect a Japanese principal of the Girls School." Hooker had succeeded her husband as principal. Hara Matsuta, the able vice principal and fervent Christian, was promoted to the position. At Seinan Gakuin, George Bouldin had been succeeded in 1933 by Mizumachi Yoshio, a Baptist deacon educated at Tokyo Imperial University and the University of Louisville. In 1935 the Convention elected its first full-time executive secretary, Kuroda Masajirō. Naomi Schell was also elected executive secretary (she and Kuroda had the same title), though she served part time.[10]

Along with the administrative burdens they assumed, the Japanese took increasing responsibility for finances. In 1933 the Seinan Gakuin church proudly dedicated a new building constructed entirely with funds raised in Japan--a first in the Convention. Rowe Memorial Auditorium at Seinan Jo Gakuin, with a seating capacity of 1,304, was built in like manner. Friends of John Rowe had been raising money for the auditorium in his memory since his funeral in 1929. It was proudly dedicated on the 10th day of the 10th month of the 10th year of Shōwa (October 10, 1935). In that same year, the first pastorium built without Board aid was erected at Yawata, and the first home mission work funded by Japanese Baptists was opened at Yukuhashi. Also in 1935, the system of assessing dues on member churches to support the Convention was dropped in favor of voluntary offerings--a change wrought mainly by the persuasive leadership of Naomi Schell. Still, a Bible Training School for women established that year in connection with the seminary was entirely dependent on funds from abroad for the first several years, and even Secretary Kuroda's salary was paid by the Board.[11]

[8]EBD, "Mission and Convention," 14. The missionary quoted is EBD.

[9]*ASBC, 1934*, 231-32; C. K. Dozier, quoted in *ASBC, 1933*, 216.

[10]MM minutes, 1934; *ASBC, 1934*, 230; *ASBC, 1936*, 203; EBD, "Lantern Lights," 15.

[11]*ASBC, 1934*, 227; *ASBC, 1936*, 203; *HFF* 20 (Sept. 1936): 18; EBD, "Mission and Convention," 15.

Charles E. Maddry, T. B. Ray's successor as the Board's executive secretary, and Mrs. Maddry visited Japan in early 1935. They were accompanied by the Jesse B. Weatherspoons of Southern Seminary. Maddry broke the ground for Rowe Memorial Auditorium. Weatherspoon, since acclaimed as the "principal figure" in the progress made by Southern Baptists in social ministries, praised the varied work of the missionaries as "wonderful."[12]

In June, during a second stay in Japan after a trip to China, Maddry helped the Mission work out a statement of its new relationship to the Convention. "The responsibilities to the churches borne by the Mission," the statement said, "have been transferred to the Seibu Kumiai [West Japan Convention]. The requests for the appointment and location of missionaries also have been transferred to that same body. All property of churches, social, and educational institutions is to be turned over to the Seibu Kumiai in proper legal form." This did not apply to the property of Seinan Gakuin, a separate legal foundation, and afterwards it was decided to set up a like foundation for Seinan Jo Gakuin.[13]

Consequently the Mission had far less business to conduct than before. The change was evident at the 1938 Mission meeting, which met at the Ray residence in Hiroshima immediately following the annual convention held in that city. The missionaries allowed "the larger proportion of the time for spiritual meditation and fellowship." Said Ernest Mills: "This is the kind of Mission Meeting I used to dream about." Mills was Mission treasurer; Franklin Ray was president.[14]

In January 1939 the Mission's legal person passed to the Convention under the name Nihon Baptist Seibu Shadan. The board of directors consisted of six Japanese and three missionaries. The Seibu Shadan had legal ownership of all property that the Mission had obtained with appropriations by the Board or with funds derived from these appropriations. The Board had not intended to transfer the ownership of missionary residences, but this had to be done to meet government requirements. So the Mission and the Convention agreed that the Seibu Shadan would hold this residence property "in trust" for the Mission and the Board. Within a decade the pattern of relationship had progressed from the Mission-centric stage through the Mission-Convention parity stage to the Convention-centric stage.[15]

The Backdrop of Ultranationalism

How do we account for so rapid and revolutionary a change? Among the several reasons that may be cited were the decline in Mission personnel and finances, the growing maturity of the Convention, and the example set by other

---

[12]Samuel S. Hill in Eighmy, *Churches in Cultural Captivity*, 205; EBD notes, 1935.
[13]EBD notes, 1935.
[14]*ASBC, 1939*, 232.
[15]Executive Board report, 24, 27 Feb. 1939, typescript, EBD papers.

Protestant bodies in attaining independence from mission boards. The most prominent and critical factor in the change, however, was political: the growing influence of militarism and ultranationalism. Changing conditions in the world and within the nation brought about a shift in the precarious balance of Japan's several power groups, giving the advantage to the armed forces. The worldwide depression, the rise of Hitler and Mussolini, the surge of Chinese nationalism, radical and violent movements within Japan--these all played into the hands of the militarists. As early as 1931, jingoistic army officers, confident that the moderate government lacked the power to restrain them, proceeded to take over Manchuria, a mineral-rich country three times the size of Japan. Manchuria was renamed Manchukuo and turned into a military police state. In 1933, as noted previously, the League of Nations condemned the takeover as an act of aggression, but the militarists simply forced Japan's withdrawal from the League and continued their plunder of the Asian mainland.[16]

In 1936-37 Japan signed the Anti-Comintern Pact with Nazi Germany and Fascist Italy. The treaty was concluded to oppose the interests of the Soviet Union, but Japan's deepening ties with the Axis Powers worsened its relationships with England and America. In 1937, furthermore, Japan launched an undeclared war against China. As stated in the Foreign Mission Board's report that year, the invasion was "legally and morally wrong--unpardonably wrong." Atrocities committed against the Chinese, including the Rape of Nanking--the wanton slaughter of 200,000 civilians and the rape of 20,000 women--aroused criticism of "the fury and unspeakable brutality and lust of unrestrained Japanese soldiers." Mission schools, churches, chapels, and missionary residences were looted and in many cases destroyed. The Board suffered heavy financial losses--$250,000 in Shanghai alone--and 50 or more Southern Baptist missionaries lost their personal and household effects.[17]

To whip up patriotic fervor and gain mass support for their expansionist ambitions, Japan's militarists began to enforce the demands of State Shinto more strictly than ever before. They convinced most Christians that paying homage to the emperor and his ancestors was not an act of worship, and that the prescribed rituals in schools and at shrines were civil, not religious, in nature. The most important ceremony held in the schools was the reading of the Imperial Rescript on Education, promulgated in 1890 by Emperor Meiji. D. C. Holtom, a Northern Baptist missionary and renowned authority on Shinto nationalism, called the rescript "the most famous and influential document yet produced in the history of modern Japan." This document made direct reference to Amaterasu Ōmikami, the Shinto sun goddess, and declared that the imperial throne was "coeval with heaven

---

[16]Reischauer and Craig, *Tradition and Transformation*, 245-50.

[17]*ASBC, 1937*, 216; *ASBC, 1938*, 179; *Japan Times*, 26 July 1984. Other estimates of the number of people massacred at Nanking range from 100,000, given in Japanese school textbooks, to 400,000, claimed by some Chinese authorities.

and earth." Known as the Bible of educational institutions, it was so sacred that it was always kept in a place of honor and security. Whenever it was read to students, the reader held it with white gloves and intoned its words with great reverence.[18]

As in other schools, this ceremony was conducted in Seinan Gakuin and Seinan Jo Gakuin, at graduation exercises and on major holidays. Effie Baker described the reading at Seinan Gakuin: "All stand with bowed heads. . . . Not a pin drops; not a noise is heard. The whole auditorium breathes as one mighty, humble subject waiting before his master, not worthy to lift his head until the proclamation is read and the scroll tied and placed securely in its special box on a special table under a silken spread. What reverence! What awe!"[19]

The two Baptist schools were required to keep a portrait of the emperor in a specially built sacred cabinet. In case of fire the head of the school was responsible for rescuing the portrait even at the peril of his life. Whenever the Rescript on Education was read, the portrait was also brought out and unveiled before the students, who made profound obeisance to it. The students were often reminded that bowing to the portrait was not the same as worshiping God, but they could hardly escape the influence of the Rescript that they came to know by heart.[20]

When the teachers and students of Seinan Jo Gakuin gathered at a neighborhood shrine for silent prayer toward the imperial palace in Tokyo, as required by government authorities, they were instructed beforehand how they should pray. They were told to ask God's blessings upon the emperor, to intercede for their country and its leaders, and to pray that they themselves might be good, loyal citizens. Seinan Gakuin successfully resisted orders to visit a shrine. According to Edwin Dozier, the school told prefectural authorities that if it was to attend patriotic ceremonies, the rites "would have to be held at shrines where historically authentic heroes were enshrined." Both Seinan Gakuin and Seinan Jo Gakuin struggled to maintain their Christian testimony, compromising only as required to avoid forfeiture of the institutions. The independent Osaka Bible College and a few other small schools closed their doors rather than submit to government controls.[21]

Textbooks on history and ethics were rewritten to glorify the emperor and the state, and teachers of these subjects were required to attend institutes and

---

[18]Daniel Clarence Holtom, *Modern Japan and Shinto Nationalism* (Chicago: University of Chicago Press, 1947), 77; Supreme Commander for the Allied Powers, *Political Reorientation of Japan* (Washington: U.S. Government Printing Office, 1949), 584.

[19]*HFF* 16 (Nov. 1932): 11-12.

[20]*Seinan Gakuin nanajūnen shi*, 1:318.

[21]Lancaster, "Autobiography," 101-2; EBD, *Japan's New Day* (Nashville: Broadman Press, 1949), 97-99; Leone Cole, *Sentenced to Life: 50 Years of Missionary Life in Japan* (Huntington Beach, Calif.: National Design Associates, 1987), 64.

conferences for training in the use of the textbooks.[22] Most missionaries were not directly concerned, but some were distressed at the tightening grip of religion-based ultranationalism. They maintained a discreet silence, lest their usefulness in Japan come to an end. "We don't want any politically minded missionaries," warned Kuriya Hiroji, president of the seminary; "they get into trouble and sometimes get deported."[23]

In 1937 the Ministry of Education published *Kokutai no hongi* (Cardinal principles of the national entity), an official commentary on the Rescript on Education. This publication, made required study for all teachers and students in higher schools, was highly explicit in setting forth the divine origin and characteristics of the Japanese people, who were all said to be kin to the divine emperor.[24] Even devout Christians could not escape the influence of such propaganda. Thus, no matter how respected Southern Baptist missionaries might be, the political climate of the times precluded their holding positions of authority over the Japanese.

Decline of the Mission

Another reason for yielding the reins of power to Japanese Baptists was the decline in Mission personnel and finances. As noted already, the death of John Rowe and the resignations of Mary Walters and Florence Conrad in 1929 had reduced the number of missionaries to 20. None had been sent to Japan since 1925 and very few to any other field, for the Seventy-five Million Campaign's shortfall had left the Board with an indebtedness exceeding $1 million. Between 1925 and 1931, by curtailing or suspending new appointments and asking missionaries returning on furlough to resign, the Board reduced its missionary force by 127, nearly one-fourth of the total. Despite such budget slashing, the great depression that struck in 1929 dashed any hopes for the Board's early financial recovery. In 1931 its debt again exceeded $1 million. In the Japan Mission therefore, the prospects for new personnel were bleaker than ever. "We appear to be a vanishing race," one member said.[25]

At so critical a time, nonetheless, the Mission was still engaged in the interpersonal warfare that contributed to the low esteem in which many pastors held the missionaries. The most conspicuous battle revolved around George Bouldin. As acting president of Seinan Gakuin, we have noted, Bouldin took a lenient stance toward the participation of its athletic teams in Sunday matches. In the words of Ozaki Shuichi, Bouldin "had within him not a mere conservatism but an evangelical freedom." However interpreted, his stance so angered the

---

[22]Lancaster, "Autobiography," 100.
[23]Quoted in EBD, "Mission and Convention," 17.
[24]Holtom, *Shinto Nationalism*, 7.
[25]*ASBC, 1931*, 258; *ASBC, 1932*, 156-57.

missionary trustees--Ernest Mills, Franklin Ray, Norman Williamson, even Ernest Walne--that they threatened to resign. When the Mission threw its support behind the trustees, Bouldin pledged outwardly to be more strict. In December 1930 he was formally installed as president of the school.[26]

In the spring of 1931 Bouldin led the school in observing its 15th anniversary, with Kelsey Dozier as featured speaker. That autumn he entertained distinguished visitors such as John MacNeill, president of the Baptist World Alliance. He was photographed with Charles and Anne Lindbergh, world-class celebrities who landed their pontoon-equipped *Sirius* at Fukuoka's seadrome and stopped overnight before flying on to Nanking. While George basked in the afterglow of these notable occasions, he was rapidly losing favor with his missionary colleagues.[27]

Drawing on his reservoir of shrewdness, Bouldin had forged a tacit compromise with the faculty and student body. Though Sunday sports were strictly forbidden while the school was in session, if the Seinan baseball team made it to the finals in the league tournament during the summer vacation and found itself obliged to play on Sunday or else concede the game, it could play. As punishment, the manager and captain of the team would be suspended from school for two weeks. In 1931, Bouldin insisted, the rule against Sunday sports was violated in less than 2 percent of cases, and severe punishment was meted out.[28]

That was not stern enough for the other missionaries. "We cannot stand for Bouldin's administration," wrote Kelsey Dozier to Secretary Ray. Ray had already reminded Bouldin that "the City of Richmond does not allow baseball matches on Sunday" and that "the Lord's day . . . is the Lord's day all over the world." In Bouldin's thinking, however, Richmond's blue laws did not apply to Japan. Besides, the fuss over Sunday athletics was a "smoke screen," he argued; the real source of friction was controlling the Japanese as "hirelings" and wasting Board money for frivolous reasons. In 1931, he told Ray, five members of the Mission proposed that a vacant Mission residence be rented to "a nice English family" at ¥900 for the year. "Two members of the Executive Committee turned it down," Bouldin wrote, "and the reasons given (I can send you the letter) are that the man was seen smoking a pipe on the street and his wife was seen on a hot day without stockings (about her own house)."[29]

Bouldin also made enemies by his lenient attitude toward the Asakai movement, then disruptive in several churches. It was his nature to accept

---

[26]Ozaki in *NBRS*, 375; EBD notes, 1930.

[27]EBD notes, 1931; *Seinan Gakuin nanajūnen shi*, 1:365; *HFF* 16 (Jan. 1932): 12. The latter two references include a photograph of the Lindberghs and Bouldin. The Lindberghs' journey is narrated in Anne Morrow Lindbergh, *North to the Orient* (New York: Harcourt, Brace and Co., 1935), but the Fukuoka stopover is indicated only in the maps and appendix.

[28]Bouldin, "Autobiography," 183-84; Bouldin to T. B. Ray, 1 Sept. 1932.

[29]C. K. Dozier to T. B. Ray, 13 June 1932; Ray to Bouldin, 13 Feb. 1931; Bouldin to Ray, 9 Sept. 1932.

diversity in Christian faith and practice. A Seinan student who worked part time for Bouldin, Kusakari Yasushi, belonged to the Asakai faction in Fukuoka Church, where Bouldin was a member. In a tense business meeting of the church, the student supported a no-confidence motion brought against Pastor Shimose. The motion failed by a single vote, with the result that 10 members of the faction, Kusakari among them, left to form an independent Asakai congregation. In that crucial business meeting, Bouldin had spoken in defense of Kusakari after the youth had been scolded by Shimose. So enraged was Shimose that he spread a rumor among Convention leaders that Bouldin himself belonged to Asakai. Though false, the rumor was damaging nonetheless.[30]

At the April 1932 Mission meeting in Beppu, five men--Walne, Clarke, Ray, Dozier, and Williamson--sponsored actions asking the Seinan Gakuin trustees to dismiss Bouldin from his posts at the school and asking the Convention-Mission cooperating committee to assign the Bouldins to Kumamoto without delay. Two reasons were cited for the actions. First was George's "improper attitude" toward the Asakai, particularly the Kure church, then in turmoil over the movement. Second was his "improper attitude"--insubordination?--toward Seinan Gakuin's trustees as displayed in their recent meeting. No mention was made of the sabbath controversy. Subsequently the trustees accepted George's resignation as president effective July 10 and denied his request to stay on as dean of the theology department.[31]

The action provoked a massive student strike in support of Bouldin. He was hailed as a progressive educator, as the one missionary who understood the students and showed them goodwill. Hara Matsuta, named acting president, tried in vain to get the students back to classes. He succeeded only after an ominous letter of inquiry had come from the Ministry of Education and the Bouldins had physically left Fukuoka. To no one's surprise, they went not to Kumamoto but in the opposite direction to their private home in Gotemba. "I hope to be spared to see brighter days," said the aging Ernest Walne. And what did the Mission and Board's 1932 report on Seinan Gakuin have to say? Neither Bouldin nor these fateful events that swirled about him were mentioned or even alluded to.[32]

Though not specified as a cause for his dismissal, it is worth nothing that Bouldin also antagonized the Mission with his fiscal policies, especially with the means used to purchase 2,640 square meters of land adjoining the athletic field. Friends of the school pledged ¥25,000 toward the purchase, and most teachers made pledges of part of their salary for 42 months ahead. With faculty consent Bouldin borrowed ¥10,000 from the teachers' pension fund set up by the Mission. When some missionaries objected to this borrowing, the Mission asked the Board

[30]*Seinan Gakuin nanajūnen shi*, 1:612-17; *ASBC, 1933*, 215.
[31]*Seinan Gakuin nanajūnen shi*, 1:612-17.
[32]Ibid., 1:608-25; EBD notes, 1933; *ASBC, 1933*, 218.

to replace the ¥10,000 with other funds on hand in Japan. The Board complied, but on December 9, 1932, Secretary Ray wrote George a letter deprecating his action as "a serious mistake" and "very reprehensible." On the same day, by sheer coincidence, the Bouldins wrote out their resignations to the Board, which later accepted them "with regret." Afterwards Bouldin faulted the Board for replacing the ¥10,000 and not letting the school handle its own affairs.[33]

George Bouldin's popularity with the Japanese ran deep. As in the case of the Jesuit Francis Xavier, his aristocratic bearing and touch of haughtiness were assets among a people steeped in the samurai tradition. So were his scholarly attributes and his tendency to side with the nationals against his fellow missionaries. "He had more ability," said Arase Tsuruki, "and he knew it. He treated the other missionaries like children." Like J. W. McCollum, Bouldin showed scant sympathy for those less competent in the language. He spoke scathingly of the veteran missionary who knew only enough Japanese to administer the Lord's Supper and pronounce the benediction. Worse still, such a missionary lives "in a big house in the style of a baron," said Bouldin, and "because he can hand over some American money every month claims the right to control the church." Whether Bouldin had a particular person in mind is unclear.[34]

Prior to the Bouldins' departure from Fukuoka, a local newspaper said as much in its own way. It laid the blame for the school's "cancer"--its Sunday sports problem--on foreign subsidy. The Japanese trustees were powerless, the paper claimed, because of their financial dependence. The basic problem was whether or not to accept aid (and control) from the Mission--as Bouldin claimed.[35]

Much in George's favor was a wife who excelled him in poise and grace and who was no less diligent in mission work. Among Maggie's many contributions were the kindergarten and social ministries in Jigyōhama, an outcaste village located on Hakata Bay between the campus of Seinan Gakuin and the Bouldin residence at Jigyō. The village had about 80 families, a people ridden with diseases, class hatred, and inferiority complexes. One day in 1929, when Maggie first took a shortcut through the village, dirty children with sore eyes and skin blemishes called her "foreigner" and threw rocks at her feet. Her response was to bring a basketful of roses from her garden and hand a rose to each child who picked up a rock to throw. At Christmastime the Bouldins planned a party for the children at their home. But when the children were let into the house, they grabbed everything off the Christmas tree and ran off with it.[36]

---

[33]Ray to Bouldin, 9 Dec. 1932; Bouldin to JBM, 8 Dec. 1932; Bouldin to Virgil Bouldin, 29 Sept. 1933; George and Maggie Bouldin to FMB, 9 Dec. 1932; Maddry to Bouldins, 13 Jan. 1933.

[34]Arase, quoted in Max Garrott interview; Bouldin to Ray, 9 Sept. 1932.

[35]*Seinan Gakuin nanajūnen shi*, 1:619.

[36]*HFF* 16 (Jan. 1932): 12.

In 1930 Maggie arranged for some of the Maizuru Kindergarten teachers to visit the village once a week and teach knitting and other skills to the older girls. In 1931, with permission from the village headman, she opened a kindergarten named Ai no Sono (Garden of Love) in the rundown public hall, using volunteers from Seinan Gakuin. Each morning 35 children, "once so dirty as not to be recognizable," were cleaned up and sent to learn a better life. Maggie persuaded a large corporation to provide a playground. She arranged for a dentist to donate 60 toothbrushes, and a doctor to examine free the eyes of 200 people and provide treatment for the many who had trachoma.[37]

Maggie herself was spared this terrible eye disease, but some of her helpers were afflicted, including Elizabeth Watkins, who succeeded Maggie as director of the Garden of Love. Watkins sometimes had to sit "for six hours a day with hot applications on my eyes." Her sight was so impaired that she had to wear glasses the rest of her life.[38]

After the Bouldins left Fukuoka and moved to their cedar house at Gotemba, George put into practice his twin concerns of evangelizing farmers and promoting self-support, concerns which he felt were grossly neglected by the Mission and the Board. He did rural work in cooperation with Kagawa Toyohiko, who in 1936 addressed a joint meeting of the Northern and Southern Baptist conventions in St. Louis. Bouldin not only preached in the chapel of the American village, of which he was chairman, but taught many Japanese how to cure ham, grow corn, raise turkeys, and make furniture. He became such a legend in the area that a television documentary made in 1979 focused on his many contributions. In 1936, with backing from the West Japan Convention, the Bouldins sought reappointment to Japan or Manchuria. The Japan Mission disapproved, and the Board turned them down.[39]

During a trip to the States in 1937, Bouldin was approached by J. Frank Norris about the possibility of extending to Japan the work of the Fundamental Baptist Mission Fellowship. Norris, a Fort Worth, Texas, pastor, was the most notorious critic of the SBC, and his Fellowship had already "taken over" two stations in China. Norris had known Bouldin since their student years together at Southern Seminary, and he had learned of Bouldin's separation from the Foreign Mission Board through Bouldin's lawyer-brother in Norris's church. George was no fundamentalist, however, and he returned to Japan as pastor of the English-speaking Union Church in Yokohama. It was one of the few sanctuaries in Japan, a friend noted, where Maggie could wear her favorite red dress. The Bouldins served there until 1941, when the threat of war forced their return to America.

---

[37]*ASBC*, 252-53.

[38]Watkins, "Autobiography," 52-53.

[39]Bouldin, "Autobiography," 185; Bouldin to Virgil Bouldin, 7 May, 29 Sept. 1933; C. L. Whaley, "Apostle of the Future," typescript, 4; Garrott to Bouldins, 1 May 1936; Maddry to Bouldin, 22 Apr. 1936; Bouldin to Maddry, 22 Feb. 1937; *ASBC, 1937*, 114; Garrott interview.

During the war George worked for the War Department as a teacher of Japanese and a research analyst. Then he and Maggie spent their remaining years in Alabama engaged in pastoral work, school teaching, and agricultural projects. George died in 1967, survived by Maggie, herself nearly blind.[40]

The resignation of the Bouldins also cost the Mission the services of Effie Baker, who lived with them while teaching music, English, and Bible in Seinan Gakuin. Effie had completed two years of graduate study in Kyushu Imperial University. Kelsey Dozier reported in June 1932 that she "seems dissatisfied and is not well perhaps." After leaving Fukuoka in July with the Bouldins, Effie returned to the States and resigned from the Board. During the Pacific War she taught Japanese language at the University of Texas.[41]

Also sacrificed were Norman and Fannie Williamson. They got along quite well so long as they worked in Kumamoto, but after moving to Fukuoka in 1928 at the urging of the Mission, their faculties were taxed to the limit. They moved only because Kelsey Dozier was in poor health and under pressure to resign, Fannie later explained, and the situation at Seinan Gakuin appeared desperate. When the Doziers moved to Kokura, Norman became treasurer of the school as well as teacher, and for two years he was dean of the seminary. In addition, he still had charge of the Fukuoka, Kumamoto, and Kagoshima fields, and he worked in the Seinan Gakuin church. It was his privilege to baptize Murakami Toraji, a Seinan student who in the 1980s served as the school's president and chancellor, and then as chairman of its trustees.[42]

In contrast to his playful son Norman as well as George Bouldin, Williamson found little favor with the students, because of his aloofness and poor command of Japanese. At the same time he lost the backing of the Mission, for he was not a man who minced his words. Under the pressures of the times some of his utterances displeased certain colleagues. Kelsey Dozier, who had worked closely with Williamson and often played tennis with him before leaving Fukuoka in 1929, had found him "very sensitive." When the Williamsons were on furlough in 1934-35 the Board dismissed them, for two men and one woman in the Mission had declared that the Williamsons' usefulness in Japan was over. "All three of them had selfish reasons," Fannie charged, without naming the opponents. "We were stabbed in the back." One of the two men, she added, wrote her husband a letter of apology and sought to make restitution.[43]

[40]Norris to Bouldin, 8 May 1937; Watkins, "Autobiography," 104-10; *JCY, 1968*, 405-6.

[41]*ASBC, 1933*, 212; *Seinan Gakuin nanajūnen shi*, 1:313-14; C. K. Dozier to Maddry, 13 June 1932.

[42]Fannie Williamson to Maddry, 26 July 1941; Murakami Toraji, interview with author, Fukuoka, 1988.

[43]C. K. Dozier diary, 18 July, 28 Apr., 19 May 1928; Fannie Williamson to Maddry, 26 July 1941; Murakami interview.

By 1941 the Williamsons had so spent themselves in pastoral work in Georgia that they were "just like an old stove all burned out on the inside." Unable to support themselves, they requested and were granted a Board pension. Their names appeared in the Board's list of emeritus missionaries from 1944 to 1947 and then were dropped. Norman died of a stroke in 1972, and Fannie died in 1985 after reaching the age of 90.[44]

Several other furloughing missionaries failed to return to Japan. In July 1932 Grace Mills died of cancer in a hospital at Long Beach, California. She had suffered much pain, having barely survived an operation in Japan. In 1934 Hooker Rowe retired in Redlands, California. She was in poor health, weakened by chronic bronchitis that seemed incurable in the damp climate of Japan. Yet she lived to the age of 83. Florence Walne, who returned to the States in 1930, studied in the University of California at Berkeley and worked at International House there. The Mission asked the Board to return her to the field, but the Board declined for lack of funds. Florence resigned in 1934, saying she did not feel led back to Japan anyway.[45]

The gloom of missionary attrition in Japan was relieved a bit in 1932 by the return of Edwin B. Dozier accompanied by his wife. The only son of Kelsey and Maude Dozier, Edwin had been born in Nagasaki, taught by his mother in a schoolroom set up in one corner of their dining room in Fukuoka, and then sent to Canadian Academy in Kobe, where he was a boy scout, school interpreter, and president of the student council. He continued his education at Wake Forest College and Southern Seminary. Shortly before seminary graduation in 1932, Edwin married Mary Ellen Wiley, a spirited mission volunteer. They sought Board appointment to Japan, and the Mission urged that they be sent out. Edwin would be what Pastor Shimose longed for, a second-generation missionary who truly loved Japan. But Secretary Ray could make no exception to the moratorium on appointments. So the WMU of Virginia, petitioned by some Royal Ambassadors whom Edwin had deeply impressed, voted to send the Doziers to Japan under its own sponsorship.[46]

Edwin and Mary Ellen arrived in Yokohama in November, stopped over at the Clarke home in Tokyo, then headed for Kyushu and the home of Edwin's parents on the campus of Seinan Jo Gakuin. Their presence, though much desired, created a minor crisis for the Mission's executive committee. Called into session at the Walne home in Shimonoseki, the committee grappled with the problem of what status and perquisites were due a couple not appointed by the Board. The Mission had assumed no responsibility for Elizabeth Watkins. The case of the Doziers

[44]Fannie Williamson to Maddry, 26 July 1941; *ASBC, 1944*, 269; *ASBC, 1945*, 228; *ASBC, 1946*, 298; *ASBC, 1947*, 131; Norman F. Williamson, Jr., to author, 27 Jan. 1986.

[45]*JCY, 1933*, 316; Florence Walne file, FMBA.

[46]*HFF* 17 (Jan. 1933): 9-10; Foy Johnson Farmer, "Helps for Teachers," photocopy, EBD papers.

seemed different, however, for they had been specifically requested by the Mission, and Edwin had joined the Mission family at birth. At length a decision was reached to assign the young couple to the vacant Mission residence on the campus of Seinan Gakuin, which was the very house in which Edwin had been reared.[47]

In the spring of 1933, when Edwin and Mary Ellen had barely settled into their strenuous teaching routine, Kelsey Dozier began to have chest pains with increasing frequency. He tried not to put undue strain on his heart, he said, in order "to live as long as possible to be of service." But new burdens fell on his shoulders again and again. "This is a world of crisis," he often said. "I want to die at work." Several meetings in which he was involved as Mission treasurer or committee member were held at his Kokura residence to save him unnecessary travel. These precautions were insufficient. On May 31, 1933, one week after a violent heart attack, Kelsey died at home. He was 54. Maude, Edwin, and Mary Ellen were with him, but Helen, his only other child, was graduating from Meredith College in North Carolina at the time.[48]

Kelsey was buried in the little cemetery on the Seinan Jo Gakuin campus. His dying message to his beloved Seinan Gakuin, "Be true to Christ," was carved in English on the gravestone. More important, the words were engraved on Seinan's tradition and are hallowed to this day as the school's motto. Among Kelsey's other parting words were these: "My life has been very imperfect, but I have tried to be faithful." Even allowing for some narrow views and other failings, such as beset all mortals, one must rank "Dozier the faithful" with the missionary giants. As founder of what is now a prestigious university, he has been eulogized in speeches, books, and documentary films, far more than any other Southern Baptist missionary.[49] The tributes are appropriate. One cannot read his voluminous diaries and correspondence without sensing that the man was genuine. In him is found a refreshing coincidence of achievement and character.

In April 1933, when Kelsey Dozier was having his ominous pains, Lucile Clarke left for the States in critical condition. She had failed to respond to two months' treatment at Tokyo Sanitarium and St. Luke's Hospital. She had a malignant growth on the lung--a sarcoma--and her limbs had begun to swell. Harvey, who accompanied her on the SS *Chichibu*, planned to take her to a specialist in San Francisco. But on May 2, one day before the ship reached port,

[47]Lois Whaley, *Edwin Dozier of Japan*, 101-5.

[48]Mizumachi, *C. K. Dozier*, 4-9, 35.

[49]Ibid., 3, 35; *ASBC, 1934*, 232. The most notable film is a one-hour documentary, "The Life of C. K. Dozier," produced and broadcast in 1986 by a Fukuoka TV station, RKB.

Lucile died. Her last message, Harvey said, was "Tell the Japanese to study the Bible and follow Christ."[50]

Lucile was interred at Atlanta, after a funeral message by Louie D. Newton, who later served as president of the SBC. Her musical rendition of "Beautiful Japan," an evangelical poem by the missionary statesman A. B. Simpson, was sung in her honor repeatedly during foreign missions week at Ridgecrest that summer. The featured singer was daughter Lucile, a talented vocalist like her mother. It was a fitting tribute to one who so often had brought "loving cheer through the melody of her voice and conviction to the heart in the melody of her life." Harvey spent some time with Lucile and his other children, including Coleman, a future missionary who was then a social worker in Augusta. Then he returned to Tokyo at the end of the summer and carried out his duties until retirement in 1936, with 38 years of service.[51]

Harvey Clarke was sorely missed by those he personally had led to Christ. These included two leading pastors, Arase Tsuruki and Yuya Kiyoki, and a postwar president of Seinan Jo Gakuin, Yoshii Masayoshi. These men had been captivated by Clarke's personality--his attractive face, warm heart, and quiet bearing. They had been moved by his tearful sermons, even though poorly read from a romaji manuscript that Clarke's helper had translated from his English version. After returning to the States, Clarke was asked, "Are you retired?" "Not until the trumpet sounds," came the reply. The summons came in 1943 at Gastonia, North Carolina. He was 75.[52]

On an autumn evening in 1934, the West Japan Convention sponsored a farewell service in the Shimonoseki church for Ernest and Claudia Walne. Seventy people gathered to honor the white-haired couple who were leaving Japan after more than four decades of service. In response to the lavish outpouring of tributes, Claudia sang "Blest Be the Tie That Binds," and Ernest made one of the shortest speeches of his career. "We are taking our bodies to America," he said, "but we are leaving our spirits in Japan."[53]

As noted before, Walne could be temperamental, dictatorial, and overbearing, especially in his declining years. These flaws notwithstanding, no one doubted the genuineness of his commitment to Japan or his love for the people. "I wish we

[50]W. H. Clarke, undated letter in Eden ms., 215; Y. Ikeda, M.D., statement, 13 Apr. 1933; *JCY, 1934*, 278-79. Lucile's last message is worded differently in *JCY*, a version often quoted. I have followed Clarke's account.

[51]*ASBC, 1934*, 232; Eden ms., 214; *HFF* 17 (Oct. 1933): 15. "Beautiful Japan" is quoted in Farmer, *Gate of Asia*, 13. A Japanese translation with Lucile's music is given in *NBRS*, 411-12.

[52]W. Maxfield Garrott, "Jubilee in Japan" (typescript, 1940), 2; Max Garrott interview; Yuya interview; *JCY, 1953*, 333.

[53]*NBRS*, 399-401.

were beginning instead of ending our career," he said, "so great are the opportunities in Japan." Yet he had achieved far more than any of his colleagues.[54]

It was said among the older missionaries, "McCollum was the preacher; Walne was the organizer." Walne indeed played a major role in structuring both the Mission and the Convention. He was also a zealous evangelist throughout his long career. He baptized many converts, sometimes at the request of a minuscule pastor who feared the high waves at the beach. He planted the seeds of the Fukuoka seminary that opened in 1907, and he taught church history there with remarkable clarity. Unlike Clarke, he could read and write Japanese as well as speak it. "Christian education ought to be attempted as early as possible," wrote Walne in 1910. He repeatedly urged the Board to provide funds for establishing Seinan Gakuin and Seinan Jo Gakuin. Moreover he pioneered in the field of Christian literature, founding the Gospel Book Store and supervising the publication of many books. One of these books, Kagawa's *New Life Through God*, sold more than a quarter million copies.[55]

The versatile Walne designed chapels and supervised their construction. He would climb up on the roof to measure the timber to make sure specifications were being followed. When the Fukuoka church's building was finished and four seminary students refused his request to clean the windows, Walne got his wife and two of his children to help him do the job. Their willingness was not surprising, for Ernest took time for his family. He was no workaholic. Unlike most of his fellow missionaries, however, he never spent his summers away from his place of work.[56]

Claudia Walne reared five children as their mother and school teacher, conducted numerous activities for Japanese women and girls, and served indefatigably as organist and soloist. And though she suffered a number of serious illnesses, she enjoyed better health than her husband when they reached retirement age. After completing their final furlough in 1935, the Walnes together became the Board's first emeritus missionaries from Japan, with credit for 43 years of service.[57]

Ernest Walne had truly spent himself in Japan. In February 1935, only a few months after settling in Berkeley, California, he suffered a heart attack that left him an invalid. The muscles of his face became paralyzed. Though robbed of his smile, Walne retained the twinkle in his eyes. Still talkative, he enjoyed reminiscing with old friends who dropped in. George W. Truett, president of the Baptist World Alliance, and J. H. Rushbrooke, Alliance secretary, called in May

[54]*JCY, 1937*, 351.

[55]Garrott, "Jubilee in Japan," 2; *JCY, 1937*, 351; "Sketch of Dr. Ernest Nathan Walne," in EBD notes, 1936.

[56]*NBRS*, 402; M. Hatano to Mrs. Walne, 9 Dec. 1936, carbon copy in possession of Murakami Toraji, Fukuoka; Florence Walne, "Expression of appreciation," in EBD notes, 1936.

[57]Claudia Walne obituary, in *Commission* 12 (Mar. 1949): 84.

1936 after visiting Japan on a round-the-world tour. John R. Sampey, president of Southern Seminary, visited in August, when en route to Japan. "I will never attend another Baptist convention," the 69-year-old Walne told Sampey with tears in his eyes. "No," replied Sampey, three years his senior, "but we will soon be attending a greater convention, you and I." Two months later Walne departed for that mammoth gathering above.[58]

Claudia Walne found solace in praying for her former coworkers. In 1941, when the clouds of war were growing darker, she wrote: "I would love to be in Japan, sharing burdens with our missionaries and my beloved Japanese Christians." In 1945 she rejoiced at the restoration of peace but mourned the death of her daughter Florence. Three years later Claudia died at the age of 80, survived by four sons and by two remaining 19th-century pioneers: Sophia Brunson and Dru McCollum.[59]

Rejuvenation of the Mission

In 1933, when the Board was beginning to recover from the effects of the depression, Edwin and Mary Ellen Dozier were appointed on the field after the death of Edwin's father. In 1934 another second-generation missionary, the "versatile and magnetic" Hermon S. Ray, was appointed with his wife Rayberta Reed Ray. Born in Hartford, Connecticut, where his parents did furlough study, Hermon graduated from Peiping (Peking) American High School in China. After receiving degrees from Furman University and Southern Seminary, he served two years as assistant to C. Oscar Johnson, the St. Louis pastor who later was president of the Baptist World Alliance. Rayberta, a native of Oregon, was a graduate of the Conservatory of Music in Kansas City.[60]

Assigned to Tokyo for evangelistic work (Harvey Clarke left in 1936), the Rays combined language study with church and student ministries. In 1937 their four-year-old daughter Aileen, first grandchild of the Franklin Rays, died of "scarlet-fever and chicken-pox complication." Rayberta also contracted scarlet fever and spent several weeks in St. Luke's Hospital. During that time Hermon's mother Daisy returned from an operation in Peking weighing a scant 85 pounds. Most of her stomach had been removed. The cluster of shocks was more than the young Rays could bear, and at the urging of Rayberta's physician, they returned to the States. Resigning from the Board, they assumed a pastorate in California and later served in Hawaii.[61]

Also appointed in 1934 was W. Maxfield Garrott, a brilliant Arkansan who had just received a Ph.D. from Southern Seminary at the age of 23. Like

---

[58]Florence Walne to Friends, 25 Dec. 1936.
[59]Claudia Walne obituary, in *Commission* 12 (Mar. 1949): 84; *JCY, 1950*, 151.
[60]*HFF* 20 (July 1936): 3; ibid. 17 (Oct. 1933): 19; ibid. 20 (Oct. 1934): 21-22.
[61]J. F. Rays' letter to "Our Folks," 1938.

Crawford Toy, Max was a born linguist. His mother knew Latin, Greek, and French, and she gave him a significant part of his early education. His father was a seminary-trained pastor. The family was musical, and Max acquired both vocal and instrumental skills. With these advantages, Max graduated from high school at 14 and from college at 18. Like his father a generation before, he entered Southern Seminary as its youngest student. Though he majored in Greek with A. T. Robertson, he was a Hebrew fellow under John R. Sampey. During a summer vacation he also picked up a serviceable command of Spanish, while supply pastor of the English-speaking Baptist church in Havana, Cuba.[62]

Max's studies at Southern Seminary coincided with the depression years when the Board had a moratorium on sending new missionaries. As chairman of the Student Volunteer Band, he promoted mission support through all means at his command. He also demonstrated his missionary concerns by preaching and playing his flute or portable organ in evangelistic meetings held on the streets and in factories. At the suggestion of W. O. Carver, he settled on Japan as his permanent mission field and made plans to teach in the seminary at Fukuoka. For his partner in the work he chose Carver's younger daughter Alice, to whom he proposed repeatedly without success. Alice spurned him and married another man. So Max was appointed and sent to the field without a spouse.[63]

Max's single state worked to his advantage in mastering the Japanese language and absorbing the new culture. After living briefly with Harvey Clarke in Tokyo, he moved into the home of Koga Takeo, a deacon in the Koishikawa church. Max ate Japanese food and often wore Japanese clothes to language school. He also spent much time with Pastor Yuya and learned to play a shakuhachi (Japanese flute) that Yuya gave him--a treasured instrument that the pastor had received from his mother.[64]

A few months after entering language school in Tokyo, Max slipped into a state of spiritual frustration. During this personal crisis he fell under the influence of the Oxford Group Movement. Founded by the American Lutheran Frank Buchman, this movement had been named after Oxford University, where Buchman had made an impact with his preaching on "world-changing through life-changing." By 1935 the Oxford Group Movement had spread among British and Canadian missionaries in Japan and had won the support of Kagawa and several other leading Christians. The movement promoted spiritual conversion through the techniques of confession, surrender, guidance, and sharing. It demanded of each convert four absolutes: absolute honesty, absolute purity, absolute unselfishness, and absolute love. Merrell Vories praised the movement as "a new Acts of the

---

[62]*HFF* 18 (Dec. 1934): 20; Delois Hamrick, "Biographical Materials Concerning William Maxfield Garrott, Missionary to Japan" (typescript, 1959), 1-7. Koga, a law graduate of Tokyo Imperial University, was chancellor of Seinan Gakuin 1961-65.

[63]Hamrick, "William Maxfield Garrott," 6-8; Dorothy Garrott, oral history, FMBA.

[64]Max Garrott interview.

Apostles." In Japan and elsewhere, Vories claimed, it brought rehabilitation to physical and moral wrecks, rebirth to spiritual degenerates, and reconciliation to broken families and estranged friends.[65]

In the words of Irvin Phelan, a Baptist businessman from Los Angeles, the Oxford Group was "not a new denomination but a new determination. The determination is to go all out for Christ, beginning at the point of surrender and going on to share that with others." Phelan promoted the movement in Japan mainly through "house parties" that featured Bible study, testimonies, quiet times, and public confessions. These meetings were conducted in English or Japanese in a number of cities, including Fukuoka, where Seinan Gakuin and the campus church experienced a revival so impressive that Norman Williamson said he had "never seen anything like it before."[66]

Max Garrott turned to Phelan for spiritual guidance. "It was the first time in my life," said Max, "that I ever tried to open my heart completely before any man." He confessed his sins, made restitution at several points, and began to seek fresh guidance for each day of his life. "Since the third day of June [1935]," he wrote to his friends, "I have been living a new spiritual life, different in kind and quality from any I have ever known before, distinguished by depth, reality, and power. . . . For the first time I have become a genuine witness to the power of Christ to change life."[67]

Edwin Dozier and Hermon Ray also fell under the movement's power. Edwin was confronted with the demands of absolute purity, a problem with which he had wrestled for many years. "On August 21st," he wrote, "I was able to surrender that with Hermon as my witness and the problem has been defeated, though I have had some pretty severe temptations." He also confessed to George Bouldin at Gotemba that he "had allowed the feelings of others to influence me to love you less than I should. . . . I want you to forgive me for being so untrue to you." Bouldin himself welcomed the emphases of the movement--with reservations about frank confession of sins--and acknowledged his indebtedness to Phelan. But the battle-scarred veteran was far less pliable than the younger missionaries. "Whether it is due to shyness or timidity," said Bouldin, "or to an exaggerated respect for personality, or to a liberal theology; whatever may be the cause I have never been able to be an aggressive evangelist. And to be honest, the recent meetings have not changed me in this respect."[68]

---

[65]Vories in *JCY, 1940*, 245; *JCQ* 9 (1934): 393-95; ibid. 10 (1935): 201-3. Buchman instituted Moral Re-Armament in 1938.

[66]Irving Phelan, *From Phelan's Note Book* (Peking, 1935, privately printed), 74; *ASBC, 1934*, 228, 231.

[67]Garrott to Friends, 10 Sept. 1935, Bouldin Collection, box 3, folder 6, no. 398.

[68]EBD to Bouldin, 4 Sept. 1935, Bouldin Collection; Bouldin statement, 2 Sept. 1935, Bouldin Collection.

Secretary Maddry had to warn the young missionaries against sending letters to the States about the Oxford Group, letters that were "creating uneasiness and wonder." Said Maddry: "It is a thing that will pass with the days." And so it did, though the movement left several missionaries changed for the better. Garrott for one never ceased to be grateful for its influence on his life.[69] The history of the Mission might have been altered for the better if the Oxford Group or something like it had swept Japan in 1925 instead of 1935.

The next missionary appointed by the Board was Dorothy Shepard Carver, who apart from her thyroid trouble was a most impressive candidate. Her father, W. O. Carver, was a world authority on missions, and her brother, George A. Carver, was a professor in Baptist-related Shanghai University. Her mother's brother, John W. Shepard, had founded the Rio Baptist College and Seminary in Brazil (his son John, Jr., became a missionary teacher in postwar Japan). Dorothy, a graduate of Mount Holyoke College and the WMU Training School, reached Japan in 1935, attended language school in Tokyo until 1937, then began teaching English at Seinan Jo Gakuin.[70]

Max Garrott, who had courted Dorothy's younger sister Alice without success, often took supper with Dorothy in Kokura before preaching at Tobata on Saturday nights. In October 1938, at last assured of the "guidance" emphasized by the Oxford Group, Max proposed marriage by passing her a slip of paper at a Kagawa meeting they attended in Tokyo. Dorothy accepted at once. The pair celebrated their engagement with a dinner party in the home of Horinouchi Kensuke, Japan's newly appointed ambassador to the United States. Max described Horinouchi and his wife, both members of Koishikawa Church, as "dynamic witnesses and soul-winners."[71]

In December, Max and Dorothy were married by her brother George in Seinan Jo Gakuin's unheated Rowe Auditorium. A deep snow covered the ground. After a honeymoon in Shanghai, the Garrotts settled in the Fukuoka home of the seminary president, Kuriya Hiroji. The Kuriyas moved out so that the newlyweds could have the house to themselves. Though overshadowed by her husband in many ways, Dorothy carried out effective ministries of her own. She led Endō Akiko to Christ and took her in when Akiko was expelled by her family. Hugging her, Dorothy said, "You are my child; I will take care of you." Later married to

[69]Maddry letter, 8 Nov. 1935, quoted in EBD notes, 1935; Mary Ellen Dozier, oral history, FMBA.

[70]*HFF* 19 (Nov. 1935): 24; Dorothy Garrott, oral history.

[71]*ASBC, 1937*, 233; *Commission* 43 (Oct. 1980): 8; D. Garrott, oral history; *HFF* 23 (Mar. 1939): 69, 73.

Matsumura Shūichi, Akiko became the most outstanding woman in the postwar Convention.[72]

Another missionary appointed in 1935 besides Dorothy was Helen Dozier. She taught music in Seinan Jo Gakuin and led in the YWA work there. A good pianist, her playing had always lifted the spirits of her father when he was alive. In 1938 Helen resigned from the Board to marry Timothy G. Pietsch, whom she had met while attending language school in Tokyo. A Baptist, he was a member of the Scandinavian Missionary Alliance.[73] After the Pacific War the Pietsches established the Tokyo Bible Center, an independent Baptist work. They were still serving there in 1989, both in their late 70s.

Alma Graves, a 1936 appointee, had been a member of the Student Volunteer Movement since her freshman year in college. A BYPU (Baptist Young People's Union) program on "Hearing God's Call" had turned her heart toward China before she felt led to Japan. Alma studied Japanese in Tokyo and then taught English in Seinan Gakuin. When Dorothy Carver married Max Garrott and moved to Fukuoka--Dorothy called it a "merger"--Alma transferred to Seinan Jo Gakuin. Even though her main work was English teaching, she completed the three-year Japanese language course on schedule, "a rare feat by anyone."[74]

Prior to 1939, all appointees in this decade were assigned to school work except Hermon and Rayberta Ray, and their stay was brief. After the loss of the Rays in 1937, Max Garrott noted that the schools were "drawing more than half of the missionary force, 70 percent of appropriations other than those for the missionaries themselves, and more than 75 percent of paid Japanese workers." Earlier, Daisy Ray had commented that the "lion's share" of available resources went to the schools, especially those in Fukuoka--Seinan Gakuin, seminary, and training school for women.[75] The subsequent history of the institutions has demonstrated, however, that the large investment of personnel and funds was prudent. Their Christian witness has been preserved and greatly expanded.

A Unique Ministry: The Good Will Center

The schools were not the whole show. In this decade a number of missionaries showed deep concern for the poor and underprivileged. Mention has already been made of Maggie Bouldin's work with outcastes in Fukuoka. At the 1929 Mission meeting, approval had been given for Naomi Schell to engage full-time in "social-evangelistic work," a long-time dream of hers. The Mission's president, John

---

[72]D. Garrott, oral history; *Seinan Jo Gakuin rokujūnen no ayumi* (Sixty-year history of Seinan Jo Gakuin) (Kitakyushu: Seinan Jo Gakuin, 1982), 313. On the Matsumuras, see Theodore F. Adams, *Baptists Around the World* (Nashville: Broadman Press, 1967), 116-19.

[73]*HFF* 19 (Aug. 1935): 26; *ASBC, 1939*, 228.

[74]EC minutes, 8 Feb. 1940; *HFF* 20 (Nov. 1936): 20; *ASBC, 1939*, 228.

[75]Max Garrott in *ASBC, 1937*, 235; Daisy Ray in *ASBC, 1935*, 225.

Rowe, in the last session he attended before his death, had proposed that the work be started in Tobata, a slum-ridden factory town adjacent to Kokura. Earlier efforts to start a church there had been disrupted, and a fresh approach was desired.[76]

Schell was aided by Nakanishi Kesako, a maternity nurse and the first volunteer for life service to emerge from the YWA movement. The two women first tried to rent a house in a slum area. Failing in this, they obtained a temporary residence and office in Miroku-machi, a high-class area "which does not welcome a settlement." While conducting a Sunday school and evangelistic services there, they surveyed the needs of the entire city. A few months later Nakanishi married Shinji Higasa, a new seminary graduate assigned to Tobata, and the couple devoted themselves to establishing a church at the Miroku-machi location. The church was organized in April 1931 with 28 charter members.[77]

In July 1931 Schell managed to rent a small house in Meiji-machi, the oldest and worst of Tobata's three slum districts. There she established Rinkōsha, sometimes translated Neighborhood Lighthouse but more often called in English the Good Will Center. A widowed member of Tobata Church served as matron of the house in exchange for a rent-free place to live. The work at the center included a Sunday school, a Sunbeam Band (Japan's first), clubs, mothers' meetings, and weekly evangelistic services. Two 60-year-old women who attended the meeting for mothers were soon baptized, the firstfruits of the new ministry.[78]

The work was supported by an annual grant of $1,800 from the Southern Baptist WMU, which had operated its own "good will centers" or "social settlements" since 1912, and by smaller gifts from the West Japan WMU. In December 1931, when the Japanese WMU launched an annual Baptist Day of Prayer for World Missions, a part of the special offering taken at that time was designated for the Good Will Center. Beginning in 1933, however, all of this offering was used for other causes, since the support from America was deemed adequate for the center.[79]

Special gifts from the Southern Baptist WMU, prodded by Maggie Bouldin and Maude Dozier, and the Heck Memorial Offering of North Carolina, Schell's home state, made possible the purchase of land and erection of a permanent building. Kelsey Dozier, though in failing health, gave daily supervision to the construction until its completion in February 1933. Schell and two Japanese women then moved into the building as full-time resident workers. With

---

[76]MM minutes, 1929; Tobata Baptist Good Will Center, *Showers of Blessing 1929-1939* (Tobata, 1939), no page numbers.

[77]*ASBC, 1931*, 253; *ASBC, 1932*, 249.

[78]Tobata Good Will Center, *Showers of Blessing*; *ASBC, 1932*, 249; M. B. Dozier, "Baptist Woman's Work," 21.

[79]M. B. Dozier, "Baptist Woman's Work," 28-33; *ESB*, vol. 1, s.v. "good will center work."

enthusiastic cooperation from the social service and police departments of the city, they opened an extensive program of community services.[80]

The people of the neighborhood were offered free use of a medical clinic, a library and reading room, a recreation room (ping pong, skittles, ring toss, various table games), and a playground (swings, slides, sand beds, jungle gym, and facilities for croquet and volley ball). For men, an English school and a Bible class were conducted at night. Women and older girls were provided opportunities for sewing, cooking, and clothes sales. A "Home Makers' Co-operative Club" was formed to purchase commodities cheaply and to sell handwork made by the women. For children there was a Sunday school, a story hour, a study hall, a savings club (an individual account was opened for each child at the post office), and a summer Vacation Bible School. A kindergarten established in 1936 had an enrollment of 70 by 1939.[81]

Schell and her coworkers, including volunteers from the Tobata church, visited shut-ins and prisoners, found jobs for the jobless, and nursed the sick back to health. They shared the light of their Christian faith through individual counseling as well as group activities. Perhaps it was due in part to the crushing load Schell carried that her hair turned completely white before she was 40.[82]

The Mission had no work among the sightless or hearing impaired, but the missionaries naturally took a keen interest in the 1937 visit of Helen Keller. Received by the emperor and empress, lauded by the prime minister and other top officials, the miracle woman (*kiseki no hito*) from America enjoyed the most enthusiastic reception that had ever been accorded a foreign visitor to Japan. In a spectacular tour of 39 cities, Dr. Keller, as she was billed (she held an honorary doctorate from Temple University), gave 97 lectures and charmed people from every walk of life. During her stay in Fukuoka May 26-28, she spoke to 1,500 students and others from Seinan Gakuin, Fukuoka Jo Gakkō (Methodist girls' school), and Fukuoka School for the Blind and Deaf. "Believe in the power within you," she told the enthralled students. "Ascertain the greatest good you can do, and do it." With her companion Pollie Thompson, Helen Keller was the house guest of Maude Dozier on the Seinan campus.[83]

Another matter of particular interest to the Mission was the inauguration of work among the Japanese in Dairen, Manchukuo, by the West Japan Convention. At the Convention's annual meeting in March 1937, one session was set aside to celebrate this new venture and to dedicate Amano Eizō as the first missionary. Nearly 80 persons were present. In his charge to Amano, President Shimose said,

[80]Tobata Good Will Center, *Showers of Blessing*.
[81]Ibid.
[82]Ibid.; M. E. Dozier, oral history; Lois Whaley, *Edwin Dozier of Japan*, 105.
[83]*Seinan Gakuin nanjūnen shi*, 1:434-36; Joseph C. Grew, *Ten Years in Japan* (New York: Simon and Schuster, 1944), 207-8; Joseph P. Lash, *Helen and Teacher* (New York: Delacorte Press/Seymour Lawrence, 1980), 643-46.

"Shake hands with the Manchurian, the Chinese, and tell them that we love them." Shimose's voice broke, and tears filled the eyes of many. Yet few if any seem to have comprehended the evils of Japanese colonialism.[84]

Missions was the theme of the entire convention, reported M. Theron Rankin, who in 1935 had been elected as the Board's first Secretary for the Orient. "The meetings were characterized," he said, "by a deep concern for the extension of God's Kingdom." Rankin also pointed out that Southern Baptists had been laboring in Manchuria for a decade when in 1937 a separate Manchukuo mission was formed with five missionaries. Twenty churches and chapels had been established. The Dairen church led by Amano was organized in December 1937 with 27 members. Max Garrott attended the organizational meeting as one of four representatives from the Convention.[85]

By 1939 this church, the only one in Manchukuo related to Japanese Baptists, had grown to 40 members. In the same year the Japan Reformed Church reported 18 churches in Manchukuo with 2,408 members, and the Methodist Church reported 8 churches with 1,007 members. The Southern Baptist mission, aimed at the Chinese rather than the Japanese, had grown to 6 churches, 24 outstations, and a membership of 2,255. It must be recognized, therefore, that the West Japan Convention's work in the puppet state of Manchukuo was small in scope, though large in symbolic value as a "foreign" mission enterprise.[86]

In 1939 three new missionaries were appointed to Japan, the first in three years. So anxious was the Mission for recruits that in 1938 it had voted to inform the Board that "we will accept the plain garden variety missionary." The appointees, however, proved to be a cut above the commonplace. Floryne Miller, one of eight children, was 32 and single. She had matured during several years' work in her father's Johnson City, Tennessee, law office and at a local newspaper, prior to attending Baptist Bible Institute, predecessor of New Orleans Baptist Theological Seminary. The other appointees were a couple from Texas, H. B. Ramsour, Jr., and Vera Mabel Ramsour. H. B., a former school teacher with the makings of a seminary president, had felt called to Japan upon hearing Cecile Lancaster speak in his church. Mabel was a pastor's daughter, and like her husband, a graduate of Southern Seminary.[87]

The new missionaries traveled to Japan on the same ship with Baker James and Eloise Cauthen, appointees to China whose names would become household words among Southern Baptists. While attending language school in Tokyo, they

[84]EBD notes, 1937.

[85]*Commission* 1 (Jan. 1938): 10; *ASBC, 1938*, 229, 252-53; Mrs. C. K. Dozier, *Trials and Triumphs of W.M.U. Work in Japan* (Birmingham: W.M.U. Literature Dept., [1932]), leaflet, no page numbers.

[86]*ASBC, 1940*, 260; *JCY, 1940*, 155.

[87]MM minutes, Mar. 1938; Dianne Barker, "Summary: The Life of Floryne Miller," typescript, 2-3; *Commission* 2 (June 1939): 179-80.

reported that the Koishikawa and Sugamo churches and their kindergartens were thriving, that the Baptist dormitory was filled with 16 boys, who met for prayer each morning. "We feel saddened," wrote Floryne Miller, "when we watch literally thousands clapping their hands and bowing before some shrine. . . . And then our hearts are made glad when on one street car we sit by a young student reading his Greek New Testament, and on another we see a shop girl hanging on to a strap with one hand and reading from the Bible she holds in the other."[88] This mingling of sadness and gladness was a mild foretaste of what the next decade had in store for these eager young missionaries and the tiny Christian minority they found in Japan.

November 5, 1939, marked the 50th anniversary of the arrival of the first Southern Baptist missionaries in Japan. In that time of hysterical nationalism, Japanese Baptists were in no position to commemorate the coming of foreigners to their country. They scheduled special evangelistic campaigns and other jubilee events for 1940, commemorating the first Baptist service held in Kyushu by a Japanese evangelist in 1890. Plans were also made, but never realized, for establishing a Baptist Rest Home for Tubercular Patients, considered a pressing need. Another concern was a serious drop in Sunday school attendance, caused mainly by the regimentation and control of pupils by the educational authorities. Pupils were required to attend patriotic functions and athletic meetings held with increasing frequency on Sundays. Moreover, many of the Sunday school teachers were being drafted into military service.[89]

Especially worrisome was the Religious Bodies Law passed by the Diet in March 1939 and due to take effect in April 1940. This law would require all religious groups to accept the "protection" and strict control of the central government or else be dissolved. To strengthen the Baptist position vis-à-vis a totalitarian regime, the West Japan and East Japan Conventions agreed to unite as one Baptist Convention of Japan, effective January 1940. The 14 Southern Baptist missionaries, though apprehensive of what lay ahead, continued to assist their Japanese coworkers as best they could in the evangelization of the empire.[90]

[88]*ASBC, 1940*, 244.
[89]Ibid., 242-43.
[90]Ibid.; *JCY, 1940*, 26-28.

8

Withdrawing and Starting Anew (1940-1949)

The Baptist Convention of Japan (Nihon Baputesuto Kyōdan) held its first general meeting January 3-5, 1940, in the ancient castle town of Himeji. The 200 delegates, said the Mission's 1940 report to the Board, "represented the ten thousand active Baptists in Japan." This was hyperbole. The nationwide Convention reported a total of 89 churches and 6,863 members, of whom 2,556 were active or resident members. Baptists still lagged far behind the Presbyterian-Reformed denomination (55,372 members), Methodists (50,505), Congregationalists (33,523), and Episcopalians (28,587).[1]

Most of the delegates to the Himeji convention, especially those from the East Japan churches, were pleased that Japanese Baptists had united. The Mason-Dixon line superimposed on the land by American missionaries a half-century before had at last been expunged. Although this achievement owed more to pressures from without than to strivings from within, the dire implications of the governmental squeeze were conveniently ignored. Max Garrott, then on furlough, told Southern Baptists that the union would mean "new vigor, new initiative, new power and effectiveness for Christ in Japan."[2]

Three main objectives were proposed for the decade ahead: "to multiply the membership of the churches by means of evangelistic campaigns; to double the number of churches; to increase self-support by placing emphasis on tithing."[3] In retrospect, these objectives sound like whistling in the dark; five years of repression and decline lay immediately ahead. But the deep-seated faith that inspired these good intentions was to have its reward after the holocaust of war, when radical changes in the spiritual climate would make the goals realistic.

Chiba Yūgorō, the towering figure among Baptists, was elected president of the new Convention. Edwin Dozier, the only Southern Baptist missionary present,

[1]*ASBC, 1941*, 261; *NBRS*, 492; *Kirisutokyō nenkan, 1981*, 447.
[2]Garrott, "Jubilee in Japan," 6; *NBRS*, 492.
[3]*ASBC, 1941*, 261.

and Marlin D. Farnum, a Northern Baptist, were elected with eight Japanese to a committee for establishing a union seminary in Tokyo. The two missionaries were also asked to serve as corresponding secretaries for communications between the Convention and the two supporting boards in America. Wrote Dozier: "The strain is great. . . . God grant that I have made no blunders."[4]

The new Convention comprised five *bukai* or district associations: Tōhoku (northern Japan), Kantō (Tokyo area), Kansai (central Japan), Naikai (Inland Sea region, including Hiroshima), and Seinan (Kyushu and Okinawa). Okinawa, a banana-shaped island 350 miles south of Kyushu, had been a Northern Baptist field since 1891. Therefore no district association was composed of West Japan Baptists exclusively.[5]

In May 1940, the trustees of the legal person that the Mission had relinquished to West Japan Baptists met to decide the disposition of property under their control. They voted to turn over all churches and pastoriums to the nationwide Convention but to retain Mission residences, the Tokyo dormitory, and some miscellaneous properties. In 1941, on the advice of Orient Secretary Rankin, the Mission residences in Kumamoto, Nagasaki, and Shimonoseki were sold and the proceeds placed in a church building fund. The residences in Tokyo and Hiroshima were given to Seinan Gakuin. The sale of these two properties, along with a summer house at Karuizawa donated by Edwin Dozier, yielded ¥172,000, which the school wisely used to purchase additional land and strengthen the endowment fund. The Mission residences at Seinan Gakuin and Seinan Jo Gakuin were retained.[6]

Japan Baptist Theological Seminary (Nihon Baputesuto Shingakkō) opened in April 1940 at an attractive dormitory in Den'enchōfu, Tokyo, overlooking the Tama River. East Japan Baptists had built the dormitory after discontinuing its seminary at Yokohama and affiliating with the theology department of Aoyama Gakuin (Methodist) in 1937. Chiba served the new Baptist institution as president and teacher of homiletics and pastoral ministry. Kuriya Hiroji, the only Japanese teacher to transfer from the discontinued Fukuoka seminary, was dean of the faculty and professor of Old Testament. The other full-time teachers included two Japanese and two missionaries. Northern Baptist D. C. Holtom, the renowned authority on Shinto, taught church history and the science of religion. Max Garrott, the other missionary, taught New Testament Greek. He assumed his duties in September after completing furlough study in New Testament and missions at Union Theological Seminary in New York. The student body consisted of nine men: two from the former West Japan Convention, four from the East

[4]EBD notes, 1940; *NBRS*, 491.

[5]*NBRS*, 492.

[6]EBD notes, 1940; *Seinan Gakuin nanajūnen shi*, 1:477-78; EBD, "Report to the Foreign Mission Board of the Southern Baptist Convention," 12 Dec. 1946 (typescript; EBD papers), 21.

Japan churches, and three Koreans from Manchuria "who wished to further their study of the Bible."[7]

The joint seminary in Tokyo admitted only male students, but the Bible Training School in Fukuoka, dating from 1935, continued to prepare women for ministry. Maude Dozier had tried unsuccessfully to move the school to the campus of Seinan Jo Gakuin and add a kindergarten department. In April 1940 approval was given by the Ministry of Education to establish the Seinan Kindergarten Teachers' School (Seinan Hobo Gakuin) in the vacated seminary building in Jigyō, Fukuoka. Fukunaga Tsugi, a pastor's widow in Kobe, was obtained as principal, and Maizuru Kindergarten was integrated into the new school for students' practical training. Nine students enrolled in the first class.[8]

In Maude's view, the new school was the kindergarten department of the Training School, parallel to the Bible department. But the Bible department had no official recognition, and it graduated its last student in March 1941. To provide a more suitable home for the Kindergarten Teachers' School, a campus site of 1,014 tsubo in Torikai, Fukuoka, was purchased for $12,048, and a spacious two-story building was erected for about $23,000. The building was dedicated on an ominously stormy day in June 1941. It was the last tangible expression of the generosity of Southern Baptist women until after the Pacific War.[9]

The older schools were thriving in 1940. When the academic year opened in April, Seinan Gakuin had an enrollment of 1,409, and Seinan Jo Gakuin had about half that number. Chapel, Bible classes, and other religious programs were conducted as usual. In May, evangelistic campaigns were led by Kimura Seimatsu, the Congregational minister trained at Moody Bible Institute and often called the D. L. Moody of Japan. At Seinan Gakuin, reported Maude Dozier, 460 students and several teachers responded to the gospel invitations. Seinan Jo Gakuin's President Hara cabled the Board that "531 girls surrendered to Christ." As in the case of Paul Kanamori's revivals in the 1920s, however, few of the converts submitted to baptism.[10]

Though Maude Dozier was overjoyed at the response to Kimura's preaching at Seinan Gakuin, she still feared for the soul and life of the school soon to pass under full Japanese control. As the founder's widow and the living voice of his spirit, Maude spoke out forcefully for the absolute ban on Sunday sports voted by the missionary-dominated trustees in 1933. In September 1939 she had called a meeting of the school's leaders--President Mizumachi and nine others--to plead that the ban be enforced even at the cost of closing the school. In the tense, five-hour meeting, she had argued that the school would cease to be "true to Christ"

[7]*ASBC, 1941*, 261; *JCY, 1940*, 169; *Seinan Gakuin nanajūnen shi*, 1:448; *NBRS*, 497-98; Hamrick, "William Maxfield Garrott," 10.

[8]*Commission* 3 (Sept. 1940), 267; *Seinan Gakuin nanajūnen shi*, 1:458-62.

[9]*Seinan Gakuin nanajūnen shi*, 1:458-62; *ASBC, 1941*, 264.

[10]*Commission* 3 (Sept. 1940), 260-61; EBD notes, 1940.

when it ceased to keep the sabbath. Maude's view did not prevail. In April 1940 the Ministry of Education, which had frowned on the ban all along, advised the school that athletic matches and other competitions should be held on Sundays, when they would not interfere with classes.[11] This directive portended stricter wartime controls to come. Seinan Gakuin survived as a Christian school by a policy of limited compromise such as the ousted Bouldin had advocated. To this day Sunday activities are restricted but not rigidly banned.

Growing Tensions and Restrictions

In the early months of 1940 the missionaries were still able to carry out their assignments without hindrance from the authorities. Franklin Ray, Mission chairman, was engaged in evangelistic work at Hiroshima, while his wife Daisy was recuperating from surgery performed in Shanghai. Ernest Mills, Mission treasurer, was teaching Bible classes in Nagasaki. Naomi Schell, though handicapped by "insidious creeping paralysis" that had begun with numbness in her hands, was working tirelessly in Tobata. Cecile Lancaster and Alma Graves were teaching English and Bible at Seinan Jo Gakuin. The three Doziers--Edwin, Mary Ellen, and Maude--were doing school and church work in Fukuoka. Elizabeth Watkins was still contributing her services at Seinan Gakuin. In Tokyo, Floryne Miller reportedly was "studying hard on the language in a class of three." H. B. and Mabel Ramsour were hampered in their study by her illness (she was pregnant at the time) that kept her in bed most of April and May.[12]

More missionaries were sent out by the Board and enrolled in the Tokyo language school. Curly-haired Oswald Quick arrived in August in the company of the Garrotts; Robert and Mary Dyer arrived in September. Bob Dyer was a warm and outgoing six-footer. His wife was a gifted mezzo-soprano. During the following months, wrote Lancaster, Mary Dyer was "busy with classes and studying and using her beautiful voice for the glory of God."[13]

The new missionaries arrived at a critical juncture in the life of the nation. Since 1937, wartime conditions had prevailed: censorship, night-time blackouts, and long lines to purchase rationed items such as milk, rice, bread, and fuel. Such annoyances had become commonplace to the old hands in the Mission. Then in the late summer and early fall of 1940, an ominous chain of events aroused the fears of young and old alike. A pro-American prime minister was toppled after only six months in office, all political parties were dissolved, and a new cabinet

[11]*Seinan Gakuin nanajūnen shi*, 1:455-57.

[12]*Commission* 9 (May 1946), 132; M. E. Dozier to author, 17 July 1987; Watkins, "Autobiography," 120; *ASBC, 1941*, 264; EC minutes of Baptist Kyōdan, 16 May 1940, EBD papers.

[13]*ASBC, 1941*, 265; Fern Harrington Miles, *Captive Community* (Jefferson City, Tenn.: Mossy Creek Press, 1987), 12.

was installed with General Tōjō Hideki as army minister. In August seven leaders of the Salvation Army, who routinely sent reports to their London headquarters, were arrested on charges of espionage. This aroused more concern among Christians than had the suppression of Jehovah's Witnesses in 1939, when 52 members were prosecuted for alleged crimes against the state. In September the government signed a tripartite pact with Nazi Germany and Fascist Italy.[14]

In the newly hostile, sometimes hysterical, climate, missionaries often heard the word *spai* (spy) uttered by people about them on the streets and buses. They were under constant surveillance by "guardian angels," the policemen assigned to track all their movements. More upsetting than these "tails" were the frequent interrogations by the "thought police." Mary Ellen Dozier and Dorothy Garrott complained that they were often interrupted while trying to tend to the needs of their babies. During visits that would last an hour or more, they were repeatedly bombarded with loaded questions. They were asked their opinion of various government policies, the war in China, the bombing of Shanghai, the role of the emperor. Mary Ellen found the harassments less persistent after learning to say, on advice of an American consul, "I don't know; ask my husband."[15]

Elizabeth Watkins accepted her guardian angel as a "big brother." He came several times a week, napped in her easy chair, helped with chores, and accompanied her and her mother when they wanted to go out. Few "tails" were so pleasant to have around, and few missionaries as unflappable as Watkins. Even if the missionary felt no fear, any Japanese servant or friend who happened to be present would shake with fright when the dreaded police started asking questions. Soon it became apparent to the missionaries that the Japanese who had contacts with foreigners were themselves harassed and threatened with dire consequences.[16]

In the frightful months of August and September 1940, missionaries at the schools were replaced by Japanese teachers. At Seinan Gakuin, Edwin Dozier lost his positions as dean of the college literary department and teacher of Bible. At Seinan Jo Gakuin, where local rightists tried in vain to close down the school because of its militarily strategic location, the three missionary trustees and the two missionary teachers were asked to resign. Alma Graves was promptly transferred to Seinan Gakuin amid fears for her safety, since she had refused to participate in the ceremonial bowing toward the imperial palace in Tokyo. Cecile Lancaster was told that she might continue to teach if she lived off campus and commuted to her classes. But because "my presence was bringing undue anxiety and suspicion to my Japanese co-workers," Lancaster resigned from the school and moved to Tokyo. She lived with the Dyers in the compound at Koishikawa, where Pastor Yuya allowed her to teach a Sunday school class of high school girls.[17]

[14]Iglehart, *Century*, 227-30.
[15]M. E. Dozier, oral history.
[16]Ibid.; Watkins, "Autobiography," 88-89.
[17]M. E. Dozier, oral history; Lancaster, "My Life," 107-8.

Increasingly restricted in their work and isolated from their Japanese colleagues, the missionaries also began to receive notices from the American embassy and consulates warning them to leave Japan at once, especially wives, children, and the elderly. They all had to face the tough question of whether or not to quit the land to which God had called them. Secretary Rankin emphasized that the decision was to be made by each missionary and not by the Board.[18]

The first to leave were Naomi Schell and Alma Graves. Earlier, the Tobata church had asked the Board to build a residence for Schell and let her remain, but the Mission was convinced that her paralysis was serious and required treatment in the States. So during a visit to Japan in September, Rankin persuaded Schell to take a medical furlough. Alma Graves was granted an early furlough in order to accompany her to the Mayo Clinic. Afterwards the stricken woman was confined to a nursing home in Asheville, North Carolina. For some time before her death in 1946 at the age of 52, Schell was unable to move any part of her body. She could communicate only with her eyes, those eyes that for so long had looked upon the deprived slum-dwellers of Tobata and conveyed to them the wondrous love of Jesus.[19]

The next to leave Japan was Ernest Mills, who was due a regular furlough followed by retirement. Mills sailed on September 15, one day after Schell and Graves. For many years afterwards, until forced to enter Baptist Memorials Geriatric Hospital in San Angelo, Texas, he was a familiar figure around the campus of Southwestern Seminary. In October, the Ramsours packed up and went to Hawaii for the birth of their first child. In November, Maude Dozier and Elizabeth Watkins sent their mothers home together from the port of Kobe. Shocked at the hostile rudeness of the Japanese officials encountered there, Maude advised her daughter-in-law to evacuate at once while she could still get passage with her two children. Mary Ellen reluctantly sailed on November 25, leaving her husband behind in a fearful web of restraints. "It was the hardest move I ever made," she said in later years.[20]

The last Mission members to depart Japan in 1940 were Franklin and Daisy Ray, who sailed in mid-December. They retired from the Board one year later. Daisy, weakened by a long history of ailments, died in 1944. Franklin lived another 23 years in Jackson, Tennessee, where he rented out part of his house to students at Union University and befriended many "preacher boys." Prior to his death at the age of 95, he was the Board's oldest emeritus missionary.[21]

The political changes that shook Japan in the summer of 1940 profoundly affected the nationwide Baptist Convention and other Christian bodies. Protestant

[18]M. E. Dozier, oral history; EBD notes, 1940.

[19]EBD to Mission members, 9 Sept. 1940, EBD papers; *Commission* 9 (May 1946), 132; M. E. Dozier, oral history; Max Garrott interview.

[20]M. E. Dozier, oral history; *ASBC, 1941*, 264; *Commission* 25 (Feb. 1962), 59-60.

[21]*ASBC, 1941*, 278; *Commission* 30 (Nov. 1967), 25.

leaders met again and again to discuss the demands and likely demands of governmental bureaucrats. The Ministry of Education instructed Christian groups that no more foreign funds could be received after April 1941. It also announced that to qualify for official recognition under the Religious Bodies Law, a denomination had to have a minimum of 50 congregations and 5,000 members. The Baptist Convention met this requirement, as did six other denominations belonging to the National Christian Council. But 16 groups in the NCC were too small to qualify, as were many others not related to the NCC. Much confusion followed. Then all denominations came under heavy pressure from government officials and Protestant ecumenists to join in forming the United Church of Christ (Nihon Kirisuto Kyōdan).[22]

The nationwide Baptist Convention, still in its infancy, met in Tokyo in October 1940 for the second and last time. Of the 173 delegates present, 29 represented the Southwestern (Seinan) Association, including Edwin Dozier, Max Garrott, and Cecile Lancaster. It was voted that the Convention and all its related churches and organizations would accept financial assistance from abroad only until March 31, 1941, after which they would be fully self-supporting. A motion to express gratitude for the generous aid received from the two mission boards in America was passed with a round of applause.[23]

The main purpose of this meeting, and its predictable outcome, was to approve the Convention's participation in the United Church. After the closing session, the delegates joined in a mass rally of 20,000 Christians on the campus of Aoyama Gakuin. There the representatives of some 35 denominations--all the Protestant bodies except Seventh-day Adventists--pledged to give their full support to the nation's war effort and to join together in a single church. Such a move was anathema to Southern Baptists. "If organic union prevails," wrote Secretary Maddry, "there will be nothing for this Board to do, but to withdraw all assistance to Japan--personnel and funds." The Board's attitude toward church union was irrelevant, however, for the door was being shut by the rulers of Japan.[24]

Celebrations and Sad Farewells

Despite the merger of Baptists and the subsequent rush toward Protestant union in 1940, West Japan Baptists carried out plans made earlier to celebrate their jubilee. As noted above, it was not feasible to play up the coming of the first Southern Baptist missionaries in 1889. Instead, the 50 years were counted from the first Baptist service held in Kyushu, a service conducted by Evangelist Gotō in Wakamatsu on November 3, 1890. The anniversary plans included the

---

[22]Garrott to Mission members, 19 Sept. 1940, EBD papers; *JCY, 1940*, 24-28. An English translation of the Religious Bodies Law is given in *JCY, 1940*, 309-25.
[23]*NBRS*, 499-502.
[24]Maddry letter, 29 Jan. 1941, quoted in EBD notes; *NBRS*, 502-3.

writing of Edwin Dozier's history of Southern Baptist work, whose English version was published under the title *A Golden Milestone in Japan*. Also included were the spring evangelistic campaigns conducted by Kimura Seimatsu in the two schools, as mentioned before, and in many of the churches.[25]

The celebrations culminated in a subdued service held on November 3 at the Fukuoka church, for which permission had been obtained from government authorities. About 150 persons attended. The service opened with the required singing of the national anthem and the offering of silent prayer towards the imperial palace. The congregation sang "A Mighty Fortress Is Our God," and special music was provided by the Seinan Jo Gakuin choir and the Seinan Gakuin glee club. Congratulatory messages were given by Chiba, who had come from Tokyo, and Rankin, who had come from Shanghai.[26]

The highlight of the program was a solemn remembrance of deceased persons who had contributed significantly to the work. Included were eight pastors, one layman, and eight missionaries. The missionaries were McCollum, Maynard, Walne, Medling, Willingham, Rowe, Dozier, and Lucile Clarke. The selection of Lucile as the only deceased woman to be honored testifies to the impact of her winsome personality as well as her role in establishing Seinan Jo Gakuin. In contrast, the name of Grace Mills, who founded the Maizuru Kindergarten, is conspicuous by its absence.[27]

Living pastors and missionaries with long years of service were honored with citations and gifts. The missionaries were Dru McCollum, Maude Dozier, Harvey Clarke, the Rays, the Bouldins, and Ernest Mills. The Bouldins stand out because they had been forced to resign by the Mission. The most surprising omissions are Claudia Walne and Hooker Chiles Rowe, both of whom had served long and well. Only three of the honored missionaries were present for the occasion: Maude Dozier, Daisy Ray, and George Bouldin. Pastor Shimose expressed gratitude for "the love, prayers, sacrifice, and gift of lives" that had been provided by the Foreign Mission Board.[28]

With so many missionaries leaving the field in the months preceding and following this anniversary celebration, it seemed that Japanese Baptists were carrying out the proposal made a generation earlier by Presbyterian Uemura Masahisa that the honorable missionaries be "clothed in brocade and returned to

[25]*ASBC, 1941*, 263.

[26]Ibid.; *NBRS*, 492-97.

[27]*ASBC, 1941*, 263; *NBRS*, 495-96. The deceased pastors honored were Kawakatsu, Sugano, Gotō, Fujinuma Ryōken, Satō, Obata Sadaie, Ozaki, and Ueyama; the layman was Tsuruhara.

[28]*ASBC, 1941*, 263; *NBRS*, 495-96. The living pastors honored were Arase, Takahashi, Shimose, Kuroda, and Amano.

their native villages."[29] Uemura's advocacy of an independent Japanese church free of missionary money and control had met with considerable opposition at the time, but in the political climate of 1940, his was the dominant view. The government not only had demanded the cut-off of foreign funds received by the churches but also was prodding the missionaries to pack up and leave.

Those missionaries still in Japan in early 1941 faced severe trials. Dorothy Garrott had to cook and heat water on a charcoal hibachi that emitted toxic fumes. The Garrotts had borrowed a kerosene heater from the Bouldins in Yokohama, but the wick burned up and no replacement could be found. Oppressed by the cold and the care of a baby under rigorous conditions, Dorothy complained to her husband that she was "so uncomfortable." "Did you come to Japan to be comfortable?" he asked. On March 6, after the U.S. consulate had issued its third warning against staying in Japan, Dorothy and daughter Elizabeth sailed for home. Cecile Lancaster followed on March 27. Max Garrott, who had been Mission treasurer since October 1940, wished to remain and serve as a link between the Baptists of Japan and those in America if war should come. "I do feel at present more strongly than in 1934," said Max, "that He wants me here."[30]

In Fukuoka, self-supporting Elizabeth Watkins faced a crisis. The demand for English instruction was dwindling; English signs were being removed from railway stations and other public places. But Watkins stubbornly insisted that God had called her to Japan and that no government official, whether Japanese or American, could force her to leave. Then restrictions tightened. She had to sever her connection with the Garden of Love. She found herself virtually confined to her home and dependent on friends to do her shopping. A family to whom she sent a note of thanks for a gift of chocolates was harassed by the police. When she realized that "my presence was causing my dear Japanese friends to suffer," Watkins conceded that God was telling her to pack.[31]

Edwin Dozier lamented that "by government decree" missionaries were prohibited from teaching Bible in the schools, preaching in the churches, and doing organized evangelistic work. "The only thing that helped keep my equilibrium and spirit as a missionary," he afterwards wrote, "was the request of two college students . . . asking me to have an English Bible study for them at the church and have personal soul-winning contacts with other students." Even Edwin became a burden to others. Whenever President Mizumachi called on the Doziers, for instance, the police would be waiting at his house to interrogate him about the visit. So on April 11, after Maude had made a rushed-up visit under police escort

---

[29]John F. Howes, "Japanese Christians and American Missionaries," in *Changing Japanese Attitudes Toward Modernization*, ed. Marius B. Jansen (Princeton: Princeton University Press, 1965), 361.

[30]D. Garrott, oral history; Max Garrott in *JCQ* 16 (1941): 54.

[31]Watkins, "Autobiography," 88-92; *ASBC, 1941*, 265.

to her husband's grave in Kokura, the three Kyushu holdouts tearfully sailed for Hawaii. Max Garrott remained, the only Southern Baptist missionary in Japan.[32]

Maude and Edwin Dozier took up residence in Honolulu for Japanese-language work. Mary Ellen, who had been waiting in North Carolina, joined her husband in May, bringing their two children and Maude's mother, Mrs. Burke. Elizabeth Watkins lived with her mother in Spartanburg, South Carolina, where she worked in a shirt factory, sold encyclopedias, and served in her home church.[33]

The four language students still in Tokyo in early 1941 had been transferred to two of the Board's five missions in China. "I think the Lord called me to Japan," Bob Dyer had said, "but I wouldn't put it past him to call me somewhere else." Though assigned to the South China Mission, the Dyers were sent to the College of Chinese Studies at Baguio in the Philippines, then an American possession. The school had been moved from Peking to avoid possible trouble with the Japanese. Oz Quick, also assigned to South China, went directly to Kweilen. Floryne Miller was transferred to the Central China Mission and sent to Shanghai to teach English in the North Gate Middle School. Since Shanghai was under Japanese control, Miller was required to wear an armband with the letter A to show that she was an American.[34]

Some of the missionaries who had left Japan in 1940 were likewise reassigned in 1941. Alma Graves became head of the English department in the Baptist college at Iwo, Nigeria. The H. B. Ramsours, who were among the 11 organizers of the Hawaii mission in December 1940, moved on to Buenos Aires, Argentina, where he taught in the Baptist seminary. They returned to Hawaii in 1946 and served there until 1960, when the Board was turning the work over to the Hawaii Baptist Convention (Hawaii attained statehood in 1959). Then Ramsour was elected president of the Mexican Baptist Bible Institute in San Antonio (now Hispanic Baptist Theological Seminary) and filled that position until his retirement in 1976.[35]

The Missionaries in Wartime

The only missionaries still assigned to Japan when Pearl Harbor was bombed in December 1941 were the Garrotts, Lancaster, and Schell. Except for Max Garrott, each was on furlough status. Garrott was one of just over a hundred Protestant missionaries and several hundred Catholic missionaries remaining in

[32]EBD, "Mission and Convention," 18; M. E. Dozier, oral history.
[33]M. E. Dozier, oral history; Watkins, "Autobiography," 93-95.
[34]Barker, "Life of Floryne Miller," 4.
[35]ASBC, 1943, 144, 158; Southwestern News, Feb. 1988, 7.

Japan when the Pacific War began. Most were interned, and all communications with the outside world were cut off.[36]

On Monday, December 8, Garrott was riding a local train to the home of Northern Baptist missionary William Axling when he learned that war had erupted between Japan and the United States. He saw the shocking headlines on a newspaper that a fellow passenger was reading. The next morning Garrott was interned ("for your own protection," the police told him) at Sumire Girls' School, a Catholic school and orphanage in Den'enchōfu, Tokyo. He was assigned to a room with 12 other American men, a room barely large enough for the cots and beds wedged into it. "Safe, well, profitably interned," wrote Max to Dorothy through the good offices of the Swiss Red Cross. Though some missionaries were tortured by police interrogators during those early months of the war, Max was not mistreated. He even had the use of his piano, which kind officials had transported from his house to the school. They also had brought a picture of his wife. Since the internees were allowed to buy food in addition to what was served them by the authorities, and some talented cooks were among them, Max soon gained back the 10 pounds he had lost doing his own cooking after Dorothy's departure. The next spring he and his fellow Americans had strawberry shortcake "running out of their ears."[37]

Humanitarian treatment was also the lot of Floryne Miller in Shanghai, who though an enemy alien was allowed to continue her teaching until February 1943. "Wouldn't it be fun," she wrote to her family in January 1942, "if this should get to you one of these days." The letter was delivered. In 1943, while awaiting repatriation, she spent seven months in Chapel Civil Assembly Center, an internment camp outside Shanghai. "Everyone is so good to us," she reported through the Red Cross.[38] Words to the contrary would have been ill-advised, of course.

Far less fortunate were those who had transferred to the South China Mission. Oz Quick was in Hong Kong when the city fell to the Japanese on Christmas Day, 1941. He had gone there for medical treatment after falling ill with appendicitis at Kweilin. Quick was committed to Stanley Prison with about 300 Americans, including four other Southern Baptist missionaries and Secretary Rankin. They had no furniture or furnishings of any kind, and food was so scarce that Rankin, already trim, lost 30 pounds during the half-year's confinement.[39]

The Robert Dyers were among eight Southern Baptist missionaries interned in the Philippines with about 500 American and British civilians. One of the eight

[36]*JCY, 1950*, 31.

[37]W. Maxfield Garrott, *Japan Advances* (Nashville: Convention Press, 1956), 118; D. Garrott, oral history.

[38]Barker, "Floryne Miller," 4-5.

[39]J. B. Weatherspoon, *M. Theron Rankin: Apostle of Advance* (Nashville: Broadman Press, 1958), 93-95.

was Rufus Gray, who was judged a spy because he had taken many pictures while in Peking (photography was his hobby) and had made friends among the Chinese. He died under torture by a Japanese intelligence unit. Bob Dyer was taken twice to the "house of horror" for interrogation, an ordeal that has haunted him ever since. As orderly to the sick in the camp's makeshift hospital and undertaker to those who succumbed to malnutrition and disease, Bob lived with the specter of death day after day. Mary Dyer helped to boost the morale of the living with her magnificent renderings of hymns, wedding songs, and "God Bless America." In 1944 the internees were transferred to Manila's infamous Bilibid Prison, from which they were liberated by American forces in February 1945. Most were on the verge of starvation. After returning to the United States the Dyers resigned from the Board. Bob taught religion at Wake Forest University until his retirement in 1983, and Mary gave private voice and piano lessons.[40]

In June 1942 Max Garrott was put aboard the SS *Asama Maru* for repatriation to his homeland in the first of two prisoner exchanges arranged through the medium of the Swiss government. The ship left Yokohama with about 430 passengers, mostly notably U.S. ambassador Joseph P. Grew and Mrs. Grew (she had refused evacuation with other dependents). At Hong Kong it picked up 370 more Americans, including Oz Quick and Theron Rankin. The exchange ship had large crosses painted bow and stern for identification, but because of a large Japanese flag painted in the center, the vessel was nearly torpedoed by an American submarine when off course.[41]

After a second stop at Saigon, the *Asama Maru* proceeded to Singapore for a rendezvous with the *Conte Verde*, an Italian ship under Japanese control that carried 600 passengers from Shanghai. The two ships steamed to the Portuguese port of Lourenço Marques in Mozambique, where 1,500 Japanese from the United States were waiting aboard the SS *Gripsholm*, a Swedish vessel leased for this trip by the American Export Line. The Japanese exchanged ships by marching from bow to bow, while the Americans moved from stern to stern. Among the 1,500 Americans, just under 600 were missionaries and their families. Forty of the missionaries were Southern Baptists, 39 from China and one--Garrott--from Japan. One of the China missionaries, Pearl Todd, later served in Japan.[42]

[40]Robert Allen Dyer, "The Power of Hunger," chapel message at Wake Forest University, Oct. 22, 1987; Miles, *Captive Community*, 60, 125, 146; Fern Harrington Miles, "Captive Community Update," 25 Jan. 1988, mimeographed, 2.

[41]John Coventry Smith, *From Colonialism to World Community* (Philadelphia: Geneva Press, 1982), 102-10; U. Alexis Johnson with Jef Olivarius McAllister, *The Right Hand of Power* (Englewood Cliffs, N.J.: Prentice-Hall, 1984), 58-59. Authors Smith and Johnson were among Garrott's fellow passengers.

[42]*ASBC, 1943*, 135; Smith, *World Community*, 102-20; Johnson, *Right Hand of Power*, 58-59.

The trip from Japan to America took 10 weeks, half of them on the *Gripsholm*. The fixed price per person was $575, regardless of what accommodations one had. This made for some irritation on the overcrowded *Gripsholm*, but all were delighted with the sumptuous American meals, showers, fresh sheets, recent news from the homeland, and the delicious atmosphere of freedom.[43]

After one stop en route, at Rio de Janeiro, the *Gripsholm* reached New York on August 25, 1942. Passengers without diplomatic status had to be screened for loyalty to the United States, a process that took several days. Three intelligence officers--from the FBI, Army, and Navy--examined each passenger, using dossiers prepared from earlier inquiries made of family members and acquaintances. Garrott met with difficulty because of his conviction that he could not take part in the war effort. He endured several hours of interrogation before he was permitted to go ashore.[44]

In the second prisoner exchange carried out during the war, 39 Southern Baptist missionaries reached New York aboard the *Gripsholm* on December 1, 1943. They included Floryne Miller and three others from China who later served in Japan: Rose Marlowe and Frank and Mary Connely. When all were ashore and assembled in the Prince George Hotel, they listened to words of welcome and counsel from Maddry, Rankin, and W. O. Carver. Maddry shared the good news that the Board had at last paid off the debt that had burdened it since 1922 and was building up a fund for a greatly expanded mission effort in the postwar era.[45]

Cecile Lancaster meanwhile had spent two years in Houston, Texas, ministering to Japanese immigrants and especially to the Nisei, the immigrants' children born in America. Reiji Hoshizaki, a Nisei student at Baylor University and a future missionary to Japan, used his booming voice to give a powerful testimony for Christ at one of her meetings. In 1943 Lancaster accepted a position as school teacher in the Gila River Project in Arizona, one of the relocation centers for some 120,000 persons of Japanese ancestry--77,000 American citizens and 43,000 resident aliens--who had been forcibly evacuated from the West Coast after the attack on Pearl Harbor. The camp consisted of many rows of white barracks that housed 10,000 parents and children. Normally, missionaries and ministers were not permitted to live on the project, but Lancaster lived there with the status of teacher. She was delighted to find Hoshizaki's family, evacuees from California, living in the next block from her own barrack. At Cecile's suggestion, Elizabeth Watkins also applied for a teaching position. She was assigned to another division of the project four miles away. These two single women and their mothers who lived with them contributed to a positive Christian witness in the camps.[46]

---

[43]Smith, *World Community*, 110; Johnson, *Right Hand of Power*, 59.
[44]Hamrick, "William Maxfield Garrott," 12.
[45]*ASBC, 1944*, 197; *Baptist Courier*, 23 Dec. 1943, 7.
[46]*Baptist Courier*, 16 Dec. 1943, 7; Lancaster, "My Life," 114-17.

About 15,000 evacuees from the West Coast were brought to the Rohwer and Jerome centers in Arkansas. At the Board's request, the Garrotts, who had taken over Lancaster's work in Houston for several months, moved to McGehee, Arkansas, to evangelize and help relocate the people at these centers. When the Home Mission Board claimed oversight of the work, the Garrotts were loaned to that board temporarily. Max preached for the Christian groups both in English and Japanese. Dorothy obtained a teaching position in one of the centers, which qualified the Garrotts to live inside the camp where they were able to serve the people more effectively.[47]

In 1941 the Japanese community in Hawaii numbered about 155,000, or 37 percent of the total population. Maude, Edwin, and Mary Ellen Dozier visited in their homes and drew many of these people to Honolulu's interracial Olivet Baptist Church, where Edwin was pastor of the Japanese-speaking congregation. Maude taught evening English classes for the Japanese, and Mary Ellen worked with Olivet's English-speaking congregation. Edwin also preached in Japanese on the radio. He and Maude both taught in the newly opened Baptist Bible School.[48]

When Japanese planes attacked Pearl Harbor on Sunday, December 7, the Doziers could see and hear the antiaircraft fire from their mountainside apartment in Honolulu. When told what was happening, Japan-born Edwin said, "It can't be! I think this is a maneuver." During the previous months he had turned down requests that he work with the American Secret Service in Hawaii, but on that first night of the war he was pressed into service for his needed skills. He was urged to accept an Army officer's commission and later to take an assignment in Washington, D.C., but during the 18 months he was employed by the government, Edwin remained a civilian and worked only in Hawaii. Though on leave of absence from the Board, he continued to lead the Japanese-speaking congregation at Olivet Church and often flew from island to island preaching to other Japanese congregations. One of these was the Waimea church on Kauai, where the father of Tom and Asano Masaki was converted from Buddhism. Both Tom and Asano (she married Reiji Hoshizaki) were appointed to Japan after the war.[49]

In April 1945, when Okinawa was under siege and the Japanese Empire had all but crumbled, two couples--Coleman and Jabe Clarke, Tucker and Elizabeth Callaway--were appointed to Japan with the understanding that they would serve temporarily in Hawaii. The Clarkes and Callaways were among the first missionaries--a group of 38 bound for 10 different countries--commissioned by

[47]*Baptist Courier*, 16 Dec. 1943, 7; D. Garrott, oral history. In 1988, to redress in part the injustice done to Japanese-American internees, Congress voted to pay $20,000 to each of an estimated 60,000 survivors (*Japan Times*, 3 Aug. 1988).

[48]*ASBC, 1942*, 234-35.

[49]Ibid.; M. E. Dozier, oral history; L. Whaley, *Edwin Dozier of Japan*, 169; *ASBC, 1943*, 201; Goki Saitō, "Life, Work, and Contributions of Edwin B. Dozier in Japan" (Th.M. thesis, Southern Baptist Theological Seminary, 1971), 39.

Theron Rankin, who in January had succeeded Maddry as the Board's executive secretary. It was not a felicitous time to identify oneself with Japan. "My parents thought I had lost my mind," said Callaway. Many of his church members saw him "as a traitor to my country."[50]

That autumn the Clarkes went to the island of Kauai, joining Cecile Lancaster and her mother who had arrived a short time before. Coleman served as pastor of the Waimea Baptist Church. The Callaways went to the pastorate of Wahiawa Church on the island of Oahu.[51]

Distress and Destruction in Japan

Though the Doziers, the Garrotts, Lancaster, and Watkins were able to put their Japan experience to good use in Hawaii, Arkansas, Texas, and Arizona, they could not forget the Japanese Baptists from whom they were separated. With all communications cut off, they could only speculate about the hardships borne by their beloved coworkers and pray for their safekeeping. Not until peace had been restored did the missionaries learn that Christians in Japan had suffered far more than they had imagined.

As noted already, Japanese Baptists had joined the United Church, which eventually comprised 34 Protestant denominations. The 34 denominations were grouped into 11 blocs or branches, of which Baptists were bloc 4. Like most other Protestants, Baptists expected the United Church to be a federation of denominations that allowed considerable autonomy in creed, mode of worship, and evangelistic work. To the contrary, the government required a thoroughly authoritarian structure, abolishing the bloc system in November 1942. The Baptist seminary in Tokyo had been closed in March 1942, and Baptists were no longer allowed any functions as a group. It should be noted, however, that the head of the United Church exercised his vast authority mainly through the representatives of the former denominations, including the Baptist leader Chiba.[52]

Baptist pastors and many other Christian leaders suffered peculiar trials in addition to the wartime disruptions experienced by nearly all Japanese. Their former friendly ties with Americans, their continuing allegiance to a foreign religion closely identified with America and England, their worship of a God seen as a rival to the emperor-god, their defeatist or pacifist attitudes toward the war effort--all these factors made them suspect in the eyes of ultranationalists. They were interrogated as often as every day, at home or in a police detention house. They were required to begin church services with a five-minute ceremony of bowing to the emperor and praying for the war heroes. No hymn could be sung

---

[50]Callaway newsletter, 1 Jan. 1986; *ASBC, 1946*, 292.

[51]*ASBC, 1946*, 286-88.

[52]Iglehart, *Century*, 233-43; EBD, *Japan's New Day*, 109-10.

that made mention of God or Christ as king or that referred to the Second Coming, a "treasonous" doctrine which inferred that Christ would judge even the emperor. The sermon, always preached against the backdrop of a national flag and often monitored by the thought police, had to be in keeping with the war effort. Many parsonages, like most other homes, were required to have a Shinto godshelf or a tablet symbolizing Amaterasu, the sun goddess and alleged ancestress of the emperor.[53]

Since Seventh-day Adventists had stubbornly refused to join the United Church, insisting on separate recognition, the 42 ministers and chief lay leaders of that denomination were arrested and jailed in 1943. Six were still in prison when the war ended. About two-thirds of the Episcopal churches had also refused to join, insisting that they were not a Protestant denomination. Several of their bishops were arrested and detained for three months. Ironically, the Christians who suffered the most were a group of ministers and lay leaders of the Holiness denominations, which obediently had joined the United Church as blocs 6 and 9. More than 100 were imprisoned, some were tortured, and eight died during incarceration or soon after release. Their "crime" was preaching the Second Coming and exalting Christ above the emperor.[54]

Most Baptists avoided persecution. They thought it better to obey government directives handed down through the United Church or local authorities than to appear disloyal. They chose to hedge the question when asked, "Which is greater, the emperor or Christ?" One pastor answered, "They are like air and water. You can't live without either of them." An exception was Namioka Saburō, president of the Northern Baptist girls' school in Himeji. He continued to teach Christianity at his school and declined to participate in shrine ceremonies, at which prayers were offered for victory. His only concession to the authorities was to send two or three girls to the ceremonies as token representatives of the school. Branded as antiwar, Namioka was summarily removed by the police and replaced by a non-Christian who converted the school along nationalist lines. Afterwards he was sent to a prison for felons, where he languished a full year and suffered extreme malnutrition.[55]

Among the 23 full-time pastors related to Southern Baptists at the start of the war, eight of the able-bodied younger men were drafted into military service or assigned to war-related civilian jobs. The last graduate of the joint Baptist seminary in Tokyo, Miyachi Osamu, served as a missionary to Palau in the Caroline Islands. His duties included "patriotic evangelism," or indoctrinating native Christians with the ethics of militarist Japan. Six pastors were lost to the

[53]Richard Terrill Baker, *Darkness of the Sun* (New York: Abingdon Cokesbury Press, 1947), 31-32; *Out of the Ashes: The Post War Decade in Japan* (Japan Missionary Fellowship of the ABFMS and the Woman's ABFMS, ca. 1956), 19, 23.

[54]*JCY, 1950,* 20-24.

[55]Baker, *Darkness of the Sun*, 49; *Out of the Ashes*, 18-25.

work by death or other reason, and three others had to evacuate to places of safety. Only six continued to lead West Japan churches throughout the war. Some of the pastorless churches met whenever possible under the leadership of the pastor's wife or a layman. Sunday schools and kindergartens were discontinued or severely reduced in size.[56]

During the last year of the war, American bombers rained destruction on more than 60 Japanese cities. Temple-studded Kyoto was spared for its cultural value as the ancient capital, and Kanazawa was saved by timely clouds, but all other major cities were heavily damaged. Three-fourths of Tokyo was leveled by fire bombs--100,000 civilians died in a single attack in March 1945--and Hiroshima and Nagasaki were demolished by the atomic bombs dropped on August 6 and 9. Japan surrendered on August 15.[57]

Out of a total of 1,184 Protestant church buildings in Japan proper, 507 were destroyed or badly damaged. Six churches related to Southern Baptists lost their buildings with their parsonages, while seven survived. The historic Fukuoka church burned to the ground in a massive air raid by more than 200 B-29s on June 19-20, 1945. The heart of Fukuoka City, whose population at the time was 322,000, was completely razed; only the periphery escaped damage. Left standing was the attractive Seinan Gakuin church built in 1935, which had been occupied by troops during the war (church services were held in the pastorium). The Hiroshima church was destroyed by the first atom bomb. The Nagasaki church suffered only broken glass, plaster, and roof tiles because the second bomb, called *Fat Man*, was a mile off target and the church was sheltered by the hill on which 26 Christians had been martyred in 1597.[58]

Christian schools also suffered heavy losses. In Yokohama, all 12 buildings of the Northern Baptist girls' school--Soshin Jo Gakko--were reduced to ashes, and the boys' school--Kantō Gakuin--lost all but one of its 17 buildings. Over 400 incendiary bombs were dropped by B-29s within the Kantō Gakuin campus. The Methodist schools in ill-fated Hiroshima and Nagasaki were demolished, and sprawling Aoyama Gakuin in Tokyo was mostly destroyed. The Methodist girls' school in Fukuoka lost its new chapel and most of its classrooms. It is remarkable

---

[56]EBD, "Report to the Board," 13-18; EBD, *Japan's New Day*, 129, 135-36. Five of the conscripted pastors rose to prominence in the postwar era: Miyoshi Toshio, Matsumura Shūichi, Arase Noboru, Ozaki Shuichi, and Kimura Buntarō.

[57]Drummond, *History*, 269.

[58]Ibid.; *Fukuoka ken hyakka jiten*, s.v. "Fukuoka shi"; EBD, "Japan Faces the Sunrise," in M. Theron Rankin and others, *Light for the Whole World* (Nashville: Broadman Press, 1948), 25-32; EBD, *Japan's New Day*, 135; *ASBC, 1948*, 110; *Time*, 10 Aug. 1970, 26. The other surviving churches, all surrounded by devastation, were Ijuin, Kumamoto, Tobata, Mt. Zion, and Shimonoseki. Others destroyed were Kagoshima, Kokura, Moji, and Nishi Sugamo.

that all three schools started by Southern Baptists were left standing, though extensive areas nearby lay in ruins.[59]

In Fukuoka's Daimyō-machi, where Seinan Gakuin had first been located, 2,800 out of 2,979 houses and buildings were destroyed. It was fortunate that the campus had been moved to Nishijin, which lay at the edge of the city outside the awful ring of destruction. Several incendiary bombs were dropped on the campus, but all except one fell into tree branches and failed to explode. The one that exploded fell on open ground, where it was quickly extinguished. At war's end the school buildings were greatly in need of repair, for most windows were broken from concussion, and all ceilings had been removed on government orders as protection against the fire bombs.[60]

Classes were conducted at Seinan Gakuin throughout the war. Trials were many, but thanks to President Mizumachi and others, the school retained its Christian character. It never had a military instructor who demanded that a Shinto godshelf be erected on the school grounds, as was the case in most other schools. In 1943 the Ministry of Education shut down the English literature department, and in 1944 the college was reorganized as Seinan Economics College. The Ministry's attempt to merge the school with two others, however, was successfully resisted. Enrollment dropped to about 200 each in the college and middle school, and classwork was reduced to a minimum since faculty and students were commandeered as labor in war-related projects.[61]

How different it was in the first year after the war. The battered campus teemed with students. Enrollment in the college and middle school more than doubled to 880, and newly offered night classes in English drew another 300 students. American G.I.s stationed in the area as occupation forces also made use of the shabby facilities. A large sign read: "Youth for Christ Rally Each Saturday Night at the Baptist Christian College."[62]

The Kindergarten Teachers' School, operating on a shoestring, survived the war only because Principal Fukunaga and her assistants were willing to live sacrificially on severely reduced wages. In 1946 the school was training more than 50 students and caring for 10 little orphans.[63]

Seinan Jo Gakuin also remained open throughout the war, though it suffered much interference from fanatical nationalists. The cream-colored Rowe Memorial Chapel was painted black and green as camouflage, and antiaircraft guns were installed on the roof. In 1943 President Hara was ordered by prefectural authorities to close the institution and distribute the students and teachers among

---

[59]Iglehart, *Century*, 287; *Out of the Ashes*, 45; T. T. Brumbaugh, *Christ for All Japan* (New York: Friendship Press, 1947), 4-15.

[60]*Seinan Gakuin nanajūnen shi*, 1:488-500.

[61]EBD, "Report to the Board," 19-22; EBD, *Japan's New Day*, 97-98.

[62]*ASBC, 1946*, 241-44.

[63]*ASBC, 1946*, 246-47; *ASBC, 1948*, 111.

other schools. The military establishment had decided to take over the whole campus as headquarters for the Western Air Defense. Backed by his PTA, Hara persuaded the authorities to allow the school to continue its distinctive program of education. Classes were moved to rented quarters in several different places off campus, including a Buddhist temple. Enrollment dropped to less than 300, and all except the first-year students were required to work in an electric factory, the railroad yards, or the arsenal. Despite these adverse circumstances, Hara managed "to conduct Christian services regularly in the corners of noisy and scornful workshops."[64]

Providence was especially kind to Seinan Jo Gakuin. Kokura--or more precisely, it is alleged, the prominent tower of Rowe chapel--was the intended target of the second atom bomb. *Fat Man* was dropped on Nagasaki instead because Kokura was covered by thick clouds that day. The school also escaped the conventional bombings that razed parts of Kokura and the adjoining cities of Yawata, Wakamatsu, and Moji. After the campus had been vacated by the Japanese army--the buildings had deteriorated and the playgrounds had been turned into sweet potato patches-- President Hara obtained permission from the American occupation authorities to resume classes there. "It was a day that we can never forget," wrote Hara in his diary, "that day when students and teachers gaily marched up the slope to Mt. Zion campus carrying desks, chairs, blackboards, etc., singing hymns of praise to our God who had brought us 'out of exile' back to our dear Alma Mater."[65]

Restoring the Ties Disrupted by War

The vital flow of information that had been severed by the war was reopened by Baptist chaplains in the occupation forces. These chaplains provided the Board and its Japan missionaries with eye-witness accounts of conditions in Japan and made available their good offices for the exchange of correspondence with Japanese Baptist leaders. Wrote Hara: "Send back our old missionaries as soon as possible and appoint new ones as many as possible." Pastor Yuya of Tokyo appealed especially for medical missionaries. He wanted the Board to establish a hospital and sanitarium with a nursing school attached, an institution that would demonstrate Christ's love for the sick and wounded, too often considered "damaged goods." Yuya also asked for missionaries "who can lead and rearrange the ways of agriculture in Japan in the future." Secretary Rankin replied that "we

---

[64]Hara letter in *Commission* 11 (Apr. 1948), 99; *ASBC, 1946*, 247; EBD, "Report to the Board," 19-20; Akiko Endo, *Ring in the New* (Nashville: Broadman Press, 1949), 68-69; Lancaster, "My Life," 150.

[65]Hara as quoted in Lancaster, "My Life," 150; *Commission* 11 (Apr. 1948), 99.

shall be glad to study these matters with you and other Japanese leaders just as soon as we can get in direct touch with you."[66]

In the early phase of the occupation, missionaries were not admitted to Japan except for a few representatives of churches and boards that had begun work before the war. The chief chaplain at General Douglas MacArthur's headquarters in Tokyo urged the Board to "send one mature, level-headed former missionary to Japan, who has had not less than eight years here." In response, the Board designated as its special emissary Edwin Dozier, who was issued a passport in July 1946 along with the required military entry permit. Leaving his family in Charlotte, Dozier sailed from Galveston in a freighter, *Kendall Fish*, and reached Kobe on October 30. He resided at the Yuya home in Tokyo, from which he made a 10-day survey trip to Kyushu in the second half of November. Among the numerous friends who greeted him was Kawano Sadamoto, a former student at Southern Seminary and a future chancellor (1955-61) of Seinan Gakuin. "When I gripped his hand," wrote Dozier, "he stood there sobbing with his whole frame shaken with deep emotion. I wept too."[67]

Dozier learned that missionaries were greatly desired: evangelistic couples for cities all over Japan, teachers in various fields for the schools in Fukuoka and Kokura, publication workers, student workers, doctors, nurses, a couple for agriculture and forestry, and a couple for animal husbandry. Except for the last two items, afterwards deleted, these personnel requests were filled over the next few years. In one discussion of missionary needs, Hara asked Dozier, "Can we count on the young lady missionaries not to use rouge and lipstick?" Dozier could give no assurance except that "they will not come like painted dolls like some of the dependents of the armed forces." The number of military dependents rose to 30,000 by the end of 1947.[68]

On November 23, 1946, Dozier met with pastors and other representatives of the West Japan churches in the faculty conference room of Seinan Gakuin College. He told the group that "Southern Baptists have received God's call to preach the Gospel in Japan and are therefore not waiting on the Japanese, Christian or non-Christian, to invite us." He explained that Southern Baptists wished "to join hands in the work with our former co-workers," but that they had refused to join the Federal Council of Churches in the United States and likewise would have nothing

---

[66]Hara to SB "breathren," 15 Dec. 1945, EBD papers; Yuya to M. T. Rankin, n.d., EBD papers; Rankin to Yuya, 3 June 1946, EBD papers. Chaplain Henry Austin wrote to EBD from Sasebo as early as 24 Sept. 1945.

[67]Chaplain Major W. H. Andrew, quoted in W. M. Garrott to EBD, 11 Jan. 1946; EBD, "Report to the Board," 5; EBD, *Japan's New Day*, 131-32.

[68]EBD, "Report to the Board," 8.

to do with the United Church in Japan. "Our desire in coming to Japan," he concluded, "is to cooperate with all who hold like faith with us."[69]

While Dozier had supper in town with PTA supporters of Seinan Gakuin, the church representatives discussed his proposal. When he rejoined their meeting, he was told that the representatives had reached a consensus. In keeping with their Baptist heritage, they would allow each church to decide whether or not to remain in the United Church. The churches that voted to withdraw could form a new organization for cooperation with Southern Baptists.[70]

After his return to Tokyo, Dozier spent many days preparing detailed reports for the Board. Since William Axling and other Northern Baptist missionaries were urging their churches not to leave the United Church, Dozier proposed the formation of a Baptist convention that would embrace the work of both Southern Baptists and Conservative Baptists. This suggestion was prompted by the report that a Conservative Baptist missionary would locate in Shimonoseki.[71] As it turned out, Conservative Baptists concentrated their work in northern Japan, and neither group sought to unite with the other.

During the cold winter months Dozier fell ill with pneumonia. In the spring, however, he was ready for "my second missionary journey," an extended trip to Kyushu that consumed most of April and May. Before leaving Tokyo he sent a gift of money to each church in Kyushu and explained in a letter that the money was a token of Southern Baptists' "esteem and affection." His schedule included numerous conferences, commencement addresses, and revivals. The evangelistic meetings that he held in Ōmuta, Nagasaki, Kumamoto, and Ijuin invariably drew large crowds and elicited many confessions of faith in Christ. Dozier was amazed and thrilled at the unprecedented interest in gospel preaching. The Japanese were responsive because their first-ever defeat in war, as General MacArthur pointed out, had brought about "the collapse of a faith," leaving a spiritual vacuum.[72]

On April 2, 1947, Dozier attended a "pastors' conference" at Seinan Gakuin Church that made history. Present were 23 Japanese and a few American military chaplains who had come as observers. The conference opened with a season of hymns, prayers, and devotional thoughts led by Chairman Kawano. Then a discussion was held on the relationship between the United Church and Baptist churches. Pastor Yuya, who before the war had so favored the United Church that Shimose Kamori called him "union crazy" (*gōdō kichigai*), explained that his Koishikawa church had freed itself from the wartime yoke by disbanding in 1944

---

[69]Ibid., 8-9. The Federal Council of Churches was superseded by the National Council of Churches in 1950.

[70]Ibid,. 9-10.

[71]EBD to B. J. Cauthen, 22 Jan. 1947.

[72]EBD, "A Supplementary Report to the Foreign Mission Board," 10 May 1947 (photocopy; EBD papers), 1-13, 19-25; Saitō, "Edwin B. Dozier," 48; Douglas MacArthur, *A Soldier Speaks* (New York: Praeger, 1965), 178.

and reorganizing as the independent Mejiro church. More recently, the Seinan Gakuin church had left the United Church by merely serving notice. It was recommended that each church follow one of these two methods to achieve independence. A discussion ensued on how the independent churches could form an association or convention for cooperative endeavors. Dozier recommended the adoption of a translated and adapted version of the 1945 constitution of the Hawaii Baptist Convention, excluding the bylaws but including the 10-article statement of faith, which was based on the New Hampshire Confession.[73]

The next day, Thursday, April 3, the group constituted itself a formal body to transact business. The roll was called, and privileges of the floor were extended to Dozier and the chaplains present. With Kawano in the moderator's chair, the representatives of 16 churches, 3 schools, and 2 social settlements voted unanimously to organize a Baptist convention. They then formed a circle. "Brother Yuya led in a fervent prayer of penitence, thanksgiving, and dedication," wrote Dozier. "Tears rolled unashamedly down many a cheek. The little Baptist Convention had been born."[74]

From among 10 suggested names, the body voted to call itself Nihon Baputesuto Remmei (Japan Baptist Convention). Adopting a constitution proved to be so complicated that it was decided to use the proposed instrument as a guide the first year while a committee prepared a revision for adoption at the next annual meeting. Officers were chosen or appointed as follows: Ozaki Shuichi, president; Edwin Dozier, vice president; Miyoshi Toshio, treasurer; Koga Takeo, secretary; and Kawano Sadamoto, executive secretary. These officers, together with the chairmen of four committees --evangelism, publications, social work, religious education--constituted the executive council.[75]

The newborn Convention's executive council met at President Ozaki's home on April 2. Here the crucial decision was reached to make the Convention work nationwide in scope. Across the Pacific, the SBC had already removed territorial limitations, having recognized the California convention of Southern Baptists as a constituent body in 1942 over Northern Baptist objections. The SBC went on to recognize the Kansas convention in 1948 and Oregon-Washington in 1949. In 1950 the Northern Baptist Convention in turn changed its name to American Baptist Convention, and the next year the SBC, while retaining its provincial name, declared its boards and agencies free to serve people anywhere in the United States. Such overlapping was not foreseen in Japan in 1947, for Northern-related churches remained in the United Church, committed to preserving their Baptist identity within its framework. Only after this compromise proved

[73]EBD, "Supplementary Report," 14-15.
[74]Ibid., 16-17.
[75]Ibid., 17.

unworkable did Northern-related churches withdraw in sufficient numbers to form the Japan Baptist Union in 1958.[76]

The executive council at Ozaki's home decided to provide personnel for the stations already occupied before entering new areas. It also drew up a priority list for rehabilitating the existing churches. Atom-bombed Hiroshima was put at the top of the list; in 1948, with a Board appropriation of $10,000, a wood-and-stucco building was erected amid the rubble near the heart of the city. This was the start of a massive program of erecting church buildings in cities throughout Japan. The executive council also decided on tentative assignments for missionaries appointed by the Board.[77]

Revival of the Mission

By June 1947 some 80 Protestant missionaries from the United States and Canada had returned to Japan, after which new personnel also began to enter. The first Southern Baptists to join Dozier were Alma Graves and Tucker Callaway, who sailed from Hawaii in July 1947. They traveled from Tokyo to Fukuoka with Dozier and Baker James Cauthen, Rankin's successor as area secretary. Dozier and Cauthen toured the old stations in Kyushu and preached to receptive crowds. Alma Graves resumed her teaching at Seinan Gakuin. Callaway did evangelistic work for a year, then left for furlough and returned to Japan with his family in 1949.[78]

In the fall of 1947, when missionary wives and children aged 12 months or above were permitted to enter Japan, the Garrott family arrived. Max immediately assumed the duties of Board representative, freeing Dozier to rejoin his own family in the States. Dozier had lost 20 pounds during the yearlong separation. The Garrotts were followed by Cecile Lancaster (with her mother), Floryne Miller, Elizabeth Watkins, and five postwar appointees: A. L. (Pete) and Bea Gillespie, W. R. (Bill) and Louise Medling, and Frances Talley. Watkins, still unappointed and unsalaried, had obtained the Board sponsorship needed for entering Japan. Most recently she had been teaching at a mountain school in northern Alabama conducted by George and Maggie Bouldin. The new appointees had been studying Japanese at the University of California in Berkeley. Earlier Pete Gillespie had made a name for himself as a dynamic youth evangelist and director of Baptist student work for the state of Kentucky. Bill Medling had the

---

[76]EBD, "Mission and Convention," 21; Barnes, *Southern Baptist Convention*, 291; F. Calvin Parker, "Baptist Missions in Japan, 1945-73: A Study in Relationships," *JCQ* 40 (1974): 35.

[77]EBD, "Supplementary Report," 26-27.

[78]W. Reginald Wheeler, *The Crisis Decade* ((New York: Board of Foreign Missions of the Presbyterian Church in the U.S.A., 1950), 85; Jesse C. Fletcher, *Baker James Cauthen: A Man for All Nations* (Nashville: Broadman Press, 1977), 188-89.

edge in language study. He was the fifth MK to return to Japan, following Florence Walne, Edwin and Helen Dozier, and Hermon Ray.[79]

Lancaster, Talley, Watkins, and the Gillespies lived in the old Maynard house at Seinan Jo Gakuin, where all but Pete taught in the school. As evangelistic missionary for North Kyushu, Pete helped start three mission points that later became churches. Watkins moved into a student dormitory and lived on the "pittance" the school was able to pay. The Medlings lived at Tamagawa in Tokyo for evangelistic work and language study until 1949, when they moved to Kumamoto, near Bill's childhood home of Kagoshima. Miller took a language refresher course in Tokyo before proceeding to Seinan Jo Gakuin in 1948 for teaching and evangelistic work.[80]

The missionaries had to have food and shelter, both hard to come by. Not only was production hampered by the destruction wrought by war, but demand had risen sharply with the repatriation of about eight million Japanese--military and civilian--from the overseas empire Japan had forfeited in losing the war. Official rations dropped to a mere 1,050 calories per person a day, about one-fifth the amount furnished to American soldiers. An illegal black market was flourishing--even salt was very scarce--and most people were living in over-crowded, unsanitary quarters. Because of these conditions, the missionaries brought with them to Japan a ton of processed food for each member of the family (this was required by occupation authorities), and in 1948 they imported seven aluminum prefabricated buildings for use as missionary residences and seven others for use as church buildings. Three missionary residences remained from before the war, and a fourth had been purchased.[81]

Lancaster brought the Dodge sedan that Texas Baptist women had donated for her use in Hawaii. Nicknamed the Texas Bronco, it served as the Mission car for Kokura. In 1949 the Fukuoka missionaries received a Jeep station wagon--the "Gospel Car"--given by several churches in South Carolina. That year the Mission asked the Board to provide automobiles for other areas. Cars were sorely needed because the public transportation system, considered adequate for missionary travel before the war (except for the Ford bookmobile), was now in shambles.[82]

Despite the shortage of housing, cars, and food, General MacArthur often called for "thousands of missionaries to Christianize Japan." The newly organized Baptist Convention asked for a minimum of 60 missionaries within the next four years. The Mission requested 400. "Missionaries today," wrote Max Garrott, "do not have to take a backseat and wait to be invited by the Japanese to work, as we

[79]*ASBC, 1948*, 110, 160. On Pete Gillespie, see Billy Keith, *What in the World is God Doing?* (Nashville: Convention Press, 1973), 45-48.

[80]Watkins, "Autobiography," 110-12; EBD, "Mission and Convention," 20-21.

[81]Kazuo Kawai, *Japan's American Interlude* (Chicago: University of Chicago Press, 1960), 135; EBD, "Mission and Convention," 20; *Commission* 11 (May 1948), 133.

[82]Lancaster, "My Life," 132; *ASBC, 1950*, 99.

felt before the war that we had to do. A missionary today can stand at the forefront of evangelistic work more freely than has been the case for a long, long time." Since institutional work was large in proportion to the church constituency, Garrott argued, many workers were needed for expansion, for establishing and strengthening churches. In response, the Board promised 100 missionaries by 1950, a number not attained until 1954.[83]

During the second half of 1948 the missionary ranks were increased by 11 members. Coleman and Jabe Clarke arrived in August with the Doziers. George and Helen Hays, Marion and Thelma Moorhead, Robert and Helen Sherer, Raymond and Inez Spence, and Lois Linnenkohl were among the 70 or more Protestant and Catholic missionaries who arrived on a bleak December 28 aboard the overcrowded, unconverted troopship *General Meigs*. The Moorheads, who had done language study at Berkeley, promptly joined the teaching ranks in Fukuoka. Marion taught evangelism in the seminary and directed the students in outreach ministries. The other newcomers settled in Tokyo for language study under difficult circumstances. "We moved in with the Medlings in a one-bedroom house," recalled Helen Hays, "and lived for weeks in the unheated living room. Cold, colder, coldest is all we remember about the first winter." Moreover, the new missionaries had to reimburse the Board for excess freight expenses equal to about a half-year's salary, and not everything they brought proved serviceable. The Sherers brought 12 dozen light bulbs at the suggestion of Edwin Dozier but found few takers for them.[84]

In 1948 Elizabeth Watkins received a letter from the Board saying she could be appointed if she passed the required physical examination. A medical form was enclosed. Watkins took the form to an American military hospital in Kokura and had an experience no less surprising than the Board's offer to appoint her.

> When I walked in, the doctor was upset. "I lost my nurse the other day. I can't give a woman a physical without a nurse. Give me that paper. What's this? Laboratory tests! I'm a busy man; I don't have time for such foolishness!" Writing "O.K." all over the paper, he gave it back to me and dismissed me. What could I do? I had no more blanks to take to another doctor. . . . I sent the report in and was immediately appointed.[85]

In August 1948 the Woman's Missionary Union of Japan was reorganized and took as its special project the Good Will Center in Tobata. As noted above, this ministry had been discontinued during the war, but the building had survived

---

[83]James M. Phillips, *From the Rising of the Sun* (Maryknoll, N.Y.: Orbis Books, 1981), 20, 144; Garrott to Rankin and Cauthen, 15 Jan. 1948; EBD, "Japan Faces the Sunrise," 24.

[84]Helen Hays, talk at Mission meeting, 1985; *Commission* 37 (July 1974), 20; Bob Sherer, talk at Mission Thanksgiving retreat, 1983.

[85]Watkins, "Autobiography," 118-19.

the bombings. The WMU leaders had the run-down facilities renovated and asked Watkins to serve as director. Accepting the position with enthusiasm, she moved into the refurbished building on Thanksgiving Day--without Mission permission. Permission was granted ex post facto, but the longtime free lance was reminded that as an appointed missionary she henceforth would be subject to Mission regulations.[86]

The first postwar Mission meeting had been held in Tokyo in the fall of 1947, soon after the arrival of a group of missionaries, and the second in Fukuoka in the spring of 1948. The 1949 meeting was held August 10-12 in Tokyo. The 26 in attendance, the largest number up to that time, included Secretary Cauthen and three new arrivals: Curtis and Mary Lee Askew, and Charles Whaley. Also present was Mrs. J. D. Jenkins, a Southern Baptist with the occupation forces who presented the Mission with a cake for its 60th anniversary. The gesture was doubly appreciated, for any food obtained from an American base exchange was welcome fare in those rigorous times.[87]

During the meeting, President Yuya of the Convention called for the Mission's full cooperation in evangelizing the nation. He expressed fears that missionaries coming in large numbers might form American enclaves and fail to assimilate the ways of Japan. Executive Secretary Matsumura stated that missionaries could and should become pastors of churches, a role denied them in the years preceding the war. Yuya and Matsumura were well received, but the Mission's commitment to cooperation seems to have been dulled by a streak of independence. The Convention's priority list for missionaries, presented at the meeting, urgently requested a couple for each of five churches, all in Kyushu. Of the five--Wakamatsu, Nagasaki, Ijuin, Kagoshima, and Saga--only the second and fourth ever got a missionary.[88]

The Mission elected Max Garrott as president, Bill Medling as vice president, and Edwin Dozier as treasurer. It adopted a budget for 1950 (a mere $1,000 was needed for Mission office and postage), approved a furlough schedule for all members, appointed a committee to prepare a Mission handbook, and took steps to accept a Karuizawa residence donated to the Mission by a retiree, Ernest Mills. The Friday night session followed dinner at the Hotel Tokyo, and the closing session on Saturday was combined with a picnic at the occupation-administered Roosevelt Recreation Grounds.[89]

The excitement of that August was by no means over. On the 25th, Charles Whaley and Lois Linnenkohl were married by George Hays in the prefab sanctuary of Tokyo's Daiichi (First) Baptist Church. Later in the month a fresh band of nine missionaries disembarked at Yokohama. Included were Reiji and

---

[86]Ibid., 120; *ASBC, 1949*, 142.
[87]MM minutes, Aug. 1949.
[88]Ibid.
[89]Ibid.

Asano Hoshizaki, who were sponsored by the Japan Convention and only partially supported by the Board. They would not be formally appointed until 1955. Also in the group were Luther and Louise Copeland, who had studied Japanese at Yale. Luther had also earned a Ph.D. there under Kenneth Scott Latourette, the famed missions historian. The Copelands went directly to Seinan Gakuin in Fukuoka. The other seven were assigned to language study in Tokyo, adding to the housing crunch there.[90]

Enlargement of the Baptist Witness

A development of lasting significance in the late 1940s was expansion of the Baptist schools in Fukuoka and Kokura. A combination of two factors made this possible: educational reforms carried out by the occupation, and large infusions of money and personnel provided by the Board.

The educational reforms carried out by the occupation authorities replaced Japan's elitist, multitrack school system with a more democratic, single-track system, whereby each level of education prepared students for the next higher level. The new structure was modeled after the American system of 6-3-3-4: six years of elementary school, three years of middle school, three years of high school, and four years of college. Compulsory education was extended from six years to nine, and the right to take entrance exams to high schools and colleges was made universal. The authorities encouraged the establishment of new universities and junior colleges so that a much larger segment of the population could enjoy the benefits of higher education.[91]

Seinan Gakuin, with its five-year middle school and three-year higher school or junior college, was reorganized into a three-year middle school for boys, a three-year high school for boys, and a two-year college that became coeducational in 1948. It applied for university status and set about enlarging and upgrading its faculty and facilities. Major responsibility for guiding the school through the transition fell on Max Garrott, who succeeded Mizumachi as president in 1948. Garrott made numerous trips to Tokyo--27 hours each way on unheated trains-- for conferences with the Ministry of Education. According to Edwin Dozier, Garrott's "untiring efforts and firm belief that qualified Christian teachers could be found for most of the teaching posts contributed to a higher percentage of Christian faculty at Seinan than in other Christian schools." A four-year liberal arts college was established in 1949, and its present name of Seinan Gakuin University was adopted in 1951.[92]

---

[90]George Hays, talk at Mission meeting, 1985; Genevieve Greer and Clara Selby Smith, comp., *Missionary Album* (Nashville: Broadman Press, 1954), 57. The other new arrivals were Ernest Lee and Ida Nelle Hollaway, Annie Hoover, Lenora Hudson, and Lucy Belle Stokes.

[91]Phillips, *Rising of the Sun*, 52-53.

[92]EBD, "Mission and Convention," 21; D. Garrott, oral history; *ASBC, 1950*, 99.

The Fukuoka seminary, reopened as an independent school in 1946 with 10 students, became the theological department of Seinan Gakuin's junior college in 1947 and of the senior college in 1949. Callaway, Copeland, Hays, and Moorhead were added to the faculty. In 1950 the Kindergarten Teachers' School became a junior college affiliated with Seinan Gakuin.[93]

Seinan Jo Gakuin was reorganized as a three-year middle school and three-year high school. President Hara obtained permission from the occupation forces in Kokura to take over an unused army hospital building on a hill adjoining the school's campus. Afterwards the property was purchased at a nominal sum from the Japanese government and developed into a permanent campus for the high school and a new junior college. This site was called the north campus; the original property used by the middle school became the south campus.[94]

The junior college was established in 1950 with two departments: English literature and home economics. A donation of typewriters by the Baptist Student Union of Texas opened the way for instruction in English typing. A surprise gift of $50,000 from the Southern Baptist WMU for a building in memory of Kathleen Mallory provided needed facilities for the expanded school. Completed in 1950, Mallory Memorial Hall still houses the administrative offices for the entire school and the chapel used by the high school and college. Portraits of the Rowes and Mallory painted for this building by a Japanese artist were first displayed at the 1949 Mission meeting.[95]

In 1949, during the break between academic years, Seinan Jo Gakuin hosted the WMU convention on March 22, the pastors' and missionaries' conference on March 29, the BYU (Baptist Youth Union) convention on March 29, and the third annual session of the postwar Convention from March 30 to April 1. This last meeting drew about 150 representatives, including 24 missionaries, from 22 churches and 3 missions. YWA (Young Woman's Auxiliary) members handled registration procedures and accepted the rice rations that participants brought for the meals.[96]

In the Convention elections Edwin Dozier, who had returned to Japan with Mary Ellen in 1948, was named associate executive secretary and chairman of the publications committee. He had served on the publications committee in 1947 when Yuya was chairman. It was at Yuya's home in Tokyo that Jordan Press was born, the successor to the prewar Gospel Book Store. From 1949 to 1951 the publication work was conducted in the renovated office of an old soap factory adjoining Dozier's residence in Yutenji (near Shibuya). The Convention's monthly organ, *Baputesuto* (Baptist), was published briefly in 1948, then suspended until 1950. A church members' manual appeared in 1949, and the first Baptist

[93]EBD, "Mission and Convention," 20-21.
[94]Lancaster, "My Life," 143.
[95]EBD, *Japan's New Day*;, 100; *ASBC, 1950*, 98; *ASBC, 1949*, 142; MM minutes, 1949.
[96]*NBRS*, 559-60; Marjorie E. Moore, *Japan's Southern Baptists* (Richmond: FMB, 1949), 2.

AMERICAN SOUTHERN BAPTISTS IN JAPAN

They total thirty-eight; a hundred were promised by 1950.

Mary Lee Trenor Askew D. Curtis Askew Elizabeth Clark Callaway

Tucker N. Callaway Jennie Sheffield Clarke Coleman D. Clarke Louise Tadlock Copeland E. Luther Copeland Mary Ellen Dozier Edwin B. Dozier

Dorothy Carver Garrott W. Maxfield Garrott Viola Boyd Gillespie Alfred L. Gillespie Alma Graves Helen Mathis Hays George H. Hays

Ida Nelle Hollaway Ernest L. Hollaway, Jr. Annie Hoover Lenora Hudson Cecile Lancaster Mary Louise Medling William R. Medling

Floryne Miller Thelma C. Moorhead Marion F. Moorhead Helen Mitchell Sherer Robert C. Sherer Inez Gilliland Spence Raymond M. Spence

Lucy Belle Stokes Frances Talley Mary Frances C. Walker William L. Walker Elizabeth Watkins Lois Linnenkohl Whaley Charles L. Whaley, Jr.

Missionaries in 1949 *(From M. E. Moore,* Japan's Southern Baptists. *Foreign Mission Bd., 1949)*

curriculum materials for the fast-growing church schools (formerly called Sunday schools) were produced for use beginning in January 1950.[97]

In August 1949 the Convention had a called meeting at Seinan Gakuin to deal with constitutional changes and other urgent matters. The 10-article statement of faith was finally approved after two years of furbishing that left it but little different from its Hawaiian model.[98] It was to serve the Convention until replaced with an all-new statement in 1979. With 688 baptisms registered in 1949, the year closed with church membership at 2,917, exceeding for the first time the prewar high of 2,776. A decade well described as "cross and resurrection" came to an end with Japanese Baptists poised to embark on their greatest era of advance.

[97]Ernest L. Hollaway, Jr., "Major Developments in Religious Education in the Japan Baptist Convention to 1961" (DRE diss., Southwestern Baptist Theological Seminary, 1965), 64, 75-76; *NBRS*, 559-60.

[98]*NBRS*, 560-61; Saitō Goki, ed., *Baputesuto no shinkō kokuhaku* (Baptist confessions of faith) (Tokyo: Jordan Press, 1980), 345-48, 386-94, 436. Saitō reproduces the full text of the Hawaiian and Japanese statements.

9

Advancing on All Fronts (1950-1959)

The Foreign Mission Board had adopted a Program of Advance in 1948 that called for increasing the number of overseas missionaries from 670 to 1,750 and doubling the annual overall budget from $5 million to $10 million. This advance was to be achieved "as rapidly as possible." To implement the program, the SBC had approved a plan by which all Cooperative Program receipts in excess of each year's budget would be used exclusively for missions. In 1950, the first year of implementation, all of the over-and-above money--$675,044--went to the Foreign Mission Board. Beginning in 1951 one-fourth went to the Home Mission Board (later adjusted to one-third), but the Foreign Mission Board continued to get the lion's share. These Cooperative Program advance funds made possible the unprecedented advance in Japan in the early 1950s.[1]

The decade opened with 45 missionaries assigned to Japan. Included were Stan and Pat Howard, late-1949 appointees who arrived in January 1950. Pat, a Baylor graduate, was not yet 21. She is the youngest Southern Baptist missionary ever sent to Japan except the unappointed Dru McCollum, who holds the record by one month. Of the 45 members of the Mission, 25 were language school students in Tokyo. The others, save for three couples, were concentrated at the prewar Baptist institutions in Kokura, Tobata, and Fukuoka. Within four years, thanks to the Advance Program, missionaries would exceed 100 in number. They would be dispersed from Kagoshima in the south to Hokkaido in the north, helping to make the postwar Convention the nationwide body it had set out to be.

The dispersion to new cities got underway in 1950 when Bob and Helen Sherer moved from Tokyo to Kobe, and Pete and Bea Gillespie moved from Kokura to Osaka. It may be recalled that the McCollums and Brunsons had lived in Kobe for language study, and that the McCollums had moved to Osaka but had withdrawn in 1891 after an abrupt change in the comity agreement with Northern Baptists. No Southern Baptist missionary had resided in either city since 1892,

---

[1]Cauthen, *Advance*, 52-53; *ASBC, 1949*, 86-87.

even though the Board had abrogated the comity agreement in 1918 and claimed the right to work anywhere in Japan.

By 1950 Japan's construction industry had recovered sufficiently for the Mission to have large Western-style houses built wherever its members were assigned after language school. About $12,000 was budgeted for each unit, including $5,000 for land purchase and $7,000 for house construction. A standard family residence had about 50 tsubo (1,800 square feet) of floor space as well as a spacious attic that could be used for meetings, and a garage with servants' quarters attached. A house built for a single missionary usually measured about 40 tsubo (1,440 square feet) including a maid's room. These sizes remained standard throughout the decade, though specifications were trimmed and budgets slightly enlarged as prices climbed steadily. The Gillespies' new house in Osaka was partially damaged by a fire that Pete afterwards called a blessing, for news reports of the fire called attention to the meetings conducted in the home and helped to boost attendance.[2]

The spirit of advance pervaded the 1950 Mission meeting, held July 24-28 on the enchanting island of Miyajima near Hiroshima. In a panel discussion on evangelism, Bill Medling displayed a map that showed southern Kyushu and northern Honshu as the neediest fields. Others viewed the challenge differently, though all were committed to a Baptist witness nationwide in scope. In some cases one's personal sense of call matched none of the priority needs indicated by the Convention or even by Mission leaders. Indeed, the issue of missionary deployment was debated with fervor. At length a bylaw was adopted stating that work assignments would be made "with the agreement of the missionary involved, after consultation with the Executive Board of the Japan Baptist Convention." Accordingly, a request of Ernest and Ida Nelle Hollaway to work in Nagoya was referred to the executive committee for negotiations with the Convention board. So also was a request of Tucker and Liz Callaway to locate in the eastern part of Fukuoka, though their weekday teaching was in the western part of the city at Seinan Gakuin. Eventually both assignments were approved.[3]

Prior to the 1950 meeting Chairman Max Garrott had sent a "Papa letter" to all members pleading for a spirit of understanding and cooperation. During the meeting Luther Copeland led Bible studies stressing unity in Christ, and Edwin Dozier called on the members to be "all things to all men" and not insist on the American way. All three men contributed to the harmony that prevailed amid the tensions rising from the rapid assimilation of new personnel.[4]

One expression of unanimity was an unprecedented action calling on the Board to appoint as regular missionaries Japanese-Americans Reiji and Asano Hoshizaki,

---

[2]MM minutes, July 1950; Watkins to Maggie Bouldin, 25 May 1951, Bouldin Collection.
[3]MM minutes, July 1950.
[4]Ibid.; Copeland to Mission, 16 July 1952.

who had come to Japan in 1949 under Convention sponsorship and partial Board support, as noted above. The Mission action ratified a similar action taken earlier by the Convention's executive committee, evidence that the Hoshizakis had won the confidence of missionaries and Japanese alike. In response, the Board undertook their full support beginning in 1951 (they opened new work in Shizuoka that year) and formally appointed them during their furlough in 1955. The appointment of the Hoshizakis paved the way for seven more Japanese-Americans sent to Japan in the years that followed.[5]

The 1950 Mission meeting closed with a stunt night program that further reduced the level of stress among the missionaries. Within a month, however, the Mission's digestive system was put to the severest test ever. On Wednesday, August 23, at 10:30 A.M., 27 new missionaries--11 couples and 5 single women-- arrived in Yokohama aboard the *President Cleveland*. This is an all-time record for the number of missionaries sent to Japan on the same ship or even in any one year. They raised the number of full-time language school students to 40, in a Mission of 68 members.[6]

The so-called class of '50 was so large that the members are most conveniently listed as on a ship's manifest:

Bradshaw, Melvin and Edith	Limbert, Mary
Campbell, Vera	Morgan, Mary Neal
Emanuel, Bill and Rebekah Sue	Nelson, Loyce and Gladys
Grant, Worth and Kathryn	Oliver, Ed and Sue
Gullatt, Tom and Mary	Shepard, John and Jean
Highfill, Virginia	Walker, Bill and Mary
Horton, Fred and Elvee	Wood, James and Alma
Knox, Martha	Wright, Morris and Joyce

The diverse backgrounds and specialties of these 27 new missionaries greatly enriched the Mission and enhanced its potential for effective ministry. Two of the additions were MKs (missionary kids). John W. Shepard, Jr., born on a Baptist campus in Rio de Janeiro, had grown up speaking Portuguese and had studied Chinese for two years at Yale before accepting a teaching assignment in Japan. Mary Culpepper Walker, the other MK, could keep one in stitches with the clipped English used at the British school she had attended in China.[7]

---

[5]MM minutes, July 1950, 8; Reiji Hoshizaki to author, 22 June 1988. The other Japanese-Americans are Ralph and Irene Honjo, Tom and Betty Masaki, Tak Oue, and George and Amy Watanabe.

[6]*ASBC, 1951*, 165; 181-83; Bill and Rebekah Sue Emanuel, *A Call Comes Ringing* (privately printed, 1955), 13.

[7]Biographical information on all 27 missionaries is found in Greer and Smith, *Missionary Album*.

Four had served in the military: Worth Grant, a navy chaplain in China and Japan; Morris Wright, a naval engineering officer in China; Ed Oliver, "efficiency expert" with the air corps of the Naval Reserve; and Fred Horton, who as a soldier in wartime Hawaii had been deeply influenced by the Doziers. All the men had been pastors, and all the women had gained work experience in a hospital, school, or church.

The single women shared a large Japanese house on the property now occupied by the Uehara Plaza and Garden apartments. The Emanuels occupied a prefab on the same property, and the other couples were assigned to the Nishiōkubo compound in Shinjuku, later the site for the Convention and Mission headquarters. Nine houses had been hastily built to supplement two prefabs and a garage apartment already standing on the property. The new houses were five-room wood-frame bungalows, much plainer and more compact than the permanent houses being built. Each had a three-mat (six-by-nine-foot) tatami room with a half-bath for a live-in maid. Every family had a maid or maids, for the average wage was about $12 a month plus meals, and there was a surfeit of applicants for the job.

The houses had no insulation against the cold, but they were equipped with gas outlets, and most occupants used small gas heaters purchased locally. Unfortunately, Tokyo's poor-quality manufactured gas added so much moisture to the air that water would run down the inside walls and form puddles on the floor. Worse still, the gas was highly noxious. One maid was found dead in her room, a victim of gas poisoning. Two new couples who reached Japan in January 1951 and moved onto the compound, Bob and Kay Culpepper and Leslie and Hazel Watson, were sickened by a heater's faulty combustion one evening while they were playing dominoes. Kay Culpepper had such a severe case of gas poisoning that she suffered a miscarriage and was never again able to conceive a child.[8]

The 12-family compound teemed with crying babies, prattling children, professional beggars, persistent job-seekers, assorted peddlers, and uniformed students attending English Bible classes. The strange communal life brought out the best and the worst in young missionaries affected by culture shock and engaged in grueling language study. They took their daily lessons in the cold and gloomy rooms of Kanda Misaki Church, headquarters of the Northern Baptist mission. This was one of three buildings used by the Tokyo School of the Japanese Language until its own facilities near Shibuya Station were completed in 1952.

Adding to the stress, 11 families had to share two station wagons for school attendance, evangelistic work, shopping trips, and medical appointments or emergencies. One of the most frequented places was the Tokyo Sanitarium

[8]Robert H. Culpepper, *God's Calling* (Nashville: Broadman Press, 1981), 90-91.

Hospital (Seventh-day Adventist), where the availability of American doctors more than compensated for the vegetarian meals served to in-patients. The several women who were pregnant showed a decided preference for the sleek Ford over the rough-riding Chevrolet. Only the Grants had their own car, a Rambler they had brought from the States. When no Mission car was available, as was often the case, one walked, bicycled, hailed a charcoal-burning taxi, or joined the bone-crushing crowds in a bus or train.

Compound life had its sunny side also. The children usually got along well with one another, and they picked up Japanese effortlessly from their nursemaids and neighborhood playmates. The missionaries met often for prayer and sharing or for relaxing games such as rook or 42. Some worked off their language-school frustrations with late-afternoon volley ball. A few had a bent for jokes and pranks. One morning a discarded Western-style commode was found in the privy-like telephone booth that served the whole compound.

All were encouraged by the positive response of the Japanese to their Christian testimony, whether given in halting Japanese or in well articulated English with or without the interruptions of an interpreter. When an English Bible class was arranged for 15 Tokyo University students, 150 asked to attend and stood in line two hours to be interviewed. Subsequently five classes were organized, and many of the students were led to attend church and become Christians.[9] So fruitful were English-language ministries that churches and missions in the Tokyo area vied for the part-time services of language-school missionaries.

Memorable Mission Meetings

A called Mission meeting held in Tokyo in November 1950, with Board Secretary Theron Rankin and Orient Secretary Baker James Cauthen present, provided an opportunity for the 27 "young sprouts" to get acquainted with their seniors and learn how the organizational wheels turned. Total attendance was 62, compared with 36 at the July meeting in Miyajima. Not until July 1951, however, did the newcomers experience a regular Mission meeting. It too was irregular in a sense, for the eight-day meeting held at the occupation forces' Tokyo Chapel Center near the Diet building left everyone exhausted, especially the language students whose nerves were already frayed. What was exhausting was not so much the meeting's length as its logistics, for the out-of-towners were crammed into the sultry little houses of the Tokyo residents. The Medlings, for instance, who came from Kumamoto with their four children and one maid, stayed with the Emanuels and their three children--one an infant--in the Emanuels' little prefab. Moreover,

[9]*ASBC, 1951*, 166.

everyone had to travel back and forth to the sessions, more than an hour each way for those staying at Tamagawa.[10]

By a strange coincidence, the worship speaker at the morning sessions was Cornell Goerner, a professor of comparative religion and missions at Southern Seminary. As noted earlier, W. O. Carver, his predecessor, was the guest speaker at the 1923 Mission meeting, another notable occasion when the Mission was gasping in a flood of new personnel. Once again the time was ripe for a confrontation between veterans and rookies that might issue in mass resignations.

Fortunately, Max Garrott, the Mission chairman, and Edwin Dozier, treasurer, both believed in the exercise of love and persuasion as preferable to political clout. Since Garrott lived in Fukuoka and had his hands full as president of Seinan Gakuin and professor in the seminary, it fell mainly to Dozier, a resident of Tokyo till 1958, to deal with impatient novices whose zeal outran their grasp of the situation. Some of the newcomers were offended by Dozier's Japan-bred mentality that seemed to accommodate the timid goals of the Convention leaders. Others resented his tendency to do jobs single-handedly. But warfare was avoided, for unlike George Bouldin, treasurer in the '20s, Dozier readily apologized for any hurt he inflicted.

Bob Culpepper never forgot how Dozier stood up in the 1951 Mission meeting "with tears in his eyes pleading with us missionaries to try to see things from the point of view of the Japanese. At that time he indicated that in like manner he had been pleading with the Japanese to try to understand the problems and viewpoints of the new missionaries." At length the truth became apparent, as Pete Gillespie put it, that "Edwin had full confidence in new and younger missionaries and did everything possible to enlist them all in the work and in the machinery of the Mission."[11]

The 1952 Mission meeting, held in Kyoto's Western-style Rakuyo Hotel August 4-8, proved to be the healing balm that was needed when the class of '50 was making the rough transition to field assignments after being drained by two torturous years of language study. There was fun aplenty. It was announced one morning that all the single women, to their surprise, would have a "husband for a day." Each wife led her husband to a single woman to be her escort until evening. Since the Mission had 31 married men but only 20 single women, some of the singles were given two escorts. At lunch in the hotel dining room, the wives sat together at a table in the corner while each single dined with her temporary husband or husbands. At the evening banquet the senior single, Cecile Lancaster, had a crown placed on her head and a wedding ring (afterwards

---

[10]Culpepper, *God's Calling*, 84; Emanuel, *A Call Comes Ringing*, 26. The July 1951 MM program, inside cover, has attendance figures for earlier Mission meetings.

[11]Saitō, "Edwin B. Dozier," 74-76.

returned) on her finger, and she was showered with baby food, baby clothes, and baby blankets.[12]

On the serious side, inspiring addresses were given by Glendon McCollough, a contract teacher at Seinan Gakuin who later headed the Southern Baptist Brotherhood; Secretary Cauthen, a resident of Tokyo in 1951-52; and Frank H. Connely, newly transferred from China to replace Dozier as Mission treasurer. A veteran of the 1931-32 Shantung Revival, Connely told how missionaries had embraced one another and their Chinese coworkers in a purge of pride, envy, jealousy, and criticism.[13]

Revival broke out on Wednesday night in a "song and testimony service" led by Marion Moorhead. All were seated in a circle, in full view of one another while they shared their experiences. The atmosphere grew electric, and all fell on their knees in prayer. "Wave upon wave of God's very special power and presence swept down upon us," said Bill Emanuel. "We were melted by it. Sin was confessed; forgiveness was sought and given; a heavenly joy was poured into our hearts." Tucker Callaway disclosed that in his struggle to learn the language he had been driven to the brink of suicide, and he had come to Kyoto with the intention of announcing his resignation. Yet he had been elected Mission chairman. "My first impulse," Callaway wrote afterwards, "was to refuse it on the ground that it was a mistake." Then he realized that there had been no nominations, that each missionary had voted by secret ballot as led by the Lord.[14]

Others who had come with thoughts of resigning gained the courage to persevere in the work with their brothers and sisters. All had been melded into one family. In the first half of the 1950s, despite the explosive growth and concomitant tensions, the Mission lost only one member--Johnni Johnson (later, Mrs. Fon Scofield)--and that due to a serious medical problem. Johnni, who was in Japan from 1951 to 1954, found a niche at the home office in Richmond in the field of communications and rose to become the Board's first woman vice president.[15]

Responding to the Nationwide Challenge

The two years of language study for the class of '50 coincided with the last two years of the occupation (1945-52) and the first two years of the Korean War (1950-53). In this period of upheaval and change it was disheartening to the new missionaries that they could not immediately seize on the opportunities for evangelism. The spiritual vacuum left by Japan's defeat in war was rapidly being filled by materialism, secularism, and the non-Christian religions, especially the

---

[12]Lancaster, "My Life," 34-35.

[13]MM program, Aug. 1952.

[14]Bill Emanuel, *I Enlisted for the Duration* (privately printed, 1979), 38; Callaway to Mission, 16 Aug. 1952; Culpepper, *God's Calling*, 84-85.

[15]*ESB*, vol. 4, 2211.

so-called new religions such as Sōka Gakkai. Christian evangelism now had to be conducted not in a vacuum, but in an arena with many fierce rivals. And with every passing year, the competition would increase.[16] Yet for two long years, most of the 27 missionaries in the class of '50 had to keep their noses to the grindstone of language study, except for very limited activities, leaving the bigger challenges to others.

The Board had planned to sponsor a three-month evangelistic campaign in 1950 led by 15 American preachers, but the project was cancelled when the Korean War broke out. In its place a three-week campaign was conducted in October with four speakers: Rankin, Cauthen, Duke K. McCall, and W. A. Criswell. McCall was executive secretary of the SBC's executive committee, and Criswell was pastor of the First Baptist Church, Dallas, Texas. These two men were available at the time because they were passing through Japan on a round-the-world tour. All four preachers got a good response. At Seinan Jo Gakuin 369 students made decisions for Christ. Meetings at two rented halls in Osaka resulted in 700 decisions, and a meeting in a Kobe movie theater, with 1,000 people present, drew 325 down the aisles during the gospel invitation. In the three-week campaign, later known as the first preaching mission, a total of 8,000 decision cards were signed, some indicating a full acceptance of Christ and others a desire to learn more about the Christian faith. During the next several months the pastors and missionaries sought to enlist these prospects in the churches. Approximately 10 percent of those who signed cards were baptized. Baptisms in Convention churches and missions in 1950 totaled 1,026, up from 688 in 1949.[17]

The second Board-sponsored preaching mission, extending over a period of six weeks in September and October of 1951, featured eight preachers, twice as many as in 1950. The services were more church-centered than in the first mission and less well attended. The quality of interest was higher. Of the 10,000 who signed decision cards, 45 percent indicated a decision to accept Christ as Saviour. As the 1950 preaching mission had been the springboard for new work in Osaka and Kobe, the 1951 meetings served the same end in Shizuoka, Nagoya, and Kyoto. This was the first year of implementing the Convention plan to establish work in all the prefectural capitals, a plan proposed by Kimura Buntarō, chairman of the evangelism committee and afterwards president of the Convention. Also in 1951, the Baptist Training Union (BTU) program was inaugurated through the evangelism department. Baptisms for the year increased to 1,293.[18]

---

[16]Cf. *JCQ* 17 (1951): 101-2.

[17]Garrott, *Japan Advances*, 131; *ASBC, 1951*, 165-69.

[18]*ASBC, 1952*, 165-71; E. Norfleet Gardner, *Journey to Japan* (privately printed, 1952), 7 and passim; EBD, "Mission and Convention," 22. The eight preachers were Cauthen; E. Norfleet Gardner, Henderson, N.C.; E. D. Head, president of Southwestern Seminary; Clyde V. Hickerson, Richmond, Va.; Roland Q. Leavell, president of New Orleans Seminary; M. Ray McKay, Little Rock; John L. Slaughter, Birmingham; and Monroe F. Swilley, Atlanta.

In June 1951 a new Tokyo headquarters building was dedicated in Kamiyama, Shibuya Ward. Offices for the Convention, Mission, and Jordan Press were located there. Second-generation preacher Arase Noboru succeeded Matsumura Shūichi as the Convention's executive secretary. Arase promoted the vision of "1,000 Baptist churches within 25 years," a dream that could have been realized had every church started another church in each five-year period. Actual goals adopted in the years since have been far more modest.[19]

In the spring of 1952, the Moorheads and Annie Hoover moved to Sapporo, becoming the first Southern Baptist missionaries on the northern island of Hokkaido. They initiated work in cooperation with Suzuki Masana. That autumn the Convention sponsored a wide-ranging campaign called New Life Evangelism (*shinsei dendō*), with the slogan "To all of Japan the light of Christ." The preaching was done, not by visiting Americans, but by 19 Japanese and 5 missionaries fluent in the language. Attendance was smaller than in the 1950 and 1951 preaching missions, but the attendance of many adults with serious motivation gave much encouragement. A number of Japanese preachers gained new confidence as evangelists. Some gave public invitations, virtually a sacrament among Southern Baptists, for the first time in their ministry.[20]

The program of advance was further strengthened in 1952 by the dispersion of the class of '50 to their field assignments. True, the majority went to Kyushu, to cities where churches had already been organized. Bill and Mary Walker were assigned to Ōita, where the Convention had started work only since the war. No Southern Baptist missionaries had lived there before. Ed and Sue Oliver moved to Kagoshima, which had had no resident missionary since Lenna Medling's departure in 1920. Personnel assigned to institutions helped to start new missions in the surrounding areas.[21]

Among the other members of the class of '50, Bill and Rebekah Sue Emanuel started work in Takamatsu on the island of Shikoku, which the Mission had claimed as its territory since 1907 but had never entered. A church was organized in 1954. Worth and Kathryn Grant chose to work in Sendai, a strategic city of 300,000 people located 200 miles north of Tokyo in the cold and conservative Tōhoku district. Their story is worth recounting in some detail as a window into the experiences of all the missionaries who served in the front lines of nationwide advance.

During their second year of language study, the Grants made several trips to Sendai--six hours each way by express train--to find suitable residence land that did not encroach on another Protestant mission's territory and whose owner was willing to sell to a foreigner. This task alone consumed more than six months

[19]EBD, "Mission and Convention," 22-23; "Mission Handbook," 1957 ed. (JBM, 1957), 93.
[20]EBD, "Mission and Convention," 22; *ASBC, 1953*, 160-65.
[21]*ASBC, 1953*, 160-65.

and produced a series of disappointments. After obtaining the land and letting the contract for their "Lottie Moon house," they had to oversee carpenters who were novices in Western-style construction.[22]

The Grants also had to cultivate good relations with other Christian groups and particularly with American Baptists, who had opened work in Sendai even before the McCollums and Brunsons first set foot in Japan. Fortunately, two missionaries who taught in Sendai's American Baptist mission school took no offense at the Southern Baptist incursion. They shared their home with the Grants for a month while the Grants' house was under construction.

The Grants further had to deal with strong opposition from longtime residents of their chosen neighborhood. The residents initiated a movement to halt construction of the house on grounds that its location on a corner lot would make it too conspicuous in the community. When Worth was summoned to a protest meeting in the home of a prominent local family, he took along Fukuhara Takeshi, the Mission's business specialist and troubleshooter. Together they faced stern demands that the house be relocated. Fukuhara asked for understanding and acceptance on grounds that the city authorities had duly registered the land transaction and issued a building permit. The meeting came to an end with neither side making any concession. "We were already the objects of hostility and had become a bone of contention," Worth recalled. "We would begin our ministry to the area surrounding our home with the proverbial three strikes against us."[23]

The Grants formally launched their evangelistic effort in November 1952 with a five-day campaign in a public hall. Curtis Askew did the preaching. A room was rented from the YMCA for Sunday morning services. After moving into their nearly finished house in December, the Grants used it as a meeting place for Sunday school and prayer services but continued to use the YMCA for worship services. The Sunday school grew until 50 to 75 children filled the attic each week. Worth started English Bible classes to draw students, and Kathryn scoured the neighborhood for women to attend the "Gospel Cooking School" that met in her kitchen weekly. A large display window that had been built into the fence surrounding the property attracted the attention of passers-by. The display included religious pictures, Bible verses, and meeting notices accompanied by words of invitation.

In November 1953, after one year of evangelistic effort, Worth baptized the first six converts--his second daughter Angela among them--in the Hirose River, which flows through Sendai. The next April he baptized Sendai-born Ōtsuki Kunihiko, a future pastor. At the age of 17 Ōtsuki had been drawn to the Grants

[22]Worth C. Grant, *A Work Begun* (printed in Tokyo, n.d.), 7-43.
[23]Ibid., 11.

and their faith by a picture of Christ on the cross displayed in the window in the fence.[24]

The Grants searched out land for a church building, and in early 1954 they obtained an excellent lot only three blocks from their home. Since Kathryn was anxious to start a kindergarten in April, the beginning of the school year, they had a temporary building erected at a cost of $500. With needed equipment provided by American military personnel in the area, the kindergarten opened on schedule with 30 children enrolled. Sunday worship services were moved to this building from the YMCA, and the congregation called as pastor Sekiya Sadao, later a seminary professor and noted archaeologist.

With an appropriation of $12,000 from the Lottie Moon Christmas offering, the Grants had a church building erected of their own design. It had a tall steeple topped with a gold-leaf cross, the cross a gift from their parents. A Southern Baptist chaplain made available through army chapel funds--military regulations were often stretched--a gift of $12,000 to pay for the pulpit furniture and pews to seat 250 people. That autumn the building was dedicated in a service attended by Sendai's mayor, who though not a Christian strongly commended the Christian faith in his congratulatory message. In 1955 the church was formally organized and received by the Convention as a member church. When the Grants left for their first furlough in America that year, more than 100 people crowded into the train station to send them off with the hymn, "God be with you till we meet again." The missionaries departed with a sense of accomplishment.[25]

The Growing Mission at Work

Meanwhile, other missionaries who had arrived in Japan in 1951 or 1952 finished language school and moved to major cities on the Japan Sea Coast and in northern Japan. In Asahigawa, Hokkaido, Dub Jackson, a firm believer in large-scale evangelism, launched work in July 1954 with a banner stretched over the city's main intersection, two-color posters placed in the bathhouses and other conspicuous locations, and 38,000 handbills inserted into the newspapers. After a kick-off dinner for the city's dignitaries, a series of meetings in the civic auditorium drew 3,500 people and registered 164 decisions. Pastor Ōtani Kenji preached, and Pete Gillespie led the music.[26]

The next year Jackson organized a music-evangelism team of missionaries and Japanese to conduct a two-week campaign. The meetings were begun in the city auditorium and continued in the just-completed church building. Daytime services were conducted in a variety of places: hospital, police station, high

[24]Worth Grant, *Japan with Love* (Buchanan, Ga.: Baptist Missionary Service, n.d.), 27-30.
[25]Grant, *A Work Begun*, 44-45.
[26]Carl M. Halvarson, *Japan's New Baptists* (Nashville: Convention Press, 1956), 75-76.

school, university, Rotary club, and Self-Defense Forces camp. A Hammond organ played by Rebekah Sue Emanuel proved to be the star attraction, but Pete Gillespie's accordion and Jackson's trumpet also delighted the crowds. As a result of the campaign the church was organized in October with 70 members, and by Christmas the membership had reached 115.[27]

Jackson promoted similar campaigns in Sapporo, Otaru, and Aomori. In Sapporo, an open-sided street car was rented for publicity purposes. Loaded with the organ, a vibraharp, and eye-catching foreigners, it clanged through the city streets "with banners streaming and music blaring." Whether because of or in spite of this show-biz approach, by the end of the decade the Sapporo church had grown to a membership of 145 and a new mission had been started in the city.[28]

A 1953 appointee, Mavis Shiver, was honored as the Mission's 100th member, the fulfillment of a Board goal for Japan. Board records indicate that Shiver raised the total only to 98 and the 100 mark was reached in 1954. The Mission, however, included the not-yet-appointed Hoshizakis in its count.[29] Shiver recruited another worker in the person of Robert Hardy, an Air Force pharmacist. She resigned in 1957 to marry Bob, and the two returned to Japan in 1959 as a missionary couple. Mary Lou Massengill, a registered nurse appointed in 1954, likewise found a husband--Wayne Emanuel, Bill's younger brother--from among the Air Force personnel in Japan. She resigned on his account in 1957, and they too returned to Japan in 1959 as an appointed couple.

In the first half of the '50s the Mission also received four single women and one couple who had been forced out of China by the Communist takeover and had come to Japan for English-language ministries. All but one of these six missionaries had been interned and repatriated on the *Gripsholm*, and all without exception had witnessed Japanese acts of cruelty toward the Chinese during the war. Yet in their new assignments they demonstrated a genuine love for the Japanese people while drawing on their China experience for specialized ministries.

Lois Glass and Pearl Todd both taught college and secondary-school English at Seinan Gakuin from 1950 to 1956. Lois Glass, a sister of Eloise (Mrs. Baker James) Cauthen, used her nurturing instincts to good advantage in working individually with young men, and she was popular with missionary children as well. Pearl Todd won the admiration of the women in the Fukuoka church with her vivacious charm and animated gestures. Both missionaries demonstrated the significance of Christian personality through their Bibles classes and personal contacts.[30]

---

[27]*ASBC, 1956*, 160; Bill Emanuel, *I Enlisted*, 52-53.

[28]Emanuel, *I Enlisted*, 53; *ASBC, 1956*, 160-61.

[29]*ASBC, 1954*, 187, 198; *ASBC, 1955*, 187.

[30]Luther and Louise Copeland, interview with author, Fukuoka, 22 June 1987: Todd obituary in *Commission* 45 (Feb./Mar. 1982), 92.

Rose Marlowe taught oral and written English at Seinan Jo Gakuin from 1950 to 1955. Her favorite course was "History of English Literature," for which she prepared her own textbook materials. As one of eight residents in the run-down Maynard House, "Miss Carpenter," as she was called, skillfully used hammer, saw, nails, and screws to put on weather stripping, add a fourth leg to the three-legged bathtub, and seal her room from invading centipedes. A Sunday morning Bible class that she taught in this house drew men and women from all over the city and often produced confessions of faith. At the time of Rose's retirement, the class enrollment was 76 and average attendance was 64.[31]

Lucy Smith, who had served in Shanghai and Hong Kong as assistant to the Secretary for the Orient, was assistant treasurer of the Japan Mission for several years and treasurer for two years. While treasurer, she fulfilled her duties as liaison to the Convention's executive committee despite her meager grasp of the language. Sitting tirelessly through the three-day meetings, often the only woman present, Lucy won high marks for fortitude. She was an evangelist also, and many young people were drawn to Christ through her English-language ministry at Mejiro Church and the friendships she cultivated.[32]

Frank Connely, introduced earlier, was Mission treasurer from 1952 to 1956, until he died of a heart attack at the wheel of his automobile. He was driving under tension because a taxi with which he had unintentionally touched bumpers at an intersection was following his car. The funeral was conducted at Tokyo Chapel Center. Interment took place in the Yokohama Foreigners' Cemetery. Connely is the only Southern Baptist missionary buried there, since John Rowe's remains were removed to Seinan Jo Gakuin after the war. Connely's China-born wife, Mary Sears, returned to the States and died of a stroke in 1958.[33]

The Mission was also saddened by the loss of three missionary children during this decade. Two infants were victims of crib death, Naomi Hoshizaki at Shizuoka in 1952, and Scott Spencer at Matsue in 1958. Ronald Whaley died in Tokyo of leukemia at the age of three. Ronald was interred at Seinan Jo Gakuin, where his parents had taught, and the other two children were laid to rest in local cemeteries. The Hoshizaki plot was later deeded to the Shizuoka church and made into a depository for the ashes of deceased church members.[34]

---

[31]Alice Johnson Tucker, "Rose of Three Countries" (typescript, 1966), 121-28; Anna Mae Smith, *Adventuring with Rose* (Georgetown, Ky.: Georgetown College Press, 1964), 39: obituary in *Commission* 43 (Apr. 1980), 39.

[32]Lucy Smith interview, oral history, FMBA; obituary in *Commission* 44 (Sept. 1981), 44.

[33]*HFF* 1 (Nov. 1916): 24; George Hays to Mission, 26 Oct. 1956; *Commission* 20 (Jan. 1957), 31.

[34]Reiji Hoshizaki to author, 22 June 1988.

New Institutions Are Born

In 1952-53 four medical doctors were sent to Japan to staff a planned Baptist hospital. These were James Satterwhite, internal medicine; C. F. Clark (Liz Callaway's brother), pediatrics; Audrey Fontnote and Martha Hagood, both specializing in obstetrics and gynecology. The two wives, Altha Satterwhite and Polly Clark, were registered nurses. The Satterwhites, formerly volunteers for Africa, had become interested in Japan in 1948 while stationed there with the U.S. Army Medical Corps. They had made the acquaintance of Pastor Yuya and caught his vision of Baptist medical work in Japan.[35]

In 1952 both the Mission and the Convention took action to establish a hospital, and a founding committee tackled the sticky problem of location. A survey of the opinions held by churches and missionaries revealed that central Japan was favored over northern Kyushu. In 1953 Coleman Clarke and Pastor Yamaji Motoi found a highly suitable location in the northwestern hills of Kyoto. It was an eight-acre, landscaped estate with quiet surroundings. On the estate stood a four-story, 32-room concrete structure with 17,000 square feet of floor space. The building had many features appropriate for a hospital: central heating, extensive plumbing, double glass walls in some rooms, sun porches, automobile entrance, and office space on the ground floor. Valued at $100,000, the estate had belonged to the Shimizu family, prominent manufacturers of X-ray machines and other scientific apparatus. The Convention obtained the property in 1953 for only $56,000, since it was to be used for a medical ministry.[36]

A small clinic was opened in 1954 under the direction of Jim Satterwhite. Construction was begun on a new building that joined to the remodeled old structure, increasing the total floor space to 32,000 square feet. When the work was completed in 1955, the Japan Baptist Hospital was dedicated and formally opened with 70 beds and a staff of 50. All 50 were Christians, an amazing feat of recruitment accomplished through churches and religious periodicals. Included were seven doctors (three Japanese and four Americans) who served in five departments: surgery, obstetrics and gynecology, pediatrics and medicine, dermatology, and urology. The next year a fourth Japanese doctor was added, and Melvin Bradshaw assumed the post of chaplain. In 1958 the hospital served 2,174 in-patients and 9,117 out-patients. Many Japanese who had no previous contact with Christianity found their way to the attractive Baptist hospital, where they encountered genuine love in health care and the transforming power of Christ.[37]

[35]*Commission* 17 (July 1954), 10; "Mission Handbook," 1957 ed., 102-3.

[36]*Commission* 16 (June 1953), 26; ibid. 19 (Jan. 1956), 17; "Mission Handbook," 1957 ed., 103.

[37]*Commission* 19 (Jan. 1956), 17; *ASBC, 1959*, 198; Halvarson, *Japan's New Baptists*, 85-88.

Another notable institution, Amagi Baptist Assembly, began to take shape in 1951 within the Woman's Missionary Society of Yokohama. The society was composed of U. S. military personnel and two missionary sponsors, Mary Ellen Dozier and Hazel Watson. When the members asked the sponsors what they could do to help the Baptist cause in Japan, Mary Ellen, after consulting with her husband, suggested that they develop a "little Ridgecrest," a Japanese version of the Southern Baptist Assembly in Ridgecrest, North Carolina. The idea was so challenging that the Yokohama women, led by Sergeant Lena Bratton, took up two offerings in one meeting, and by 1952 they had raised about $2,000.[38]

Since more money was needed, these women encouraged the men of the Kantō Baptist Military Fellowship to share in the project. Colonel Rupert Elliott and others promoted the fund till it grew to $7,365. The money was turned over to the Convention for the purchase of a 10-acre site that had been chosen by Edwin Dozier and his coworker at Jordan Press and duly inspected and approved by Sergeant Bratton and other military representatives. The property lay on a small plateau 1,300 feet above sea level, near Mount Amagi in the center of Izu Peninsula (south of Tokyo). Bounded by two rivers, it touched on the main highway (then unpaved) at the Sambonmatsu bus stop, named for a cluster of three giant pines that towered overhead. Townsend Harris had rested beneath these trees in 1857 while en route from the U. S. legation in Shimoda to the shogun's palace in Edo (Tokyo).

Two wooden buildings were constructed in 1953 with a Board grant of $25,000. The main building had an auditorium and dining facilities on the first floor and Japanese-style sleeping accommodations on the second. A one-story annex provided additional sleeping space, making a total capacity of 200 guests. The assembly was dedicated in January 1954 as Amagi Sansō (Amagi means "heavenly castle," Sansō means "mountain villa"). This name was also given to the bus stop some years later when the three ancient pines were cut down for safety and the name Sambonmatsu lost its relevance.

American military personnel not only donated the purchase price of the land but also raised additional funds to build a staff house, grade and gravel roads, beautify the grounds, and equip the buildings. In 1955 the Board made a second grant of $25,000 for a third structure, later called Building No. 2, which raised the assembly's capacity to 300. The original structures have since been replaced by two three-story concrete buildings, and a chapel, dining hall, and gymnasium have been added to accommodate the Christian groups of many denominations that keep the facilities occupied the whole year round. In the early years Amagi Sansō

[38]Hollaway, "Religious Education," 180-182; Halvarson, *Japan's New Baptists*, 88-89; "Mission Handbook," 1957 ed., 101-2. See also "Retreat Grounds Presentation Service," program dated Apr. 6, 1952.

was called a "deep freeze" in winter and a "furnace" in summer, but now the main buildings have central heating and air conditioning.

From its beginning Amagi Sansō served as the permanent site of the annual meetings of both the Convention and the Mission, and many of their related organizations and committees met there often. Of the 14,000 guests registered in 1959, for example, about half attended Baptist meetings.[39] Among the missionaries and especially their children, "going to Amagi" meant going to Mission meeting, the most exciting event of the year. All went by train, for in the 1950s few highways were paved and expressways were but a dream of the future. Residents of Tokyo and points north would muster in the special waiting room at Tokyo Station for hugging and handshaking before boarding an express train for Shuzenji. The missionaries and their children, together with the Japanese maids that some brought along to care for infants, would nearly fill a reserved-seat coach, forcing the other passengers to endure three hours of high-decibel English-language chatter. At Shuzenji the party would transfer to a chartered bus for the hour-long bumpy ride over a narrow winding road that was dusty if not muddy. Upon arriving at Amagi Sansō, this Tokyo group would have joyous reunions with those who had come from points south and west. Everyone would hail the arrival of a hired truck that brought trunks, baby beds, and other large items from Mishima Station, the collection point for shipped baggage.

Amagi Sansō was highly conducive to the development of a strong sense of family unity in the Mission. It offered a secluded and homey setting that no hotel could provide. Children could roam freely about the buildings and spacious grounds, which became increasingly familiar with the passing of the years, leaving many enduring and treasured impressions. When an untimely rainy spell kept the hyped-up youngsters indoors all week, everyone alike tried to be patient and cheerful, even the mothers who had to iron their diapers dry.

Accommodations were sparse in those early years, but finicky missionaries learned to bring air mattresses (with pump and patches), electric fans (with double sockets for the electric cord hanging from the ceiling), makeshift curtains, eye shields, ear plugs, and other paraphernalia conducive to comfort. Individual rooms were separated by fusuma (sliding paper doors), which children tended to fling open when an occupant was undressed, and which, even when tightly closed, seemed to amplify the noises made by snoring adults or fussy babies in adjoining rooms. The Japanese-style communal bathing offered therapeutic relaxation for all but a self-conscious few, and rare entertainment for some, as when the "Single Sisters Society" conducted the "nightly water follies."

The facilities at Amagi allowed a program of activities in Mission meetings more extensive than ever before. Fun night, talent night, dress-up banquet, daily Vacation Bible School, and outdoor recreation--softball, volley ball, hiking--all

---

[39]Hollaway, "Religious Education," 251.

found a niche. Even full-fledged field days were held, with sack races, egg throws, and tug-of-wars. A swimming pool was opened in 1958. When heavy-weights Stan Howard, Marion Moorhead, Curtis Askew, and Bud Spencer dived into the water simultaneously for the adult swimming race, it was reported, they produced "a sonic boom and tidal wave." The pool was poorly constructed, unfortunately, and had to be deactivated in the next decade. The year 1958 also featured the first piano recital, with 27 MK performers, and a Girl's Auxiliary coronation presided over by a guest celebrity, Juliette Mather. In that same memorable year, talent night was climaxed by the "Charleston Trio, straight from the Roaring Twenties," performed by Vera Campbell, Mary Gullatt, and Thelma Moorhead.[40]

At one Mission meeting a male quartet sang some impromptu ditties to the tune of "Sixteen Tons." Bob Culpepper recalled some of them as follows:

> I was born one morning when the sun didn't shine,
> I picked up my Bible and I got in line.
> I filled out 16 questionnaires the Board to console,
> And the psychiatrist said, "Well bless my soul."

Chorus:

> You load 16 tons and what do you get?
> Another day older and deeper in debt.
> St. Peter, don't you call me cause I can't go,
> I owe my soul to the Foreign Mission Board.

Another stanza referred to Coleman Clarke's notorious driving habits:

> If you see Coleman coming, you better step aside.
> Other men didn't, and other men died.
> One fender's of iron and the other's of steel;
> If the right one doesn't get you, the left one will.

Even the business sessions, however sober the agenda, were often punctuated by humorous remarks that checked any build-up of tension. By the end of the 1950s, the burgeoning Mission had become an extended family of brothers and sisters, aunts and uncles. Most members felt closer to these spiritual kin than to blood relatives in America. Surely no other mission in the world, it was often remarked, had been melded into a fellowship so divine. One may recall that in the 1910s the Mission fellowship was seriously disrupted by a remark by Bessie

---

[40]MM "unofficial minutes," 1958, 7-11.

Maynard to the effect that young missionary wives should not be in a hurry to bear children. In the 1950s such a remark heard during Mission meeting would likely have appeared in the "unofficial minutes" with other chuckles.

Maturing Through Conflict and Accommodation

Yet serious tensions did arise, if not over the bearing of children, certainly over the educating of children. In 1959, for example, a couple asked to move to Tokyo for evangelistic work so that their children could attend ASIJ (American School in Japan). Missionaries were then dispersed among 25 cities in 22 prefectures, far short of the goal of a presence in all 46 prefectures, and it was Mission policy to make permanent assignments to Tokyo only for specialized ministries. Parents without access to military or other English schools were expected to teach their own children the elementary grades with correspondence course materials from the Calvert School of Baltimore. They were expected to place their older children in the dormitory at Canadian Academy in Kobe or Christian Academy in Tokyo.

The couple in question rejected these options and also declined to place their children with a family in Tokyo where they could attend ASIJ. A serious confrontation arose between the couple and the executive committee. Finally, a compromise was reached by which the family was assigned to a city in the outskirts of Tokyo within commuting distance of ASIJ.

Still, missionary-missionary relationships were less delicate and less often strained than missionary-pastor relationships. A missionary assigned to field evangelism was usually teamed with a Japanese pastor just out of seminary. It was demonstrated convincingly that a missionary and a national working together could develop a church more rapidly than either working alone. But they made an odd pair. There was a glaring disparity between them in physical height, standard of living, personal habits, and perception of the task to be accomplished. Under the Japanese system of delayed ordination, the young pastor usually had to demur to the ordained missionary for baptizing converts and administering the Lord's Supper. Often the missionary saw the pastor as more concerned with study and status than with soul-winning, while the pastor viewed the missionary as success-oriented and having "a zeal for God but not according to knowledge [of Japanese culture]."

Serious conflicts developed in a number of places, and the Mission's personnel committee had to deal with charges against individuals brought directly to the committee or indirectly through Convention leaders. Usually the conflict could be resolved by the process of reassignment, but in at least one case the Convention leaders came close to asking that an individual leave Japan. "We have now very bad impression about missionaries in general," a pastor wrote in English, "because of that one missionary."[41]

In 1954 missionaries outnumbered Japanese workers 100 to 55. Not until 1959, when there were 123 missionaries and 126 nationals, did the majority shift to the other side.[42] At conferences and conventions the foreigners were highly conspicuous, and some were mindlessly clannish. Whenever a Convention board, agency, or committee met, a missionary was present as a non-voting liaison member, whose responsibility was to transmit pertinent information both ways and gain needed experience in Convention operations. The Mission stations and committees, however, met without benefit of Japanese participation, and Convention leaders usually attended Mission meetings only for short periods to extend fraternal greetings. The rationale for this lopsided pattern was that business sessions conducted by missionaries dealt mostly with their own logistics as expatriates, while the meetings of Convention bodies dealt with matters of mutual concern.

The Mission yielded to the Convention's overall direction of the work but retained certain prerogatives. Missionary assignments were recommended by a joint Mission-Convention personnel committee, voted by the Mission or its executive committee "subject to Convention approval," then ratified by the Convention's executive committee. The most sensitive responsibility borne by the Mission was recommending the Convention's budget requests to the Board. Good stewardship of Southern Baptist resources required that each request be reviewed with care, and the Board considered its agency on the field--the Mission--as best qualified to check out details and express an informed opinion. In reality, the Mission rubber-stamped the requests except in rare instances. Still, Pastor Yuya likened the Convention to the lower house of the Diet (Parliament) and the Mission to the upper house. All requests had to pass through the upper house, he said, to reach the executive office in Richmond, where the final decisions were made.[43] The intermediate, seemingly intrusive, role of the Mission implied to some pastors that the Board lacked confidence in Japanese Baptists.

Huge sums of money were involved, for it was with Board grants that Seinan Gakuin and Seinan Jo Gakuin were greatly enlarged, that a hospital, assembly, and office building were erected, that chapels and pastor's homes were built throughout the country. Secretary Maddry had believed in "letting the turtle grow its own shell," but neither Rankin nor Cauthen subscribed to this philosophy. They were committed to helping the Convention's churches and institutions to the fullest extent possible.[44]

[41]Watanabe Kunihiro to George Hays, [1956], JBM.

[42]*ASBC, 1955*, 182; JBM annual report, 1959.

[43]Yuya interview.

[44]Garrott, *Japan Advances*, 135-36.

By the late 1950s, land prices and building costs in Japan had increased so greatly that even with a drastic reduction in the size of land and buildings for churches, the Board could not meet the needs of the 10 or 15 seminary graduates who entered pioneer work each year. This crisis arose at the very time some of the postwar missionaries had come to feel they had gained sufficient experience to start churches with only lay assistance. When a missionary requested a budget for a modest lot and building, such a budget was available from the Board only through the Convention, and the waiting list was long. Delay was all the more irksome for a missionary eager to get started immediately after a furlough in order to have a full five years to develop the church before the next furlough.

There was no little grumbling at the system of placing a highly-trained missionary on the field at considerable cost and then providing no tools for the work beyond a small allotment for petty expenses available through the Mission. Without a specific place to start new work, said Loyce Nelson, "I can rotate at the churches and missions [in Hiroshima], but it is largely a waste of time, talent, and money."[45] It was said only half jokingly that the missionary was little more than a pastor's chauffeur or *kaban-mochi* ("briefcase carrier"). In truth, some felt inadequately used, an attitude incomprehensible to pastors who wondered aloud why missionaries did so little visiting and personal work in the neighborhoods where they lived. As we shall see, these problems were addressed in the 1960s with capital grants for missionaries' exclusive use, and in the 1980s with tighter supervision of missionaries' work.

A matter of deep concern to some of the postwar missionaries was the Convention's membership in the National Christian Council of Japan. It was proposed that the Mission call attention to "the dangers involved in our connection with the N.C.C. and the strong stand taken by . . . the Southern Baptist Convention against such cooperation with unionizing [*sic*] bodies." At the 1954 Mission meeting the general affairs committee, chaired by George Hays, was asked to make a study of the NCC and express "their opinions as to whether the membership the Convention now holds is beneficial to our Baptist program." The committee did the necessary research and interviews but split on the issue. In 1955 the majority reported to the Mission that the NCC in Japan was not parallel to the NCC in the United States, that the prewar West Japan Convention had held full membership, and that current Convention leaders regarded the NCCJ as "an important factor of Baptist prestige, a strategic opportunity for our Baptist testimony, and a stimulating source of information and inspiration for our Baptist work." The majority further noted that the Convention leaders were fully aware of potential dangers in the relationship (they had experienced the wartime United Church) and that any action by the Mission on this matter would be improper. Attached to this report was the minority opinion of Frank Connely, who argued

---

[45]Nelson statement in author's notes.

(Upper) Kanazawa Baptist Church, 1955, typical of churches built in the '50s.
(Lower) Church school at Kanazawa missionary residence, ca. 1955. *(Photos by author)*

that the NCCJ ties should be severed. The Mission accepted the entire report and laid the matter to rest.[46]

Other Events in the Later '50s

Of the 52 churches organized in the 1950s, the most significant from the Mission's point of view was Tokyo Baptist, organized in 1958 as its first English-language church. The origins of this work may be traced back to 1946, when Southern Baptists among the U.S. military personnel in the Tokyo area began to form fellowship groups. Though many of them were active in Protestant chapel programs, they craved the warm, unstructured services they had known in their churches back home. Gradually the scattered groups were melded into one Baptist Military Fellowship at Tokyo Chapel Center, where Sunday school and worship services were conducted on Sunday afternoons. Participants came by bus, car, and train from such widely scattered places as Washington Heights, Camp Zama, Yokohama Air Station, Tokorozawa Army Base, and the air force bases at Tachikawa, Johnson, and Yokota. The end of the occupation in 1952 had no immediate effect on the fellowship, since American bases and military activities remained intact under treaty arrangements with Japan.[47]

In 1958, under the leadership of Air Force Major Galen Bradford, later a missionary associate in Japan, the fellowship made preparation for becoming a full-fledged church. Meeting on Sunday afternoon, January 5, 1958, at Keisen Church, the group organized formally as Tokyo Baptist Church, with 57 charter members. Dub Jackson was called as pastor. On Easter Sunday the congregation moved into a surplus quonset hut hastily erected at the church's present site in Shibuya. Members pitched in to renovate the hut's interior and make it respectable for worship. They also gave sacrificially for a new building. With aid from the Board, a three-story, $150,000 structure was completed in August 1959. In November it was dedicated with a week-long, star-studded program. Music was provided by the Japan Philharmonic Orchestra and the Fifth U.S. Air Force Band. With a little persuasion, the *Japan Times* marked the occasion with a four-page supplement on "Tokyo's newest church."[48]

Various developments in the Convention also were of particular interest to the Mission. In 1955 Shirabe Masamichi and his wife were sent as "foreign" missionaries to Okinawa, an island under American administrative control from 1945 to 1972. Their work at Shuri was supported by the WMU-sponsored Christmas offering, and in 1958 a church building was completed there with funds

---

[46]Reports of the General Affairs Committee on the NCCJ to the EC and Mission, 23 Feb., 31 May, July 1955.

[47]F. Calvin Parker, "In God's Master Plan," in Tokyo Baptist Church's 20th anniversary booklet, 1978.

[48]Ibid.

provided by the Convention without Board assistance. In 1956 Ernest Hollaway was elected associate secretary of the Church School Department, and the next year Morris Wright was elected to the same position in the Training Union Department. Also in 1957, the Convention elected Arase Noboru as its first full-time secretary of evangelism (Coleman Clarke afterwards became his associate) and sponsored New Life evangelistic campaigns throughout the nation. The campaigns put into practice some of the methods taught by C. E. Autrey of Southwestern Seminary in regional conferences held earlier in the year. They also had the support of the Youth Department, which sent evangelistic "caravans" to pioneer areas and even to Okinawa.[49]

In October 1957 the Board voted to "encourage the Japan Baptist Convention and our Japan Mission in planning for a major city-wide evangelistic campaign for Tokyo, the world's largest city, in 1959, the centennial of evangelical missions in Japan." The plans for a large Tokyo campaign fizzled, but evangelistic meetings were conducted in 1959 on a nationwide scale. Eight Southern Baptist leaders, including Ramsey Pollard, president of the SBC, were featured speakers. They also took part in the dedication services for Tokyo Baptist Church and in Convention-sponsored programs conducted in Tokyo and Fukuoka to commemorate the 70th anniversary of Southern Baptist work in Japan. The centennial celebrations of the larger Protestant community elicited only a token response from members of the Mission or Convention.[50]

All church-related organizations got a boost during this banner year. Japanese adaptations of SBC Sunday school and Training Union manuals were published by Jordan Press, thus inaugurating the study course system of leadership training. The Woman's Missionary Union published a manual and sponsored a series of conferences led by WMU leaders Marie Mathis and Alma Hunt. Maines Rawls of the Sunday School Board led a month of Training Union conferences. BTU was so well promoted that 80 percent of the churches had adult unions.[51]

In this same year a reorganization of the Convention brought all departments, boards, agencies, and institutions under three divisions: education and service, evangelism-missions, and institutions. An enlarged staff, including missionaries

---

[49]Edward E. Bollinger, *The Cross and the Floating Dragon: The Gospel in Ryukyu* (Pasadena: William Carey Library, 1983); *Zen Nippon ni Kirisuto no hikari o* (The light of Christ to all Japan) (Tokyo: Nihon Baputesuto Remmei, 1980), 6-9; EBD, "Mission and Convention," 23-25.

[50]Winston Crawley to George Hays, 11 Oct. 1957; Hollaway, "Religious Education," 230; EBD, "Mission and Convention," 25; Winston Crawley, *New Frontiers in an Old World* (Nashville: Convention Press, 1962), 95. The visiting speakers other than Pollard were G. Kearny Keegan of the Sunday School Board; Winston Crawley and James G. Stertz of the FMB; seminary professors T. B. Maston and W. H. Souther; and pastors Herschel H. Hobbs, T. A. Patterson, and E. H. Westmoreland.

[51]Hollaway, "Religious Education," 214-23. The Training Union movement declined in the next decade and virtually died. The Japanese name, *Kunren kai*, was never well regarded, and some aspects of the organization failed to take hold in the churches.

as associate secretaries, required additional space. To meet this need a new Convention-Mission office building was erected on the Nishiōkubo compound where the garage apartment and two prefabs had stood. Earlier, a Mission committee's recommendation that this property be set aside as a servicemen's center had failed. The two-story ferroconcrete building--a third story was added later--housed the Mission office in the rear portion of the second floor. Dedication services were scheduled for January 1960.[52]

So ended a decade in which the number of Convention churches nearly tripled, rising from 24 to 67, membership more than quadrupled, from 2,917 to 13,035, and total gifts soared from ¥3,286,891 to ¥50,899,906. In 1959 the 67 organized churches were sponsoring and cultivating another 100 congregations, called missions, most of which would become churches in the decade ahead.[53] The Convention's work had expanded into all 46 prefectures save one, Toyama, which was to be entered in 1960. The Mission, whose own number had grown from 45 to 123, had played an indispensable role in this nationwide advance.

[52]Ibid., 198-207.
[53]Zen Nippon ni, 31-33.

10

Coping with Change (1960-1969)

The decade of the '60s opened with Japanese politics in a state of turmoil. In January, Prime Minister Kishi Nobusuke and President Eisenhower signed a revised Japan-U.S. Security Treaty that was strongly opposed by the Socialist and Communist parties and their supporters among workers and students. In May, Kishi and his ruling Liberal-Democratic Party pushed through the necessary ratification in the Diet. Antitreaty demonstrations that had begun in 1959 now turned violent. Platoons of snake-dancing students clashed with riot police in the streets of Tokyo and forced their way into the Diet building. So massive were the demonstrations--as many as 100,000 participants at a time--and so tense the atmosphere that Eisenhower's planned visit to Japan had to be cancelled. Kishi was attacked and wounded at his official residence and later forced to resign. In the most shocking scene of all, Asanuma Inejirō, chairman of the Socialist Party, was fatally stabbed by a 17-year-old rightist on the stage of Tokyo's Hibiya Hall while the audience watched in horror.[1]

Kishi's successor as prime minister, Ikeda Hayato, helped to defuse the tension by announcing a highly popular "income doubling plan" for the decade. No one could foresee that the economy would grow so fast that Japanese incomes would double within 7 years instead of 10. It so happened that in this decade the whole capitalist world enjoyed the longest sustained economic boom on record. Relations between Japan and the United States took an upward turn in 1961 after John F. Kennedy was inaugurated president. Kennedy was immensely popular with the Japanese, most of whom mourned his death in 1963. Kennedy's ambassador to Japan, Edwin O. Reischauer, also won popular acclaim. Born and reared in Tokyo, the son of Presbyterian missionaries, Reischauer had an insider's grasp of Japan and enjoyed close rapport with its leaders.[2]

---

[1]*JCY, 1960*, 3-21; *JCY, 1961*, 1-3.
[2]*JCY, 1961*, 1, 9; Phillips, *Rising of the Sun*, 29; Edwin O. Reischauer, *My Life between Japan and America* (New York: Harper & Row, 1986), 7-8, 161-304.

For Baptists, the decade got off to a sunny start with the January 1960 dedication of the new Convention and Mission office building in Shinjuku. "The office is really the 'kitchen' of the work rather than the 'headquarters,'" said Convention president Yuya Kiyoki, "and those who work there are 'servants' rather than 'directors.'" He regarded the building as more a gift from God than a gift from the Board, since Southern Baptists had given the money primarily to God and secondarily to the Board.[3]

In June, on the day after the most violent of the anti-Security Treaty demonstrations, the cornerstone was laid for another building--Tokyo Baptist Student Center--that some Convention leaders regarded as more a gift from the Board than a gift from God. They would have preferred to use the money for churches. But a missionary couple had been assigned to student work in Tokyo, and the Board and the Mission both thought the Convention should have a student center. Regardless, an excellent location was found for the center within a few minutes' walk of a subway station and four universities. In November the new building was dedicated to the primary purpose of "leading students to Christ." The task was a major challenge, for Tokyo had 300,000 college students from all parts of Japan.[4]

Evangelism was indeed the chief emphasis of the year, as of most years. It was taken up at Mission meeting under the theme, "Go Forward." It was discussed at length in station meetings. In December, 12 single women gathered in Tokyo for their own evangelistic conference, at which they not only discussed such matters as visitation and Bible classes but engaged in serious dialogue with Convention leaders.[5]

During 1960 the Convention opened new work in Toyama, completing its expansion to all the nation's prefectures. At the same time it urged the establishment of a second congregation in each prefecture that had only one. The Convention also started its first radio broadcast, "Baptist Hour," a 10-minute program aired in Fukuoka each Sunday morning until 1966, after which it was moved to the Tōkai district. With still greater vision and determination, the Convention launched a five-year advance movement to double the number of churches from 70 to 140. Unlike Ikeda's income-doubling plan that ran ahead of schedule, the goal was not reached until 1969, at the end of a second five-year movement whose aim was to double the effectiveness of the churches rather than the number.[6]

[3]JBM annual report, 1960.

[4]Hollaway, "Religious Education," 230-31; Crawley, *New Frontiers*, 115.

[5]"Report of Single Women's Evangelistic Conference," 28-29 Dec. 1960.

[6]*JCY, 1961*, 88-89; John Shepard to Winston Crawley, 13 May 1965; JBM annual report, 1965; EC minutes, 29 June-1 July, 1966; "Japan Baptist Convention Summary, 1947-1986"; Egasaki, *Hachijūnen no ayumi*, 107.

The New Life Movement

The most spectacular event of the decade, the 1963 New Life Movement, began to take shape in the January 1960 meeting of the Convention's executive committee, when an action was taken to invite Billy Graham to conduct a citywide crusade in Tokyo. The plan called for the Convention to sponsor the crusade but to enlist the support of other denominations. Matsumura Shūichi, chairman of the Convention's evangelism committee, was asked to head the invitation committee.[7] "Let's shout!" exclaimed Dub Jackson, who had been lobbying for the crusade. Jackson's church, Tokyo Baptist, provided $1,500 as traveling expenses for Matsumura to attend the SBC's May 1960 meeting at Miami Beach and present the invitation to Graham. The famed evangelist tentatively agreed to conduct the crusade.[8]

Matsumura carried to Miami a 16mm color film, *The Tokyo Challenge*, which Jackson had produced through a cinema company at a cost of only $2,000. The movie highlighted the dynamics of a great city preparing to host the 1964 Olympics and played up the timely opportunity afforded for mass evangelism. Jackson had asked the Board to show the film at the Miami convention but had been refused on grounds that the Board's program was already full. Had there been time, the Board's staff would have preferred to show a new movie on Lottie Moon. So after the convention had opened, Jackson telephoned SBC president Ramsey Pollard and urged that the film be shown. Pollard publicly asked Baker James Cauthen to include it in the foreign missions presentation. This put Cauthen in an awkward position. Reluctantly he consented, against the advice of his own staff. Consequently a large number of the 13,612 delegates at Miami were confronted with *The Tokyo Challenge*.[9]

Jackson worried about having offended both Cauthen and his secretary for the Orient, Winston Crawley, by going over their heads with a direct appeal to Pollard. But Cauthen was magnanimous as usual, accepting the reality and pledging his support for the crusade. When Crawley passed through Tokyo in July and Jackson raised the sensitive matter with him, Crawley "said he'd forgotten all about it."[10]

Graham's tentative acceptance of the invitation was followed by a surge of publicity that embarrassed him. His friend Bob Pierce of World Vision had conducted a citywide crusade in Osaka in 1959 and was planning one for Tokyo in 1961. Just before Matsumura's departure for Miami, however, Jackson had

---

[7]EC minutes, 19-22 Jan. 1960.

[8]Jackson to George Hays, 30 Jan. 1960; JBC EC minutes, 19-22 Jan. 1960; Jackson to author, 20 July 1960.

[9]Billy Keith, *Shinsei: New Life for Asia* (Tokyo: Jordan Press, 1963), 22; Fletcher, *Baker James Cauthen*, 238-39.

[10]Jackson to author, 20 July 1960.

heard that the 1961 crusade was being cancelled. Matsumura had conveyed this intelligence to Graham. But it proved erroneous, and the announcement of a Graham crusade in 1963 threatened to aggravate mounting opposition to the 1961 crusade. A group of younger pastors, mostly in the United Church, was accusing Pierce of representing "American imperialism" and violating the separation of church and state by renting the city-owned Tokyo Gymnasium for religious purposes. So Jackson apologized to both Pierce and Graham for the mix-up and promised to withhold further publicity on the Graham campaign until after Pierce's crusade had ended in June 1961.[11]

In June 1961 Jackson was again consumed with the Tokyo challenge. His Japanese colleagues commended his zeal but asked him "to exercise restraint in his promotional activities." Before month's end, however, he met with Prime Minister Ikeda at Travis Air Force Base in California (Ikeda was en route home from a visit to Washington). Texas-born Jackson presented the prime minister with a pair of cowboy boots, a cowboy hat, and an honorary Texas citizenship. The unusual meeting had been arranged through the good offices of Vice President Lyndon Johnson and other influential Texans. Photographs of the encounter were used to promote the crusade in Japan.[12]

Meanwhile the Baptist General Convention of Texas agreed to underwrite the "big Tokyo pow-wow," as one pastor called it, with the needed personnel and $300,000 for expenses. After some hesitation, the executive committee of the Japan Convention accepted the offer. The Texas-Tokyo linkup seemed incongruous (Jackson's cable address in Tokyo was TEXBAP), but if the big state and the sprawling metropolis had nothing else in common, they had the same population--about 10 million each. By the end of 1961, plans had been revised to make the Tokyo crusade the kick-off for a nationwide effort--the New Life Movement--to share Christ with all 94 million Japanese. In response, Texas Baptists, noted for their big churches and unabashed triumphalism, increased their financial pledge to $500,000. The Foreign Mission Board also threw its support behind the expanded movement.[13]

So exciting were the reports emanating from Tokyo, Dallas, and Richmond that other Southern Baptist agencies and individuals wanted a piece of the action. The Radio and Television Commission sent films to be dubbed into Japanese and shown on television. The Brotherhood Commission made available its director of promotion, James M. Sapp, to speak at a Layman's Leadership Conference held in July 1962 as preparation for the New Life Movement. When some missionaries objected to Sapp's coming because of his tobacco habit--Japanese Baptists frown

[11]Jackson to Pierce, 4 July 1960; Jackson to Graham, 6 July 1960; *JCY, 1961*, 35-38.

[12]Coleman Clarke to Crawley, 6 June 1961; "Tokyo-Texas Meet," in Golden Gate Baptist Theological Seminary, "News and Information," n.d.; *New Life*, 15 Jan. 1963, 2.

[13]Jackson to Ramsey Pollard, 1 June 1960; "Billy Graham Evangelism Committee Meeting," 4-5 Dec. 1961; Crawley to George Hays, 11 Mar. 1963.

more on smoking than drinking--Sapp pledged to abstain while in Japan and won clearance from the Foreign Mission Board. The Home Mission Board sent its evangelism director to speak at a January 1963 planning conference.[14]

The Layman's Conference of July 1962, which featured Sapp, helped to set a spiritual tone for the Convention's annual meeting held in the following month. The tone of the meeting was crucial, for delegates were confronted with two items on the agenda that seemed to conflict with each other. One was a plan of reorganization, to take effect in January 1964, that would reduce expenditures drastically and propel the Convention toward self-support. The plan was approved. The other item was ratification of the executive committee's decision to sponsor the New Life Movement. This proposal aroused heated debate. Opponents argued that the Convention should not accept massive foreign aid at a time when it was striving for financial independence. Yet others who were at best cool toward the New Life Movement felt that commitments had been made which, if retracted, would cause all Japanese Baptists to lose face. Although appalled at the aggressive tactics of Matsumura and a few others in obligating the Convention, they voted aye or abstained from voting. It was with "considerable difficulty," reported Edwin Dozier, that the executive committee pushed through its recommendation.[15]

Hard feelings persisted until December, when the venerable Pastor Yuya "switched sides" in favor of the movement. At this, the opposition among pastors virtually melted away.[16] A number of missionaries harbored lingering resentment that the regular Mission channels for decision-making were being ignored, that even Mission officers were not being informed of decisions that directly involved the whole missionary body. The New Life Movement committee and staff, led by Matsumura and Jackson, seemed to function independently. With the onset of 1963, nevertheless, nearly all pastors and missionaries became heavily involved in local preparations.

The Texas Convention raised $500,000 as planned. Except for $10,000 retained for bills payable in Texas, it remitted the full amount to Japan through the Board. Out of this $490,000, $200,000 was paid to Dentsū, a leading advertising agency. Dentsū was retained to publicize the New Life Movement through newspapers, magazines, TV, radio, and outdoor advertising. One of the agency's highly regarded contributions was an attractive logo designed for this purpose.[17]

Nearly a dozen celebrities were recruited by the New Life Movement committee to attract the eyes and ears of the nation. The most recognizable was movie idol Charlton Heston. While visiting Tokyo in December 1962 to boost one

[14]Clarke to Truett Myers, 11 Sept. 1961; Myers to Clarke, 19 Sept. 1961; Crawley to Charles Whaley, 19 May 1962; *New Life*, 1 Feb. 1963, 2. The evangelism director was Vernon Yearby.

[15]Dozier to Crawley, 14 Aug. 1962.

[16]Whaley to Shepard, 12 Mar. 1962.

[17]Crawley to Hays, 11 Mar. 1963; *New Life*, 15 Jan. 1963, 2.

of his films, Heston read the Christmas story from the Bible on a nationwide television program sponsored by the New Life committee.[18]

The movement proper was conducted over a five-week period from March 30 to May 5, 1963. It was launched with a five-day crusade in Tokyo for which Billy Graham had been billed as preacher. Since Graham had fallen ill and cancelled his Orient trip on doctor's orders, five different speakers were substituted. The first four meetings, held nightly in Waseda University's cavernous Memorial Auditorium, featured Akbar Haqq of India, J. T. Ayorinde of Nigeria, T. A. Patterson of the United States, and Ozaki Shuichi of Japan. The fifth and climactic rally, held in Kōrakuen Baseball Stadium, featured Baker James Cauthen, who had spent much of the afternoon giving out handbills in front of a busy railway station. These same speakers were used for three-day citywide meetings held in Sapporo, Nagoya, Fukuoka, and Kokura.[19]

Attendance at the rally in Kōrakuen Stadium was reported as 9,000 in *Newsweek* and 15,000 in the *Mainichi Daily News*. Even the two official English publications of the New Life Movement gave different figures: 10,000 in *New Lifeline* and 13,000 in *New Life*. These discrepancies point up the problem of reliable figures for such large gatherings. Even the stadium's seating capacity was variously given as 35,000, 40,000, or 50,000. Whatever the correct figure, only the infield section was filled at the rally. By contrast, a Billy Graham rally in the same stadium in 1967 drew an estimated attendance of 36,000 to 40,000.[20]

Though deprived of the magic name of Billy Graham, the Tokyo meetings utilized an impressive array of fame and talent. The Japan Philharmonic Orchestra and a 400-voice choir offered special music. The vice president of Liberia, W. R. Tolbert, Jr., spoke about his Christian faith, as did several Olympic champions and other well-known athletes. Baseball stars were given such prominence that one critic wrote: "The spiritual content of this crusade . . . seems likely to set a new low. 'Be a Baptist and win success at baseball' seems to be the theme."[21]

The big-applause getters in the citywide crusades and various other meetings over a month-long period were the 35 members of the Hardin-Simmons University Cowboy Band. They wore gold shirts, purple bandannas, faded levis, scarred leather chaps, cowboy boots, and 10-gallon hats. Their music offended the fine-tuned ears of some Japanese, but the colorful garb, rebel yells, and unique "cow-step" marching seemed adequate compensation for the off-key playing. Regardless, their well-meant efforts were said to make Christianity look like "a three-ring circus." Eugene A. Nida, a Baptist missiologist and specialist in Bible translation,

[18]*New Life*, 1 Jan. 1963, 2.

[19]*New Lifeline*, n.d.

[20]*Newsweek*, 19 Apr. 1963, 61; *Mainichi Daily News*, 4 Apr. 1963; *New Lifeline*, vol. 1, no. 7, n.d.; *New Life*, 5 Apr. 1963, 2.

[21]*Yomiuri*, 18 Feb. 1963; *New Life*, 5 Apr. 1963, 2.

(**Upper**) Dub Jackson with Prime Minister Ikeda, 1961. (**Lower**) New Life Movement information desk, Hotel Okura, Tokyo, 1963. *(Photos from Billy Keith,* Shinsei: New Life for Japan. *Courtesy of Jordan Press, Tokyo)*

later remarked that the use of these student entertainers "proved a disaster, for they alienated far more than they ever attracted to the gospel."[22]

The big-city rallies paved the way for smaller eight-day meetings held in 150 Convention churches and missions--all but five churches and some of the smaller missions. Over 500 Americans, mostly from Texas, made up the 150 teams. A typical team consisted of one preacher, one musician, and one or two laypersons. All the participants were divided into four larger teams, designated as A, B, C, and D. Team A (27 teams) served the first week, and Team D (43 teams) served the fourth and final week. Before leaving home the participants read an 18-page paper, "Preparing for Your Mission to Japan," written by Ernest Hollaway, and after reaching Japan they attended an orientation session at Tokyo Baptist Church. These preliminaries doubtless reduced the number of bobbles made by the visitors.[23]

Missionaries were heavily involved. Day after day they entertained, chauffeured, interpreted, counseled. One wife said, "My major work is opening the door at midnight letting my husband in the door." Though physically exhausted and sometimes exasperated at foul-ups and failures, most missionaries were pleased with the outcome of the meetings. "Never have we seen the devil work any harder," said Lucy Smith, "but somehow the Lord overruled his efforts and wonderful things happened."[24]

The "wonderful things" included 22,651 decisions, of which 10,402 were decisions for baptism. As a result, Convention baptisms for the year 1963 reached an all-time high of 1,778. This achievement was offset in 1964, when baptisms dropped to 968, the lowest number since 1949. The spiritual climate in Japan had changed radically since 1951, when a preaching mission with nine preachers had registered 10,000 decisions and contributed to a 10-fold increase in baptisms over the year before. In the case of the New Life Movement, well-planned follow-up meetings were held three weeks and five weeks after the close of the large crusades, but contact was lost with many who had made decisions.[25]

In the conservative Hokuriku district, the initial response seemed incredible: 120 decisions at Kanazawa, 100 at Fukui, and 66 at Toyama. But only a handful of seekers attended the follow-up meetings. The three pastors wrote a stack of letters and visited many homes, learning to their dismay that the people who had signed decision cards no longer wanted to become Christians or attend church. The pastors concluded that the sermons had been too direct and offensive and the

[22]*New Life*, 15 Feb. 1963, 4; "A Brief Evaluation of the New Life Movement in Japan," in "Mission Actions, 1963," 54; Eugene A. Nida, "My Pilgrimage in Mission," *International Bulletin of Missionary Research* 12 (Apr. 1988): 64.

[23]"New Life Movement Scrapbook," JBM.

[24]Keith, *Shinsei*, 150.

[25]"Report of Evangelism Study Committee," in "Mission Actions, 1963," 50; "Japan Baptist Convention Summary, 1947-1986."

invitations too emotional and compulsive. For whatever reasons, the lasting results were meager. After six months there had been two baptisms at Kanazawa, four at Fukui, and none at Toyama. All six of those baptized had been seekers before the New Life Movement.[26]

Throughout the Convention, in fact, the success of the movement was seen less in the number of persons truly converted than in the number of churches and missions strengthened and renewed. The visiting teams had helped bring revival to struggling congregations all over Japan. In the words of Tucker Callaway, the team at Nara, for instance, "had come to an obscure new mission and put it on its feet."[27] The movement also produced some of the Japanese ministers who serve the churches today.

In a follow-up activity of the New Life Movement, 10 pastors were invited to the United States in the summer of 1964 to observe evangelistic and educational work in a variety of churches. Several other activities, though not linked directly with the movement, seemed to thrive in its spiritual wake. In 1964 the Convention appointed Togami Nobuyoshi and his wife Kimiko as missionaries to Brazil and sent them to New Orleans Seminary for a year of study prior to entering upon their new work. A major attraction of Brazil as a foreign field was its 600,000 people of Japanese descent, the largest number in any country other than Japan.[28] As noted before, the prewar Convention had sent the Amanos to Manchukuo, a puppet state controlled by the Japanese military, and the postwar Convention had sent the Shirabes to Okinawa (their work was incorporated into the home mission program in 1967). The Togamis were the Convention's first missionaries sent to a country truly foreign.

A three-year Sunday school crusade launched in 1965 strengthened 10 "pilot churches" and then scores of other churches that learned by example the value of a properly led, fully-graded church school. The year 1965 also marked the beginning of nationwide brotherhood conventions. In 1966 a committee was established on evangelizing the deaf, and in 1968 the Convention was divided into 13 associations to give more responsibility to local areas and encourage more cooperation in evangelistic efforts.[29]

Whatever the immediate and long-range benefits of the New Life Movement, questions naturally were raised about the huge expenditure, an estimated $1,650,000. Could not the money have been better used, some asked, to buy land and build chapels for new congregations? The obvious answer was that the funds would not have been made available for that purpose. A large share of the spiritual benefits went to the foreign participants themselves, who were overjoyed

---

[26]Author's notes from his Oct. 1963 meeting with Hokuriku pastors.

[27]Tucker N. Callaway, "Our Nara Team" (1963, mimeographed), 8.

[28]*JCY, 1964*, 111; Egasaki, *Hachijūnen no ayumi*, 89; *Zen Nippon ni*, 12.

[29]FMB, "Evangelism and Church Development," no. 8, Dec. 1966; Egasaki, *Hachijūnen no ayumi*, 89; *Zen Nippon ni*, 13-15.

at the response to their testimony in an alien culture. One preacher thought he had been a part of "the greatest spiritual movement since Pentecost." Two musicians returned to Japan as permanent missionaries.[30]

The most effective witness in the New Life Movement was given by lay people representing various businesses and professions. Bankers witnessed to bankers, doctors to doctors, merchants to merchants. They handed out tracts, visited in homes, testified in church services. These laypersons sounded more authentic than the professional preachers, and the Japanese were impressed that they would leave their work and come to Japan at their own expense to share a simple but earnest testimony for Christ. Gifted musicians also won favor, for good music transcends the language barrier and reaches the soul.[31] So when team-evangelism meetings were resumed on a smaller scale in 1966, laypersons and musicians were requested from America, but most of the preaching was done by Japanese pastors and missionaries. In the fall of 1967, for instance, the team members sent from America included 27 musicians and laypersons but only 4 preachers. This pattern has since prevailed over that of the 1963 extravaganza.

New Strategies Are Developed

For some missionaries, the New Life Movement was a temporary respite from the sense of frustration they had felt since the late 1950s. Two couples had resigned in 1961 (both were later reappointed) for virtually opposite reasons. One husband, Melvin Bradshaw, felt that the work in Japan was too heavily subsidized and too tainted with Southern Baptist and American ways. The other husband, Bill Emanuel, thought the Mission had given in to the Convention's "gradualist" approach to evangelism. The Convention was failing to utilize missionaries adequately while insisting on the right to control their work assignments, Bill charged, and its leaders did not want missionaries to succeed because the Japanese would lose face.[32]

Both viewpoints were held by other missionaries on the field. Pete Gillespie, for example, in his 1961 Mission meeting address entitled "A Preacher's Dilemma in Japan," faulted the Mission for its "passive accommodation" to the Convention. Such a policy should be scrapped, he said, because it had yielded but meager results. He called for a new approach of "positive affirmation," by which missionaries would work alongside the nationals, not under them. The Mission, he asserted, should conduct radio and TV programs, operate large Baptist centers, and do mass evangelism. Many who heard him could appreciate these sentiments

---

[30]K. Owen White, "Where is the Lord God of Elijah," in White papers, box 1, folder 15, SBC Historical Commission; "Brief Evaluation," 53-54. The musicians were Beryle Lovelace and Darrell Mock.

[31]"Brief Evaluation," 56.

[32]Dozier, "Mission and Convention," 26.

coming from Gillespie, one of the most gifted preachers in the Mission. None other than W. A. Criswell once told him, "Pete, you can preach!"[33]

Rebuttal came from Tucker Callaway, who aired his views most eloquently in a sermon about "walls" delivered at Mission meeting in 1963. Callaway warned against erecting a dividing wall between the Mission and the Convention, or between missionaries with conflicting attitudes toward the Convention. He argued that the Mission's current posture, which he called "active accommodation," had been vindicated by the Convention's remarkable growth. Callaway compared their relationship to a fruitful marriage in which each partner must forego some freedom in order to produce and rear children. Both the Mission and the Convention, he argued, should forego a measure of freedom in order to produce and nurture churches.[34]

Pastor Yuya had often said that the missionary should relate to the national as an old-fashioned wife relates to her husband. Such a wife gives up her name and career to work for her husband's advancement. She is his best critic, though always tactful and never nagging. She is not zealous to reform him, for she accepts him as he is. And his success is her joy and crown. For Yuya, the analogy was ironically suited to the Mission-Convention relationship, for in Japan "the wife controls the purse strings."

Against this background, Coleman Clarke took Callaway's reference to the marriage relationship as implying servility on the part of one partner rather than mutual equality. "We are co-workers under God," he thundered. Among those who stood with Gillespie and Clarke on this issue were some who had expected a colossal "breakthrough" in evangelism through the New Life Movement and now felt that the work had reverted to "business as usual." They were discontented if not frustrated. A spirit of unrest pervaded the Mission.[35]

To deal with the crisis, a special Mission meeting--in reality a strategy conference--was called in November 1963. Eight Convention representatives participated during a part of the five-day conference. Papers were read, problems were discussed, suggestions were made. With expert guidance from Winston Crawley, the relationships of Board, Mission, and Convention were carefully explored. At the conclusion a statement was adopted expressing the Mission's appreciation and support for the Convention and asking for a joint study on two questions: "(1) How can missionary personnel be used most effectively in evangelizing Japan and in strengthening the work of the Convention? (2) How can the resources of the Mission and of the Board be used so as to promote the

---

[33]A. L. Gillespie, "A Preacher's Dilemma in Japan," 1961, mimeographed. Criswell's remark was quoted by Gillespie to the author.

[34]Tucker N. Callaway, "Mission Meeting Sermon," July 1963, mimeographed.

[35]Parker, "Baptist Missions in Japan," 38; Ralph Calcote, "The Development of CAPEO and PEP" (1970, mimeographed), 1.

genuine independence of the Convention and its churches and at the same time to promote the spread of the gospel to all the people of Japan?"[36]

Though the fall meeting was cathartic in allowing vent to frustrations, it was disappointing to some in that no changes were made in the basic working policies of the Mission. A number of missionaries feared that subsequent talks with the Convention would merely reconfirm the status quo. During the months that followed, rumors spread that the "missionary exodus" then affecting the missions of several other denominations might spread to Southern Baptists. Among the books in vogue at the time were *The Unpopular Missionary* and *Missionary Go Home.*[37]

In 1965 Gillespie wrote another paper to argue that the fundamental issues had not been resolved. Among his recommendations: that the Mission adopt a budget for direct evangelism done by "those missionaries choosing to work under Mission direction instead of Convention direction," and that it "set up its own Evangelism Committee to direct this new category of missionary."[38] In response, the Mission's executive committee established a special study committee with Gillespie as chairman.

After much study and many consultations, the special committee recommended that the Mission "undertake a Cooperative Advance Program of Evangelistic Operations in full partnership with the Japan Baptist Convention." This program, mercifully called CAPEO, was approved at the 1965 Mission meeting. Some members who opposed it in principle voted for it out of sympathy for those who might be lost to the work without it. The program statement, while reaffirming the traditional principles underlying the Mission's work of evangelism, greatly expanded the boundaries set in the past. The key sentence read: "The Mission shall seek especially to study and recommend experimental projects in church development and evangelism and to project work in cooperation with local churches or Convention agencies." The reference to "experimental projects" was innovative, but the proposal that the Mission "project work" was radical and revolutionary. The intention was that the Mission would provide funds directly for missionaries to start churches. Accordingly, the executive committee requested from the Board $8,000 to establish a revolving loan fund called the Pioneer Evangelism Property Fund, or PEP fund for short.[39]

At the 1966 Mission meeting, action was taken "to use funds from the Pioneer Evangelism Property Fund to purchase small plots of land (40-60 tsubo) [one tsubo is 36 square feet] for the purpose of beginning and implementing the growth of new missions for which the missionary is delegated as pastor or responsible

---

[36]"Statement Adopted by the Mission," Nov. 16, 1963, mimeographed.

[37]Calcote, "CAPEO and PEP," 1; Richard H. Drummond, "A Missionary 'Exodus' from Japan?" *Christian Century* 82 (26 May 1965): 672-74.

[38]A. L. Gillespie, "A Preacher's Continuing Dilemma in Japan," 1965, mimeographed.

[39]Calcote, "CAPEO and PEP," 3-6.

person by the local church." It was further voted that the PEP fund could be used "to provide a temporary removable building where needed at a cost not to exceed $2,000." The land purchased by the Mission was to be loaned to the missionary rent-free for a period of up to five years. During this period the missionary was to lead the congregation to practice Christian stewardship and form a relationship to the Convention through which a permanent location could be provided. When this was accomplished, the temporary property was to be sold and the money returned to the PEP fund.[40]

Further consultations with the Convention led to the formation of a joint evangelism study committee. The Convention representatives on this committee spoke bluntly: "Did the missionaries really want to win souls or did they want to administer an organization?" They stressed anew that churches had been developed most rapidly where missionaries and Japanese pastors had worked together. The work had slowed down, they said, because the Mission had stopped deploying missionaries to the outlying prefectures and Japanese pastors had been left to work alone. As for missionaries starting work on their own, the Convention representatives argued that "missionaries gather around themselves quite a different kind of person than those who gather around a Japanese pastor, and in many instances these two do not mix. . . . The fault is not with the missionary, but rather with the motivations of those that come about them."[41]

Despite these reservations, the Japanese expressed sympathy for the plight of missionaries and recognized the necessity of their obtaining "tools" on an enlarged scale through the Mission's own budget. They gave assurance that work begun by missionaries in temporary quarters provided by PEP funds would be given "the same consideration as any other work in Convention priority lists for capital needs." As expected, the Japanese emphasized the importance of prior consultation with all parties concerned and the wise use of lay leadership. Surprisingly, they suggested more flexibility in the size of land tracts and recommended that the temporary building be larger than that specified by the Mission. Small, cheap buildings, they said, "did not create in the communities respect and confidence that more permanent structures engendered."[42]

After hearing the report of the joint committee, the Mission in 1966 amended CAPEO policies to allow the purchase of up to 100 tsubo of land instead of 60, and to allow up to $5,000 for a building instead of only $2,000. The land budget was set at $10,000 but raised to $15,000 a few years later. The standard building size was fixed at 30 tsubo. In keeping with its new responsibilities, the Mission also dissolved its evangelism study committee and established a permanent evangelism committee as a subcommittee of the executive committee. This was

[40]Ibid., 6-7.
[41]Edwin B. Dozier, "Resume of the Mission and Convention Evangelism Study Committees Joint Meeting," Feb. 1964, typescript.
[42]Ibid.; Calcote, "CAPEO and PEP," 8-10.

made the largest subcommittee, with one member from each of the five stations: North Japan, Tokyo, Kansai, Central Japan, and Kyushu. The other two subcommittees were finance, with four members, and personnel, with three members. The property and transportation committees had been dissolved and most of their duties turned over to the stations or to the business manager, who had been added to the office staff in 1964.[43]

Executive committee agendas underwent a dramatic change. For the first time since the 1930s, the committee gave major attention to evangelistic activities, needs, and opportunities. PEP missions were soon established in Fukuoka, Keihan (Kyoto-Osaka), and Nagoya. In 1969, $15,000 was granted from the fund to construct a basement-level student center in the front yard of the Nagasaki church.[44]

In the same year the Mission also took the liberty of launching its own radio project in Osaka, a nightly five-minute program produced by Gillespie and called "Chapel in Music." The radio project drew fire from the Convention's executive secretary and evangelism secretary. They protested that it had been approved by neither the Kansai Association nor the Convention's evangelism committee, but only by some of the local pastors. Osaka was the wrong place for the project, they argued, because the existing discord among pastors and churches would be exacerbated. Even prior to this time there had been complaints that CAPEO projects were being conducted without the consultation agreed on between the Mission and Convention.[45] The radio project continued, nevertheless, and friction persisted, but it cannot be denied that CAPEO brought new vigor to the Mission. Some members came to feel for the first time that they were a part of the cutting edge in evangelism and church growth. The "missionary exodus" that some had expected was not averted entirely, but apparently it was reduced in scale.

Inside the Mission Family

By the mid-1960s the Mission had developed an elaborate set of policies on housing and transportation. The policies could be implemented with little or no debate. Concerning transportation, we have noted that in the early 1950s language school students and a few others shared in car pools. Automobiles were scarce because they had to be brought from the States and the missionaries bringing them had to show proof of prior ownership for at least six months. In 1957 a made-in-Japan car--a Toyopet--was purchased on an experimental basis, and by the early

---

[43]Calcote, "CAPEO and PEP," 10-11. An outstanding contribution of the Evangelism Study Committee was the compilation of *The Missionary and His Work*, published in Fukuoka in 1962.

[44]Unsigned letter to Bob Culpepper, 15 Jan. 1972.

[45]Bee and Pete Gillespie, "Annual Report, 1970-71," mimeographed; Curtis Askew to Melvin Bradshaw, 15 Dec. 1969; Ralph Calcote, "CAPEO: Its Development and Meaning" (1970, mimeographed), 5.

'60s the switch from imports to domestics was virtually complete. New missionaries and those returning from furlough were routinely provided with a new car. Families with two or more children could select a Cedric or Crown, while smaller families and single missionaries chose a Bluebird or Corona. In 1967 automatic transmission was made optional on all Mission cars. This meant an additional outlay of ¥50,000 on a new Corona and a slight increase in gasoline charges. Previously allowed for medical reasons only, this option was no longer considered a luxury. The frequent shifting of gears required in heavy city traffic tended to wear out both clutch and driver all too quickly.[46]

In the 1960s the Mission installed central furnaces in new houses and floor furnaces in older houses regardless of the location. In earlier years missionaries had provided heating equipment at their own expense except in the northern areas of Hokkaido or Tōhoku. House and lot sizes were reduced from the standard of the 1950s. Instead of buying lots in excess of 300 tsubo, the Mission was buying in the range of 100 to 150 tsubo. In 1960 the 50-tsubo standard for houses was reduced to 45 tsubo for a large family, 40 tsubo for a small family, and 25 tsubo for a single person. Carports were often substituted for enclosed garages, and separate quarters for maids were no longer provided. These reductions were mandated by spiraling inflation. By the end of the '60s, land prices had increased by 12 to 15 times since 1955 and construction costs had tripled.[47]

In this decade the chief responsibility for implementing policies lay with the stations. In 1964 the Mission chairman, John Shepard, stated that there had been "a gradual dissipation of standards" resulting in "breaches of policy" on the part of the stations. Especially was this true in the construction of houses. "We have in some cases," Shepard wrote, "moved far away from the handbook." On the one hand, he pointed out, policy revisions had not kept pace with rapidly changing circumstances, and on the other, the maturing Mission tended to value personal preference above uniformity. The pendulum was to swing back toward uniformity by increasing the authority of the business manager and creating the post of Mission administrator, as related in the next chapter.[48]

In earlier years, when the Japanese economy was still recovering from the war, the Mission had purchased many large residence lots at relatively low prices. Much of the property was located in central, high-growth areas. In the 1960s, therefore, the Mission realized a considerable profit each time it replaced an older piece of property with one that was smaller and less centrally located. With Board approval the money gained in these transactions was placed in the Land Purchase Supplement Fund. Since the Board appropriation for a new residence lot was only $7,000, usually insufficient for purchasing even 100 tsubo, this fund was drawn

---

[46]Jack Smith to Bradshaw, 15 May 1967; Bradshaw to Crawley, 2 June 1967.
[47]"Mission Handbook," 1969 ed., B-15; *Program Base Design* (JBM, 1973), 167-70 (hereafter cited as *PBD*).
[48]Shepard to author, 6 July 1964.

on to make up the difference. The fund was also used to supplement house budgets and to build high-rental apartments, beginning with Uehara Plaza in 1969. The apartments were profitable, for they could pay for themselves within a few years and help meet future housing needs of the Mission.

Unlike the Mission as a whole, most missionaries had no property holdings to fall back on in the fight against inflation. During the first half of the '60s, while Japanese incomes increased dramatically, missionary salaries declined in purchasing power despite cost-of-living adjustments made by the Board. No longer could a family have a full-time maid, and even part-time help put a strain on most budgets. These financial restraints made it more difficult for mothers to get the language, though they could hire baby-sitters at Mission expense while attending classes at language school. Middle-aged couples found that teen-agers were a greater financial burden than small children, especially after they entered college, where expenses far exceeded Margaret Fund allowances provided by the Board. Families that formerly had eaten out two or three times a week, enjoyed steak or roast at home, and supported worthy causes over and above their tithe--all on Board salary--now found themselves in a "critical financial situation," much like the missionaries caught in the spiraling inflation that followed World War I.[49]

A fortunate few had private wealth, such as inherited property, or received regular gifts from individuals or churches and perhaps the free use of a car and house while on furlough. A few had military pensions and shopping privileges on U.S. military bases. Some could send their children to state colleges without paying out-of-state tuition. The less fortunate had to accept financial inequality as a fact of life.

A crisis struck several families in 1965 when tax officials ordered the Mission to start withholding taxes on child schooling allowances. Included were travel expenses and dormitory fees as well as tuition. This requirement more than doubled the withholding tax of couples with several children in school. Medical expenses were also declared taxable, and about the same time a number of missionaries had to start paying local resident taxes. Since it was Board policy to refund income taxes in excess of what the missionary would pay if in the United States, relief was forthcoming, but not soon enough for several frantic couples. Everyone rejoiced at a substantial salary increase granted in January 1966. It restored the missionary's purchasing power to the level of four or five years before, though not to the bounteous standard of the '50s.[50]

Missionaries suffered a variety of woes. In 1966 Dub and Doris Jackson were at home in Mitaka when Typhoon Ida picked up the entire roof of their house, rafters included, and hurled it against a high wire fence across the road. The fence, designed to stop golf balls rather than house roofs, buckled and collapsed.

[49]Shepard to Crawley, 8 Sept. 1965.
[50]Author to Mission, 7 May 1965; author to Crawley, 3 Dec. 1965.

Several other missionaries had rugs and furniture damaged by rain after tile or metal roofing was blown from their houses.[51]

Burglaries and break-ins were reported from time to time, and window bars were authorized for vulnerable dwellings if desired by the residents. Calvin and Harriett Parker had cash, jewelry, or other items taken from their home six times within a span of two decades, and Lenora Hudson had two burglaries in one month. Wayne and Mary Lou Emanuel were robbed by two teenage intruders who tied them up at knife point and threatened to kill their baby (Bart) if they told the police. No one was injured, and the stolen items were later recovered. Violent crimes were and still are less common in Japan than in the United States. But one couple suffered an attack so serious that it bears telling in some detail.

On Saturday, January 8, 1966, Coleman and Jabe Clarke were surprised when a high school boy they knew appeared at their door after 10 P.M. with a suitcase. The student said he had just returned from spending the Christmas-New Year's vacation at his home in Fukuoka and would be going to his lodging the next day. The Clarkes invited him to spend the night, as they had done a few times before. He was a member of Shibuya Mission, where Coleman was pastor, having joined by transfer from Fukuoka Church the previous October. The Clarkes knew that the husky boy was sometimes impolite, but on that fateful Saturday night they had no reason to suspect that he was lying. Actually the boy had been in Tokyo for over a week. Moreover, he had told a girl friend that soon he would be in the top newspaper stories throughout Japan. Concealed in his suitcase were black kid gloves, a face mask, and a dagger.[52]

Early the next morning Coleman was aroused from sleep by the sound of a dining room chair being overturned. He ran to the dining room, still shadowy dark with its curtains drawn, and saw the upset chair. Suddenly the boy emerged from the study, where he was hiding, and jumped Coleman from behind, stabbing him repeatedly on the head, face, and neck. In the fierce struggle that ensued the boy lost his dagger but immediately replaced it with one of two butcher knives he earlier had taken from the kitchen.

The commotion aroused Jabe. Just as she left the bedroom the student met her and forced her back in. He struck her repeatedly and knocked her to the floor but did not stab or cut her. When Coleman lurched in and flipped on the light, the youth, wielding a 12-inch butcher knife in his left hand, forced both Coleman and Jabe onto the bed. He kept shouting, "I'm going to kill you. I don't like Americans." (It was later learned that his sister had married, and been deserted by, an American G.I.) Coleman reminded him of Christ's forgiving love.

---

[51] Author to Mission, 26 Sept. 1966.

[52] Coleman Clarke, "An Account of the Attempted Murder of Jabe and Coleman Clarke," 1966, typescript, FMBA; Jabe Clarke, "An Account of the Tragic Occurrence of January 9, 1966," typescript, FMBA. The author was a neighbor of the Clarkes at the time and was called to their home immediately after the incident described.

Jabe saw that Coleman was badly hurt. "He was literally bathed in blood," she said later. "It was running from the top of his head down his eyes, forehead, nose, ears, neck, everywhere." Indeed, Coleman had been stabbed 19 times, though amazingly not in a vital organ. "Let me get a doctor," Jabe pleaded. The boy ordered them into the closet, one at a time, but Coleman, his strength fast ebbing, reached for the phone. When the boy closed in on him, Coleman wrested the knife from him. Jabe seized the opportunity to escape from the room and run for help to the neighborhood police box a block away. The flustered youth attempted to recover the knife from Coleman but only managed to break the blade in two. He then ran to the Clarkes' car and tried to start it with the keys he had taken earlier from Jabe's pocketbook. When it failed to start, he fled on foot, leaving the car's ignition on and the windshield wipers swishing back and forth over dry glass. The police apprehended him at day's end.

The Clarkes spent more than two weeks in Tokyo Sanitarium Hospital recovering from physical and psychological wounds. The injury done to them was compounded by false allegations. A newspaper stated that Coleman had scolded the boy and implied that the missionary had brought the attack on himself. The police assumed that the boy had intended only to steal; when caught red-handed he had temporarily gone berserk and used a kitchen knife for self-defense. After detectives had finished their investigation at the Clarke residence, however, a missionary checking the house discovered the bloody dagger actually used to stab Coleman, a dagger the boy had brought to the home with him. The police had missed it.

The Clarkes declined to bring charges against the student, asking instead that he be provided with whatever psychiatric treatment was needed. A juvenile court released him to the custody of his parents on probation for one year. Coleman and Jabe returned to the States for further recuperation and then resigned from the Board because of their apprehension of a repeat attack. They served as missionaries to Japanese in New York City with the Metropolitan Baptist Association. Reappointed to Japan in 1972, the Clarkes served in Miyazaki until their retirement in 1976.

Throughout the 1960s missionaries and their children were beset with various medical problems that required special leaves, furlough extensions, or resignations. In 1962 Ed and Sue Oliver lost their son Mark, who had been born in 1960 with a heart condition.[53] And during this decade three missionaries in active service were called to their reward.

Loyce Nelson took medical leave in 1962 to enter Baylor University Hospital in Dallas. The next year, at the age of 38, he succumbed to leukemia. "Loyce died as he lived with a smile on his face," said his wife Gladys, "and his last words were of apology to the nurses for the trouble he had been." Loyce had

---

[53]C. F. Clark to Franklin Fowler, 30 Jan. 1962.

served as Mission chairman and tireless evangelist. Fittingly he had been awarded a D.D. degree by Ouachita University, where he had been president of his class.[54] Gladys, left with two sons, resigned from the Board. In subsequent years she was remarried, ordained a minister, and elected area director for American Baptist missions in South Asia.

A 1964 appointee, Bill Hashman, fell ill while a language student in Tokyo. He was preparing to teach at Seinan Gakuin and assist in its athletic program (he held a master's degree in physical education). Earlier he had been active in Seinan Gakuin Church while stationed near Fukuoka as an Air Force officer. When it was learned that he had Hodgkin's disease, a cancer of the lymph system, Hashman was sent to Seattle for treatment. So intense was his pain that Jim Satterwhite accompanied him to administer drugs en route. Hashman died in a Seattle hospital in 1968, when he was 37. He was survived by his wife Jeanie and four children.[55] Three years later Jeanie resigned from the Board.

Edwin Dozier suffered a heart attack in 1959 while attending a pastors' and missionaries' conference in Kyoto. In 1960 he went through the strain of helping settle a 100-day teachers' strike at Seinan Jo Gakuin. After the chancellor was forced to resign, Dozier wisely declined the school's request that he assume the post, but he continued to carry heavy responsibilities at Seinan Gakuin, where he was a seminary professor and head of the junior college department. In 1965 he was elected chancellor of that institution. In 1969 he bore the brunt of vicious attacks by radical students, who forced him to hear their strident charges against the school. On April 23 they wrecked his office, leaving the portrait of his father, Kelsey Dozier, soiled and torn. Edwin kept at his job until May 10, 1969, when he died of myocardial infarction. He was 61. He had outlived his father by almost seven years.[56]

The funeral was held in an overflowing Seinan Gakuin Church, where a missionary quartet sang "When all my labors and trials are o'er."[57] Then Edwin was laid to rest next to his father in the little cemetery at Seinan Jo Gakuin. At the close of the interment service a Japanese friend remarked that the radical students had killed Dozier. The bereaved Mary Ellen thought so too. But she continued to serve in Fukuoka until after she had reached 65, the age for retirement.

Edwin Dozier had been awarded a D.D. by Wake Forest University in 1955 and the Fourth Class Order of the Rising Sun by the Japanese government in

[54]Gladys Nelson, quoted in George Hays to Matsuda Shōzō, 12 Mar. 1963; Dale Cowling, "Funeral Message for Loyce N. Nelson," 13 Mar. 1963, mimeographed, JBM; Crawley to Whaley, 9 Dec. 1963.

[55]Author to Mission, 4 Mar. 1966; author to Mission, 9 Mar. 1966; Culpepper to Mission, 14 Mar. 1966. "FMB News," 28 Aug. 1968.

[56]Lois Whaley, *Edwin Dozier of Japan*, 251-54; "Report of Seinan Gakuin trustees," 12 Sept. 1969.

[57]Fred Horton to James Belote, 4 May 1969.

1968. Highly regarded in the Convention, he had once come within four votes of being elected president, a post that has never been held by a missionary. In 1983 he was honored posthumously as "man of the way" in a biography written by Lois Whaley.[58]

"The Ranks are Thinning," declared a 1968 editorial in *Japan Baptist News*, a Mission monthly. The Mission lost some 40 members in the decade of the '60s, most by resignation for medical reasons, including "severe depression." Various maladies cited in the records often accompanied job dissatisfaction or interpersonal conflicts--conflicts between missionaries or between missionaries and nationals. The increase in physical comforts since the '50s seems to have been offset by greater psychological hardships. As if they had not suffered enough, some resignees were mindlessly called "quitters" for "leaving the ranks."[59]

Despite the heavy losses in this decade, the Mission grew in number from 123 to 140. The growth owed much to the Board's creation of new categories of personnel, especially that of missionary associate. An associate was one who because of age or other factors did not meet the full requirements for career appointment.[60] Among those sent to Japan in this category was the Mission's first business manager, Jack Smith, a retired lieutenant colonel. Also sent were missionary journeymen, young college graduates enlisted for two-year English-language assignments. Japan's first journeyman, Elaine Stan, came in 1965 to teach in Kyoto International School. Summer student workers also proved valuable, though they were not included in the count of missionaries.

Meeting Needs and Creating Problems

Another significant development in the '60s was the multiplication of English-language churches from one--Tokyo Baptist--to seven. In 1961 Kantō Plains Church was organized west of Tokyo near U.S. Air Force bases, and Yokohama International was organized near a U.S. Navy housing area. In the same year a mission of Tokyo Baptist was opened at Misawa in northern Honshu, near an Air Force base. In 1964 this mission was organized into Calvary Baptist Church. Each of these four churches gave birth to a Japanese church, and all eight congregations were still active in 1989. Three other English-language churches were established in the '60s but discontinued due to a shift of U.S. military personnel away from their areas. These were Chōfu, now a Japanese church; Nakagami, near

---

[58]Greer, *Missionary Album*, 51; L. Whaley, *Edwin Dozier of Japan*, 264-65.

[59]Austin W. Farley to Worth Grant, 10 Aug. 1968; Marion Moorhead to Crawley, 26 Feb. 1963; Moorhead to Whaley, 5 Mar. 1963; Hays to Belote, 25 Nov. 1969.

[60]On "supplementary personnel," see Winston Crawley, *Global Mission* (Nashville: Broadman Press, 1985), 151-52.

Tachikawa Air Base; and New Life, which briefly served Itazuke Air Base in Fukuoka.[61]

In 1960 Bud and Doris Spencer transferred to Okinawa to lead the English-speaking Central Baptist Church in Naha. This marked the beginning of the Southern Baptist mission in Okinawa and the start of fruitful cooperation between American and Southern Baptist missionaries within the framework of the Okinawa Baptist Convention. Eventually four English-language congregations became a part of the convention, three sponsored by Southern Baptists and one started by black military personnel.[62]

The churches in Japan proper formed an English-language Church Association and sponsored various ministries such as an annual Family Inspiration Week at Amagi Assembly. An English-language church committee elected by the Mission served as a liaison between the churches and the Mission, Convention, and Board, processing financial and personnel requests from the churches and assisting in other ways. The churches were led to give generously to the Convention's cooperative offering and to repay Board loans into the Convention's revolving loan fund. When a newly organized church applied for Convention membership, however, as it was expected to do, opposition was voiced, though not enough to block its acceptance. The opposition seems to have stemmed in some instances from resentment over the disparity between the English-language and Japanese churches. The former contributed much larger sums to the Convention's cooperative offering. In 1968, for example, the English-language churches gave 30 percent of the total.[63] They also baptized far more converts. The overriding source of friction, however, was the military makeup of most of the churches. They were linked with the widely resented American bases in Japan.

Given the background of Japan's aggressive war against China and its ruinous clash with the United States, it was no surprise that many Japanese Baptists strongly opposed the military establishment. Moreover, American bases continued to be an irritant, with military personnel frequently involved in accidents that killed or injured Japanese. Even though no one was hurt when a U.S. Phantom jet fighter from Itazuke Air Base crashed into a building at Fukuoka University, the public was so incensed that the base was forced to close.[64] Hostile feelings were particularly strong after 1964, when America's involvement in the Vietnam War escalated dramatically, reaching its peak in 1969. Even the missionaries could not escape the repercussions from this fateful entanglement.

One Mission member who was pastor of a Japanese congregation was asked by his deacons to resign in favor of a national, on grounds that people were

----

[61]"Bird's Eye View of English Language Churches," 1972, typescript.

[62]Bollinger, *Cross and Floating Dragon*, 229. Bollinger, an American Baptist missionary, was pastor at Central Church prior to the coming of the Spencers.

[63]"Convention Finance Committee Meeting," 25-27 Jan. 1971, mimeographed.

[64]Reischauer, *My Life*, 255.

Kindergarten graduation at Kanazawa Baptist Church, ca. 1964. Author at right rear.

refusing to come to church. "Sorry," they would say, "but when we listen to an American pastor, we start thinking about what the Americans are doing in Vietnam, and we can't endure it." At the Convention's annual meeting in 1968, Max Garrott, while making a plea for more evangelistic efforts, quoted something Billy Graham had said in his Tokyo crusade the previous autumn. When Garrott finished, a pastor stood up and said that Garrott should be rebuked for using the quote. "Should we listen to Billy Graham," he asked, "when Billy Graham is on record as supporting the war in Vietnam?" No one rose to Garrott's defense, nor was anything further said on the matter.

This incident notwithstanding, Garrott enjoyed immense respect among the Japanese. Except for Edwin Dozier, whose birth and upbringing in Japan put him in a special category, Garrott is the only missionary ever elected to the postwar Convention's executive committee. Several other Mission members were elected to lesser committees in the 1960s, and some held major positions in Convention-related institutions. A still larger number attended the annual meetings and showed a keen interest in the work of the Convention as a whole.

As has often been pointed out, missionaries could be highly critical of nationals. A few who worked in institutions sometimes found that they could not submit to Japanese management without violating their conscience. When the Kyoto hospital came under Japanese control in the '60s and a number of changes were made for financial reasons--it was suffering "teen-age growing pains," and salaries and other operating costs were soaring--some missionaries complained that medical standards had been lowered intolerably. The situation was exacerbated by venomous outbursts and spatting among some of the missionaries involved. Over the next few years three of the four doctors--all but C. F. Clark--and several nurses left Japan permanently.[65]

Other missionaries were miffed in 1969 when the Convention's executive committee approved the plans of three institutions to accept government aid. The institutions were Seinan Gakuin, Seinan Jo Gakuin, and the three-year-old Japan Baptist School of Nursing in Kyoto. "We judge it to be proper," the committee agreed, "to accept aid for the public service function which is a rightful responsibility of the state." No aid was to be accepted for the seminary, of course, whose character and purpose would forbid any dependence on the state.[66]

Worth Grant, who worked at Jordan Press for eight years during this decade, publicly lamented the apparent lack of interest in publishing evangelistic books and tracts. He also objected to the "tardy (six months old) payment of bills to the Baptist Sunday School Board for Sunday School literature for the English speaking churches, which had been paid for in advance." Grant commended Jordan Press, however, for some of its titles, especially *Christian Marriage and the Family* by

[65]JBM annual report, 1962.
[66]Max Garrott, "The Convention and Its Institutions," spring 1970, liaison report, JBM.

George Hays, which won a recommendation from Japan's Ministry of Education and went through six printings.[67]

Missionaries were no more dissatisfied with the Convention and its institutions than they were displeasing to their Japanese colleagues. There seemed to be no end to complaints about their attitudes and activities. One congregation petitioned the Mission to remove the "senseless old woman" who was alleged to hinder the work with her reckless zeal. An executive secretary described some missionaries as too forceful and insistent when they made proposals. Pastor Yuya found one man's attitude repugnant. "If you disagree with him," Yuya said, "his response is 'You don't have faith' or 'That's a sin.'"

In 1969 the Convention's personnel committee refused to prepare the priority list of missionary needs requested each year by the Mission and the Board, stating that the list had been disregarded so often as to be useless. The personnel committee cited "the marked tendency of missionaries to choose places that have little or no connection to what Convention leaders deem as strategic and high priority." Apparently the charge was never refuted.[68]

In 1967 the Mission had voted to encourage couples whose children were grown to consider work opportunities in outlying areas. But no pressures were ever applied, and the clustering of missionaries in central areas continued to bother Convention strategists. Sizing up the problem, one Mission wit compared missionaries to manure. "When spread out," he said, "they do good; when piled up, they raise a stink."

Unlike the '50s, when several couples in outlying areas taught their own children with Calvert School materials and in a few cases sent them to Japanese schools, in the '60s most parents insisted on living near an English school, and a few demanded a particular school. A major reason for this trend was the growing emphasis on quality education in America, especially as it affected Baptist colleges and universities. A number of Baptist schools that formerly accepted any high school graduate had grown selective, some of them highly selective. To be assured of acceptance, MKs now had to submit good SAT or ACT scores.

American military schools were still available in several places, including Fukuoka, but their number was decreasing. To fill a void or meet new needs, international schools had been established in Kyoto (1957), Sapporo (1958), Hiroshima (1962), and Nagoya (1963). Some years would elapse before these schools could offer the higher grades. Most children of high school age, and some of middle school age, attended one of the older schools in Tokyo, Yokohama, or Kobe. Dormitory facilities were available at Christian Academy in Tokyo and Canadian Academy in Kobe, as noted earlier, but not at Tokyo's American School

---

[67]Grant to Colleagues, 20 May 1968; Grant, *A Work Begun*, 82; JBM mailout, 13 Mar. 1970.
[68]Fred Horton to George Watanabe, 3 Oct. 1969; *PBD*, 1973 ed., 162.

in Japan, the choice of many parents. So in 1962 the Mission opened its own dormitory in Mitaka near ASIJ.

Baptist Dormitory, as it was called, looked like a dream come true. Built by Homat Homes, the neat and spacious two-story building accommodated a dozen or more students of both sexes in middle or high school. Sadly, the operation was soon plagued with troubles, dashing the dream of a Christian home environment for MKs. The supervisors were changed rather often, and some of them were quite the opposite in discipline and manner. Some were considered too strict and some too permissive. The parents and the trustees sometimes clashed on how the dormitory should be run or how a controversial rule should be worded. It was agreed, for example, that smoking should be strictly prohibited in the dormitory and on the premises. But should a student be retained who smoked off the premises, in violation of the Japanese law forbidding the use of tobacco by minors? The trustees said no, which caused a family to move to Tokyo against their wishes. So divisive and irresolvable were various issues that twice during the decade the trustees voted to close the facility. Each time they then yielded to parents' demands that it be kept open. To complicate matters, sometimes a parent with a child in the dormitory served as a trustee, contrary to what some considered a sound administrative principle. At any rate, the dormitory was sadly disruptive of the Mission's fellowship.

The MK problem came to the fore in a shocking manner at the 1969 Mission meeting. The meeting was held July 29 to August 1, not at Amagi Sansō, but at the Kokusai Takamatsu Hotel on Shikoku. On the closing night some of the young people held a "drinking party" in the hotel annex where they were staying. Descriptions of what took place ranged from "drinking only a tiny amount of whisky in a coke" to heavy drinking that left the imbibers "dead drunk" and "staggering." Some children who witnessed the scene "spent the night sitting in the hall, afraid to return to their room." The incident caused grave concern throughout the Mission for its effect on the smaller children and on the Christian witness in Takamatsu.[69]

That autumn the dormitory supervisors sent five boys home for one week because of improper conduct. Subsequently the trustees expelled three of the boys for the remainder of the school year. The charges included smoking, theft of several items (even an airplane propeller from a nearby airfield), wrongful possession of dormitory keys that provided access to the girls' section, obscene writing and speech, damage to property, and intimidation of younger boys with threats of bodily harm. Some parents expressed regret that they had opposed the closing of the dormitory years before. At the end of the 1969-70 school year, in which 12 students had been accommodated, the dorm was closed "for lack of applicants." The facility was turned into a guest house and later sold.

---

[69]Carroll and Frances Bruce to Curtis Askew, Aug. 1969.

Appropriately, it seems, the Convention's special emphasis in 1969 was reaching middle and high school students. Associational youth retreats and work camps were conducted, associational conferences were held on the meaning and methods of youth evangelism, and a study group was organized to consider the problems and needs of youth work. The Convention also observed the 80th anniversary of Southern Baptist work in Japan with evangelistic meetings, conferences, celebrations, and the publication of a pictorial history.[70]

Another highlight of 1969 was the first graduation exercises of the Japan Baptist School of Nursing. Sixteen young women, all Christians, received their diplomas. All 16 passed their national board exams, and 10 remained to serve at the Baptist hospital. The school was off to a good start.[71] But for many other institutions, Seinan Gakuin included, 1969 was a year of student protests and strikes. Baptists braced themselves for more trouble to come.

[70]JBM annual report, 1969. The pictorial history was *Baputesuto Senkyō hachijūnen no ayumi*, edited by Egasaki Kiyomi.

[71]JBM annual report, 1969.

11

Planning and Appraising the Work (1970-1979)

The year 1970 seemed like another 1960: tense, stormy, bloody. In a drama more grisly and shocking than the 1960 assassination of Socialist Party chairman Asanuma, the famed right-wing novelist Mishima Yukio committed ritual suicide (harakiri) at the Tokyo headquarters of the Ground Self-Defense Forces. It was his way of protesting Japan's abandonment of an emperor-centered militarism. When Mishima had plunged the dagger into his abdomen, an aide standing behind him with raised sword lopped off his head--a conventional act of mercy. The aide then performed harakiri on himself and was beheaded by a second aide.[1]

The most volatile issue of the year was the Japan-U.S. Security Treaty, which in June would be automatically extended for another 10 years unless abrogated by either country. Linked with it in the public mind was the government-sponsored world exposition that opened in Osaka March 15. Opponents charged that Expo '70, as it was popularly called, was a "festival of capitalism" slickly timed to distract from the planned extension of the Security Treaty. Resolutions opposing both the treaty and the exposition had been introduced at the Baptist Convention's 1969 annual session, but each resolution had failed, mainly on grounds that the Convention should not speak out officially on political issues. Baptists, like most other Christian groups in Japan, included supporters of the ruling Liberal-Democratic Party as well as the Socialist Party and others.[2]

One resolution adopted at the 1969 convention protested the construction of a Christian Pavilion at Expo '70. The pavilion in question was sponsored by the Catholic Bishops' Conference as well as the National Christian Council, of which the Convention was a member. It had been conceived as a bold experiment in ecumenical evangelism, an attempt to bear witness to Christ among the 30 million visitors expected at the exposition. Some critics viewed it as an intolerable compromise with a "corrupt" Japanese government. Others questioned the

---

[1]*Japan Times*, 26 Nov. 1970.
[2]Phillips, *Rising of the Sun*, 35; *Baputesuto* (Baptist), July 1969, 9.

involvement with Roman Catholicism: the pavilion had official ties with the Holy See and was located accordingly among the pavilions of foreign governments. Though interpretations varied, the majority of Baptists saw it as violating the principle of church-state separation.[3]

The Christian Pavilion opened as scheduled despite Baptist antagonism and more vehement protests from a strident minority within the United Church of Christ. This minority insisted so adamantly on an apology from those who had carried out the project that the churches were polarized, and many functions of the United Church were paralyzed for years to come. The Baptist Convention was spared this fate.

The Baptist World Congress in Tokyo

Another hot issue for Japanese Baptists in 1970 was the Baptist World Congress that met July 12-18 in Tokyo's Budōkan (Martial Arts Hall). Held for the first time in the Orient, the congress was hosted jointly by the Convention, the Japan Baptist Union (related to the American Baptist Churches in the U.S.A.), and the Japan Baptist Church Association (related to the Baptist General Conference of America). A resolution opposing the congress had failed at the Convention's 1969 session, but a disgruntled minority representing 15 churches had organized the Tokyo Joint-Struggle Council to further their cause. They charged that the congress would detract from the fight against the Security Treaty and Expo '70 while ignoring such crucial problems as the Vietnam War, America's occupation of Okinawa, and Japanese "imperialism" in Asia. The theme of the congress, "Reconciliation through Christ," they argued, "has nothing to do with elegant talks nor with gaudy national costumes."[4]

The Joint-Struggle Council members demanded and were granted two public debates with the Convention's executive committee at a Tokyo church. At these debates they grilled committee members individually, making sharp accusations. At the second session they refused to allow Matsumura Shūichi to speak, though he was a vice president of the Baptist World Alliance and director of local arrangements. Nor did they allow questions from the floor until 2:40 A.M., when only 70 out of 220 attenders remained. Their tactics won little favor, and their attempts to control other meetings proved less successful. At a pre-congress rally held at Tokyo Baptist Church, when a Joint-Struggle Council member jumped to

---

[3]*Baputesuto*, July 1969, 9; *Japan Times*, 28 Nov. 1969; F. Calvin Parker, "Ecumenism and the Evangelization of Japan," *Japan Missionary Bulletin* 30 (Jan./Feb. 1976): 21; Phillips, *Rising of the Sun*, 37.

[4]Anti-BWA Action Committee, "To the Attendants of 12th BWA," 17 July 1970, mimeographed; *12th Baptist World Congress* (Tokyo, 1970), inside front cover.

the platform and demanded that the program be changed to a debate, congress supporters quickly subdued him.[5]

At the congress itself the tactics employed by dissidents were nonviolent and but slightly disruptive. Anti-congress handbills were distributed daily, many of which lambasted Billy Graham, the speaker for the closing session. Graham was called a "positive supporter of Nixon's Vietnam war policy" and "one of those who advocate killing the people."[6]

The congress drew 8,672 registrants, including 1,347 from Japan. Nearly every activity went smoothly, thanks in part to the Mission's role. Marion Moorhead was co-director with Matsumura, and eight other Southern Baptist missionaries served on committees. Still others helped with the music, pageantry, and small meetings. Charles Whaley interpreted several times for a Moscow pastor. Nearly all Mission members in Japan at the time availed themselves of the rare opportunity to join in the warm fellowship with Baptists from every part of the world.[7]

Elizabeth Watkins wore a tiny pin symbolizing the Fifth Class Order of the Precious Crown, awarded by the emperor for her contribution to education. She had obtained permission from the Board to remain in Japan beyond her 70th birthday (April 21) in order to attend the congress. Watkins beamed when Matsumura presided at a session speaking English, for he had been one of her students when a freshman at Seinan Gakuin.[8]

Partner-Church Evangelism

Prior to and following the congress, hundreds of Baptists from Texas and Hawaii dispersed throughout the country for "partner-church" evangelistic meetings and other witnessing activities. In Sapporo a three-night citywide campaign drew crowds of 800, 1,000, and 1,200. Musical groups from several Baptist colleges performed on television and at Expo '70, in both the Christian Pavilion and American Park.[9] These events held in tandem with the congress had been arranged by Dub Jackson, who had resigned from the Mission and the Board to promote team evangelism worldwide. In 1972 Jackson organized the World Evangelism Foundation for this purpose.

One partner-church relationship linked First Baptist Church, Amarillo, Texas, with Akatsuka Church, Tokyo. Fifty-four members from Amarillo conducted a week-long campaign at Akatsuka and invited their partner church to reciprocate.

---

[5]The author was present at these meetings.
[6]Anti-BWA Action Committee, "We Accuse Billy Graham," 18 July 1970, mimeographed.
[7]*Baputesuto*, 20 Aug. 1970, 6; *12th Congress*, 10-11; Charles and Lois Whaley, report to MM, 1970.
[8]Watkins, "Autobiography," 245-46.
[9]Dub Jackson to Mission, 3 July 1970.

Not until 1975 was Akatsuka able to respond, but then it went all out and sent 56 members to Amarillo for an eight-day crusade. Among them was Virginia Highfill, the church's minister of education, who rendered valuable service as an interpreter.[10]

The partner-church plan incited controversy in Japan. It was debated throughout the Convention's annual meeting in August 1970. The 19 Japanese churches involved were accused of violating the Convention's principles of autonomy and cooperation by forming "unequal partnerships" for financial gain, since their American counterparts had provided most of the funds for the evangelistic meetings. They were said to have circumvented the one accepted route by which the Convention received aid from Southern Baptist churches, namely, through the Board via the Mission. For a bloc of churches within the Convention to accept charity through another route was branded as "noncooperative" and even "traitorous."[11]

An action was taken which, while acknowledging the independence of each local church, affirmed that "churches of this Convention will not make private requests or suggest financial needs directly to churches of the Southern Baptist Convention." The post-convention executive committee stated further that a lack of respect had been shown for "independence and cooperation" and "the accepted route for financial transactions." "It was unfortunate," the committee concluded, "that the partner-church program was carried out at this juncture and in this way."[12]

Ironically, some of the censored churches were the most generous contributors to the Convention's cooperative offering, and some of their critics were themselves receiving aid in one form or another. Many missionaries viewed the fracas as a fresh demonstration that Japanese Baptists lacked the tradition of grassroots democracy and a genuine respect for local church autonomy. It was noted that the Convention still held title to most church property, though a growing trend was for the churches--especially those with kindergartens--to assume legal ownership. Both the Convention and the individual churches seemed vertically structured with an ascending hierarchy of authority, reflecting the pattern of Japanese society as a whole.

Seminary Strife

In the fall of 1970 the battlefield shifted to the seminary campus in Fukuoka, where most Convention ministers were trained. The seminary was--and is--a part of Seinan Gakuin University, which was plagued by student rebellions in 1969,

---

[10]Highfill to Mission, 12 June 1975; *Commission* 39 (Jan. 1976), 4-8.

[11]Melvin Bradshaw to James Belote, 22 Sept. 1970; author's notes.

[12]"Report of the 1970 (24th) Japan Convention Annual Meeting," JBM; "Statement Issued by the Convention Executive Committee," 25 Aug. 1970, JBM.

as noted in connection with Edwin Dozier's death. The rebellions were nationwide in scope, affecting private and public universities alike, though carried out by a militant minority and not by the majority of students. At Aoyama Gakuin University (Methodist) in Tokyo and Kantō Gakuin University (American Baptist) in Yokohama, the theology departments became so involved as to self-destruct over a period of time.[13] Neither has been reopened. Belatedly, though no less ominously, a group of dissident students at the Fukuoka seminary called a strike in September 1970.

The seminary had 34 students: 23 in the theology department of the university and 11 in an unaccredited Bible school. The striking students numbered only 10 at first and never exceeded 11, but they forced the cancellation of all classes until January 1971. With the backing of a few area pastors, they assailed the faculty for not speaking out jointly against the Vietnam War, the Security Treaty, the Baptist congress, Expo '70, and government efforts to nationalize Yasukuni Shrine, where the war dead are enshrined. A theology that does not address such issues is invalid, the students declared; any evangelism that does not attack the evil structures of society is incomplete.[14]

These social activists declared that the seminary was bankrupt and not salvageable, that the faculty should resign en bloc to clear the way for a new beginning. George Hays had the misfortune of being seminary dean at the time. On October 7, citing "two instances of misunderstanding related to the language," he resigned the position, no longer confident that he could negotiate with the students.[15] Hays was succeeded by Professor Sekiya, who, one may recall, had worked in Sendai with the Worth Grants.

Numerous meetings were held, some of them loud and boisterous, in quest of reconciliation. Position papers were demanded of each faculty member, and each was interrogated as though an accused heretic at an inquisition. No exceptions were made of the three missionary teachers: Hays, Bob Culpepper, Vera Campbell. Culpepper returned from an emergency furlough in November 1970, in the midst of the turmoil, and went on trial as the others had done. All three handled themselves well and helped the seminary to survive. When the new school year opened in April 1971, however, total enrollment was down to 22. Not until the next decade did it reach 34 again.[16]

[13]Reischauer and Craig, *Tradition and Transformation*, 299; Phillips, *Rising of the Sun*, 38-39, 74.

[14]Robert H. Culpepper, "Interpretation of the Seminary Problem" (JBM, 1971; mimeographed), 1, 7; George H. Hays, "Second Report to the Mission on the Seminary" (JBM, Nov. 1970; mimeographed), 3-4.

[15]Hays, "Second Report," 3.

[16]Culpepper, "Interpretation," 4; Robert H. Culpepper, "Chronicle of Some Leading Events in the Seminary Crisis" (JBM, 1971; mimeographed), 2; Culpepper, *God's Calling*, 192-95.

Ozaki Shuichi has said that the most tragic result of the strike was the loss of some very promising students to the gospel ministry. If so, a close second was the loss of Ozaki himself to the seminary faculty. This New Testament scholar, second-generation preacher, and sometime interpreter to Billy Graham resigned during the struggle. Consequently, he was scathingly denounced as irresponsible and harassed by late-night phone calls. Dean Sekiya also got calls at night. The harassments came to an end when Ozaki's daughter Yōko, the seminary librarian, was struck and killed by a train--an apparent suicide. So great was the shock that 16 years were to pass before Ozaki accepted an invitation to speak at the seminary, though he lived in Fukuoka all this time.[17]

Towards a Self-supporting Convention

The tension between conservatives and social activists surfaced again at the Convention's 25th annual meeting in 1971. The tension was visible, for example, when representatives of new churches applying for membership were asked, "At what points is the gospel of Christ at odds with the government and society of Japan?" But the chief focus of attention was financial independence. "The time has come for us to stand on our own feet," Arase Noboru had said to a missionary group. "We have been riding in your car, and our legs are weak. Now we must get out and walk to make our legs strong." The delegates were presented with a five-year plan by which the Convention would become self-supporting in its operating budget in 1977. The plan embodied a formidable challenge, for about 85 percent of the 1971 budget was being provided by the Board. So revolutionary was the proposal, in fact, that the session in which it was adopted lasted till one o'clock in the morning.[18]

The plan called for a streamlined, economical Convention structure effective from 1973. The executive committee was reduced in size, most standing committees were abolished, and drastic cuts were made in the office staff. Institutions, churches, and various organizations were told to support themselves as best they could. The women's department, which in 1970 had celebrated the 50th anniversary of Baptist women's work, was replaced by the Japan Baptist Women's Union. Matsumura Akiko called the new organization an "unofficial auxiliary" of the Convention, more like the WMU of the SBC. It continued to sponsor the annual Christmas offerings that played a major role in the support of home and foreign missions.[19]

---

[17]Culpepper, *God's Calling*, 198-99; Ozaki Shuichi, interview with author, Fukuoka, 1987.

[18]Arase, quoted by author in *Commission* 34 (Sept. 1971), 20; Melvin Bradshaw, "A Profile in Faith," 29 Oct. 1971, typescript.

[19] Matsumura Akiko, interview with Home Interview Team, 17 July 1975, FMBA; *ASBC, 1971*, 118.

Among the institutions, Jordan Press became an independent company in 1974, with the Convention as major shareholder. Seinan Gakuin and Seinan Jo Gakuin still received token support from the Board, though directly from the Mission rather than through the Convention. Far more important for the two schools were the missionary teachers provided free of charge. The hospital required more than token aid for some years, while the nursing school, with the weakest financial base of all, continued to depend heavily on the Board for its very survival. It became a permanent item in the Mission's operating budget, typically drawing $80,000 in 1979.[20]

As for the seminary, which obviously lacked the means of self-support, the Convention decided to accept a declining Board subsidy from 1977 to 1981, after which the school's operating budget would be free from dependence on foreign funds. In 1978 a nationwide Men's Association (Brotherhood) was organized with financial support of the seminary as one of its major objectives, and Seminary Week, observed each summer with appropriate publicity and a special offering, was added to the Convention's calendar of activities.[21] Still, the seminary remained heavily dependent on missionary teachers, since eight full-time faculty members were required for accreditation, and only five were Japanese.

The Convention's 1971 decision to attain self-support within seven years seems all the more daring in light of its depressing statistics at the time. Between 1967 and 1971, active church membership had declined from 10,885 to 9,842, average attendance at Sunday morning worship services from 8,611 to 6,761, and average church school attendance from 15,391 to 12,150 (most pupils were children who did not attend the adult worship services). During the same period annual baptisms had dropped from 1,258 to 650, and in 1972 the number fell to 604, the lowest ever recorded for the postwar Convention (statistical reports begin with the year 1949). Moreover, between 1964 and 1971, membership figures for the Royal Ambassador-Girl's Auxiliary organizations, made up of middle and high school students, had plummeted from 2,283 to 666, and those of the college-age youth organizations had fallen from 3,596 to 2,818. True, membership of the men's and women's organizations had grown steadily during these years. But this further pointed up the churches' declining appeal to the younger generation.[22]

During the race toward self-support, however, the Convention recovered much of its lost vigor. Offerings increased fivefold between 1968 and 1977. In 1977 Sunday worship attendance exceeded 9,000 for the first time, and church school attendance reached a record high of 15,808. Baptisms likewise increased but fell short of the 1,000 mark. The RA-GA and youth groups also grew, though

[20]MM minutes, 1978.
[21]*Zen Nippon ni*, 20-21; *PBD*, 1980 ed., 72.
[22]*Zen Nippon ni*, 31-32.

not to the level of the 1960s.[23] Several reasons may be cited for the upturn after the years of decline.

Serious pollution problems in the early '70s and the oil crisis of 1973 aroused among the Japanese people a deeper concern for religious values. This "religion boom" benefited Christians along with Buddhists and others.[24] The return of Okinawa to Japan (1972), normalization of diplomatic relations with the People's Republic of China (1972), and the end of the Vietnam War (1975) served to reduce political tensions in the Convention and the churches. Furthermore, the challenge of emancipation from dependence on foreign subsidy seems to have inspired a recommitment to evangelism and spiritual growth.

In 1977 the Convention celebrated its newly won financial independence with 30th anniversary gatherings at Tokyo Baptist Church, Rankin Chapel in Fukuoka, and Amagi Sansō. The featured speaker at all three meetings was Douglas Hudgins, chairman of the executive committee of the SBC. Afterwards an official letter was sent to the Board expressing appreciation for four major contributions to the Convention since its founding in 1947. According to the letter, the Board had (1) sent "more than 300 dedicated and well-trained missionaries," (2) provided the financial assistance needed after a devastating war, (3) imparted "the spirit of evangelism and missions," and (4) taught the importance of religious education, especially through the Sunday school. Consequently, the letter stated, the Convention had grown from 16 churches in 1947 to 174 churches and 72 missions, with a total membership of 24,607. "No other major denomination in Japan," it added, "has shown such remarkable growth."[25]

In 1979, as this turbulent decade drew to a close, the Convention adopted a long-range plan that focused on nationwide cooperation in pioneer evangelism. It also adopted an entirely new statement of faith in place of the one modeled after that of the Hawaii Baptist Convention. The Convention further noted that increasingly, churches were using their own funds for repairing or rebuilding old auditoriums and educational buildings originally provided by the Board. This was attributable to a growing spirit of Christian stewardship as well as a thriving Japanese economy.[26]

Changes in Mission Strategy and Structure

The maturing of the Convention in this decade was paralleled by revolutionary changes in the Mission. Between 1970 and 1975 the Mission was transformed into a virtually new organization, one characterized by systematic long-range planning

---

[23]Ibid.; "Directional Planning Guidelines," JBM, 1978.

[24]*Commission* 34 (Sept. 1971), 20.

[25] Matsumura Shūichi (JBC president) to Cauthen, 3 Aug. 1977. The letter is quoted in *Royal Service* 73 (Oct. 1978), 11.

[26]JBM annual report, 1979; articles in *Baputesuto*, Sept., Oct. 1979.

and periodic evaluation of its work. Two streams of influence converged to produce the change. One was the Convention's resolve to end its dependence on Board subsidies by 1977 and establish its identity as an autonomous, self-supporting body. Japanese leaders perceived that it was in their own interest that the Mission should do evangelism not only through the Convention but alongside the Convention as a fraternal partner. Negotiations between the two bodies produced a document entitled "Points of Agreement," which was approved in 1972 at a full Mission meeting and the annual Japanese convention. The effective date coincided with the launching of the Convention's new streamlined, frugal organization in January 1973.[27]

The document affirmed that the Convention and Mission "will continue to engage in cooperative evangelism in Japan, respecting the spirit of our method of cooperation to the present." The Convention, it continued, "will assume the basic responsibility for carrying out pioneer evangelism, church development, and institutional and other projects." The Mission would cooperate with the Convention in such projects, the document added, "and may engage in evangelistic projects on its own. It will report to the Convention and discuss with them the substance of each of the Mission's projects." Provision was also made, as indicated already, for the Mission to provide financial aid directly to an institution.[28]

The new agreement gave the Mission more freedom to do work "on its own" than the CAPEO concessions of the '60s (see page 220). Unlike CAPEO, which most pastors never comprehended, this agreement had the advantage of formal approval by the Convention in a general session. The Mission's habit of consulting with the Convention but disregarding its advice now seemed to have formal if not moral sanction. However that may be, the more fraternal relationship with the Convention called for new Mission planning.

The other stream of influence contributing to a major overhaul of the Mission flowed from a new Board emphasis on strategy, first expressed in a 1970 study prepared by Winston Crawley, then director of the overseas division. "The essence of strategy," Crawley wrote, "is the managing of resources for greatest effectiveness." He called attention to the "great importance" of long-range planning. "The most relevant study of strategy," Crawley emphasized, "will . . . take place intensively and repeatedly on the fields."[29]

In response, the Japan Mission appointed a strategy study committee, with Morris Wright as chairman. The committee's assignment was to prepare study materials and recommendations concerning long-range strategies. Using research data obtained from the missionaries and other sources, the committee produced 14

---

[27]The text of "Points of Agreement" is given in *PBD*, 1973 ed., 132.
[28]Ibid.
[29]Winston Crawley, "Report of Director of Overseas Division," 14 May 1970; Crawley to Mission chairmen, 9 July 1970.

study papers on topics of major concern. Brief composite reports were presented to the July 1971 Mission meeting, which also received updates on CAPEO and the Convention's planned reorganization.[30]

In December 1971 the strategy study committee had a three-day work session with W. L. Howse, Jr., the Board's newly appointed East Asia Programming Consultant. Howse, a former seminary professor and Sunday School Board executive, introduced the concept of a program base design (PBD) to undergird the planning process.[31] Favorably impressed, the committee voted to use the PBD as the format for presenting its study materials to the Mission. It asked Calvin Parker to write this document, then made available for his use the summaries and original data of the 14 study papers. Throughout the writing process the full committee functioned as an editorial board, and Howse's *East Asia Planning Manual* served as a step-by-step guide.[32]

The program base design was developed as follows:

Why does the Mission exist?
   1. Biblical Foundations
   2. Historical Background
   3. Philosophy
   4. Needs
   5. Intentions

What is the Mission's work?
   6. Program Structure
   7. Relationships

How should the Mission do its work?
   8. Organization
   9. Human Resources
   10. Physical Resources
   11. Financial Resources
   12. Administrative Guidance

---

[30]*PBD*, 1973, i.

[31]Ibid.; *Commission* 41 (Mar. 1978), cover III; *Facts and Trends*, Apr. 1978, 4.

[32]W. L. Howse, *East Asia Planning Manual* (Hong Kong, 1972), 1-2. The decision to use one writer for the PBD instead of a team of writers as in other East Asia missions had as its aim a consistency in style and content. In effect, it also prolonged the writing process. This was gainful, for the writer and the strategy study committee had access to the materials produced more quickly by the other missions. Moreover, drafts of the 12 sections could be circulated in their logical order of development, and feedback could be obtained from the whole Mission throughout the process of writing and revising.

Sections 1 through 5 were discussed and tentatively approved at the July 1972 Mission meeting. Sections 6 through 8 were treated similarly at a special Mission meeting in November 1972. Then at the July 1973 meeting, the entire PBD--202 pages--was adopted for the 1975-77 planning cycle. This brought to a close the work of the strategy study committee.[33]

Of particular interest to the missionaries were the more practical sections of the PBD that touched on everyone's work: Intentions, Program Structure, and Organization. The Intentions section stated the overall purpose of the Mission: "to develop Christian disciples and churches through witness and ministry." Ministry was understood as directed to the whole person, since one's spiritual condition is affected by such problems as physical pain, emotional stress, and social alienation. The purpose statement was followed by seven objectives related both to the purpose and to the primary or priority needs identified in the previous section. Each objective was augmented with one or more dated, measurable goals.[34]

The section on Program Structure listed and described six specific programs in which the Mission was engaged. These were (1) starting and strengthening churches; (2) Christian witness in educational institutions; (3) Christian witness in medical institutions; (4) English-language churches; (5) Christian encounter ministry; and (6) Christian ministry to families. Missionaries were asked to identify with the program that represented their principal work assignment. A seventh program, Christian witness through radio, had been seriously considered but dropped in favor of treating this ministry as a project. This meant that radio work was to be supported with capital funds and not placed in the Mission's operating budget. This work was made a project because the Mission was about to start an experimental program, "Songs in the Night," beamed to Japan at midnight from the Far East Broadcasting Company's 250,000-watt medium-wave transmitter on Cheju Island, South Korea.[35]

The new organization replaced the Mission's geographical stations with six divisions, each to plan and conduct one of the six programs. Each division was to nominate its own leader, prepare its own PBD, and bring its goals, action plans, and budgets to the 1974 Mission meeting. Transcending the divisions was a full-time administrative staff, composed of administrator, treasurer, business manager, and research and design consultant. The administrator was to lead the Mission in planning, conducting, and evaluating its work. The R & D consultant was to assist the divisions with research and design activities and oversee experimental projects. By the end of the 1973 Mission meeting the four staff members and six division leaders had all been selected.

---

[33]*PBD*, 1973 ed., i-ii.
[34]Ibid., 114-15.
[35]Ibid., 119-27. Response to the Cheju broadcasts was so meager that they were dropped after one year.

Another feature of the new organization was a reduction of the executive committee from 15 members to 7. The subcommittees were abolished. The work of the evangelism committee fell mainly to the Division of Starting and Strengthening Churches. The responsibilities of the personnel committee passed into the hands of the administrator, aided by the division leaders as a consulting group. The duties of the finance committee were assumed by the business manager and the treasurer. Only the work of the general affairs committee remained largely with the smaller executive committee.[36]

Since the PBD was not fully implemented until January 1975, the geographical stations and the 15-member executive committee continued to function through 1974. To make the transition to the new system, it was necessary for the administrative staff and division leaders to assume their duties in 1973 and operate as best they could with a two-track system. The first administrator, Melvin Bradshaw, was absent on furlough in 1973-74, but Morris Wright served as acting administrator during this crucial period.

In October 1973 division leaders and staff members held a four-day conference in Tokyo to study leadership principles and coordinate their planning. This was followed by a November conferences for writers of division PBDs and a March 1974 seminar on research. Mission representatives also attended management and planning seminars sponsored by other organizations in Japan and participated in Baptist conferences and workshops in Taiwan and Korea. Some of these activities were led by Morton Rose of the Sunday School Board. Annie Ward Byrd, a retiree of the same board, assisted in the tedious work of rewriting old Mission policies and procedures and writing many new ones, all in line with the PBD and a newly prescribed format. Fifty-three policy statements were adopted in 1973; many others followed over the next several years. They were published in the Mission's loose-leaf "Operations Manual" with its constitution and bylaws. This manual, together with the PBD, replaced the venerable "Mission Handbook."[37]

In 1974 the Mission office was moved from the Convention headquarters building in Shinjuku to the Mission-owned Shibuya Baptist Building, which had been used for conferences and committee meetings since its completion five years before. In 1969 Tokyo Baptist Church had enlarged its basement fellowship hall with a $10,000 gift from Fred Lange, a generous supporter after whom the hall had been named. At the same time, to better utilize the land, the Mission had built a two-story structure over the basement extension. Beginning in 1974 the first floor was used for the traditional functions of the Mission office, mainly accounting. The second floor accommodated the Mission administrator as well as conferences and other activities. A three-story annex constructed in 1974 provided space on the second floor for the R & D consultant and the research center library.

---

[36]Marion Moorhead to Mission, 1 Jan. 1975.
[37]Author's notes of 1973-74 meetings; "Operations Manual," JBM, 1973.

A lounge was located on the first floor, and printing and storage facilities on the third. The move to Shibuya was deemed necessary for the Mission's enlarged operations, though it resulted in a spatial and symbolic distancing of the Mission's leadership from that of the Convention. Mutual consultations became less frequent.

Not everyone was happy with the "new ways for new days" that had been urged on the Mission by a Board-sponsored team of experts. No one wanted the Mission to do its work willy-nilly or to dissipate its energy and resources in trivial pursuits. But more than a few members looked askance at the complex overhaul it had undergone. Some thought the new system might usurp the leadership role of the Holy Spirit. Some lamented the demise of the stations and the segregation of congenial neighbors into different divisions. Several flatly declined to join any division. Others who did join balked at having to prepare a job description, personal work goals, and an individual budget. Others were reticent to have their work evaluated by a fellow missionary. Even the administrator, Melvin Bradshaw, voiced serious discontent. "I have had a growing sense of disillusionment," he wrote, "with the proliferation of administration in our new organization--both in man hours consumed and budgets required. . . . Our new Mission thrust also has a tendency to substitute activities for deeper personal and Mission needs." Bradshaw submitted his resignation as administrator in June 1975 and was replaced at the July Mission meeting with Stan Howard. In September the Bradshaws announced that they were resigning from the Board. "My call to missionary service," Melvin explained, "had become static and stale."[38]

The untimely resignation of the first administrator in 1975 was followed by a turnover of the administrative staff in 1976. Treasurer Charles Whaley resigned to become dean of the Tokyo Baptist Seminary, an association-sponsored evening school that graduated its first class that year. The R & D consultant, Calvin Parker, accepted a call to the pastorate of Shibuya Church. The business manager, Morris Wright, resigned in protest against objectionable actions taken by the executive committee and was reassigned to general evangelism. Then the Mission elected Morris as part-time interim administrator during Stan Howard's four-month furlough in the autumn. At year's end, the Wrights transferred from Japan to the Caribbean area, where Morris served as curriculum coordinator.[39]

The unsettled state of affairs was reflected in a number of actions taken by the Mission or executive committee and afterwards rescinded. Some were trivial, such as approving and then disapproving the purchase of a large one-year-old car. Others were weighty. On December 5, 1975, the executive committee voted to

---

[38]Bradshaw to Moorhead, 10 June 1975; Melvin and Edith Bradshaw to "Co-laborers," 30 Sept. 1975; MM minutes, July 1975, action 157.

[39]Whaley to Hays, 18 Mar. 1976. For details on Tokyo Baptist Seminary, see Charles L. Whaley, "Development of a Pilot Program of Theological Education in Tokyo," D.Min. project report, Southern Baptist Theological Seminary, 1976.

provide land and building budgets for the English-language Nakagami Church, then meeting in three rented houses just outside Tachikawa Air Base. It also set up land and residence budgets for the new missionary pastor, Bill Emanuel. The budgets totalled more than $600,000. The Emanuels, who had expected to begin a one-year furlough in September 1976, chose to begin furlough immediately-- they qualified for eight months--in order to be in Japan for the construction projects in the fall of 1976. After their departure, the pastor of Kantō Plains Church protested the huge allocations for a church near a base that was expected to close and already had dozens of empty buildings. In response, the executive committee specified that the church building "be of prefab type design so as to be easily moved." Then in June 1976 the committee rescinded all actions related to Nakagami. Yet the Emanuels were not informed of this decision until their return to Japan in late August. In October the church disbanded. Said Bill Emanuel: "[We] sent the members that we had left at Nakagami to Kantō Plains Church."[40]

Earlier the English-language Chōfu Church had disbanded and left its large building in the hands of a Japanese congregation, which now wanted to buy the property from the Mission at a low price. Again the Mission vacillated, voting one way and then reversing itself. Finally it decided to give the building to the church, deed the lot to the Convention, and sell 80 tsubo of adjacent land to the church on easy terms.[41]

The executive committee voted to construct a 10-unit apartment building on property adjacent to Seinan Gakuin University in Fukuoka. This action too was later rescinded; the project was never carried out. Two residences were constructed near Christian Academy in Higashi Kurume, Tokyo, providing for two families with children an alternative to the secular and expensive American School. The construction was authorized only after much dallying by the Mission. About the same time the guest house in Kyoto that had been built in the 1950s with missionary contributions was closed, and the executive committee voted to establish a guest apartment in a Kyoto duplex. Even this action was rescinded though eventually carried out.[42]

The Mission was more decisive in administering Tokyo rental properties. A second apartment complex was built at Uehara, called Uehara Garden, and five of its eight units were leased to the Nigerian Embassy, which still occupied them in 1989. Plans were also made (and later carried out) to build apartments on the Kamiyama property, which had the highest potential as an income producer.[43]

The year 1975 was significant not only as the first year of a three-year planning cycle under a new Mission structure but as the start of the last quarter

[40]EC minutes, 1975, actions 293-96; ibid., 1976, actions 89, 91; Emanuel, *I Enlisted*, 207; Kenneth Bragg (Kantō Plains pastor) to Mission, 24 Dec. 1975.

[41]MM minutes, 1976, action 169; EC minutes, 1976, action 128.

[42]EC minutes, 1975, actions 245-46.

[43]Calcote to Mission, 14 Apr. 1978.

of the 20th century. A Twenty-five Year Strategy Study Committee that had been appointed by the executive committee submitted to the Mission a report entitled "Dreams of a Quarter-Century." The report was based on papers prepared by members of the Mission staff and executive committee as well as a questionnaire sent to members of the Mission.[44]

The report urged upon the Mission a strategy whose objective was "the evangelization of every person in Japan by the end of the century." This could be accomplished, the report said, through the use of mass media, the development of Baptist centers in 30 to 40 population centers, and the utilization of multiple evangelistic methods. It was recommended that the Mission have no "official" connection with the Convention, that it work "in cooperation with the churches and associations and district conventions, rather than through the 'Episcopalian' framework which now exists within the Convention." The report called for "the churches controlling the Convention and not the Convention controlling the churches."[45]

Because of the nature of the report--conglomerate, visionary, provocative-- the Mission merely voted to accept it without acting on it. This did not mean a lack of respect for Pete Gillespie, chairman of the committee and compiler of the report. As suggested before, Gillespie's discontent with the work in Japan was exceeded only by his dedication to it. Surprisingly, he claimed to have "no special calling to be a missionary." "As far as I'm personally concerned," he said later, "I don't see any difference in coming to Japan or in going to Virginia from Tennessee. To me it's all the same."[46] Unlike Jack Brunson, however, Gillespie stayed on the field 31 years, reaching the age of retirement.

In retrospect, the most interesting part of the report is the pessimistic forecast "that with resignations and retirements, plus fewer appointments, the number of missionaries will probably be reduced within 12-15 years to 80-100 instead of 160-200 we have dreamed of having." Within 12 years, in fact, the Mission would exceed 200 members. Gillespie died in 1983, too early to see his dream fulfilled.[47]

As pointed out above, the Mission suffered a great deal of confusion in the first few years under the PBD, when difficult adjustments had to be made. The turnover in staff members was nearly matched by a turnover in division leaders. Yet much was accomplished, and that mainly through the divisions, which achieved some worthy goals. The following section will describe briefly the activities of each division during the five-year period ending in 1979.[48]

---

[44]"Dreams of a Quarter-Century," report of Twenty-five Year Strategy Study Committee, 1975, mimeographed.

[45]"Dreams," 2-5.

[46]A. L. Gillespie, interview with Warren Johnson, Oct. 1972, FMB.

[47]"Dreams," 2; Gillespie obituary in *Commission* 46 (Dec. 1983), 67.

[48]The following section makes extensive use of the Mission administrator's reports, 1975-79.

Six Divisions at Work

The Division of Starting and Strengthening Churches (DSSC) had more than 50 members working in 28 cities. Coleman Clarke called this program the "granddaddy" of all the work, since it majored on activities the whole Mission had been involved in from early times. The division provided evangelistic teams--preachers and musicians--for churches requesting them. It offered specialized clinic teams in the fields of music, education, evangelism, lay training, and stewardship. It conducted evangelism conferences in Kagoshima and Nagasaki. Other activities included in-service-training, personal witnessing clinics, film evangelism training, and the publication of materials on church education and music.[49]

DSSC members led six pioneer missions in various cities and prepared to start new missions in Yokosuka and Nokata (Fukuoka). These two represented a step forward in cooperative evangelism, for each was a joint effort of the Mission, the Convention, an association, and a local church.[50]

In 1977 the DSSC assumed responsibility for the Mission's radio programs in Kansai and Hokkaido, which since 1975 had been conducted as special projects under the nominal supervision of the R & D consultant. Accordingly, the radio budget ($38,200) was moved from the category of capital funds to the division's operating budget. An argument flared over whether to continue the Hokkaido broadcast. The station that aired the morning program had moved it to an earlier slot--from 6:30 to 6:00--and responses from listeners had dwindled from 1,482 in 1975 to 367 in 1977. The DSSC voted to drop the program but later rescinded the action. The division also sponsored a short-wave broadcast from Guam, and with designated gifts from Carl T. Bahner, Max Garrott's brother-in-law, it aired brief Scripture-reading programs in Tomakomai and Nagasaki.[51]

The Division of Christian Witness in Educational Institutions (DCWEI) had its members concentrated at Seinan Gakuin in Fukuoka and Seinan Jo Gakuin in Kita Kyūshū, though one member taught briefly at International Christian University in Tokyo. The division's first leader, Joy Fenner, described the members' Christian witness to students and fellow teachers as their "piggyback task," since most had full-time duties assigned by the schools. Some members served as chaplain or director of religious activities at their school. Nearly all taught Christianity courses or extracurricular Bible classes and tried to follow up

[49]DSSC report, 1977; DSSC minutes, 1977.

[50]The six missions were Nishino (Sapporo), Hirabari (Nagoya), Motomachi (Sapporo), Tsurusaki (Ōita), Tomakomai, and Isahaya. On Nokata, see Culpepper, *God's Calling*, 235.

[51]Author to Bonita Sparrow, SBC Radio and TV Commission, 14 June 1977. Bahner was professor of chemistry at Carson-Newman College.

converts and seekers after graduation. As Max Garrott said, "Evangelism is a natural and normal part of the work of a Christian teacher as a Christian."[52]

Missionaries at Seinan Gakuin University helped to establish a sister-school relationship with Baylor University in 1971. After an international division was inaugurated in 1972, the student exchange program was rapidly expanded to include six colleges in the United States and two in France. Besides Baylor, the Southern Baptist schools involved were Ouachita University, Oklahoma Baptist University, and William Jewell College. Since these schools had a much higher percentage of Christians than Seinan, they contributed to Seinan's program of evangelism through the students they both sent and received for one year of study.[53]

The Division of Christian Witness in Medical Institutions (DCWMI) was centered in Kyoto at the Baptist hospital and School of Nursing. The division had only four members: C. F. Clark, pediatrician; Polly Clark and Mary Lou Emanuel, nurses; and Bob Hardy, chaplain. Emanuel was superintendent of the nursing school, and Polly Clark taught there. Nearly all the nursing students who were not Christians when they entered were baptized before they graduated. In 1979, 17 of the students went to America on a study trip, and a sister-school relationship was established with William Carey College in Hattiesburg, Mississippi. One concern of the division was the inadequate follow-up of hospital patients, only partly due to a shortage of personnel to carry out this ministry. Clark, who sometimes doubled as hospital superintendent, lamented that there was no "decent church" in Kyoto--no church to which one could refer prospects with confidence that their spiritual needs would be met. To provide such a place, he and Polly helped to organize Kitayama Church near the hospital.[54]

The Division of English Language Churches (DELC) was composed of missionaries working full time with those churches as pastor or other leader. At first there were six churches in the Tokyo-Yokohama area and one in Misawa, but as noted previously, the Chōfu and Nakagami churches were disbanded, reducing the total to five. While the number of American servicemen in mainland Japan (excluding Okinawa) had decreased from 71,500 in 1958 to 27,000 in 1977, the number of civilian foreigners had risen sharply, and Tokyo Baptist Church was packed each Sunday with expatriates. Rapid turnovers in membership, a perennial problem faced by all the churches, was less severe with civilian than with military personnel. At the end of the decade, for example, Kantō Plains had 753 members with 173 active, while Tokyo had 339 members with 103 active. The five

---

[52]Garrott is quoted in the division's PBD, 17. Fenner left the Mission in 1980 to become director of Woman's Missionary Union in Texas.

[53]*Seinan Gakuin nanajūnen shi*, 2:727-37.

[54]JBM annual report, 1979; *Commission* 42 (Feb. 1979), 3-6.

churches continued to sponsor family inspiration week at Amagi Sansō and to cooperate in other activities.[55]

The Division of Christian Encounter Ministry (DCEM) operated friendship houses in Fukuoka, Kyoto, and Kobe, harbor evangelism among seamen at Yokohama, a sports facility in Urawa, and local ministries in 12 places. Fukuoka Friendship House had become self-supporting with a popular program of English classes and other income-producing activities. The division's aim, said its first leader, Jim Watters, was to "witness to those people who are outside--geographically or culturally--the area of witness of our churches."[56] An understanding had been reached with the Convention that friendship houses would introduce people to existing churches and not become churches themselves.

The Division of Christian Ministry to Families (DCMF) contributed to family life enrichment through marriage encounter and other programs. As Helen Sherer pointed out, the division ministered "to and through" families, including missionary families. It established relationships with more than 50 "international families," mostly Japanese who had lived abroad. As a special service, it also prepared much-needed information packets for new appointees to Japan. The DCMF was composed only of women--17 in number--until Helen's husband Bob joined and paved the way for a few other males.[57]

In 1975 representatives of two divisions, Starting and Strengthening Churches and Christian Encounter Ministry, formed a joint committee known as the Metropolitan Project Planning Committee. It recommended a new Mission project called Japan Baptist Communication Service, whose purpose was to be a "multi-media ministry." Although the Convention and Mission had engaged in short term radio and television ministries in various parts of Japan since the 1950s, an overall strategy had been lacking. Only the Kansai and Hokkaido radio programs were in any sense permanent, and both suffered from inadequate follow-up. The committee proposed, therefore, that the Communication Service procure or develop quality materials--printed, audio, and video--and train missionary personnel to make maximum use of these materials.[58] With Mission and Board approval, the project was conducted for three years, beginning in 1978. It resulted in the establishment of the permanent Communication Center described in the next chapter.

As the Mission neared the end of the first three-year planning cycle, an evaluation was made of the innovations with particular attention given to Mission structure. Considerable support was shown, especially by school-related missionaries in Kyushu, for a return to some type of area organizations. So at the 1978 Mission meeting it was voted that "on a trial basis . . . we hold meetings by

---

[55]20th anniversary brochure of Tokyo Baptist Church, 1978; author's notes.

[56]Author's notes, 1973; *Commission* 42 (Feb. 1979), 7-8.

[57]Author's notes, 1973; report of the DCMF, 1977.

[58]"Communication Services Project," 1977, JBM.

areas (four) for sharing, discussion, and brainstorming." In 1979, however, no action was taken to continue these meetings or to modify the organization in effect since 1975. One reason is that the Division of Christian Ministry to Families began to sponsor fellowship meetings in each area and an annual Thanksgiving retreat at Amagi Sansō for the whole Mission. In 1979 this division also sponsored a Mission-wide men's retreat that drew an attendance of 38.[59]

An Intimate Look at the Mission Family

In the early years following the Pacific War, as we have noted, missionaries worked with confidence and optimism among a people bewildered and depressed. By 1970, the situation had reversed. The Japanese were confident and optimistic, and many missionaries were bewildered and depressed. The Protestant missionary force in Japan was declining sharply. Southern Baptists, barely holding their own, were not immune to stress and uncertainty. Upheavals in the Convention were unsettling, and the 1970 world Baptist congress, like the 1963 New Life Movement, was followed by a spiritual and psychic let-down.

In 1971 a charismatic evangelist from Canada, Les Pritchard, conducted a timely series of renewal conferences in Japan that attracted large numbers of missionaries, both Catholic and Protestant. Participants were led to pray for "the baptism of the Holy Spirit," and many spoke in tongues for the first time. About 12 Southern Baptists were caught up in the movement, somewhat as Edwin Dozier and Max Garrott had been caught up in the Oxford Group Movement that swept Japan in the 1930s. The new Southern Baptist charismatics, claiming that their deepest personal needs had been met, brought their spiritual exuberance to the July 1972 Mission meeting, only to be confronted by others who regarded glossolalia as weird and divisive if not heretical. Providentially, it seems, Bob Culpepper had been chosen to lead the customary time of prayer and sharing. Deeply interested in Pritchard's ministry, Culpepper had attended charismatic prayer meetings in Tokyo, Kyoto, and Fukuoka, and he had begun a serious theological study that was later developed into the book *Evaluating the Charismatic Movement*. Himself not a tongues-speaker, Culpepper was able to play a mediating and healing role as testimonies were given from "both sides of the charismatic divide."[60]

Pritchard visited Japan occasionally over the next several years, conducting well-attended seminars in the major cities. His 1973 seminar in Kyoto, held in an Anglican church, drew about 300 people. "What a wonderful time it was," exclaimed a Southern Baptist couple, "filled with the anointing of His Holy Spirit and the praises of our Lord Jesus Christ." The couple joined with pastors and

---

[59]MM minutes, July 1978, action 113; JBM annual report, 1979.
[60]Culpepper, *God's Calling*, 204-9. *Evaluating the Charismatic Movement* was published by Judson Press in 1977.

missionaries of many denominations to form an Agape Kai ("love meeting") that met monthly for fellowship and prayer.[61] This couple later resigned from the Mission, and some other members ceased speaking in tongues. Southern Baptist participation in Japan's charismatic movement gradually faded away.

Another 1972-73 visitor to Japan, Everett Barnard, a psychologist from the Sunday School Board, helped missionaries understand and deal with their personal problems from a different perspective. Barnard gave personality profile tests to members of the Mission and met with them privately to interpret the results. He traveled to several areas to render this service and to give counsel when appropriate.

In 1978 missionaries saw themselves through the eyes of Janice and Mahan Siler, counsellors from Winston-Salem, North Carolina, where Mahan was director of the School of Pastoral Care at Baptist Hospital. The Silers spent six weeks in Japan conducting family life enrichment conferences in several areas and one in conjunction with Mission meeting. After returning to America they wrote a follow-up report that identified with professional precision the strengths and weaknesses of the Mission.[62]

The Silers were impressed with the importance of the Mission as a family--an extended, functioning family that satisfied some of the deepest needs of its members. But some members, they noted, especially among the field evangelists, were still searching for their place within the Mission and its work in general. Second- and third-term missionaries seemed to be doing less well than first-termers. The older ones, while subject to "the general mid-life kind of stress," were far enough into the Japanese language and ministry to experience the severity of their limitations in an alien culture. The Silers described this state as "delayed" or "deferred" shock. Their observations were supported by Foreign Mission Board findings that missionaries were vulnerable to the "middle age syndrome," a significant factor in resignations.[63]

The Silers called for "more mutuality and partnership" within marriage. Wives especially, they pointed out, wanted more interpersonal fulfillment in their marriage relationship, which often felt more like co-existence. Since there was little opportunity for missionaries to deal with anger and frustration directly with the Japanese, resentment often built up within the marriage and the family, a resentment potentially explosive.[64] Though not mentioned in the Silers' report, it should be noted that six of the couples who had resigned from the Mission during the previous two decades had also divorced after their return to America. At least three more of the couples divorced later on.

---

[61] *Team Thrust Ministries* (brochure, n.d.), 3, 8.

[62] Janice and Mahan Siler, "Report on Enrichment Ministry to Japan Mission Family," 1978, photocopy, JBM.

[63] Ibid.; Crawley, *Global Mission*, 77-78.

[64] Siler, "Report on Enrichment Ministry."

Finally, Janice and Mahan Siler "sensed a significant level of fatigue, heaviness and over-seriousness among many of the missionaries." This was especially true of those who had very high expectations for themselves and their ministry. Such persons "grappled often with impotency, failure and guilt." Conflict of this nature is not uncommon in people with a religious vocation, the Silers indicated, but it was all the more conspicuous in a place like Japan where one consumed much time and energy on the basic necessities of life. Their advice to missionaries: play and relax.[65]

Deaths in the Family

There is a time to laugh and dance, as the writer of Ecclesiastes said, and there is also a time to weep and mourn. Several times during this decade the Mission grieved over the loss of a family member. In October 1970 the only daughter of Bill and Louise Medling, Carol Ann, a student at Memphis State University, plunged to her death from the roof of a six-story dormitory. Police ruled it a suicide. Carol had been having emotional disturbances since July, when she took a single dose of psilocybin with a group of young people on the way to a pop concert. The drug had induced a complete change of personality and deep depression that required hospital treatment. Carol had since shown marked improvement. At the time of the tragedy she was staying in the hospital at night but commuting to school by day.[66]

"We know that the drug she took induced a torment that was horrible and frightening," wrote her parents, then on furlough in Memphis. "We feel she either thought she saw something from which she was running or something beyond the roof for which she was reaching." Carol had prayed with Bill and Louise on several occasions, and "her face in death was peaceful and unmarred." Born in Japan in 1950, Carol attended high school in Okinawa, where she was a member of the National Honor Society and the National Thespian Society.[67] Bill and Louise had transferred to Okinawa in 1965 as the first Board missionaries assigned to Japanese language work. Though technically in a separate mission at the time, the Medlings nevertheless remained a part of the Japan fellowship. As related in the next chapter, the Okinawa and Japan missions were afterwards consolidated.

On October 9, 1971, the three-month-old daughter of George and Amy Watanabe, Melanie Midori, died at Kyoto University Hospital. The postmortem examination, reported C. F. Clark, "indicated that she had three serious heart defects that even heart surgery could not have corrected anywhere in the world." The funeral at Rokkō Mission in Kobe was followed by a cremation service in

[65]Ibid.
[66]Bill and Louise Medling to Friends, 24 Oct. 1970.
[67]Ibid.; unidentified newspaper clipping attached to ibid.

Kyoto. On October 16 the Watanabes left for furlough and took the remains to Hawaii for burial in the family cemetery. In October 1972, when the Watanabes were settled in Nagoya to begin a new work, another daughter, Beth Mieko, was likewise born with a congenital heart condition. She lived only three days.[68]

The death of Maude Burke Dozier on January 13, 1973, deserves mention here, though she was not in active service at the time. After the Pacific War she had continued to serve in Hawaii until her retirement from the Board in 1951. Then to be near her two children, Edwin and Helen, she returned to Japan, where she endeared herself to the postwar generation of missionaries. Ill health forced her to leave in 1964 and spend her remaining years in a Texas nursing home. In 1961 she had received the West Japan Culture Award, and in 1967 she was granted the Fifth Class Order of the Precious Crown, the same decoration afterwards bestowed on Elizabeth Watkins. Maude Dozier's ashes were brought to Japan by Jesse Fletcher, a Board staffer scheduled to come at the time, and buried at Seinan Jo Gakuin beside the remains of her husband. A memorial service at Seinan Gakuin honored Maude as the school's "mother," as founder of the Kindergarten Training School that had been integrated into the university, and as a woman mighty in prayer.[69]

On June 25, 1974, five days after his 64th birthday, Max Garrott died at the North Carolina Baptist Hospital in Winston-Salem following a coronary by-pass operation. He had been under the care of a heart specialist in Fukuoka since January, suffering from angina. Garrott elected the risky surgery because it offered the only hope for continuing to serve in Japan. The operation was done successfully, doctors reported, but because of previous damage to the heart muscle, Max died afterwards while in intensive care, without regaining consciousness.[70]

Much has been written about Garrott in previous chapters, for he looms large in the Mission's history. In 1972 he resigned the chancellorship of Seinan Jo Gakuin, which he had held since 1962, in order to return to seminary teaching and devote more time to a Bible translation project. Within a year, however, he was elected chancellor of Seinan Gakuin. Garrott accepted, feeling that he could not decline an opportunity to strengthen the Christian witness of this highly influential institution. His term as chancellor was cut short by death. In recognition of his signal contribution to education, the Japanese government conferred on him posthumously the Third Class Order of the Sacred Treasure.[71] Garrott has the distinction of being the only person to serve as chancellor of both Baptist schools and chairman of both boards of trustees.

---

[68]Clark report on Melanie Watanabe, n.d., JBM; "Jabas News," Oct., Nov. 1972.

[69]*Seinan Gakuin nanajūnen shi*, 2:98-101; Mary Ellen Dozier newsletter, n.d. [1973].

[70]JBM mailout, 11 Jan. 1974; Franklin Fowler to C. F. Clark, n.d., JBM; Dorothy Garrott, oral history.

[71]*Japan Times*, 24 Aug. 1974.

Garrott was a legend in his time. Once when giving the chancellor's address at a Seinan Gakuin University commencement, properly attired in a morning suit, he shocked the audience by standing on top of the podium to emphasize a point. At a Convention annual meeting, when a Japanese pastor said that churches could not be started without land and building, Garrott shouted *"Bakayarō!"* So offensive is this term, usually translated "You fool," that its onetime use by Prime Minister Yoshida Shigeru in a Diet debate almost toppled his government. Yet Garrott's use of this obscenity was tolerated--he could be excused as a foreigner-- and later it was praised by a Convention president, Okamura Shōji, as a shock that was needed at the time. Indeed, Garrott's stress on house churches eventually won Convention-wide support. On another memorable occasion, when the Convention leadership was under attack by radical students and pastors, Garrott rebuked the critics by demonstrating with his own hand that to point a finger at another person was to point three fingers at oneself.

Dorothy Garrott brought Max's ashes to Japan for interment in the little cemetery at Seinan Jo Gakuin. A phrase from John 4:37, "To do the will of Him that sent me," was inscribed on his gravestone in Japanese. Dorothy continued to do mission work in Fukuoka until retiring in 1977. Upon her death in Louisville in 1982, her remains likewise were brought to Japan and laid beside those of her husband. At this latter burial service the bereaved family was represented by Matsumura Akiko, a convert and spiritual daughter of Dorothy's who had risen to become president of the Asian Baptist Women's Union and a vice president of the Baptist World Alliance.[72]

The retirement of Dorothy Garrott in 1977, along with that of Alma Graves in the same year, brought to a close the service of prewar missionaries in Japan. They were an outstanding lot. Mention has been made that imperial decorations were conferred on Maude Dozier, Edwin Dozier, Elizabeth Watkins, and Max Garrott. Two others were likewise honored. In 1952 Cecile Lancaster, vice president of Seinan Jo Gakuin, received the Fifth Class Order of the Sacred Treasure. In 1968 Alma Graves, noted for her mastery of ikebana and her skillful direction of Shakespeare dramas at Seinan Gakuin, received the Fourth Class Order of the Sacred Treasure.[73]

After the death of Max Garrott, the trustees of Seinan Gakuin offered the chancellorship to Luther Copeland, professor of missions and world religions at Southeastern Seminary in North Carolina. The Copelands had been missionaries from 1948 to 1956, and Luther had been chancellor of Seinan Gakuin for three of

---

[72]Dorothy Garrott to Friends, Feb. 1976; program of Dorothy's burial service, 18 Dec. 1982.
[73]The Order of the Rising Sun, bestowed on Edwin Dozier, is granted to men only. The Order of the Precious Crown, bestowed on Maude Dozier and Elizabeth Watkins, is granted to women only. The Order of the Sacred Treasure, bestowed on Lancaster, Graves, and Garrott, is granted to both men and women. The decorations are ranked from first to eighth class, according to the degrees of meritorious service. See *Kodansha Encyclopedia of Japan*, s.v. "decorations."

those years. After visiting the school to look over the situation, he decided to take the job again. Luther and Louise were reappointed by the Board. As they described it, the Copelands "went home" to Japan and Fukuoka, where they served a full term before "retirement" and several visiting professorships in the United States. Luther was chancellor of Seinan Gakuin from February 1976 through March 1980, his salary paid by the school. Striving "to maintain and strengthen the school's Christian character," he led the institution to adopt a new constitution stressing the importance of Christian education and requiring three-fourths of the trustees to be Christians.[74]

One more death should be noted. James Belote, area secretary for East Asia, was stricken with a fatal heart attack on March 4, 1975, while playing tennis in Richmond. He was 61.[75] Though never a missionary to Japan, Belote was mourned as though a member of the family. He was succeeded by George Hays, his field representative who earlier had won the Mission's respect as chairman, treasurer, and seminary teacher specializing in Christian ethics. One of only three from the Mission to become a Foreign Mission Board bureaucrat (the others are Johnni Johnson Scofield and a journeyman, Robert Shoemake), Hays served ably as area director until his retirement at the end of 1985.

[74]"FMB Digest," 1-15 Mar. 1982.
[75]*Religious Herald*, 15 Jan. 1976.

12

Crossing Over the Peak (1980-1989)

The lead article in the February 1980 *Commission* had an arresting title set in large bold letters: "Who'll Fill Their Shoes in Japan? Age Catches up in the 1980s." Written by Lois Whaley, the Mission's press representative, the article pointed out that since it was still the custom in Japan to remove one's shoes before entering a church building, one could determine how many people were gathered inside by counting the shoes at the door. "At a meeting of the Japan Baptist Mission," the article continued, "one might count as many as 130 pairs of shoes in the doorway, if all were able to attend. . . . By 1990 at least 50 pairs of those shoes--that's 38 percent--may be left vacant due to retirement among the missionaries. Fifty missionaries will reach the initial retirement age of 65 by 1990."[1]

The article then introduced all 50 of these veterans--Lois Whaley included--and described their heavy involvement in the evangelization of Japan. Three couples--Copelands, Culpeppers, Moorheads--were scheduled to leave Japan as early as 1980 or 1981. Luther and Louise Copeland had majored on educational evangelism at Seinan Gakuin. So had Bob and Kay Culpepper, who also had started and developed three churches in Fukuoka during the 28 years that Bob taught theology. Unlike the Copelands, however, the Culpeppers were leaving Japan prior to retirement age so that Bob could fill a vacancy at Southeastern Seminary. Marion and Thelma Moorhead had taught at both Seinan Gakuin and Seinan Jo Gakuin, opened new work on Hokkaido, and filled various positions in the Mission. Since 1963 they had led the strategic English-language Tokyo Baptist Church, Marion as pastor and Thelma as minister of counseling.

The 44 persons scheduled to leave Japan after 1981 had likewise made notable contributions to the work. Virginia Highfill, for example, who was to retire in 1984, had effectively applied her specialties in church evangelism, religious education, and WMU work. After Lois Whaley's article was published, Highfill

---

[1]*Commission* 43 (Feb. 1980), 4.

became the only woman in the history of the Mission to hold the office of chairman (the term was never changed to chairperson). "Can it be," Whaley asked in concluding her article, "that somewhere God has 50 spiritual and intellectual giants, either Japanese or missionary, who can step into the shoes of these who have served so faithfully?"[2]

Not many readers of the *Commission* could have skipped these challenging words. The article was attractively illustrated with pencil sketches of 21 of the 50 missionaries, and 10 of the sketches adorned the magazine's cover. One thing is certain: the article had its desired effect. At the beginning of 1980 the Mission numbered 122 career missionaries, 14 associates, and 18 journeymen, or a total of 154 members. In 1987 the total reached an all-time high of 206. The number of two-year journeymen remained constant, with about half replaced annually, but more than 70 new career and associate missionaries were added, far more than enough to offset resignations as well as retirements. In 1986, when five missionaries left for retirement and three others resigned, 22 recruits arrived on the field, the most since 1950. Some of the new arrivals cited Lois Whaley's article as a decisive factor in their call to Japan.[3]

The challenge of replacing Japan's large band of greying personnel coincided with the full implementation of Bold Mission Thrust, a program of missions advance developed by the SBC and its agencies in the second half of the 1970s. The SBC had voted in 1976 to set as "its primary missions challenge that every person in the world shall have the opportunity to hear the gospel of Christ in the next 25 years." For its part the Foreign Mission Board had adopted specific goals to be reached by the end of A.D. 2000. These included 5,000 missionaries serving in 125 countries, 10,000 persons involved annually in volunteer programs and projects, and a tenfold multiplication of churches, church members, and baptisms on the mission fields.[4]

The number of missionaries and volunteers increased so rapidly that in 1987 the Board adopted new goals for the year 2000 of 5,600 missionaries and 20,000 volunteers. In 1988 the number of missionaries was said to have increased 44 percent during the 12 years of Bold Mission Thrust, reaching a total of 3,839. The Japan Mission's growth to a record 206 members reflected this overall increase.[5]

A lesser factor in the Mission's growth was its merger with the Okinawa Mission on January 1, 1981, after approval by the Board on the recommendation of both missions. The merger increased the count for Japan by nine persons, all connected with English-language churches. Subsequently, the Mission assigned two couples to Okinawa for Japanese-language ministries and strengthened its ties with the growing Okinawa Baptist Convention. Between 1981 and 1989 the

[2]Ibid., 11. On Highfill, see ibid. 44 (Apr. 1981): 39-47.
[3]*ASBC, 1980*, 92; *ASBC, 1988*, 128; JBM annual report, 1986.
[4]*ESB*, vol. 4, s.v. "Bold Mission Thrust."
[5]*Commission* 51 (June/July 1988), 47.

number of churches increased from 19 to 24, and membership doubled from 1,212 to 2,431. The Okinawa Convention retained its separate identity from both the Japan Baptist Union and the Japan Baptist Convention and continued its relationship with the American Baptist Foreign Mission Society in addition to that with the Southern Baptist Foreign Mission Board.[6]

The rapid influx of new missionaries made the 1980s seem like a replay of the 1950s. Once again Mission meetings teemed with little children. To accommodate the growing number of families, the facilities at Amagi Assembly had to be supplemented with rooms at two hotels in nearby Yugashima. Mission housing throughout the nation had to be supplemented with an increasing number of rentals. Fortunately, the Mission still had disposable properties and income-producing rental units that generated funds needed for new construction and additional rentals. In 1981, for example, when $105,000 was received from the Board for construction needs, $1,441,639 was generated on the field, most of it from property sales. In 1983 the 15 rental units in Tokyo produced over $400,000, but this was less than enough for two new residence budgets at the usual amount of $250,000 each. In 1987 the housing crunch was so acute and budgets so tight from the sharp decline of the dollar against the yen, that the Mission was forced to call for a drastic reduction in new appointments. The number dropped to one couple in 1988 and three couples in 1989.[7]

The rapid growth of the '80s made possible a wider distribution of Mission personnel. Missionaries were assigned to places like Shimonoseki and Matsue that had been vacated many years before. In 1987 a couple took up residence in Sasebo, previously occupied only by Kelsey and Maude Dozier in 1907-8. Other couples moved to cities never before occupied, such as Tsuchiura, near the newly developing university/science city of Tsukuba. Toyama, regarded by Convention leaders as the weakest link in the chain of churches joining every prefecture, had Reiji and Asano Hoshizaki in residence prior to their retirement in 1984.

At the annual Mission meetings, where newcomers were formally recognized and welcomed, retirees were somewhat pampered. They were presented with gifts while cameras flashed, and allowed time on the program to make a farewell speech. The gifts were no surprise to the recipients, for they had been at liberty to select a hand-painted folding screen or anything else within a ¥50,000 limit. But the speeches often amazed the listeners, most of whom knew nothing of the devastated, preaffluent Japan to which the aging "boat people" had come.

Tom and Mary Gullatt, who gave their farewell speeches at the 1984 Mission meeting, chose not to reminisce about their early adventures and misadventures, but to describe their recent partings from Japanese friends. As is customary in

[6]EC minutes, Dec. 1980; *Kirisutokyō nenkan, 1982*, 422; JBM annual report, 1989. See also "The Okinawa Baptist Convention: A Historical Overview," JBM, 1988.
[7]MM reports, 1983; JBM annual reports, 1987-89.

The Commission

FOREIGN MISSIONS JOURNAL, SBC/FEBRUARY 1980

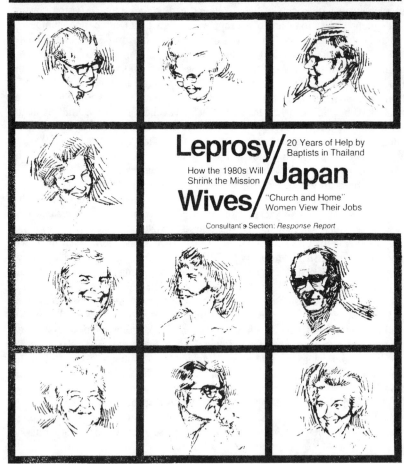

Leprosy / 20 Years of Help by Baptists in Thailand

How the 1980s Will Shrink the Mission / **Japan**

Wives / "Church and Home" Women View Their Jobs

Consultant's Section: *Response Report*

Soon-to-retire missionaries on *Commission* cover. *Counterclockwise from upper right:* Bob Sherer, Mary Gullatt, Tom Gullatt, Betty Faith Boatwright, Bob Culpepper, Rebekah Sue Emanuel, Ed Oliver, Mary Elizabeth Ray, Bob Boatwright, Jean Shepard. *(Sketches by Dan Beatty)*

Japan, the Gullatts had been feted at sayonara parties in each of the five churches where they had served, most notably in Mito. The Mito church had originated in their home, and the Gullatts had been connected with it for about 25 of their 34 years in Japan. The people had come to love Tom for his humility and faithfulness, and Mary for her sparkling humor. So the church elected Tom pastor emeritus and proceeded to honor both in a grandiose manner.

As revealed by the Gullatts in their speeches, they were given an all-expense trip to Okinawa. They were written up in three newspapers, and Tom was interviewed on four radio stations. On Friday night, June 8, 1983, the first service of a weekend revival with Tom as preacher, NHK--Japan's public broadcasting company--telecast a five-minute segment of the meeting live on "News Center," which had a potential audience of 40 million. The segment included interviews of Tom and Mary and Japanese leaders of the church. To telecast live, NHK had brought heavy equipment to the church and installed a transmitter on the tallest building in the city. After the last service of the revival on Sunday morning, June 8, the Gullatts were photographed with 100 well-wishers at a climactic party. The church memorialized the farewell events with a set of 130 slides, 100 copies of a sermon tape, and 1,300 copies of a 20-page, full-color bilingual booklet.[8]

It yet remained for the Gullatts to go to Tokyo, attend Mission meeting at Amagi, and fly to Georgia. Steeped in Japanese culture, they knew the importance of leaving Mito by train so that friends could send them off in the traditional manner. But since they also needed to drive their Mission car to Tokyo, Tom rose early on their day of departure, drove the baggage-filled car to the station where their train would make its first stop en route to Tokyo, and hopped a train back to Mito. At the proper time the Gullatts were standing in the depot, encircled by a throng of well-wishers who bowed one by one and presented bouquets and gifts. After boarding the train they waved to the crowd until cut off from view. Then 20 minutes later, to the astonishment of other passengers who had witnessed the send-off, the Gullatts detrained with their armloads of presents and walked to their waiting car.

Dottie Lane, who retired in 1987 with 36 years of service, learned that her Japanese Baptist friends were not content to give her a grand send-off. A delegation of 24 visited the First Baptist Church of Sturgis, Kentucky, to express their thanks for Dottie's fruitful ministry. This was the church that had nurtured her commitment to missions as a youth and had sent her to Japan in 1951.[9] Dottie was further pleased that retirees and other former missionaries to Japan began holding an annual reunion in her area at Jonathan Creek Baptist Assembly. Attendance reached 54 in 1989. Their ties to one another are deep, as are their ties

[8]*Baputesuto*, 1 Sept. 1984, 15; *Ai no hi* (Sun of love), Mito Baptist Church, 1984.
[9]*Commission* 50 (Oct./Nov. 1987), 5.

to Japan. More than a dozen persons in this group--Dottie Lane and the Gullatts among them--have returned to Japan one or more times as short-term volunteers.

Though words of regret were often heard in this decade when a missionary left Japan for retirement or resignation, the greatest outpouring of sorrow followed the death of a comrade in Tokyo. On Saturday morning, March 28, 1981, Gene Clark suffered chest pains while playing tennis on the American School courts near his home. He lost consciousness en route to a hospital, and upon arrival was pronounced dead of a heart attack. He was 54, too young to have made Lois Whaley's list of missionaries expected to retire by 1990.[10]

At the funeral service held the next evening, Chōfu Church overflowed with an estimated 500 mourners. Gene's favorite hymns were sung, including "Just As I Am," and a portion of a recording was played of the last sermon he had preached, "Now is the Day of Salvation." In the funeral address Pastor Hotai Ken paid tribute to Gene's evangelistic zeal. "He used the phone, he witnessed in restaurants," Hotai said, "and he asked people at the tennis courts, 'Do you know Christ? Please come to church.' . . . He had a vision of seeing this building full of people." Gene had often challenged the Chōfu church to build a congregation of 300 people.[11]

Gene's body, after embalmment at the U.S. Air Force base in Yokota, was flown to Avon Park, Florida, for another funeral service and interment on April 3. Afterwards, Dorothy Clark resigned from the Board. The loss of Gene and Dorothy from the Mission was partially compensated in 1987 when their daughter Maggi and her husband, David Davis, were assigned to Nagasaki as journeymen.

The Mission at Work

A revised edition of *Program Base Design*, issued in 1980, incorporated a number of actions taken at the 1979 Mission meeting. These actions narrowed the major thrust of the Mission to urban penetration, church starting, and student evangelism "during the remainder of the century." Among these three emphases, urban penetration was made the central focus for the 1981-83 planning cycle. A workshop on urban evangelism was conducted at Amagi Sansō, and specific strategies were worked out for concentrating on seven urban areas.[12]

The 1980 PBD also carried a rewording of the Mission's purpose statement. It read: "To bring people in Japan to a saving faith in Jesus Christ as Lord, introducing them into the fellowship of local Baptist churches and involving them in Christian growth and service." This wording expanded on the original 1973 statement but left out its direct reference to the developing of churches.

---

[10]Dick Horn to Mission, Apr. 1981 mailout.

[11]Bob Hardy to Mission Family, 8 Apr. 1981; JBC executive secretary's column in *Baputesuto*, May 1981.

[12]*PBD*, 1980 ed., 73, 115.

Apparently the omission was a matter of wording, not intention, for among the stated "tasks" of the Mission the first was "to start churches." Still, the deficiency in the purpose statement grew conspicuous in the following years as the Board put heavier stress on "evangelism that results in churches." So in 1986 the statement was changed to read: "We will proclaim the gospel of the Lord Jesus Christ through witness and ministry in cooperation with the Japan Baptist Convention and the Okinawa Baptist Convention so as to make Christian disciples and to establish strong Baptist churches." This purpose was reinforced with the objective, "to engage in evangelism that results in churches."[13]

It is significant that the stated intention of starting churches was tactfully balanced with a reference to cooperation with the two Baptist conventions. In 1979 the Japan Convention had set a long-range goal of 1,000 churches, with at least 250 churches and 250 missions by 1989, the centennial of Southern Baptist work in Japan. In 1984 these goals were modified to 50,000 believers and 500 churches with a less definite target date. Convention leaders urged missionaries to work for the attainment of these goals.[14]

Among the missionaries, however, doubts were aired that the Convention really meant business. Some felt that the Convention was so absorbed in looking after itself that it could never conduct a "bold mission thrust." In the view of these doubters, the Mission was bound by a commitment to "participate in the starting of churches" only at the discretion of Japanese Baptists, when what was needed was freedom for the Mission to start churches whenever and wherever it chose. In 1984 administrator Stan Howard expressed the frustration of many when he spoke of "a state of inertia" in the Mission directly related to the philosophical problem of "how we relate to the Convention."[15]

Another matter of concern in the Mission was its own organizational structure. The flaws had become more pronounced with the passing of the years. A proposal to make the administrator and division leaders voting members of the executive committee was referred to a special committee and then rejected.[16] A quite different proposal, supported by most school-related missionaries, would have replaced the six functional divisions with three geographical divisions, in order to reunify and strengthen work that had become fragmented. This proposal also failed, though as we shall see, a similar plan was implemented in 1989. Until the end of 1988, the Mission continued to work primarily through the six divisions, with the mildly revised PBD as compass and guide.

The Division of Starting and Strengthening Churches, as in the previous decade, provided teams for special evangelistic meetings, conducted clinics in such specialties as religious education and church music, and established new missions

---

[13]Ibid., 116, 114; JBM annual report, 1986.
[14]*PBD*, 1980 ed., 73; JBM annual report, 1984.
[15]Administrator's report, Aug. 1984.
[16]See MM minutes, 1985, action 122.

and witnessing places. The number of division members serving as pastor of a church or mission in a given year rose as high as 22. Their contributions came into focus each year when new churches were received into the Convention, for invariably a number of the churches bore the marks of missionary leadership. Of the seven newly organized churches received in 1984, six had been led by missionaries during all or a part of their history.[17]

Of six new missions started in 1984, three had missionary pastors. The most notable was Fukuma in Fukuoka Prefecture, the first known mission to have three mother churches (Fukuoka, Nagazumi, and Taguma). Charles Whaley served as pastor the first four years, which coincided with his term as chancellor of Seinan Gakuin. Services were conducted in a house purchased by a Seinan Gakuin professor for the express purpose of starting a new church in a fast-growing residential area. In 1986 a building was erected with grants of ¥20 million from the Mission, ¥11 million from the Convention, and ¥3.35 million each from the three mother churches.[18] Fukuma was very fortunate, for most missions started during this decade had to meet in rented quarters while spiraling land prices all but quenched any hopes of getting a building of their own.

The DSSC played a prominent role in the Partnership Evangelism crusades held in the fall of 1983 with 165 participants from Southern Baptist churches. The participants arrived in three separate groups and were divided into smaller teams for services in 67 churches and missions. Conducted with Convention approval and under the umbrella of Bold Mission Thrust, this undertaking was the largest in the Mission's history except for the New Life Movement of 1963.[19]

Another significant activity of the DSSC was promotion of the highly successful discipling program, MasterLife. Don Heiss introduced the program to Japan after attending a 1980 workshop at Ridgecrest by invitation of the Board. In 1983 the program's originator, Avery T. Willis, Jr., conducted a workshop in Kobe for 96 missionaries and nationals from East Asia, including 11 Japanese. Over the next three years the materials were translated into Japanese. Beginning in 1986 area workshops were conducted annually, with more than 10 held in 1989, when there were 35 Japanese group leaders. MasterLife was added to the curricula

---

[17]JBM annual report, 1984. Nokata Church in Fukuoka, a joint project of the Mission, Convention, and Nagazumi Church, was started by Bob Culpepper and subsequently led by Ralph Calcote. Hirabari Church in Nagoya was begun and led for many years by Reiji Hoshizaki. Yokosuka Church had Tak Oue as pastor. Tama Newtown was started by Les Watson in a gymnasium, and Nishi Tokyo, developed as a mission of the English-language Kantō Plains Church, had Ed Oliver as pastor. The sixth church, Kita Sendai, was begun under Convention-wide sponsorship, but Bob Boatwright was one of its first leaders.

[18]Ibid.; EC minutes, 1986, action 81.

[19]JBC executive secretary's column in *Baputesuto*, Dec. 1983, JBM mailout.

of the Tokyo seminary and the new Kyushu Baptist Seminary, the latter an independent Bible school established by a group of Baptist pastors in 1988.[20]

The Division of Christian Witness in Educational Institutions continued to work through the Baptist schools in Fukuoka and Kita Kyūshū. At Seinan Gakuin, Luther Copeland was succeeded as chancellor by Murakami Toraji, who as a Seinan student had been baptized by Norman Williamson. In 1983 the school conferred an honorary doctorate on former missionary James E. Wood, Jr. Wood had served with distinction as executive director of the Baptist Joint Committee on Public Affairs and as professor of church-state studies at Baylor University. In 1984 Chancellor Murakami was succeeded by Charles Whaley, and in 1988 Whaley was followed by Tanaka Teruo, a Baptist lay preacher who had been a student at Stetson University and an exchange professor at Baylor. In each case the chancellor was elected by the trustees after receiving written nominations from the faculty and staff.[21]

During Whaley's tenure Seinan Gakuin erected an eight-story multipurpose building, purchased 18 acres of reclaimed land near the campus at a cost exceeding $50 million, installed a pipe organ in Rankin Chapel, and celebrated its 70th anniversary with Coretta Scott King as main speaker. After Whaley was succeeded by Tanaka, the trustees elected Leroy Seat as head chaplain of the 9,400-student institution, a position previously held concurrently by the chancellor. Seat was one of several missionaries who had been dean of religious activities for the university. Their efforts to improve chapel programs had helped increase attendance to an average of 350 daily.[22]

At Seinan Jo Gakuin, Vera Campbell, vice chancellor since 1980, was elected chancellor in 1986. She was the first woman to head the school after the resignation of Carrie Hooker Rowe in 1932. For a time Campbell was also acting president of the junior college. In 1985 she led in forming a sister-school relationship with her alma mater, Tift College in Georgia. The relationship was soon shifted to Mercer University, which absorbed Tift, and in 1988 Seinan Jo Gakuin began sending students to Mercer for summer English studies. It also purchased additional land with a view to opening a four-year college in 1993, with courses in nursing and medical welfare. Total enrollment in 1989 was 3,282.[23]

The Division of Christian Witness in Medical Institutions still had no more than four members, all serving at the Baptist hospital or nursing school in Kyoto. Each year the missionaries helped distribute hundreds of Bibles and large

---

[20]"MasterLife News," Dec. 1987, JBM mailout; "MasterLife Report," May 1988, JBM mailout; "Japan Mission Report," Aug. 1988; JBM annual report, 1989.

[21]The author taught at Seinan Gakuin 1980-89.

[22]"Japan Mission Church Growth Study," loose-leaf, 1987, IV, 109-13, 119-20.

[23]Ibid., IV, 113-18; 23. Seinan Jo Gakuin report, Sept. 1985, JBM mailout; Vera Campbell, "Seinan Jo Gakuin to Become a Four Year College," typescript, 1989; *Kōhō Seinan Jo Gakuin*, no. 44 (18 Oct. 1989), 3.

quantities of other Christian literature to patients and their families. It was encouraging for them to recall that the Convention's executive director, Matsukura Osamu, had become a Christian while a patient in the Baptist hospital. The missionaries also assisted in the CPE (clinical pastoral education) program conducted in cooperation with Dōshisha University since 1977. Mary Lou Emanuel, nursing school director, took 30 nursing students to Birmingham, Atlanta, and Nashville for a study/observation program. They sang and gave testimonies in several churches and hospitals. Preparations were underway to merge the nursing school with the four-year course at Seinan Jo Gakuin.[24]

In 1989 the 155-bed hospital registered 2,313 inpatients and 3,912 outpatients. Plans were made to reduce the general beds to 105 in order to provide a 98-bed facility for the elderly, and then to restore the 50 general beds in a second phase of building. A home for the elderly built in 1983 adjacent to the hospital had 90 occupants.[25]

The Division of English Language Churches changed its name to English Language Ministries early in the decade when it absorbed the chaplaincy ministry at Tokyo's 2,057-room New Otani Hotel. By agreement with Dub Jackson, founder of this hotel ministry, the New Otani continued to provide free of charge a chapel in the hotel's garden and a deluxe suite for the resident chaplains. In 1981 the number of English-language churches increased to seven, due to the merger of the Japan and Okinawa missions. In 1985 an eighth congregation was started in Kobe. The Kobe church, like Tokyo and Yokohama, was civilian in makeup. Kōza, Central, Calvary, and Kantō Plains churches were predominantly military, and Zama was about half and half.[26]

The Division of Christian Encounter Ministries (formerly, Ministry) worked through four subdivisions: friendship house evangelism, student evangelism, home encounter evangelism, and harbor evangelism. Harbor evangelism was conducted in Yokohama, and home encounter evangelism was conducted at numerous places through English classes, cooking classes, and discipleship groups. The most significant growth in this decade was recorded in the other two ministries, friendship house evangelism and student evangelism.[27]

New friendship houses were opened in Tokyo, Toyonaka, and Sapporo. The Tokyo facility utilized one unit of a new apartment complex built by the Mission at Kamiyama in 1983. The Toyonaka ministry was conducted in remodeled maids' quarters. The newest work, started in Sapporo in 1986, utilized space in one Mission residence and the remodeled maids' quarters of another, the latter called "The Open Door." Of the six friendship houses operating in 1989, only Fukuoka had a building designed exclusively for its ministry. The modern two-story

[24]"Church Growth Study," IV, 103-4; JBM annual report, 1988, 1989.
[25]JBM annual report, 1989.
[26]Commission 48 (Feb./Mar. 1985), 58-59; "Church Growth Study," IV, 122-23.
[27]"Church Growth Study," IV, 130-33.

(Upper) Charles Whaley at Seinan Gakuin, 1984. Behind him is the school's motto: "Seinan, be true to Christ." **(Lower)** Max Love leaving Tokiwadai Church, 1984. *(Photos by Don Rutledge/Foreign Mission Board, SBC)*

structure, complete with a counseling suite and a worshipful chapel, was built in 1985 at a cost of $490,000. A budget of this size was available because the city paid the Mission about $500,000 for 88 tsubo of land appropriated for widening the street.[28]

Student evangelism was conducted in several locations, most notably in Tsukuba and Sendai. Tsukuba was especially challenging because of its 50 research centers with 6,500 specialists and its national university with 12,000 students. Tsukuba University strictly prohibited religious and political activities on campus, but a missionary gained entrée for Christian witness by participating in the school's chorus, English club, and sports program. He was asked to lead a Bible study on the first chapter of the Gospel of John because the chorus was singing an oratorio based on that chapter. In Sendai a missionary couple formed a Sendai U. (Send-I-You) club that sponsored homestay programs in the United States. During spring vacations they cultivated Japanese students from several universities in the city by placing them in the homes of cooperating Southern Baptist church members.[29]

The Division of Christian Ministries (formerly, Ministry) to Families changed its name in 1986 to express more accurately what its members were doing. The new name: Division of Evangelism and Ministry through Church and Home. The work was conducted through action groups with clearly defined responsibilities, including the Mission's prayer calendar and telephone prayer chain, presentation of gifts to MKs graduating from high school, Mission fellowships, information packets for new missionaries, and family life enrichment.[30]

Assisting and supplementing the six divisions was the Japan Baptist Communication Center, established in 1981. It occupied a portion of the Mission office in Shibuya until 1983, when new office and studio facilities were provided at Kamiyama. The center produced and distributed Japanese versions of the discipling programs MasterLife and Survival Kit, as well as audio and video cassettes on such topics as "How to Teach Adult Sunday School" and "Introduction to Christianity." In 1988 it provided a Japanese-language version of the American video series on "Active Parenting."[31]

For several years the Communication Center conducted the two radio broadcasts formerly under DSSC supervision: the five-minute early morning program in Sapporo and the twice-daily 15-minute shortwave program aired from Guam by the Pacific Broadcasting Association. In 1987, for financial reasons, the short-wave broadcast was dropped and the Sapporo program was turned over to the Hokkaido Baptist Association under terms of a diminishing subsidy from the

---

[28]Ibid.; FMB action approving sale of Fukuoka property, 12 Dec. 1984; JBM mailout, Mar. 1985; *Commission* 49 (May 1986), 5.

[29]"Japan Baptist News," Feb. 1987; JBM annual report, 1988.

[30]"Church Growth Study," IV, 121.

[31]JBM annual reports, 1981-88.

Mission. The two programs had consumed more than half of the center's 1986 operating budget of $130,000, at a time when the declining value of the dollar was forcing the Mission to reduce expenditures. The disengagement from radio work freed the Communication Center to concentrate on its other ministries.[32]

In 1987 another new building was completed on the Kamiyama property to house the Mission office. The office building in Shibuya was sold to Tokyo Baptist Church for $100,000. The Kamiyama office and other construction projects were financed mainly by the disposal of residential lots in expensive areas. In 1988 the Mission sold a lot in Takamatsu for $528,000 and one in Sendai for $3,600,000.[33] The Japan Convention likewise took advantage of high property values in 1988 when it decided to sell its headquarters in Shinjuku and build a new office complex in the satellite city of Urawa. Construction was to begin in 1990.

Adopting a New Strategy

In February 1986 Foreign Mission Board president Keith Parks made a report to the Board of such import that a cassette-tape recording was sent to missionaries around the world. The report called for a more serious response to the challenge of Bold Mission Thrust, with its overarching objective of sharing the gospel with all the world by the year 2000. "Southern Baptists must take a more positive role of leadership," Parks declared. To transform his vision into reality, the Richmond staff was reorganized with focus on a 10-member Global Strategy Group that would develop and coordinate outreach on a worldwide scale. Four of the strategy group's members were vice presidents representing the four main regions of the world. One of their assigned duties was to supervise, counsel, and evaluate the area directors in their region. The area directors themselves were required to live on the field instead of in Richmond as previously, and they were given more authority for directing their missions.[34] Sam James, who had succeeded George Hays as East Asia director in January 1986, moved his office from Richmond to Hong Kong in late 1987.

In 1986 the Mission responded to the Board's initiative by launching a two-year Japan Mission/Church Growth Study. It approved a five-member committee to conduct the study, with Tak Oue as coordinator. In addition, the Mission approved an outside evaluation team of four members to give direction to the study and bring recommendations based on it. The team's chairman was Jerry

---

[32]Ibid.

[33]FMB actions, 15 June, 12 Oct. 1988.

[34]Keith Parks, "Report to the Board," 12 Feb. 1986; *Intercom*, Mar. 1987, 1; ibid., Oct. 1987, 3.

Rankin, a former missionary to Indonesia who in 1987 became area director for South Asia and the Pacific.[35]

The study committee provided each missionary unit and each team member with a thick binder for letter-size papers and sent out about 400 pages of materials over the next two years. The materials were divided into four categories: (1) church growth principles, cross-cultural communication, and mission methodology; (2) culture, society, and religion; (3) other churches of Japan; and (4) Japan Baptist Convention and Japan Baptist Mission (the Okinawa Convention was included in this category though not named in the title). The materials included articles and extracts from various publications; research papers, book reviews, and interview reports written by members of the Mission; questionnaires for missionaries, English-language churches, and pastors and church members of both conventions; and compilations of results of the questionnaires. A few items were sent out after the evaluation team had compiled its report in the spring of 1988.

Meanwhile the Board developed new strategic objectives that were disclosed in February 1988. One of these was to "redeploy missionary personnel to assure concentration of the missionary force on primary evangelism and ministry." Subsequently it was specified that 70 percent of career missionaries would be assigned to church planting and direct evangelism. Although it was stated that 10 years would be allowed for achieving this goal and that it was a worldwide goal, not necessarily applicable to every mission, alarming rumors circulated, and some missionaries not in field evangelism began to feel like second-class citizens. In April, Sam James acknowledged "a level of anxiety and frustration that I never thought was possible in our area." He sought to reassure missionaries that strategies would be developed in which each person would be a vital part.[36]

In this atmosphere of uncertainty, the evaluation team members interviewed most missionaries in Japan and some key pastors and prepared their report in the form of observations and recommendations. Then they traveled to selected cities with the area director, Mission administrator, and survey committee coordinator for one-day meetings with members of the Mission. At each meeting the report was distributed one section at a time--first the observations in a particular category, followed by the recommendations in that category--and solemnly read aloud by team members taking turns. After this exercise had run its course by mid-afternoon--the report was 103 pages long, in single-spaced typescript-- questions were allowed and fielded by the team members and the area director.[37]

As the questions seemed to indicate, probably the most common reaction was a feeling of being overwhelmed by the mass of observations and recommendations

---

[35]The other team members were missionaries Bob Davis of Hong Kong, Burton Cook of Taiwan, and Steve McCord of Korea.

[36]James to East Asia missionaries, 4 Apr. 1988.

[37]See Jerry Rankin et al., "Japan Mission/Church Growth Study Outside Evaluation Team Report," JBM, 1988.

dished out at one serving. By contrast, materials prepared by the survey committee had been served in digestible portions over a two-year span. The team's report, moreover, to the extent that it could be assimilated on the spot, conveyed far more than information of interest to missionaries. Despite assurances to the Mission that "the challenge of what you do with it is in your hands alone," the report was backed by higher authority and destined to impact each life.[38] Some missionaries felt anger, fear, confusion, or resentment, though others felt challenged or relieved.

The former area director, George Hays, after interviewing all members of the Mission in 1980, had said bluntly that missionaries were not doing enough personal witnessing and discipling, nor were they affirming one another as much as they should.[39] Yet his observations were mild compared with the evaluation team's litany of missionary failings.

The recommendations following the observations called for a complete revamping of Mission structure: the dissolution of divisions into area support groups and the creation of a "centralized administrative authority."[40] Also urged were stricter language requirements, reassignment or relocation of many missionaries, a drastically reduced presence in institutions, and the involvement of all missionaries to some degree in starting new churches. In the weeks that followed, when the report could be studied in detail, some missionaries suffered depression and insomnia.

Various negative reactions were shared by phone or letter. The "established church growth criteria" and "missiological principles" undergirding the report struck some missionaries as too narrowly conceived.[41] The objective observations expected of outsiders were said to be freighted with subjective opinions, some of which betrayed a limited understanding of Japan. The omission of any reference to other Christian groups disappointed some readers, especially since the survey committee had distributed a large quantity of materials on these groups, and one of the strategic objectives of the Board was to "seek to cooperate with other Great Commission Christians in world evangelization."[42] Indeed, the evaluation team's report bore so little relationship to any of the materials distributed earlier that one member of the survey committee charged that their two years of work had been ignored.

Probably the most flak came from missionaries at Seinan Gakuin, who denounced a number of statements about the school as biased or misinformed. "There have been recommendations from the Board of Trustees," one statement said, "to elect a non-Christian Chancellor of Seinan Gakuin University." In

[38]Ibid., Introduction, 3.
[39]Hays to Mission, 30 Jan. 1981.
[40]Rankin, "Team Report," Structure, Recommendations, 4.
[41]Ibid., Introduction, 2.
[42]Keith Parks to missionaries, 9 Feb. 1988.

rebuttal, Leroy Seat pointed out that the trustees themselves elect the chancellor, who must be a Christian as specified in Seinan Gakuin's constitution.[43] Long-time board members confirmed that the question of changing or making an exception to the requirement had never been discussed, and they expressed shock that the baseless rumor had spread. The evaluation team later retracted its statement.

On the positive side, the evaluation team's report, though written under pressure of time, embodied the most comprehensive evaluation of the Mission ever attempted and the boldest, most radical plan yet devised for transforming the Mission into a prolific producer of churches. It applied to Japan in concrete terms the newly adopted global strategy of the Board, including the plan to have 70 percent of all missionaries assigned to church planting and direct evangelism. It promised relief from the fragmentation of work and ministry that had afflicted the Mission since the formation of divisions in 1975. It offered a streamlined administration less costly in money and time. Furthermore, the report spoke to the needs of many who wanted more supervision, more motivation, more visible fruit, and more freedom from restraints allegedly imposed by the Convention and its pastors.

At the 1986 Mission meeting, which had launched the two-year project, it had been voted "that Mission Meeting 1988 deal with a final evaluation of the study and act on recommendations that come as a result of that study." To allow adequate time for this purpose, another action had authorized the June 1988 executive committee to handle most of the business that normally would be brought to the Mission in session. In response, the executive committee acted with proxy votes from other missionaries and cleared the 1988 Mission meeting agenda for the evaluation team's recommendations. Without explanation, the June 1988 executive committee minutes were entitled "Mission Meeting 1988," and the full meeting of the Mission held July 25-29 at Amagi Sansō was billed as "Strategy Conference 1988."[44]

An August news release from the Board stated that "challenges from some missionaries were expected at the July strategy conference but did not material-ize."[45] Actually quite a number of proposals were challenged, and some of the votes were very close. What failed to materialize were sharp or even rude confrontations that might have followed the earlier rumblings of discontent. Several factors account for the deceptively peaceful atmosphere that prevailed.

At the annual meeting of the SBC in May, the candidate of the fundamentalist coalition was elected president for the 10th year in a row. His election signified that the process of bringing SBC agencies in line with fundamentalist agendas

[43]Rankin, "Team Report," Auxiliary Ministries, Observations, 1; Seat to Mission, 27 June 1988, 3.
[44]MM minutes, 1986, actions 105-7; EC minutes, June 1988; MM program, July 1988.
[45]Commission 51 (Sept. 1988), cover IV.

would be brought to completion. Some missionaries feared that the Foreign Mission Board would be bound by a narrower philosophy of missions, different from the comprehensive, holistic approach of the past. Meanwhile the Board circulated "Some Basic Observations," one of which stated that the missions would "lose autonomy in some areas particularly those areas which call for implementation of global strategy."[46]

In June, it was announced in the executive committee minutes that the area director himself would serve as moderator of the strategy conference and his associate for Korea and Hong Kong would serve as parliamentarian--roles that had always been performed by members of the Mission.[47] When questions were raised about the legitimacy and wisdom of this plan, the executive committee ruled that it was not a violation of the Mission's bylaws, adding that it would free all missionaries to participate fully in the discussions. The cumulative effect of these developments in the SBC and in the Mission was to discourage active opposition to the proposed changes. It seemed futile to resist a process that had the momentum and force of a juggernaut.

The manner in which the conference was conducted also served to temper opposition. During the first two days the recommendations of the evaluation team were recast into motions by six working groups to which missionaries had been assigned in advance. Although complaints were heard that the presence of the team members inhibited frank discussion, these working groups modified some of the less realistic proposals, rendering them less controversial.

The groups meetings were followed by a two-day plenary session. Moderator Sam James asked that to keep things moving, no one be permitted to speak more than once to a motion. The body so voted, without reference to parliamentary requirements for limiting debate. James also obtained "common consent" that substitute motions from the floor be disallowed. Then 133 motions from the six small groups were distributed one sheet at a time, and with harelike speed brought to the floor for immediate disposition. Discussions were restrained, because words once uttered could not be defended when contradicted by another speaker. All motions were passed by a simple majority, even those concerning organizational changes. A number of motions were amended, several were passed by a slim margin, and a few were referred to an implementation committee. Not one motion was defeated.

Some missionaries said later that they had acquiesced in the questionable proceedings lest a confrontation with the respected area director shatter the peace to no good end. They were reticent to challenge him before dozens of first-term missionaries, to whom the director's Board-given authority implied a superior wisdom. If the Mission chairman or another missionary peer had wielded the gavel

---

[46]Stapled papers beginning with "Global Statistical Overview," n.d., 8.
[47]EC minutes, June 1988.

and parliamentary rules had been strictly observed, the proceedings would have slowed down and debate would have heated up. How--or whether--the end product would have differed will never be known.

It should be observed further that the recommendations of the evaluation team formed a single package, one far more comprehensive than the 1972-73 recommendations of W. L. Howse and his associates from the Sunday School Board. The Howse team had dealt with management, not missiology. The Jerry Rankin team dealt with both. The Howse team had encouraged the Mission to apply the principles of good planning and administration to all the work it was conducting. The Rankin team, backed by a more compelling authority, told the Mission to alter radically what it was doing and prescribed the machinery and methodology to effect the change. No one was prepared to offer an alternate plan equally comprehensive in scope.

Viewed in historical perspective, the July 1988 meeting marked the demise of a Mission that had functioned since 1900 as an autonomous body, operating both within the framework of Board policy and in accordance with its own constitution and bylaws. A new Mission was created, effective January 1, 1989. It was a swift metamorphosis. The previous major changes had been approved in the two Mission meetings of 1972-73, with a called meeting in between, and implemented in 1975. The revolutionary changes adopted at a single meeting in 1988 allowed a transitional period of less than six months. Disorder was inevitable. The 1989 budgets and objectives, adopted in June, had been hammered out by and for divisions that ceased to exist at the end of 1988.[48]

The Mission at the Century Mark

The new Mission of 1989 was shaped by the 133 actions passed at Strategy Conference 1988. In accordance with actions subsumed under "structure," the Mission was organized into six "area support groups." To distribute the missionaries among the area groups as evenly as possible, greater Tokyo was divided into two regions, and Okinawa, which had not been a part of the Mission in the earlier years of geographical stations, was combined with Kita Kyūshū and Shikoku. The other three areas were northern Japan (Hokkaido-Tōhoku), central Japan (Chūbu-Kansai), and Fukuoka in union with western and southern Kyushu. The area support groups met "primarily for prayer, sharing, planning, coordination and evaluation of local area planning and ministries." Each group elected a coordinator, and the six coordinators formed the Mission's executive committee together with the administrator as chairperson. Gone was the traditional office of Mission chairman, dating from 1900.[49]

---

[48]EC minutes, June 1988, appendixes B and C.
[49]Strategy Conference minutes, 1988, actions 1-8.

The administrator had "authority for all matters of personnel, budget and strategy within the Mission." Directly under the administrator were two evangelism directors, one for northern Japan and the other for southern Japan. Though not on the executive committee, they had delegated authority to correlate personnel, budgets and strategy for their respective spheres of three areas each. The administrator and the two evangelism directors formed the Mission's "administrative team."[50]

The new organization was tailored to fit the "more directive" stance of the Board. The administrator and evangelism directors were elected by the Mission, but the administrator was nominated by the executive committee "in close consultation with" the area director, and the evangelism directors were nominated by the executive committee "in consultation with" both the area director and the administrator. Moreover, the administrator was "directly responsible" to the area director, and the administrative team served as the Mission's primary planning group "in consultation with" the area director.[51]

Plans proposed by the administrative team had to be "presented for approval to the executive committee or to the Mission in annual Mission meeting." The option was significant. Only by a close majority vote in the July meeting was the executive committee authorized "to give final approval to strategy plans, personnel and budget requests," an authority formerly reserved for the Mission as a whole. The change had been recommended by the evaluation team to increase efficiency and "to free up the time at Annual Mission Meeting for priority emphasis on prayer, fellowship, and mini-functional conferences for missionaries."[52] In the view of some, Mission members relinquished the long-cherished right to debate and vote on crucial matters that affect their lives and work (the right was partially reasserted in the 1989 Mission meeting), and thus devalued a democratic process their forebears had bequeathed not only to the missionaries but to the Convention and its churches. In the view of others, new hierarchical controls were needed to ensure accountability, since missionaries had not been sufficiently restrained from "goofing off" or "doing their own thing."

Max Love, Mission administrator since 1986, held the same position in the new organization. Japan-born Tak Oue, coordinator of the church growth study committee, was elected evangelism director for northern Japan. Bob Sherer, second-generation missionary, was named director for the southern half of the country. These three leaders composed the Mission's "centralized administrative authority."[53]

The second most revolutionary change after Mission structure was the adoption of a "base staffing pattern"--afterwards called "missionary personnel deployment

---

[50]Ibid., actions 9-26.
[51]Ibid., actions 11, 23, 25..
[52]Ibid., actions 25, 121; Rankin, "Team Report," Structure, Recommendations, 6-7.
[53]Strategy Conference minutes, 1988, actions 22, 79-80.

plan"--for determining how many missionaries were needed and where they would be deployed. The plan included strategic assignments for at least 80 missionary units (a unit is a married couple or a single person). The evaluation team, while acknowledging that the number 80 was somewhat arbitrary (the "at least" was added at the strategy conference), felt that it was reasonable and appropriate for two reasons: the narrowing focus of the work to evangelism that results in churches, and the exorbitant costs of maintaining personnel in Japan. The Mission had 92 units when the plan was adopted.[54]

The 80 positions included 46 church planters, 8 church developers (consultants in educational and musical evangelism), 8 outreach ministers (including campus and center workers), 6 teachers in educational institutions, 5 staff members, 4 teachers in theological education or leadership training, and 3 administrators. These positions were arranged in four tiers according to their strategic importance. In filling assignments, priority was given to a higher tier.[55]

The Mission's 1987 report to the Board had called attention to the "urgent need" for teachers at Seinan Gakuin and Seinan Jo Gakuin and a replacement for the missionary doctor at Baptist Hospital--C. F. Clark--upon his retirement in 1990. The deployment plan adopted in 1988 was based on a different perception of need. The doctor was not to be replaced, nor the teachers in excess of three at each school. The area director gave assurance, however, that none of the seven missionaries assigned to Seinan Gakuin or the five assigned to Seinan Jo Gakuin would be forced to resign or transfer to other positions. Rather, the reduction to three at each school was to be achieved by attrition. Provision was also made for other missionaries serving in assignments outside the new deployment plan--some complained of their "second-class" status--to continue with special permission of the area director.[56]

These provisions did not mean that some persons were unaffected by the new strategy. All missionaries, regardless of their primary assignment, had to "be engaged in evangelistic witnessing and be involved in outreach efforts for church planting." This requirement implied that it was more important to bring a new church to birth than to prevent an old one from dying. No longer was a missionary to serve as pastor of an established Japanese church, and even pastoral assignments to new work were limited to a period of two to five years. Some missionaries were to pool their talents in pioneer evangelism teams for concentrated efforts on new urban areas.[57]

In the category of "methodology," both conventional and innovative methods of pioneer evangelism were enjoined. New groups were to be encouraged from the

[54]Rankin, "Team Report," Base Staffing Pattern, 1-3; Strategy Conference minutes, 1988, 31-33.

[55]Strategy Conference minutes, 1988, action 132.

[56]JBM annual report, 1987; Strategy Conference minutes, 1988, actions 38, 97-101.

[57]Administrator's report, Oct. 1989; Strategy Conference minutes, 1988, actions 39-44.

outset to assume full responsibility for rental of meeting facilities (hitherto borne by the Mission) and to engage in further outreach ministries. One action taken by the Mission affirmed women "who feel led to start outreach points and mission points."[58] A few women already had served as mission pastors.

Under the rubric of "lifestyle," strategy for missionary deployment was to be "enhanced by, not controlled by, options for missionary housing." Mission policy for MK schooling had to be "compatible with overall strategy for evangelism and budget constraints." As missionaries became more mobile, they would have to make greater use of rental housing, and more mothers and fathers would have to teach their own children or participate in team-teaching arrangements. A part-time educational consultant was chosen to assist families in these matters.[59]

The evaluation team had recommended that the Mission establish an MK dormitory and suggested that the Christian Academy in Tokyo would be an appropriate place for it. A working group at the strategy conference altered the recommendation to a motion to establish dormitories at both the Christian Academy in Tokyo and the Canadian Academy in Kobe "according to need." After debate on the floor the motion was referred to the implementation committee.[60] The issue brings to mind the ill-fated Baptist dormitory of the 1960s. It was unclear whether the Mission would attempt this precarious business again or continue to utilize existing facilities. As several discussions in the strategy conference revealed, child schooling was a major concern, along with parenting in general in an alien culture. Missionaries often fail as parents, as did William Carey, David Livingstone, Alexander Duff, and others who neglected their children.[61]

Another major topic in the lifestyle category was language learning. One action stated that "all missionaries are expected to achieve facility in Japanese." The words sound familiar and trite, but they were endowed with new significance. Even veterans, like everyone else, were to be tested in 1990 for the proficiency required in their assignments. Some were fearful. There seemed to be no more place for a Rose Marlowe or a Lucy Smith, whose effectiveness as evangelists was due in part to their inability to speak Japanese. Prospective converts who understand English are sometimes put off by missionaries who insist on using their limited Japanese.[62]

Various other changes can be mentioned only briefly. Friendship-house ministries, in a radical departure from the past, were to be conducted "in cooperation with local Baptist churches for the purpose of establishing new churches."

[58]Strategy Conference minutes, 1988, actions 55-61.

[59]Ibid., actions 62, 66, 127.

[60]Ibid., action 76.

[61]Ruth A. Tucker, *From Jerusalem to Irian Jaya: A Biographical History of Christian Missions* (Grand Rapids: Zondervan Publishing House, Academie Books, 1983), 119, 136, 150.

[62]Strategy Conference minutes, 1988, action 92; Administrator's report, Oct. 1988, Dec. 1989.

The harbor ministry was discontinued because it did not "contribute to evangelism that results in churches." Missionary involvement in the Baptist hospital was limited to a part-time associate chaplain. Subsidy for the nursing school, the one institution partly supported by the Mission, was to be reduced by 20 percent annually after 1989 (one reason for the school's planned merger with Seinan Jo Gakuin). All career-appointed missionaries in staff positions in English-language churches were to be redeployed into Japanese work, since the Board now expected these churches to become self-supporting and to provide their own leadership.[63]

Finally, under "Mission-Convention relationships," ties with the Japan and Okinawa conventions were reaffirmed. As one expression of these ties, missionaries were urged to attend at least one Convention-sponsored conference a year as well as annual associational meetings. A joint Mission-Convention committee, consisting of the Mission's administrative team and several Japan Convention leaders, began to meet monthly as "a forum for communication, planning, and clarification of issues of mutual interest." Less formal contacts were maintained between the Mission and Okinawa Baptist leaders. The Mission's relationships with the two conventions were redefined so that "personnel are used in the primary evangelization roles instead of secondary church support roles." Moreover, the Mission resolved to "take initiative in the task of evangelism which results in churches." The deployment of missionaries, which at one time required Convention approval and at another time consultation, was now determined by the Mission's own strategy.[64]

A former executive secretary of the Convention accused the Mission of violating the mutual agreement of 1973. More diplomatically, the current executive director expressed his concern that missionaries would start missions without mother churches, which could complicate the transition to Japanese leadership. Another leader referred to the Mission's new emphasis on missionary mobility as "parachute evangelism."

The Convention missions committee expressed fears that the number of "problem" churches--those with fewer than 19 members or with a budget under ¥4 million--would be increased as a result of the Mission's new church-planting strategy. About 77 churches, one-third of the total of 215, were said to fit this description in 1988. But the missions committee also recognized that the Mission's new strategy could contribute to reaching the goal of 500 churches and 50,000 members. It commended the strategy in general but urged more flexibility and some modifications, such as allowing a missionary who has led a new congregation for five years to continue longer if circumstances so demanded. These and other issues were subject to negotiation in the joint committee.[65]

[63]Strategy Conference minutes, 1988, actions 101-4, 117; Rankin, "Team Report," Auxiliary Ministries, Recommendations, 6.

[64]Strategy Conference minutes, 1988, action 94.

[65]Oral report of Kitahara Sueo, 28 Oct. 1988, Seinan Gakuin seminary, Fukuoka.

In the Mission, a minority continued to question the validity of actions taken at the 1988 Strategy Conference. For the area director to serve as moderator, they argued, was a violation of the Mission's constitution. At the 1989 Mission meeting, presided over by administrator Max Love, it was moved that all the actions in question "be rescinded and that those motions be reintroduced to this body (JBM) for consideration." The motion failed, 35 to 81. Afterwards a motion was passed to "accept and affirm the action of the Mission in allowing a non-resident member to be moderator pro tem during the discussion of business during that Mission Meeting." The parliamentary dispute was thus settled, though discord remained.[66]

In other business, the Mission asked the Board "to reconsider the decision to withdraw pastoral support for missionary pastors of English Language churches." There was little expectation that the Board would do so. But the Mission voted to extend from 1990 to 1993 the deadline for the pastors to be redeployed into Japanese work. Tokyo Baptist Church, which had long depended on a Board-supported missionary as pastor, initiated action to acquire clear title to its property--valued at $250 million--which was registered in the Mission's name. Approval was obtained from the Mission and the Board.[67]

The Mission resisted Board efforts to sell properties in Japan for the purpose of supplementing the Board's global fund, the interest from which was used for housing and other capital needs throughout the world. The Board desisted when it became apparent that the proceeds from property sales would be heavily taxed if taken out of the country and the Mission's commitment to evangelism in Japan might be jeopardized. Property sales continued to make possible the relocation of missionaries to more strategic areas.[68]

As mentioned before, one couple was appointed to Japan in 1988 and two couples in 1989. All attracted attention, and not merely because they represented a dramatic slowdown in additions to the Mission. The 1988 couple, Tony and Cindy Ludlow, were products of the ultraconservative Mid-America Baptist Seminary in Memphis, the first missionaries appointed to Japan under the new Board policy of accepting graduates of seminaries not controlled by the SBC. Jacob and Poong Ja Shin, both born in South Korea, were the first appointees for evangelism among Koreans in Japan. John and Rhonda (Bennett) Wright, were the sixth and seventh Japan MKs in the history of the Mission, and the first of these appointed as a married couple.[69]

The last couple appointed to Japan in this decade, David and Pat Lee, natives of Taiwan, drew widespread publicity in the United States because both were ordained ministers. Earlier in the year the Board's trustees had rejected a couple,

---

[66]MM minutes, 1989, actions 21, 17.
[67]Ibid., actions 30-31; EC minutes, 21-22 Sept. 1989, action 36.
[68]EC minutes, 4-5 Dec. 1989, action 44.
[69]*Commission* 52 (May 1989), 68; Administrator's report, Aug., Oct. 1989.

both ordained, despite their recommendation by the Board's staff. In that case the wife had been ordained in a church whose association strongly opposed the ordination of women. Pat Lee was touted as proof that the trustees "honestly practice the board policy that ordination neither qualifies nor disqualifies a candidate." Some Baptists were unimpressed. One former missionary, noting the Board's report that "he is to develop churches; she will serve in a church-and-home role and work with women and children," asked why Pat Lee, who speaks five languages, was not assigned the "church developer" role. The first ordained woman ever appointed to Japan, Pat was one of about 10 among the Board's 1,890 female missionaries.[70]

The slowdown in appointments to Japan was accompanied by further retirements and resignations. The Mission's membership, which had peaked at 206 in 1987, fell to 196 in 1988 and 180 in 1989.[71] Given the new deployment plan and the SBC troubles back home, the downward trend was no surprise.

On August 4-5, 1989, about 1,400 Baptists gathered in Seinan Gakuin's Rankin Chapel to celebrate the centennial of Southern Baptist work in Japan. The celebration was jointly sponsored by the Convention and Mission. Visitors were present from the United States, Indonesia, South Korea, Singapore, and Thailand. They heard a 150-voice choir and several speakers, including Bill O'Brien of the Foreign Mission Board. Fukuoka was hot, and Rankin Chapel uncooled, but participants testified that the joy and challenge of the occasion far outweighed the discomfort.[72]

In October, two waves of evangelistic teams from Mississippi, a total of 117 persons, conducted week-long partnership crusades. Similar crusades were planned for 1990. The Convention, meanwhile, continued to promote its 1987-90 theme of "A Strong Foundation and Active Churches." This theme was to be followed by a four-year emphasis on church planting. The Convention planned to use the interest on funds gained from property sales to assist churches and associations in obtaining land and building for new missions. It continued to support two missionary couples in Indonesia and to sponsor a volunteer missionary couple in Thailand. Japanese Baptists were giving high priority to evangelism and outreach. A century of Southern Baptist teaching and example was bearing fruit.

---

[70]*Commission* 53 (Feb./Mar. 1990), 69; *Biblical Recorder*, 3 Feb. 1990, 9.
[71]*ASBC, 1989*, 105; *Book of Reports, SBC, 1990*, 75.
[72]Administrator's report, Sept. 1989; *Seinan Gakuin Daigaku Kōhō*, 2 Nov. 1989.

13

Conclusion: Using Strategy and Means

In 1792 William Carey published *An Enquiry into the Obligations of Christians to Use Means for the Conversion of the Heathens*. In its 87 pages he argued against the widespread belief that Christ's command to "preach the Gospel to every creature" had been fulfilled in the first century and that the fate of the non-Christian world lay in the hands of God alone. Carey insisted that the Great Commission was still binding on Christians and required the use of strategy and means.[1] Later, at Serampore, India, in collaboration with William Ward, a printer, and Joshua Marshman, an educator, Carey developed pioneer strategies that have been highly influential in the modern missionary movement.

Only since the 1970s has the Japan Baptist Mission engaged in strategic planning on a formal and continuing basis. But it has always had a strategy in the looser sense of methods--the how of doing mission work. That strategy has always been determined primarily by the philosophy and aims of the Foreign Mission Board.

When the Board opened work in Japan in 1889, as noted earlier, one of its rules read: "The oral communication of the gospel, the formation of churches, the training and ordination of a native ministry, the translation and circulation of the Scriptures and the extension of missionary work by the aid of native laborers, supported, as far as practicable, by the natives themselves, shall be regarded as the chief business of its missionaries." This statement expresses clearly how the Board thought Japan and its other mission fields should be evangelized. Yet the Board allowed its missionaries "the widest liberty as to methods to be adopted on their fields, believing that they are in their respective fields, other things being equal, the best judges of such methods."[2]

---

[1] Kenneth Scott Latourette, *A History of the Expansion of Christianity*, vol. 4 (New York: Harper & Brothers, 1941), 67.
[2] Tupper, *Decade*, 69; Cauthen, *Advance*, 85.

The Board's strategy reflected the pioneering work of Carey, Marshman, and Ward, the Baptist trio at Serampore. It embodied the refinements of Congregationalist Rufus Anderson, America's greatest mission strategist of the 19th century. With Henry Venn of England, Anderson formulated the mission objective as developing churches that were self-governing, self-supporting, and self-propagating. He emphasized self-propagation above self-support, as did Southern Baptists (note the "as far as practicable" in the Board's statement). Anderson also taught that converts should be organized into churches at once, without waiting for them to reach the standard expected of American Christians. He gave low priority to education and social reform. Education, he believed, should be fostered only in the vernacular and for the sole purpose of developing an able ministry and laity for the churches and their own mission outreach.[3]

In Japan, J. W. McCollum demonstrated the Anderson (and Board) strategy most vividly. He preached incessantly and only in the vernacular, disdaining English-language ministries. He organized churches without delay in Osaka, Moji, and Fukuoka. He promoted Christian stewardship and encouraged churches to cover local expenses. "Our policy," he said, "is building self-supporting churches." To ensure self-propagation, McCollum trained Japanese workers in his home, at retreats, and through the Fukuoka seminary he helped to establish in 1906. Like his early colleague Brunson, he frowned on general educational work. Mac advised the Baptist annual conference of 1896 to "organize Christian schools when we have a Christian constituency who want them, not before."[4]

By 1910, the year of McCollum's death, the Southern Baptist missionaries were committed not only to direct evangelism and theological training but to a program of academic and collegiate work. "The inefficiency of some of our workers," they reported, "is one cause of our lack of progress. . . . The day of small men, poorly equipped, is over in Japan."[5] The Board, however, though supportive of mission schools in China and elsewhere, withheld the needed permission because of the long-term financial obligations it would entail. The Mission kept pressuring the Board and at length obtained funds for opening a boys' school in 1916 and a girls' school in 1922. The Mission was made more aware than before that its strategy, especially when educational work was involved, was controlled by the availability of Board funds, which in turn was dependent on economic conditions in the homeland.

The Mission's strategy was further determined by comity agreements with Northern Baptists. Thanks to its involuntary confinement to Kyushu, the Mission concentrated its meager forces on a manageable area and put down deep roots that later nourished a ministry nationwide in scope. In 1908 Northern Baptists

[3]*Encyclopædia Britannica*, 1970 ed., s.v. "missions"; Beaver, "History of Mission Strategy," 25-26.

[4]EBD, "Mission and Convention," 3.

[5]Ibid., 6.

amicably yielded southwestern Honshu and Shikoku, and in 1918 they grudgingly conceded a share of Tokyo that the Mission had gained by cooperating in the joint seminary. It was in 1918 that the Board unilaterally revoked the comity agreement. This action was the culmination of a growing rift between Northern and Southern Baptists over ecumenical cooperation with other denominations. "Southern Baptists have the right," declared Secretary Love, "to work anywhere in the Empire." Afterwards the Board advised that although the Mission was free to assign missionaries anywhere, it would be wise not to enter any field already occupied unless the Baptists there requested assistance.[6] The asserted right to a nationwide presence was not exercised until after World War II, when Northern Baptist-related churches chose to remain in the United Church and not function as a separate denomination.

Prior to the historic Edinburgh missionary conference of 1910, Protestant missions worldwide were paternalistic in outlook and practice. It was not unusual that McCollum and his colleagues hired pastors and evangelists and exercised full authority over their work. After 1910, Protestant mission strategists emphasized the independence and authority of the national churches, and the major missions in Japan began to yield control of the work to Japanese leaders. Southern Baptists, having come on the scene late, dallied until the 1930s, and even then were unconvinced that their national colleagues had reached sufficient maturity. During that decade, nevertheless, they were forced by nationalist sentiment and government pressures to yield the reins in rapid stages until even the ownership of missionary residences had passed to the nationals.

In 1940 it became painfully evident that political factors, and especially war, played a significant role in the Mission's strategy. Southern Baptists were absent in the early years of Protestant missions when Christianity was still banned as politically subversive, but they were affected by Japan's wars with China and Russia. These wars closed some doors to Christian evangelism and opened others. In the tension-filled months preceding the Pacific War, the missionaries were pestered as enemy aliens and severely restricted in their work. Then for four anxious years they were cut off from their adopted land. Even their national colleagues were rendered almost helpless by the demands of an ideologic and militarist government that was itself increasingly desperate as its vaunted empire crumbled.

Japan's defeat in the Pacific War opened the doors for Christian evangelism more widely than ever before. The Allied--mostly American--occupation removed the legal restrictions on religious freedom and, in contradiction to its avowed principle of the separation of church and state, facilitated the renewal of Christian missionary activity. Concurrently the Board was blessed with a rapidly growing income. It dispatched personnel in unprecedented numbers and acquired vast

---

[6]Ibid., 8, 10.

property holdings throughout Japan. Land prices were depressed at the time, and landowners needed cash.

This historic opportunity for advance in Japan was enhanced by the Communist takeover of China. The takeover closed to Southern Baptists their oldest and largest mission field. The diversion of funds and personnel from China to Japan played a considerable role in the expansion of prewar schools, the establishment of a hospital and other institutions, and the construction of hundreds of homes and buildings. Moreover, the fear of Communist aggression against Japan itself contributed to stronger ties with the United States and a friendlier reception for American missionaries.

The Board and the Mission agreed that Japanese Baptists should be assisted to the full extent that funds could be made available. So plentiful were the funds that spacious buildings were provided for tiny new congregations. When this strategy was questioned by some other missions that exercised restraint in order to encourage self-support, Edwin Dozier argued that the strategy was justified by its obvious result. The Baptist Convention was the fastest growing denomination in Japan.

Japan recovered quickly from the ravages of war, aided by a benevolent occupation, the resourcefulness of its people, and timely spurs to its economy. Its extraordinary economic growth became the envy of the world. Prices rose steadily in the 1950s and '60s, but wages increased more rapidly than prices. When prices stabilized in the '70s, wages continued to increase until the Japanese enjoyed a standard of living comparable to that of advanced Western nations. Land became increasingly scarce, however, and disproportionately expensive. Consequently the proven strategy of starting churches by first providing land and a building had to be scrapped, except for occasional projects with pooled funds from the Board and the Convention. Both the Mission and the Convention became financially dependent on property holdings in inflated areas, which could be sold to buy property in less expensive areas.

Land became especially scarce in greater Tokyo, where the population increased to more than 30 million. In 1989 the average price of residential land was $689 per square foot. This converts to about $15 million for a mere half-acre. Commercial land averaged more than eight times as much.[7]

As Japan prospered, the people grew less responsive to the gospel. The ratio of Christians--Protestant and Catholic--to the total population increased from 0.5 percent in the early '50s to about 1 percent in the late '60s. Since then it has remained at the same or a smaller ratio, well under the 1.5 percent achieved by Roman Catholics in the early 17th century. The growth rate for Baptists slowed

---

[7]*New York Times*, 25 Mar. 1990; *Asheville Citizen-Times*, 22 Apr. 1990; *Asiaweek*, 27 July 1990, 39. Greater Tokyo includes metropolitan Tokyo, Yokohama, 24 other cities, 6 towns, and 9 villages.

but did not flatten. In 1989 the combined membership of the Japan and Okinawa Baptist conventions was 31,000, or 3 percent of the nation's one million Christians. If eight smaller Baptist bodies are included, the total was 40,000, or 4 percent. Baptists remained a tiny minority among the tiny minority of people called Christians.[8]

Why have Christians been stymied in their efforts to gain a larger share of the population? Why have converts been so few? Numerous reasons have been adduced, from which three may be cited as major barriers to the gospel. One is the tribal makeup of the Japanese people, the most homogeneous of the major nations of the world. Their unique language is radically different from Western languages. Their ethics require loyalty and conformity to one's company or other primary group. They are a relatively closed society, with less than 5 percent of the population having any regular contact with foreigners. To such a people Christianity is indeed an alien and a stranger. Becoming a Christian may seem like a betrayal of one's parents and ancestors, a denial of one's heritage and identity. Conversion may seem unnatural, even shameful.[9]

Another barrier is the negative image of Christianity that the Japanese get from school textbooks and other literature, from movies and TV. Because of the high level of education, nearly everyone is acquainted with the darker side of Christian history: crusades, inquisitions, religious wars, colonialism, opium trade, slavery, racial discrimination. In recent years affluence has enabled millions of Japanese to experience so-called Christian societies for themselves. In 1989 alone, nearly one-tenth of the population traveled abroad.[10] Some travelers get a favorable impression of certain Christians they encounter, but for many, the negative image is confirmed.

A third major obstacle to evangelism is the exclusive nature of the Christian faith itself. It is the non-mixer among the religions of Japan. One can be a Buddhist and a Shintoist at the same time, but neither if one is a Christian. This absoluteness is expressed in the saying that Buddhism soothes and stimulates like tea, but Christianity intoxicates and enslaves like strong drink. The Christian demand for total allegiance poses a threat to personal freedom, to the all-important bond with one's company, or to the Sunday rest or recreation highly valued among a people who often work six days a week.

Since ancient times the Japanese people have demonstrated an unusual capacity for selective absorption of foreign cultures. They have exercised discrimination in their borrowing, and what they have absorbed they have modified and adapted to their native heritage. Buddhism, for instance, has undergone extensive reshaping to reconcile it to Shinto and other traditions. In the case of Christianity, Christmas

---

[8]*Kirisutokyō nenkan, 1990*, 512-13.
[9]*PBD*, 1973 ed., 87, updated.
[10]*Asiaweek*, 5 Jan. 1990, 5.

has been indigenized but not Easter; the marriage ceremony has won favor but not baptism. The exclusiveness of the gospel remains an offense and a stumbling block.

Christians have employed a wide range of strategies for overcoming these formidable barriers, including strategies frowned on by the majority. One indigenous group of churches has baptismal pools ready at all times for whoever is willing to submit to the ritual and thereby become a Christian. Even a Southern Baptist missionary was pressured to receive baptism on the spot when he visited the churches' headquarters. This group's statistical claims are no less impressive than deceptive. Other groups engage in militant, sectarian evangelism by which they subtly break down resistance and gain excessive control over the lives of converts, even breaking up marriages and families. Their tactics alienate many from the gospel and add to the negative image of Christianity.

The more respectable strategies generally have been effective when employed with the highest competence. Certain missionaries and Japanese Christians have specialized in radio and TV broadcasting, especially for preevangelism and indirect evangelism, for seed-sowing and image-building. The more talented among them have produced worthwhile programs. Baptists have never excelled in this field, and the strategy adopted by the Mission in 1988 dismisses it as too expensive.

Other groups have contributed to Christian advance with their expertise in literature evangelism. Despite notable pioneering efforts by Ernest Walne and Edwin Dozier, Baptists later fell behind in this area. The Mission's new strategy emphasizes the role of the Communication Center in providing literature as well as audio and video tapes, but much of this responsibility is to be discharged by evaluating and recommending materials published by others.

Some missions have specialized in social reform and welfare ministries. They have striven for human rights, justice, and the relief of all kinds of suffering. Some missionaries have even been instructed by their boards to join in demonstrations and strikes when Christian principles are at stake. Southern Baptists, to the contrary, have distanced themselves from activities with political implications. To do otherwise would violate the policies of their Board. With some notable exceptions, they have shown little understanding of, or interest in, the complex social problems in Japan. The Mission has not worked with outcaste groups since before the Pacific War, the Good Will Center was closed in the early '60s, and missionary participation in the hospital ministry has virtually been terminated. But thanks to Mission achievements of the past, the hospital it founded continues to minister to the sick, and the Convention it brought to birth upholds the holistic approach to evangelism, with genuine concern for the total person.

The Convention works for justice primarily through four special committees. The Yasukuni Shrine committee opposes government efforts to nationalize this Tokyo shrine dedicated to 2.4 million war dead. It protests against all government-sponsored Shinto rites, especially the Daijōsai, by which a new emperor traditionally acquires divinity. This rite is planned for Emperor Akihito in November 1990.[11] The pollution committee strives for a clean environment. The South Korea committee points up human rights violations in South Korea and discriminatory acts against the 682,000 ethnic Koreans living in Japan, nearly half of them in the Osaka area.[12] The buraku committee deals with the discrimination suffered by the two to three million burakumin, descendants of the outcastes in feudal Japan.[13] The Mission has never shown interest in any of these issues, though some of its individual members have. It is further worth noting that neither the Mission nor the Convention, in sharp contrast to the SBC, has ever made an issue of abortion or homosexuality, both widely practiced in Japan.

Various other missions specialize in direct evangelism and church planting. Most of them have little property, no institutions except perhaps a Bible school, and no large organized constituency. Hundreds of missionaries work in this manner, and many of them are trained in the church growth methods identified with the late Donald McGavran or a missiologist influenced by him. These missionaries have produced scores of churches that are either independent or linked with a small chain of like churches, and often related to the Japan Evangelical Association. A 1988 survey of JEA-related churches planted during the previous 10 years revealed that nearly half the 162 churches responding had shown little or no growth, or had declined. One major conclusion was drawn from the survey: the key variable in determining the effectiveness of church planting is the church planter.[14]

Southern Baptists have demonstrated throughout their history in Japan a knack for starting new congregations. In recent years this was a major achievement of the Division of Starting and Strengthening Churches. The Mission has enjoyed a considerable advantage over most other church-starting groups. That advantage is a historical bond with a strong, nationwide Convention that provides guidance and stability to its member churches along with the opportunity for wider fellowship and participation in a comprehensive program of missions. The Mission's new strategy reaffirms that bond, while failing to make full use of its accumulated wisdom and expertise. Whatever real or perceived faults the Convention may have, it is a significant part of the Protestant scene in Japan. Excluding certain fringe groups whose statistics are unreliable and not recognized by the *Kirisutokyō nenkan* (Christian yearbook), even with only 29,000 members the Baptist Convention ranks third among Protestant bodies, exceeded only by the United Church and the Anglican-Episcopal Church. Only one other body, the Evangelical Lutheran Church. has even half the membership of the Convention.

---

[11]*Kodansha Encyclopedia of Japan*, s.v. "Yasukuni Shrine"; Nishikawa Shigenori, "The Daijōsai, the Constitution, and Christian Faith," *JCQ* 56 (Summer 1990): 132-35.

[12]See *Asiaweek*, 4 May 1990, 18-20.

[13]See *Kodansha Encyclopedia of Japan*, s.v. "burakumin."

[14]Japan Church Growth Institute, "Shocking Need for Church Planting in Japan," 1988.

Another advantage the Mission enjoys is its tie with influential schools and a hospital. Japanese institutions esteem their historical roots and honor their founders. Seinan Gakuin, Seinan Jo Gakuin, and Japan Baptist Hospital not only promulgate their Christian heritage but also endow the brand name of Baptist with legitimacy and recognition. Moreover they provide a unique forum where missionaries may share their faith. Karen Schaffner, an assistant professor at Seinan Gakuin University, described this advantage:

> The school provides me with an office where I can meet with students and faculty members. The school provides a budget for materials and activities as well as a meeting place for Bible studies and other religious activities held on campus. I am given opportunities to speak to more students in chapel than would be in attendance at six or eight church *tokuden* (special evangelistic) meetings. Some students come to chapel because they are in my classes, others because I'm a foreigner, but they leave confronted with who Jesus is and what they are going to do with Him. The school provides a community in which I can give both incarnational and intentional witness to the Christ who is in me. I don't have to join a sports club or go house to house. I am where the students are. Students know who I am, why I am here and where to find me. And I have no trouble finding them.[15]

Schaffner, who teaches German as well as Christian Studies, is one of several assistant chaplains at the school. Similar forums for missionary witness are provided at Seinan Jo Gakuin and the Baptist hospital. Since it is generally acknowledged that students, women, and the physically ill are the most responsive segments of Japanese society, the Mission's new strategy is somewhat inconsistent in that it aims at a reduced missionary presence in the very places where witnessing opportunities offer the greatest potential.

True, starting churches is a proven method of evangelism. Even in America, denominations that show an increase in membership invariably show an increase in the number of churches. Still, the Mission's new strategy runs the risk of diverting missionaries to church planting who are better equipped for other vital tasks, and who may become disillusioned when they fail to measure up to expectations. Some Convention leaders fear a proliferation of weak, dependent churches.

Convention leaders also worry about the triumph of the fundamentalist party in the SBC. The Mission is controlled by the Foreign Mission Board, which in turn is controlled by the SBC. Probably the Mission will show increasing restraint in its cooperative relationship with the Convention, a body that tolerates theological diversity. The same is true of the relatively new relationship with the

---

[15]Statement written in 1988.

smaller Okinawa Convention. The Mission likely will decline in influence as well as membership as it moves toward a theological stance acceptable to only a minority of Japanese Baptists. The possibility remains that the SBC's pendulum will swing back the other way in the early part of the next century. Again, SBC moderates may form a new convention or sponsor their own missionary work in Japan. Whatever happens, the SBC, described in 1948 as "the last hope, . . . the only hope for evangelizing this world on New Testament principles," will be preoccupied for some time with saving itself.[16]

What is the future of Christian evangelism in Japan? Is this country a "bottomless swamp," as Catholic novelist Endō Shūsaku suggested, where evangelistic efforts will always bog down? Secretary H. A. Tupper once told McCollum, "Look a hundred years ahead."[17] If Tupper could view the church in Japan today, doubtless he would be disappointed, given his triumphalist expectations. But his words are still relevant, especially in a country whose businessmen criticize their American counterparts for emphasizing short-term profits. Some Japanese banks offer home buyers 100-year mortgage loans that can be passed down through generations, an offer unheard of in the United States.

Great Commission Christians, like these profit-minded businessmen, might do well to take the long view. Bold Mission Thrust notwithstanding, it is unlikely that the evangelization of Japan will show spectacular results by A.D. 2000. Given current trends in Protestant and general population growth, 100 years may be required for the church to reach 5 percent of the population. Some hopeful analysts speculate that Christianity may have some measurable influence on Japanese society by A.D. 2100.[18]

The huge investment of Western personnel and funds in the evangelization of Japan has produced a permanent community of Christians who will continue to reach out to their fellow citizens. They will be assisted by non-Western missionaries, who, on a worldwide basis, are expected to outnumber Western missionaries within a few years. South Korean Christians, backed by flourishing churches, have begun to transmit their zealous spirit to the Japanese, breaking through the deep-seated prejudice against Koreans. Probably the tens of millions of Christians in China will join them in the decades ahead. Perhaps Japan will grow increasingly open to a faith offered by the neighbors who in ancient times provided its Buddhism, Taoism, and Confucianism.

Whatever scenario the future may hold, the door remains open for foreigners to share their faith. Unlike as many as 119 nations of the world, Japan does not restrict traditional missionary residence or evangelism. Western missionaries,

---

[16]The quotation is from L. E. Barton, in Leonard, *God's Last and Only Hope*, 2.
[17]EBD, "Mission and Convention," 3.
[18]Marvin Eyler, "Research, Motivation, Training, and Mobilization," *JCQ* 56 (Winter 1990): 3.

with strategies informed by a century or more of learning experiences, can still make a contribution. In the era of Heisei, perhaps they will see their own "accomplishment of peace."

Appendix 1

Chronology

1859   First Protestant missionaries enter Japan; John ROHRER, Crawford TOY, and John JOHNSON are appointed to open Southern Baptist work.

1860   John & Sarah Rohrer sail from New York August 3 but are lost at sea; Johnson's health fails; Toy is detained by threat of war.

1861   Civil War erupts, forces shelving of Southern Baptist plans for Japan.

1873   American Baptist Missionary Union opens Japan mission, organizes first church in Yokohama.

1889   Jack & Sophia BRUNSON, J. W. & Dru McCOLLUM arrive November 5 to open Southern Baptist work, begin language study in Kobe.

1890s

1891   McCollums organize church in Osaka; new comity agreement with ABMU restricts Southern Baptist work to Kyushu.

1892   Brunsons and McCollums move to Kokura, take charge of ABMU work begun in northern Kyushu in 1890 with Gotō Mutsuo as evangelist; Jack Brunson baptizes Sugano Hanji, a Gotō convert; Brunsons resign and return to U.S.; Ernest & Claudia WALNE arrive in Kokura.

1893   Walnes move to Fukuoka, teach national workers with Kawakatsu Tetsuya as interpreter; McCollums move to Moji, organize first Baptist church in Kyushu on October 4 with 30 members.

1894   Nathan & Bessie MAYNARD arrive in Fukuoka; missionaries visit military hospitals and camps during Sino-Japanese War.

1895   Maynards move to Kokura; McCollums settle in Fukuoka.

1896   Walnes locate in Nagasaki, begin work also in Sasebo.

1897   J. W. McCollum instructs evangelists, promotes stewardship, builds first Southern Baptist residence at 96 Daimyō-machi, Fukuoka.

1899   Harvey CLARKE and Lucile Daniel arrive separately, marry in Yokohama on Thanksgiving Day, settle in Kumamoto; "Mrs. Maynard's House" is built in Kokura.

1900s

1900   Japan Baptist Mission is formally organized in Fukuoka January 23.

1901   George & Elizabeth HAMBLETON arrive; Lottie Moon teaches in Fukuoka while refugeeing from Boxer Rebellion in China; second Baptist church in Kyushu is organized in Fukuoka.

1902   Calder & Bessie WILLINGHAM arrive; Hambletons begin work in Kagoshima; churches are organized in Kumamoto, Sasebo, Nagasaki.

1903   Mission legal person is approved; Walne opens Gospel Book Store (Fukuin Kan) in Nagasaki; Kokura and Kagoshima churches are organized; Southwestern Association (Seinan Bukai) is formed with seven churches and three missions.

1904   Franklin & Daisy RAY arrive; Russo-Japanese War breaks out.

1905   Ernest Walne starts associational monthly, *Seikō* (Starlight), with Chiba Yūgorō as editor.

1906   George & Maggie BOULDIN, Kelsey & Maude DOZIER, John & Margaret ROWE arrive; Hambletons resign.

1907   Paul & Lenna MEDLING arrive; Willinghams resign; Fukuoka Baptist Seminary opens with Chiba as president.

1908   Southern Baptist field is enlarged to include Shikoku and southwestern Honshu, with Hiroshima City as northern boundary.

1909   John MONCURE arrives; McCollums resign; Southern Baptist-ABMU joint mission meeting approves single monthly paper and union seminary.

1910s

1910   Ernest MILLS is appointed on the field; Maynards resign; J. W. McCollum dies; Bessie Willingham dies; Tokyo Baptist Seminary opens with George Bouldin on faculty.

1911   Calder Willingham returns to Japan with second wife Foy; Kelsey Dozier opens Fukuoka Night School in vacated seminary building.

1912   Grace Hughes of ABMU marries Ernest Mills, joins Mission; Lottie Moon dies aboard ship in Kobe harbor; Moji becomes first self-supporting church.

1913   Grace Mills starts Maizuru Kindergarten in Fukuoka.

1914   Ernest Mills begins railroad evangelism.

1915   Hooker CHILES (later Mrs. Rowe) arrives.

1916   Kelsey Dozier founds Seinan Gakuin (Southwestern Academy) in Fukuoka with 105 students.

1917   Kelsey Dozier succeeds Jō Inohiko as principal of Seinan Gakuin; Kanamori Tsūrin conducts evangelistic meetings.

1918   Norman WILLIAMSON and Frances FULGHUM arrive; Calder Willingham dies; Mission withdraws from joint seminary; Board frees Mission from comity agreement; Southwestern Association is reorganized as West Japan Baptist Convention (Seibu Kumiai); Seinan Gakuin moves to Nishijin campus; Fukuoka Night School is discontinued; Koishikawa (Tokyo) church is organized.

1919   Fannie McCall arrives, marries Williamson; Florence WALNE is appointed on the field; Clarkes move to Tokyo for student work; Paul Medling dies in Kagoshima.

1920s

1920   Cecile LANCASTER arrives; Lenna Medling resigns; Margaret Rowe dies; Convention launches five-year campaign; Convention-wide WMU is organized at Fukuoka.

1921   Four couples--Griffin & Vecie CHAPMAN, Willard & Minta NIX, Roscoe & Sadie SMITH, M. H. & Ruth TREADWELL--and four single women--Effie BAKER, Florence CONRAD, Leita HILL, Naomi SCHELL--arrive; Foy Willingham resigns; John Rowe and Hooker Chiles are married; Seinan Gakuin adds higher school (college); Convention opens work among Japanese in Shanghai.

1922   Collis & Hester CUNNINGHAM arrive; Rays move to Hiroshima; John Rowe founds Seinan Jo Gakuin (Southwestern Girls' School) in Kokura with Hooker Rowe as first principal; Treadwells resign; Hill dies in Tokyo.

1923   Phoebe LAWTON and Mary WALTERS arrive; Seinan Gakuin opens seminary department with George Bouldin as dean; BYPU work begins.

1924   Nixes resign; first daily vacation Bible schools are held.

1925   Lolita HANNAH arrives; Mission meeting reveals sharp divisions.

1926   Chapmans, Cunninghams, Smiths, and Lawton resign; first YWA conference is held.

1929   Conrad and Walters resign; John Rowe dies in Gotemba; Schell starts Good Will Center in Tobata.

1930s

1930   Baptists cooperate with Kagawa Toyohiko's Kingdom of God Movement.

1931   First WMU-sponsored "Day of Prayer" is held in December.

1932   Edwin & Mary Ellen DOZIER arrive under sponsorship of Virginia WMU; Baker resigns; Grace Mills dies; Asakai movement causes havoc in several churches.

1933   Edwin & Mary Ellen Dozier are appointed on the field; Bouldins resign; Kelsey Dozier dies in Kokura; Lucile Clarke dies en route to U.S.

1934   Hermon & Rayberta RAY, Max GARROTT arrive; Florence Walne resigns.

1935   Dorothy CARVER (afterwards Mrs. Garrott) and Helen DOZIER arrive; Walnes and Hooker Rowe retire; Hannah resigns; Mission turns over most work to Convention; WMU becomes auxiliary to Convention; Maude Dozier founds Women's Training School in Fukuoka.

1936   Alma GRAVES arrives; Harvey Clarke retires; Amano Eizō is sent to Dairen, Manchuria, as Convention's first foreign missionary.

1937   Hermon Rays and Williamsons resign; Japan launches war against China.

1938   Helen Dozier resigns, marries Timothy Pietsch.

1939   Floryne MILLER, H. B. & Mabel RAMSOUR arrive; Mission property is turned over to Convention.

1940s

1940   Bob & Mary DYER, Oz QUICK arrive; West and East Conventions merge, open joint seminary in Tokyo; missionaries begin to leave Japan.

1941   Remaining missionaries leave except Max Garrott; joint Convention enters United Church; Pacific War begins December 8 (December 7 in U.S.).

1942   Max Garrott is repatriated on *Gripsholm*; Baptist bloc in United Church is dissolved; Japan Baptist Seminary is closed.

1944   Koishikawa Church disbands, reorganizes as Mejirogaoka Church outside United Church.

1945   Pacific War ends, Allied occupation begins; Southern Baptist military chaplains enter Japan.

1946   Edwin Dozier returns to reestablish Southern Baptist work.

1947   Japan Baptist Convention (Nihon Baputesuto Remmei) is organized in Fukuoka April 3 with 16 churches; Jordan Press is established; Garrotts, Graves, Lancaster, and Miller return; Tucker CALLAWAY, Pete & Bee GILLESPIE, Frances TALLEY arrive; Edwin Dozier rejoins family in U.S.

1948   Doziers return; Coleman & Jabe CLARKE, George & Helen HAYS, Marion & Thelma MOORHEAD, Bob & Helen SHERER, Raymond & Inez SPENCE, Lois LINNEN-KOHL (afterwards Mrs. Whaley) arrive; Elizabeth WATKINS is appointed in Japan;

WMU convention is held; BYU (Baptist Youth Fellowship) is organized.

1949 Curtis & Mary Lee ASKEW, Liz (Mrs. Tucker) CALLAWAY, Luther & Louise COPELAND, Ernest & Ida Nelle HOLLAWAY, Reiji & Asano HOSHIZAKI, Stan & Pat HOWARD, Annie HOOVER, Lenora HUDSON, Lucy Bell STOKES, Charles WHALEY arrive; Seinan Gakuin gains recognition as senior college.

1950s

1950 A record 27 new missionaries arrive, namely, Melvin & Edith BRADSHAW, Vera CAMPBELL, Bill & Rebekah Sue EMANUEL, Worth & Kathryn GRANT, Tom & Mary GULLATT, Virginia HIGHFILL, Fred & Elvee HORTON, Martha KNOX, Mary LIMBERT, Mary Neal MORGAN, Loyce & Gladys NELSON, Ed & Sue OLIVER, John & Jean SHEPARD, Bill & Mary WALKER, James & Alma WOOD, Morris & Joyce WRIGHT; Lois GLASS, Rose MARLOWE, Pearl TODD transfer from China; first preaching mission is held; Convention begins nationwide expansion; Seinan Jo Gakuin opens junior college.

1951 Hannah BARLOW, Ralph & Gena CALCOTE, Bob & Kay CULPEPPER, Dub & Doris JACKSON, Dottie LANE, Calvin & Harriett PARKER, Leslie & Hazel WATSON arrive; Lucy SMITH transfers from China; second preaching mission is held; Convention-Mission office building is dedicated in Shibuya, Tokyo.

1952 Audrey FONTNOTE, Carl & Ruth HALVARSON, Frances HORTON, Virgil & Donabel McMILLAN, Jim & Altha SATTERWHITE, Bud & Doris SPENCER arrive; Frank & Mary CONNELY transfer from China; Allied occupation ends; Convention conducts New Life Evangelism meetings, opens work in Hokkaido and Shikoku.

1953 C. F. & Polly CLARK, Martha HAGOOD, Mavis SHIVER (later Mrs. Hardy) arrive.

1954 Gerald & Jo Beth FIELDER, Mary Lou MASSENGILL (later Mrs. Wayne Emanuel) arrive; Amagi Baptist Assembly (Amagi Sansō) is dedicated.

1955 Dewey & Ramona MERCER arrive; Japan Baptist Hospital is established in Kyoto; Baptist Training Union is begun; Shirabe Masaji is sent to Okinawa as Convention missionary.

1956 Charles & Anne MARTIN, Tom & Betty MASAKI, Evelyn OWEN arrive; Frank Connely dies; kindergarten association is organized.

1957 Gene & Dorothy CLARK, June COOPER, Don & Joyce HEISS, Bertha MARSHALL arrive.

1958 Bob & Betty Faith BOATWRIGHT, Corky & Juanita FARRIS, Frank & Wynon GILLHAM arrive; first English-language church, Tokyo Baptist, is organized.

1959 Mary CANNON, Ted & Pat COX, Milton & Julia DUPRIEST, Wayne EMANUEL, Charlie FENNER, Robert HARDY, Mack & Carolyn MOBLEY, Jo RANDALL, Bill & Mary WARMATH arrive; Convention is reorganized into three major divisions; 70th anniversary of Southern Baptist work is celebrated with mass meetings in Tokyo and Fukuoka and nationwide evangelistic campaigns; new Convention-Mission office building is erected in Shinjuku, Tokyo.

1960s

1960 Dwight & Anne DUDLEY, Ken & Audrey WOOD arrive; Spencers transfer to Okinawa for English-language ministry, begin Southern Baptist mission there; Convention launches five-year movement, enters last of 46 prefectures, starts "Baptist Hour" radio broadcast in Fukuoka.

1961 Preston & Audie BENNETT, Carroll & Frances BRUCE, Earl & Tookie FARTHING,

Billy & Mona KEITH, Archie & Elaine NATIONS, Larry & Marcella SOUTHER-LAND, Rennie SANDERSON arrive; first nationwide BSU (Baptist Student Union) retreat is held at Amagi Sansō.

1962   Galen & Arline BRADFORD, Annie Sue CLIFT, Anita COLEMAN, Harry & Barbara GRIFFIN arrive; Max Garrott is installed as chancellor of Seinan Jo Gakuin; Baptist Dormitory opens in Mitaka, Tokyo.

1963   Harold & Vicki PRICE, Jack & Velma SMITH, Jim & Darlene WATTERS arrive; Loyce Nelson dies; New Life Movement is conducted with nearly 600 foreign participants; Convention names Togami Nobuyoshi as missionary to Brazil.

1964   Bill & Jeani HASHMAN, Ken & June HAYES, Max & Flo LOVE, Dan & Beverly O'REAGAN arrive; number of churches reaches 101.

1965   Beryle & Elouise LOVELACE arrive; first journeyman, Elaine Stan, arrives; Medlings transfer to Okinawa; Asia Sunday School Crusade is launched; Togamis begin work in Brazil.

1966   George & Annette COX, Pratt DEAN, Ralph & Irene HONJO, Leroy & June SEAT, Doris WALTERS, Blake WESTERN arrive; team-evangelism meetings are held; School of Nursing opens in Kyoto.

1967   Joy (Mrs. Charlie) FENNER is added to Mission; Convention incorporates its Okinawa work into home missions program.

1968   Ken & Faye BRAGG, Tom & Dot GRAHAM, Darrell & Norma Lea MOCK, George & Amy WATANABE arrive; Bill Hashman dies; Convention is divided into 13 associations.

1969   Roy & Jean FRIERSON, Floyd & Lela MAYBERRY, Price & Mary MATHIESON, Hugh & Norma YOUNG arrive; Edwin Dozier dies in Fukuoka.

1970s

1970   Rita (Mrs. Pratt) DEAN is added to Mission; Paul & Sue BENEDICT, Bob & Kathleen HOLLAND, Tak & Lana OUE, Mike & Bonnie SIMONEAUX, Ed & Sharon SMITH, Mary SWEDENBURG arrive; Baptist World Alliance meets in Tokyo.

1971   Wayne & Linda HASENMYER, Bill & Pat ROBERTS, Bob & Claudia SHERER arrive; Roy & Anna Marie EDGEMON transfer from Okinawa.

1972   Okinawa reverts to Japan; first friendship houses are opened in Fukuoka and Kyoto.

1973   Bill & Linda HOLLAWAY, Dick & Joanie HORN arrive; Mission adopts program base design and formal agreement with Convention; harbor evangelism is begun in Kobe.

1974   Bill & Christine HAILEY arrive; Max Garrott dies; Mission office is moved to Shibuya, Tokyo.

1975   Gerald & Brenda BURCH arrive; Mission enters first planning cycle with new structure of six divisions.

1976   James & Martha COLVIN, Mike & Cathy MEADOWS arrive.

1977   Wayne & Kay Ellen DECKERT, Sherwood & Margaret MOFFETT, Charles & Mary Elizabeth RAY, Malcolm & Edyth STUART, Neil & Susan TUTTLE arrive; Convention becomes self-supporting in its operating budget.

1978   Janie ELLIS, John & Nancy NORTON, Becky P'POOL, Charles & Jane WESTBROOK arrive.

1979   Bob & Gail GIERHART, Bob & Maureen ULLOM, Tony & Marsha WOOD arrive.

1980s

1980   Elton & Marylou BOST arrive; Wayne & Dorothy MADDOX transfer from Okinawa.

1981   Cole & Beth COCHRAN, Richard & Marilyn CURTIS, Jack & Barbara DARLEY, Dennis & Judi FOLDS, Ray & Ardith FRANKLIN, Chuck & Chere GAFFORD, Bill & Shirley KARR arrive; Okinawa Mission is merged with Japan Mission, adding Palmer & Donna FLETCHER, Elton & Dottie GRAY, Spencers.

1982   Freddie & Deborah DAVIS, Bob & Babs DILKS, Merl & Vivian ESTEP, Joe & Hazel Dean GRIFFIN, Ron & Lydia HANKINS, Phyllis MAYO, Jean TEAGUE, Keith & Sue VAUGHN, Carlton & Cornelia WALKER, Charlie & Darlene WILLIAMS arrive; Gene Clark dies in Tokyo.

1983   Barbara AKINS, Frank & Josie GARVER, Gene & Nancy HINES, Hershel & Liz JOHNSON, Ed & Nan JORDAN, Ron & Cindy REYNOLDS arrive; Convention sponsors partnership crusades.

1984   Gary & Carolyn BARKLEY, Dave & Jamea CRUM, Steve & Phyllis GOSS, Danny & Jan HINSON, Gary & Joanie MAYFIELD, Don REID, Karen SCHAFFNER, Delane TEW, Bill & June WARDLAW, Tom & Carol WHALEY arrive.

1985   Dennis & Debbie CONNELL, Mark & Kristy EDLUND, Tom & Carol KENNEDY, Larry & Kean MILLER arrive.

1986   Charles & Mary BARHAM, Jim & Linda BOBO, Mike & Janet BROOKS, Robert & Linda CALHOUN, Ron & Joan CAPPS, Floyd & Becky FRENCH, Randy & Janice HICKS, Hank & Linda LEE, Rick & Barbara PHIPPS, Jim & Dale RUSSELL, Milton & Jeanna SMITH arrive; Japan Mission/Church Growth Study is launched.

1987   Fred & Nancy CAMPBELL, Dave & Robin JOHNSON, Peggy JOHNSON, Bob & Renae ODELL, Kyle & Margaret PERRIN, Mark & Linda WHITWORTH arrive; Mission office is moved to Kamiyama in Tokyo.

1988   Bill & Nancy WALKER arrive; Mission meeting is devoted to strategy conference.

1989   New Mission organization and policies take effect January 1; Tony & Cindy LUDLOW, Jacob & Poong Ja SHIN arrive; David & Pat LEE, John & Rhonda WRIGHT are appointed; Mission and Convention celebrate centennial of Southern Baptist work with special meetings and team evangelism.

Appendix 2

Roster of Missionaries

This roster includes all career and associate missionaries appointed to Japan by the Foreign Mission Board, SBC, from 1859 to 1989. Journeymen are listed in Appendix 3. Student semester missionaries, special project personnel, and volunteer personnel are not listed.

Underlined names are commonly used given names. Names in brackets are surnames acquired by marriage after completion of service in Japan .

Years of service begin with the year of appointment or transfer to Japan, and end with the year of resignation or retirement from the Board, or transfer to another field. The year of appointment may be earlier than the year of arrival given in the Chronology. The years are only indicated for a wife when they are different from those of her husband. The letter *e* stands for *emeritus*, a status given those who continue in service until retirement at age 62 or above.

Types of assignment are adapted from *Missionary Directory, 1989* and *Overseas Personnel: Foreign Mission Board Directory, Nov. 1989-Oct. 1990.* Preference is given to the more precise terminology used in the former. For missionaries in service in 1989, the current assignment is indicated. For others, the assignment may be the last one filled or the one for which the missionary is particularly noted.

The date of death, if available, follows the abbreviation *d.*

Name	Home State	Date of Birth	Years of Service	Type of Assignment
AKINS, <u>Barbara</u> Lynn	TX	12-14-51	1982-	Student worker
ASKEW, David <u>Curtis</u> <u>Mary Lee</u> Trenor	MS MS	12-27-21 07-21-21	1947-72	Gen Evangelist Church & Home
BAKER, <u>Effie</u> E [Rogers]	TX	04-09-95	1921-32	Col Teacher
BARHAM, <u>Charles</u> S <u>Mary</u> M Kveton	AR TX	04-16-37 12-31-40	1985-	Eng Lang Min Church & Home
BARKLEY, <u>Gary</u> Wayne <u>Carolyn</u> A Vincent	TN GA	07-17-55 10-05-57	1984-	Theol Teacher Church & Home
BARLOW, <u>Hannah</u> Lee [Bain]	VA	11-03-26	1951-62	Gen Evangelist
BENEDICT, <u>Paul</u> W Jr <u>Sue</u> Ellen Suddath	NC GA	03-16-25 02-26-30	1969-	Gen Evangelist Church & Home

Name	Home State	Date of Birth	Years of Service	Type of Assignment
BENNETT, E <u>Preston</u>	TX	05-08-30	1961-	Gen Evangelist
<u>Audie</u> Ercanbrack	TX	01-07-30		Church & Home
BOATWRIGHT, C S (<u>Bob</u>)	GA	08-10-24	1958-89e	Gen Evangelist
<u>Betty Faith</u> Williams	GA	04-22-26		Church & Home
BOBO, James Jay (<u>Jim</u>)	TX	08-18-42	1986-88	Friendship Hse
<u>Linda</u> Sue Stansberry	OK	08-02-49		Church & Home
BOST, Thomas <u>Elton</u>	TX	11-15-50	1979-	Student worker
<u>Marylou</u> Woolsey	TX	11-15-48		Church & Home
BOULDIN, <u>George</u> W	AL	09-21-81	1906-33	School Adm
d. 02-13-67				
<u>Maggie</u> Lee	TN	08-05-82		Church & Home
BRADFORD, Leo <u>Galen</u>	TX	08-14-19	1962-70	MK Dormitory
E <u>Arline</u> Younger	TX	06-18-24		MK Dormitory
BRADSHAW, <u>Melvin</u> Joel	VA	01-01-25	1950-61 1963-74	Hosp Chaplain
<u>Edith</u> Claytor	WV	12-05-25		Church & Home
d. 06-26-90				
BRAGG, <u>Ken</u>neth Raymond	GA	03-28-31	1967-78	Eng Lang Min
<u>Faye</u> Grace Helms	NC	04-10-29		Church & Home
BROOKS, Michael L (<u>Mike</u>)	GA	03-04-56	1985-	Gen Evangelist
<u>Janet</u> Moseley	GA	08-31-57		Church & Home
BRUCE, Robert <u>Carroll</u>	KY	06-22-29	1961-71	Eng Lang Min
<u>Frances</u> Kirkpatrick	KY	01-24-30		Church & Home
BRUNSON, John A (<u>Jack</u>)	SC	04-17-62	1888-92	Gen Evangelist
d. 11-22-43				
<u>Sophia</u> Boatwright	SC	07-09-64		Church & Home
d. 03-09-53				
BURCH, <u>Gerald</u> Wayne	AL	04-21-44	1975-	Gen Evangelist
<u>Brenda</u> Gail Bailey	AL	01-26-44		Church & Home
CALCOTE, <u>Ralph</u> Victor	MS	09-12-23	1951-86e	Gen Evangelist
<u>Gena</u> Myrle Wall	LA	12-06-19		Church & Home
CALHOUN, <u>Robert</u> Luther	TX	09-11-45	1986-	Gen Evangelist
<u>Linda</u> June Wallace	TX	11-27-51		Church & Home
CALLAWAY, <u>Tucker</u> Noyes	GA	09-06-18	1945-67	Theol Teacher
d. 01-21-87				
Elizabeth Clark (<u>Liz</u>)	TN	03-26-20		Church & Home
CAMPBELL, <u>Fred</u>dy Vander	TN	01-18-49	1987-	Gen Evangelist
<u>Nancy</u> Gail Miller	IL	08-24-52		Church & Home
CAMPBELL, <u>Vera</u> Leona	GA	08-24-21	1950-	School Adm

Name	Home State	Date of Birth	Years of Service	Type of Assignment
CANNON, <u>Mary</u> Dunning	NC	05-06-32	1959-75	Gen Evangelist
CAPPS, <u>Ron</u>ald Wayne	TX	07-23-54	1986-	Gen Evangelist
<u>Joan</u> Ellen Partsch	MO	10-16-53		Church & Home
CHAPMAN, J. <u>Griffin</u>	KY	12-22-95	1921-26	Gen Evangelist
<u>Vecie</u> King	TX	09-13-96		Church & Home
CHILES, Carrie <u>Hooker</u>	(See under ROWE)			
CLARK, <u>C</u>larence <u>F</u>ord Jr	TN	06-20-25	1953-	Physician
Pauline Watts (<u>Polly</u>)	NC	09-28-25		Nurse
CLARK, <u>Gene</u> Austin	NC	05-25-26	1957-81	Gen Evangelist
d. 03-28-81				
<u>Dorothy</u> E. Lawhon	FL	09-30-26	1957-82	Church & Home
CLARKE, <u>Coleman</u> Daniel	Japan	03-19-11	1948-67 1972-75e	Gen Evangelist
Jennie Sheffield (<u>Jabe</u>)	GA	01-17-11		Church & Home
d. 12-16-82				
CLARKE, William <u>Harvey</u>	GA	07-04-67	1898-36e	Gen Evangelist
d. 02-21-43				
<u>Lucile</u> Daniel	GA	06-20-76	1899-33	Church & Home
d. 05-02-33				
CLIFT, <u>Annie Sue</u>	TN	11-29-31	1961-68 1971-75	Nurse
COCHRAN, William <u>Cole</u>man	MO	09-01-53	1980-89	Communications
<u>Beth</u> Irene Smith	LA	11-02-51		Church & Home
COLEMAN, Wilma <u>Anita</u>	TN	10-31-29	1962-	Col Teacher
COLVIN, <u>James</u> Robert	NC	04-11-44	1976-83	Hosp Chaplain
<u>Martha</u> Ellen Mooney	VA	08-25-47		Church & Home
CONNELL, <u>Dennis</u> Wilson	NC	05-20-52	1985-	Gen Evangelist
Deborah Spence (<u>Debbie</u>)	NC	07-27-54		Church & Home
CONNELY, <u>Frank</u> Hutchins	MO	08-02-90	1952-56	Treasurer
d. 10-23-56				
<u>Mary</u> Sears	China	09-07-94	1952-57e	Church & Home
d. 01-04-58				
CONRAD, <u>Florence</u>	TX	03-04-97	1921-29	Col Teacher
COOPER, Nell <u>June</u>	NC	05-31-28	1957-	Music Promoter
COPELAND, Edwin <u>Luther</u>	WV	01-24-16	1948-56 1975-81e	School Adm
<u>Louise</u> Tadlock	NM	06-05-23		Church & Home

Name	Home State	Date of Birth	Years of Service	Type of Assignment
COX, <u>George</u> F	SC	12-01-30	1966-72	Gen Evangelist
Rose <u>Annette</u> Young	SC	07-27-36		Church & Home
COX, Theodore Olan (<u>Ted</u>)	IN	01-30-24	1959-87e	Gen Evangelist
<u>Pat</u>ricia Roberts	IN	02-13-28		Church & Home
CRUM, David L (<u>Dave</u>)	MO	09-03-51	1983-	Gen Evangelist
<u>Jamea</u> Sue Smith	MO	12-25-51		Church & Home
CULPEPPER, Robert H (<u>Bob</u>)	GA	12-08-24	1950-80	Theol Teacher
Kathleen Sanderson <u>Kay</u>	VA	08-12-24		Church & Home
CUNNINGHAM, <u>Collis</u>	GA	08-31-90	1922-26	Col Teacher
<u>Hester</u> Faulkner	AL	09-21-00		Church & Home
CURTIS, <u>Richard</u> Wayne	TX	03-13-43	1980-	Treasurer
<u>Marilyn</u> Louise Haas	KY	05-27-45		Friendship Hse
DARLEY, <u>Jack</u> Wayne	AL	09-24-49	1980-	Teacher
<u>Barbara</u> Ruth Kohn	AL	05-10-50		Church & Home
DAUGHERTY, Robert J (<u>Bob</u>)	TN	03-22-24	1973-89e	Eng Lang Min
Lillian <u>Myrtle</u> Dabney	KY	09-15-28		Church & Home
DAVIS, Fredrick Floyd Jr (<u>Freddy</u>)	FL	07-11-52	1981-	Gen Evangelist
<u>Deborah</u> L. Rush	MS	09-19-55		Church & Home
DEAN, <u>Pratt</u> J	AL	03-13-34	1966-	Gen Evangelist
<u>Rita</u> Joyce Duke	AL	04-14-32	1970-	Church & Home
DECKERT, <u>Wayne</u> Benjamin	CA	08-09-47	1977-	Gen Evangelist
<u>Kay Ellen</u> Green	MO	12-01-47		Church & Home
DILKS, C Robert (<u>Bob</u>)	AR	01-29-53	1981-	Gen Evangelist
Barbara Blass (<u>Babs</u>)	AL	05-28-53		Church & Home
DOZIER, Charles <u>Kelsey</u> d. 05-31-33	GA	01-01-79	1906-33	School Adm
<u>Maude</u> Burke d. 01-13-72	NC	09-18-81	1906-51e	WMU Promotion
DOZIER, <u>Edwin</u> Burke d. 05-10-69	Japan	04-16-08	1933-69	School Adm
<u>Mary Ellen</u> Wiley	NC	08-16-07	1933-74e	Church & Home
DOZIER, <u>Helen</u> [Pietsch]	Japan	06-10-10	1935-38	Teacher
DUDLEY, <u>Dwight</u> N	FL	08-26-32	1960-76	Gen Evangelist
<u>Anne</u> Grace Vinson	TX	01-10-31		Church & Home
DUPRIEST, <u>Milton</u> Eugene	TX	08-20-27	1959-64	Eng Lang Min
<u>Julia</u> LaVaughn	TX	05-18-31		Church & Home

Name	Home State	Date of Birth	Years of Service	Type of Assignment
DYER, Robert A (<u>Bob</u>)	LA	04-05-13	1940-41	Lang Student
<u>Mary</u> Mills	NC	03-01-15		Lang Student
EDGEMON, Le<u>roy</u> T Jr	TX	07-11-34	1968-75	Eng Lang Min
<u>Anna Marie</u> Wilson	TX	02-05-35		Weekday Min
EDLUND, <u>Mark</u> Howard	CO	07-05-50	1984-	Col Teacher
<u>Kristy</u> Mae Kroese	AZ	11-06-54		Church & Home
ELLIOT, Dorothy M (<u>Dot</u>)	NC	08-15-24	1973-89e	Gen Evangelist
ELLIS, <u>Janie</u> Mae	NC	11-04-44	1977-86	Secretary
EMANUEL, Beverly P (<u>Bill</u>)	OK	09-03-24	1950-61 1963-86e	Gen Evangelist
<u>Rebekah Sue</u> Jackson	OK	05-08-24		Church & Home
EMANUEL, <u>Wayne</u> E	OK	03-14-29	1958-	Gen Evangelist
<u>Mary Lou</u> Massengill	KY	08-09-28	1954-57 1958-	Nurse
ESTEP, William <u>Merl</u>	KY	11-10-45	1981-88	Col Teacher
<u>Vivian</u> Lee Heldreth	OK	08-13-47		Church & Home
FARRIS, Theron V (<u>Corky</u>)	TX	07-04-27	1957-64	Gen Evangelist
<u>Juanita</u> Peacock d. 10-14-64	TX	10-28-21	1957-64	Church & Home
FARTHING, <u>Earl</u> D	NC	08-29-32	1960-66	Gen Evangelist
Lovie (<u>Tookie</u>)	NC	12-01-30		Church & Home
FENNER, <u>Charlie</u> W	TX	11-28-29	1959-66 1967-80	Teacher
<u>Joy</u> Lynn Phillips	TX	03-03-29	1967-80	Church & Home
FIELDER, Lennox <u>Gerald</u>	China	04-26-26	1954-78	Col Teacher
<u>Jo Beth</u> McKneely	TX	08-13-28		Church & Home
FLETCHER, J <u>Palmer</u> Jr	DC	05-27-37	1974-87	Youth Worker
<u>Donna</u> Lee McDonald	TN	01-03-42		Church & Home
FOLDS, <u>Dennis</u> Gerald	LA	11-22-40	1980-	R&D Consultant
Judith (<u>Judi</u>) A Synco	AR	08-31-44		Friendship Hse
FONTNOTE, <u>Audrey</u> V	NE	01-18-23	1952-70	Physician
FRANKLIN, <u>Raymond</u> Edwin	TX	09-28-53	1980-	Gen Evangelist
<u>Ardith</u> Mildred Miller	TX	12-27-54		Church & Home
FRENCH, <u>Floyd</u> Lee	OR	10-09-47	1986-	Gen Evangelist
Rebecca Smith (<u>Becky</u>)	TX	08-28-53		Church & Home

Name	Home State	Date of Birth	Years of Service	Type of Assignment
FRIERSON, Leon <u>Roy</u>	GA	07-10-29	1968-72	Eng Lang Min
Ellen Jeanine Mays (<u>Jean</u>)	GA	01-10-33		Church & Home
FULGHUM, Sarah <u>Frances</u> d. 02-18-73	GA	05-29-90	1918-28	Col Teacher
GAFFORD, Charles E (<u>Chuck</u>)	TN	05-07-31	1980-	Gen Evangelist
<u>Chere</u> Edell Northcutt	OK	12-15-36		Church & Home
GARROTT, Wm <u>Maxfield</u> d. 06-25-74	AR	06-20-10	1934-74	School Adm
<u>Dorothy</u> Carver d. 09-07-82	KY	10-10-09	1935-77e	Church & Home
GARVER, <u>Frank</u> Edwin	NC	07-10-30	1982-89	Eng Lang Min
<u>Josie</u> Ray Sessoms	NC	08-15-32		Church & Home
GIERHART, Robert D (<u>Bob</u>)	CO	02-20-51	1978-	Gen Evangelist
<u>Gail</u> Chiemi Morihara	HI	07-23-52		Church & Home
GILLESPIE, A L (<u>Pete</u>) d. 10-05-83	TN	05-18-12	1946-77e	Gen Evangelist
Viola Rose Boyd (<u>Bee</u>) d. 09-27-82	IN	01-19-19		Church & Home
GILLHAM, Moudy <u>Frank</u>	TX	09-21-31	1958-65	Eng Lang Min
Hazel <u>Wynon</u> McKinley	TX	12-08-30		Church & Home
GLASS, <u>Lois</u>	China	11-25-07	1950-56	Col Teacher
GOSS, B Stephenson (<u>Steve</u>)	NC	11-07-49	1983-88	Gen Evangelist
<u>Phyllis</u> Jeanne Johnson	NC	11-28-51		Church & Home
GRAHAM, Thomas W (<u>Tom</u>)	FL	09-13-35	1967-	Music Promoter
Minnie <u>Dot</u> Easterlin	SC	01-13-41		Church & Home
GRANT, <u>Worth</u> C	NC	10-16-18	1950-71	Literature Min
<u>Kathryn</u> Stephens	SC	08-18-20		Church & Home
GRAVES, <u>Alma</u> O'Norean	LA	02-23-07	1936-40 1947-77e	Col Teacher
GRAY, <u>Elton</u> Pierce	TN	06-05-34	1970-	Gen Evangelist
Dorothy Marie Eavenson (<u>Dottie</u>)	MS	04-08-30		Church & Home
GRIFFIN, <u>Harry</u> Dee	OK	01-16-25	1962-69	Eng Lang Min
<u>Barbara</u> Terry	OK	04-10-29		Church & Home
GRIFFIN, <u>Joe</u> R	TX	12-20-22	1981-87e	Eng Lang Min
<u>Hazel Dean</u> Lester	TX	12-17-23		Church & Home

Name	Home State	Date of Birth	Years of Service	Type of Assignment
GULLATT, <u>Tom</u> Dean	GA	03-20-20	1950-85e	Gen Evangelist
<u>Mary</u> Studdard	GA	02-25-20		Church & Home
HAGOOD, <u>Martha</u>	AL	10-15-23	1953-66	Physician
HAILEY, William M (<u>Bill</u>)	TX	01-27-31	1974-81	Eng Lang Min
Mary <u>Christine</u> Wilson	VA	03-03-35		Church & Home
HALVARSON, <u>Carl</u> Maurice	CO	09-12-22	1952-60	Gen Evangelist
<u>Ruth</u> Ayres	KS	05-13-24		Church & Home
HAMBLETON, <u>George</u> F	OH	05-31-70	1900-06	Gen Evangelist
<u>Elizabeth</u> Spaulding	KY	01-27-78		Church & Home
HANKINS, Jerry <u>Ronald</u>	AL	09-25-50	1981-	Gen Evangelist
<u>Lydia</u> Barrow	GA	08-23-54		Gen Evangelist
HANNAH, <u>Lolita</u> Irene	TN	01-29-03	1925-35	Teacher
HARDY, Robert D (<u>Bob</u>)	KY	04-29-29	1958-	Assoc Area Dir
<u>Mavis</u> Gladys Shiver	AL	06-11-26	1953-57	Gen Evangelist
			1958-	Church & Home
HASENMYER, <u>Wayne</u> Leon	IN	12-15-46	1971-79	Gen Evangelist
<u>Linda</u> Lee DeMar	KY	11-08-47		Church & Home
HASHMAN, William (<u>Bill</u>)	CA	08-02-31	1964-68	Lang Student
d. 08-27-68				
<u>Jeani</u> M Jackson [Smith]	WA	06-15-33	1964-71	Church & Home
HAYES, C <u>Kenneth</u>	KY	01-03-28	1964-68	Music Promoter
<u>June</u> Snider [Tischler]	KY	04-06-32		Church & Home
HAYS, <u>George</u> H	MO	10-10-20	1948-73	Theol Teacher
			1973-75	Field Rep
<u>Helen</u> Mathis	KY	01-14-20		Church & Home
HEISS, <u>Don</u>ald R	OH	04-04-27	1957-	Gen Evangelist
<u>Joyce</u> Sheckler	OH	08-13-27		Church & Home
HICKS, <u>Randy</u>	AL	11-10-48	1985-	Gen Evangelist
<u>Janice</u> K McCullough	AL	05-17-53		Church & Home
HIGHFILL, <u>Virginia</u>	NC	05-08-22	1950-84e	WMU Promoter
HILL, <u>Leita</u> Mae	GA	03-20-92	1921-22	
d. 03-18-22				
HINES, Blaney <u>Eugene</u>	NC	10-18-46	1982-	Gen Evangelist
<u>Nancy</u> Kay Balentine	SC	02-21-54		Church & Home
HINSON, <u>Danny</u> William	LA	07-01-55	1983-	Friendship Hse
<u>Janice</u> Sue Parker	TN	10-06-52		Church & Home
HIX, <u>Glenn</u> Luther	NC	09-23-25	1971-76	Eng Lang Min
<u>Mabel</u> Blackwell Green	AL	02-22-22		Church & Home

Name	Home State	Date of Birth	Years of Service	Type of Assignment
HOLLAND, Robert Miller (Bob)	KY	08-22-34	1969-73	Teacher
Kathleen Gail Thompson	KY	07-04-37		Church & Home
HOLLAWAY, Ernest Lee Jr	AR	11-30-19	1949-68	Ch Ed Promoter
Ida Nelle Daily	IL	06-18-21		Church & Home
HOLLAWAY, R William (Bill)	AR	05-15-44	1972-76 1980-86	Friendship Hse
Linda Frances Louton	FL	11-08-44		Church & Home
HONJO, Ralph S	HI	03-21-37	1966-72	Gen Evangelist
Irene Harada	HI	06-02-37		Church & Home
HOOVER, Annie	AR	10-21-23	1949-	Gen Evangelist
HORN, Richard N (Dick)	TX	01-06-40	1972	Eng Lang Min
Joan K Ezell (Joanie)	NM	04-25-41		Church & Home
HORTON, Frances	FL	12-21-25	1952-87e	Gen Evangelist
HORTON, Frederick M	PA	05-27-18	1950-84e	Col Teacher
Elvee Wasson	LA	11-21-23		Church & Home
HOSHIZAKI, Reiji	CA	02-06-18	1955-84e	Gen Evangelist
Alice Asano Masaki	HI	05-11-23		Church & Home
HOWARD, Stanley P Jr	MO	12-20-22	1949-87e	Mission Adm
Patsy Ruth McGee	TX	02-11-29		Church & Home
HUDSON, Lenora C	TX	08-22-18	1949-71	Col Teacher
HUNTER, William Hal	FL	05-29-19	1975-77	Eng Lang Min
Esther Strange	FL	10-09-22		Church & Home
JACKSON, William H Jr (Dub)	TX	04-23-24	1951-64 1965-69	Gen Evangelist Eng Lang Min
Doris Shirley	TX	04-27-23		Church & Home
JOHNSON, Betty Jane (Johnni) [Scofield]	KY	09-12-22	1951-54	Literature Min
JOHNSON, David A (Dave)	AL	02-08-49	1986-	Col Teacher
Robin Elliott	MS	01-22-49		Church & Home
JOHNSON, Hershel Conrad	VA	10-28-35	1982-	Col Teacher
D Elizabeth Wells	NC	11-29-39		Church & Home
JOHNSON, John L d. 03-02-15	VA	08-12-35	1859-60	
Julia Anna Toy d. 01-16-30	VA	12-30-42		
JOHNSON, Peggy H	VA	09-26-31	1987-	Secretary

Name	Home State	Date of Birth	Years of Service	Type of Assignment
JORDAN, H Edward II	LA	09-30-46	1982-	Bus Manager
Nancy Grayce McKennon	MO	07-08-48		Church & Home
KARR, Clarence William	TX	09-15-50	1980-84	Ch Ed Promoter
(Bill)				
Shirley Ann Jackson	TX	06-14-51		Church & Home
KEITH, Billy P	OK	08-19-34	1961-68	Gen Evangelist
Mona Pigg	TX	06-17-35		Church & Home
KENNEDY, Wm Thomas (Tom)	LA	06-18-52	1985-	Hosp Chap
Carol Lynn Snead	LA	09-06-52		Friendship Hse
KNOX, Martha Elizabeth	MO	02-07-21	1950-63	Good Will Ctr
LANCASTER, Cecile E	TX	01-01-96	1920-61e	School Adm
d. 01-02-86				
LANE, Dorothea K	KY	02-03-24	1950-87e	Gen Evangelist
(Dottie)				
LAWTON, Phoebe [Faucett]	SC	12-13-97	1923-26	Teacher
LEE, David C.	Taiwan	02-27-45	1989-	Gen Evangelist
Patricia Y. Chiu (Pat)	"	08-06-48		Church & Home
LEE, Henry G Jr (Hank)	MS	01-08-47	1985-	Gen Evangelist
Linda Ione	LA	12-06-49		Church & Home
LIMBERT, Rosemary	AR	04-29-22	1950-68	Col Teacher
[Samsom]				
LOVE, Max H	GA	01-08-32	1964-	Mission Adm
Flora Gardner	GA	08-21-35		Church & Home
LOVELACE, Beryle C	TX	07-27-28	1965-	Music Promoter
Eva Elouise Roberts	TX	06-27-28		Church & Home
LUDLOW, M Anthony (Tony)	AR	07-25-57	1988-	Gen Evangelist
Cynthia K Goad (Cindy)	TN	10-30-57		Church & Home
McCOLLUM, John W (Mac)	AL	06-05-64	1889-09	Gen Evangelist
d. 01-23-10				
Drucilla Collins	AL	01-14-69		Church & Home
d. 01-20-63				
McMILLAN, Virgil O Jr	AL	01-17-23	1952-68	Gen Evangelist
Donabel Pitts	AL	04-08-26		Church & Home
MADDOX, Wayne R	VA	07-02-25	1969-	Friendship Hse
Dorothy Rogers	TN	04-06-30		Friendship Hse
MARLOWE, Elizabeth Rose	KY	04-21-90	1950-55e	Col Teacher
d. 02-18-80				

Name	Home State	Date of Birth	Years of Service	Type of Assignment
MARSHALL, Bertha Jane	IN	11-27-31	1957-67	Nurse
MARTIN, Charles L Jr	AL	01-26-23	1956-62	Student worker
Anne Crittendon	TX	02-07-22		Church & Home
MASAKI, Tomoki	HI	08-08-25	1956-79	Hosp Adm
			1983-	Gen Evangelist
Betty Takahashi	HI	08-24-30		Church & Home
MASSENGILL, Mary Lou	(See under EMANUEL, Wayne)			
MATHIESON, E Price	TX	01-26-36	1968-72	Col Teacher
Mary Darden	TX	02-07-39		Church & Home
MAYBERRY, Floyd I	MO	10-03-25	1968-74	MK Dormitory
Lela Cantrell	MO	06-01-28		MK Dormitory
MAYFIELD, Gary Wayne	TX	03-11-47	1983-	Gen Evangelist
Joan Ann (Joanie)	TX	12-23-49		Church & Home
MAYNARD, Nathan	MD	12-25-58	1894-10	Gen Evangelist
Bessie Harlowe	VA	06-04-61		Church & Home
d. 12-12-34				
MAYO, Phyllis	MD	10-21-53	1981-82	
MEADOWS, Michael G (Mike)	TX	04-07-47	1975-82	Music Promoter
Jane Catherine (Cathy)	TX	01-05-49		Church & Home
MEDLING, Phillip Paul	TN	06-12-80	1907-19	Gen Evangelist
d. 12-31-19				
Lenna Rushing	TN	10-02-81		Church & Home
d. 12-24-42				
MEDLING, Wm R (Bill)	Japan	05-28-14	1946-79e	Gen Evangelist
Mary Louise Gulley	TN	01-06-15		Church & Home
MERCER, Dewey E	KY	08-20-29	1955-	Gen Evangelist
Ramona Hall	TN	09-12-28		Church & Home
MILLER, Floryne Tipton	TN	07-25-07	1939-41	
d. 01-18-86			1946-72e	Gen Evangelist
MILLER, Larry Leland	CA	11-21-53	1984-	Music Promoter
Kean Lynne	CA	05-23-56		Church & Home
MILLS, Ernest O	WI	03-04-73	1910-40e	Gen Evangelist
d. 01-01-62				
Grace Hughes	MO	07-01-72	1912-32	Kindergarten
d. 07-16-32				
MOBLEY, Marion A (Mack)	GA	11-12-27	1959-80	Gen Evangelist
Carolyn Ham	GA	04-25-30		Church & Home

Name	Home State	Date of Birth	Years of Service	Type of Assignment
MOCK, <u>Darrell</u> A	OK	07-04-20	1967-86e	Music Promoter
<u>Norma Lea</u> Thomas	OK	03-01-26		Weekday Min
MOFFETT, E <u>Sherwood</u> Jr	LA	04-04-47	1976-	Teacher
<u>Margaret</u> Jane Denton	TX	07-18-47		Church & Home
MONCURE, <u>John</u>	VA	04-02-80	1909-13	Gen Evangelist
d. 1930				
MOORHEAD, <u>Marion</u> F	SC	04-23-17	1946-82e	Eng Lang Min
<u>Thelma</u> Chandler	VA	01-11-17		Church & Home
MORGAN, <u>Mary Neal</u>	KY	04-21-24	1950-73	Gen Evangelist
[Clarke]				
NATIONS, <u>Archie</u> Lee	LA	11-13-29	1960-67	Theol Teacher
Lois <u>Elaine</u> Sheffield	NC	12-11-28		Church & Home
d. 05-05-75				
NELSON, <u>Loyce</u> Neil	AR	04-01-24	1950-63	Gen Evangelist
d. 03-11-63				
<u>Gladys</u> Mosley	AR	02-05-26		Church & Home
[Peterson]				
NIX, <u>Willard</u> Voniver	NC	11-07-96	1921-24	Gen Evangelist
<u>Minta</u> Oxford	LA	08-04-97		Church & Home
NORTON, <u>John</u> Edward	AL	03-18-48	1977-	Col Teacher
<u>Nancy</u> Janell Turner	FL	08-18-51		Church & Home
ODELL, John Robert (<u>Bob</u>)	TX	12-03-58	1987-	Gen Evangelist
Elise <u>Renae</u> Sellers	AL	09-30-58		Gen Evangelist
OLIVER, <u>Edward</u> L	FL	04-06-25	1950-90e	Gen Evangelist
Susan (<u>Sue</u>) Pyles	KY	02-22-25		Church & Home
O'REAGAN, <u>Daniel</u> W	TX	12-20-30	1964-82	Gen Evangelist
<u>Beverly</u> Broussard	LA	02-16-31		Church & Home
OUE, <u>Takahiro</u>	Japan	08-05-43	1969-	Evang Director
<u>Lana</u> O'Banion	KY	02-07-46		Church & Home
OWEN, <u>Evelyn</u> Wood	AL	07-15-30	1956-	Gen Evangelist
PARKER, Franklin <u>Calvin</u>	FL	11-27-26	1951-89e	Theol Teacher
<u>Harriett</u> Evelyn Hale	TN	10-17-24		Church & Home
PERRIN, Jay <u>Kyle</u>	OK	02-25-32	1987-	Col Teacher
<u>Margaret</u> Lois Joplin	OK	04-26-32		Col Teacher
PHIPPS, Richard W (<u>Rick</u>)	IL	09-01-47	1986-	Music Promoter
<u>Barbara</u> Gail Jernigan	FL	01-23-47		Church & Home
P'POOL, Rebecca L	NM	01-25-50	1977-82	Col Teacher
(<u>Becky</u>) [Trainham]				

Name	Home State	Date of Birth	Years of Service	Type of Assignment
PRICE, <u>Harold</u> Lee	TX	06-12-32	1962-69	Ch Ed Promoter
Victoria Hardegree	GA	05-31-32		Church & Home
(<u>Vicky</u>)				
QUICK, Oswald J (<u>Oz</u>)	MO	08-23-15	1940-41	Lang Student
RAMSOUR, <u>H B</u> Jr	TX	01-11-11	1939-40	Lang Student
Vera <u>Mabel</u> Howard	TX	04-07-14		Lang Student
d. 11-30-85				
RANDALL, Mary <u>Josephine</u>	AL	07-22-27	1958-79	Student worker
RAY, <u>Charles</u> Augustus	TX	02-20-22	1971-72	Eng Lang Min
			1977-	
<u>Mary Elizabeth</u> Gilbert	MS	06-29-24		Church & Home
RAY, <u>Hermon</u> S	CT	09-30-07	1934-37	Gen Evangelist
<u>Rayberta</u> Reed	OR	08-19-10		Church & Home
RAY, J <u>Franklin</u>	MS	01-15-72	1904-42e	Gen Evangelist
d. 09-13-67				
<u>Daisy</u> Pettus	AL	07-15-74		Church & Home
d. 10-22-44				
REED, K <u>Don</u>	TX	06-07-32	1983-86	Eng Lang Min
d. 11-30-86				
REYNOLDS, <u>Ron</u>ald James	FL	05-15-53	1982-	Gen Evangelist
Cynthia Darlynn (<u>Cindy</u>)	FL	07-12-55		Church & Home
ROBERTS, Wm P (<u>Bill</u>)	AL	08-09-39	1971-81	Music Promoter
<u>Patricia</u> Ann Barr	MS	05-17-40		Church & Home
ROHREK, <u>John</u> Q A	MD		1859-60	
<u>Sarah</u> Robinson	PA			
ROWE, <u>John</u> Hansford	VA	11-13-76	1906-29	Gen Evangelist
d. 08-12-29				
<u>Margaret</u> Cobb	TX	11-29-83	1906-20	Church & Home
d. 04-05-20				
Carrie <u>Hooker</u> Chiles	MS	01-28-83	1915-35e	School Adm
d. 09-11-66				
RUSSELL, James D (<u>Jim</u>)	NC	10-30-52	1985-	Gen Evangelist
Vanessa <u>Dale</u> Woodside	NC	08-20-55		Church & Home
SANDERSON, <u>Rennie</u> [Otani]	MS	10-18-27	1960-69	Music Promoter
SATTERWHITE, James P(<u>Jim</u>)	NC	05-10-21	1952-75	Physician
<u>Altha</u> Smith	NC	03-02-21		Nurse
SCHAFFNER, <u>Karen</u> June	TX	06-25-52	1983-	Col Teacher
SCHELL, <u>Naomi</u> E	NC	09-21-93	1921-46	Good Will Ctr
d. 02-23-46				

Name	Home State	Date of Birth	Years of Service	Type of Assignment
SCHOOLAR, <u>John</u> Earl	MS	05-22-30	1968-72	Eng Lang Min
<u>Clara</u> Huckaby	TX	12-04-30		Church & Home
SEAT, <u>Leroy</u> Kay	MO	08-15-38	1966-	Theol Teacher
<u>June</u> Tinsley	MO	06-30-37		Church & Home
SHEPARD, <u>John</u> W Jr	Brazil	07-21-21	1948-83e	Col Teacher
<u>Jean</u> Prince	IL	11-14-21		Church & Home
SHERER, Robert C (<u>Bob</u>)	AL	09-15-17	1948-66 1972-84e	Gen Evangelist
<u>Helen</u> Mitchell	IL	10-11-21		Church & Home
SHERER, Robert H (<u>Bob</u>)	IL	11-04-45	1971-	Evang Director
<u>Claudia</u> Beth Kruer	MO	10-10-46		Church & Home
SHIN, <u>Jacob</u> Suktae	Korea	03-15-36	1989-	Gen Evangelist
<u>Poong Ja</u> Kim	Korea	05-16-39		Church & Home
SHIVER, <u>Mavis</u> G	(See under HARDY)			
SIMEONEAUX, M S (<u>Mike</u>)	LA	05-06-39	1969-81	Music Promoter
<u>Bonnie</u> Jean Rushing	MS	03-10-41		Church & Home
SIMMONS, JAMES M (<u>Jim</u>)	MI	04-03-40	1977-83	Gen Evangelist
Marilyn <u>Camille</u> Bishop	AR	07-23-47		Church & Home
SMITH, <u>Jack</u> Arthur	IL	08-02-21	1962-68	Bus Manager
<u>Velma</u> McLaughlin	TX	12-27-23		Church & Home
SMITH, James <u>Edward</u> Jr	OK	03-12-44	1969-	Gen Evangelist
<u>Sharon</u> Sue Craig	OK	01-06-44		Church & Home
SMITH, <u>Lucy</u>	MO	09-24-98	1951-65	Treasurer
d. 05-27-81				
SMITH, <u>Milton</u> Ray	TN	10-13-50	1986-88	Eng Lang Min
<u>Jeanna</u> Elaine	TN	06-08-50		Church & Home
SMITH, <u>Roscoe</u> C	TN	05-19-94	1921-26	Theol Teacher
d. 08-01-78				
<u>Sadie</u> Wilson	TN	01-19-98		Church & Home
d. 1983				
SOUTHERLAND, Lawrence M Jr (<u>Larry</u>)	SC	03-13-29	1961-70	Col Teacher
Bessie <u>Marcella</u> Brown	SC	05-30-31		Church & Home
SPENCE, <u>Raymond</u> Morris	TX	01-15-18	1948-55	Gen Evangelist
<u>Inez</u> Gilliland	TX	01-01-20		Church & Home
SPENCER, Alvin E Jr (<u>Bud</u>)	IL	07-23-23	1952-85e	Eng Lang Min
<u>Doris</u> Scalf	NC	01-04-23		Church & Home
STOKES, <u>Lucy Bell</u> [Ma]	OK	11-03-21	1949-61	Gen Evangelist

Name	Home State	Date of Birth	Years of Service	Type of Assignment
STUART, <u>Malcolm</u> W	AL	08-02-13	1977-78e	Eng Lang Min
<u>Edyth</u> Boyd	TX	08-13-05		Church & Home
SWEDENBURG, <u>Mary</u> S	AL	02-09-43	1969-	Gen Evangelist
TALLEY, <u>Frances</u>	NC	01-04-16	1946-62e	Gen Evangelist
TEAGUE, P <u>Jean</u> McSwain [Cabaniss]	NC	11-30-33	1982-87	Col Teacher
TEW, C <u>Delane</u>	AL	09-27-56	1983-	Friendship Hse
TODD, <u>Pearl</u> d. 12-08-81	GA	11-02-90	1950-57e	Col Teacher
TOY, <u>Crawford</u> H d. 05-12-19	VA	03-23-36	1859-61	
TREADWELL, <u>M A</u>	AL	04-27-91	1921-22	Lang Student
<u>Ruth</u> Espy	GA	07-29-93		Lang Student
TUTTLE, Robert <u>Neil</u>	NC	01-06-50	1977-80	Gen Evangelist
<u>Susan</u> Marie Spencer	KS	02-17-49		Church & Home
ULLOM, Robert Lynn (<u>Bob</u>)	WV	01-03-44	1978-89	Gen Evangelist
Sylvia <u>Maureen</u> Powell	GA	05-10-45		Church & Home
VAUGHN, <u>Keith</u> B	KY	07-23-44	1981-86	Music Promoter
<u>Sue</u> A Younce	OH	07-24-43		Church & Home
WALNE, <u>Ernest</u> N d. 10-31-36	MS	01-20-67	1892-35e	Literature Min
<u>Claudia</u> McGann d. 12-06-48	KY	01-26-68		Church & Home
WALNE, <u>Florence</u> d. 1945	Japan	04-19-95	1919-34	Literature Min
WALKER, <u>Carlton</u> E Jr	VA	04-09-54	1981-	Gen Evangelist
<u>Cornelia</u> Graham	KY	04-01-54		Church & Home
WALKER, William Levi II (<u>Bill</u>)	KY	03-17-23	1949-88e	Gen Evangelist
<u>Mary</u> Culpepper	China	06-12-26		Church & Home
WALKER, William Levi III (<u>Bill</u>)	Jpn	02-16-52	1987	Gen Evangelist
<u>Nancy</u> E Williams	TX	10-27-56		Church & Home
WALTERS, <u>Doris</u> L	NC	02-24-31	1966-88	Friendship Hse
WALTERS, <u>Mary</u> [Brooks]	FL	09-08-96	1923-29	Literature Min
WARDLAW, William (<u>Bill</u>)	AR	07-26-46	1984-	Gen Evangelist
<u>June</u> Marie Mills	FL	06-21-47		Church & Home

Name	Home State	Date of Birth	Years of Service	Type of Assignment
WARMATH, William C (Bill)	MS	05-18-27	1959-67	Eng Lang Min
Mary Cox	AR	05-12-29		Church & Home
WATANABE, George H	HI	01-09-38	1967-	Gen Evangelist
Amy Konishi	HI	01-30-44		Church & Home
WATKINS, Elizabeth T	SC	04-21-00	1948-70e	Good Will Ctr
d. 10-15-83				
WATSON, Leslie	TX	06-17-17	1950-86e	Gen Evangelist
Hazel Tunstead	NJ	01-04-19		R&D Consultant
WATTERS, James (Jim)	OK	01-18-32	1962-84	Friendship Hse
Darlene Ryburn	OK	01-26-31		Church & Home
WESTBROOK, Charles N	SC	12-06-47	1978-89	Gen Evangelist
Doris Jane Derrick	SC	09-30-48		Church & Home
WESTERN, Blake W	OK	01-07-35	1966-	Gen Evangelist
WHALEY, Charles L Jr	GA	08-10-22	1949-89e	School Adm
Lois Linnenkohl	GA	06-19-21	1948-89e	Church & Home
WHALEY, Thomas W (Tom)	CA	12-21-54	1984-	Gen Evangelist
Karol Ruth	CA	11-20-55		Church & Home
WHITWORTH, Mark Todd	MO	06-15-54	1986-	Gen Evangelist
Linda Sue Rounds	MO	07-10-54		Church & Home
WILLIAMS, Charles H Jr (Charlie)	AL	12-23-55	1981-	Gen Evangelist
Elizabeth Darlene	AL	06-06-55		Church & Home
WILLIAMSON, Norman F	GA	01-10-88	1918-36	Theol Teacher
d. 1972				
Fannie McCall	GA	07-18-90		Church & Home
d. 11-01-85				
WILLINGHAM, Calder T	GA	03-03-79	1902-07	Gen Evangelist
d. 03-03-18			1911-18	
Bessie Hardy	VA		1902-07	Church & Home
d. 03-19-10				
Foy Johnson [Farmer]	NC	10-06-87	1911-21	Gen Evangelist
d. 05-29-71				
WOOD, James E Jr	VA	07-29-22	1948-56	Col Teacher
Alma Leacy McKenzie	VA	09-19-18		Col Teacher
WOOD, Sydney Kenneth	PA	03-22-27	1960-65	Gen Evangelist
Audrey Ell Richmond	LA	04-06-30		Church & Home
WOODS, Tony Ray	TX	01-30-48	1978-	Gen Evangelist
Marsha Glee Smith	CO	06-13-50		Church & Home

Name	Home State	Date of Birth	Years of Service	Type of Assignment
WRIGHT, <u>John</u> S.	TX	02-15-56	1989-	Gen Evangelist
<u>Rhonda</u> L. Bennett	CA	03-15-57		Church & Home
WRIGHT, <u>Morris</u> J Jr	TX	04-10-22	1950-76	Ch Ed Promoter
<u>Joyce</u> Hickman	TX	08-19-26		Church & Home
YAGI, <u>Dickson</u> Kazuo	HI	05-11-37	1971-	Col Teacher
<u>Ellen</u> Ogawa	CA	10-08-34		Church & Home
YOUNG, <u>Hugh</u> H	GA	01-17-33	1968-	Col Teacher
<u>Norma</u> Lucas	KY	10-02-35		Church & Home

Appendix 3

Roster of Journeymen

Journeymen are auxiliary personnel on two-year assignments. They are selected from among college graduates under 30 years of age. The journeymen are listed below with their years of service in Japan. Surnames acquired by marriage after completion of service, if known, are enclosed in brackets.

Adams, Steve	1986-88
Alexander, James M.	1966-68
Allmon, Susan [Mullis]	1969-71
Anderson, Mary Lynn	1969-71
Aunspaugh, G. Allan	1982-84
Baker, Deborah [Kailer]	1978-80
Barmer, Greg	1986-88
Barrow, Lydia [Hankins]	1975-77
Bayne, Pam	1985-87
Benner, Dawn	1988-90
Blattner, Carol	1982-84
Boggs, Samuel	1971-73
Bounds, Bethany [Christman]	1977-79
Brown, Cherri	1981-83
Brown, Donna [Boatwright]	1980-82
Buckingham, Susan [Dorner]	1976-78
Burns, Margaret	1986-88
Cadenhead, Shirley [Riggs]	1975-77
Carrier, Suzanne	1973-75
Carson, Jan	1986-88
Carswell, Carla [Beard]	1980-82
Clark, Paul H.	1989-
Combs, Anita [Lee]	1967-69
Cookson, Daniel	1982-84
Cooley, Sharon	1984-86
Cooper, Rhonda	1980-82
Crook, Susan [Fergus]	1986-88
Curtis, Carol	1986-88
Daffern, Elaine [Graves]	1973-75
Dakin, Paul	1980-82
Davis, David B.	1987-89
Davis, Mary Margaret (Mrs. David)	1987-89
DuCharme, Peggy R.	1989-
Duncan, Cathy [Young]	1979-81
Dunn, Rebecca	1978-80

Eades, Terry	1975-77
Emundson, Marilyn [Hesser]	1979-80
Evans, Rosalie	1980-82
Feather, Deanna L.	1988-90
Ferrington, Darryl	1975-77
Ferrington, Mary Catherine (Mrs. Darryl)	1975-77
Finklin, Robin [Pendergrass]	1982-84
Finch, Gail	1984-86
Fleming, Connie [Bunch]	1974-76
Fletcher, Steven Ted	1988-90
Foster, William Jr.	1979-81
Frazier, Jerry	1976-78
Friday, Lynn	1986-88
Fuller, Molly	1985-87
Gellerstedt, J. Robert	1978-80
Gierhart, Robert	1973-75
Givens, Sherri R.	1988-90
Goodroe, Susan	1981-83
Griffin, Warren	1988-90
Gross, Shirley	1982-84
Gwathmey, Ellen	1972-74
Haigler, Kim	1986-88
Hankins, Ron	1975-77
Harrington, Anne	1983-85
Harris, Lynne	1982-84
Hartley, Sherrie [Mills]	1984-86
Hayes, Bruce M.	1988-90
Hemmings, Christina	1984-86
Hendrix, Brian	1985-87
Herrell, Sharon [Starwalt]	1967-69
Hickman, Diane [Shoemake]	1967-69
Holland, Eleanor	1971-73
Holland, Karen (Mrs. Russell)	1980-82
Holland, Russell	1980-82
Holland, Susan [Ziglar]	1980-82

Holley, Ellen [Burnette]	1984-86
Holt, Katherine [Black]	1970-72
Hooks, Susan	1981-83
Hortin, Mary Jane [Lim]	1975-77
Horton, Sheryl [Swindler]	1982-84
House, Janice [LaRoy]	1975-77
Huffman, Marilyn	1976-78
Hughey, Susan	1983-85
Humble, David	1979-81
Johnson, Anne (Mrs. Wilson)	1978-80
Johnson, Shirley	1966-68
Johnson, Wilson	1978-80
Jones, Ann	1984-86
Keck, Lee [Daniels]	1973-75
King, Karen	1982-84
Kirkwood, Virginia [Bullis]	1979-81
Kitts, Iva Nell [Edwards]	1977-79
Lail, Paulette B.	1988-90
Leavell, James	1967-69
Leavell, Judith (Mrs. James)	1967-69
Lee, Tina	1986-88
Long, Philip	1984-86
McAuley, Jane [Wright]	1966-68
McCombs, Ann	1986-88
McCoy, Frieda	1987-89
McFerron, Jerry	1979-81
Martindale, Shawna	1988-90
Maugans, Ruth [Nolen]	1982-84
Meador, Patricia	1966-68
Miller, Catherine	1981-83
Miller, Michael S.	1989-
Moran, Douglas	1977-79
Morgan, Christine [Cooper]	1971-73
Nakanishi, Stanley	1979-81
Nelson, Glynis	1968-70
Newell, Curt	1971-73
Odell, Renae (Mrs. Robert)	1985-87
Odell, Robert	1985-87
Odom, Rebecca	1968-70
Olson, Carole	1968-70
Palmer, Ellen	1981-83
Parker, Janice	1976-78
Pendergrass, Paul	1983-85
Pentz, Gloria [Gellerstedt]	1979-81
Perry, Elizabeth	1987-89
Phillips, Robert	1974-76
Pickler, Karen	1979-81

Pinkard, Susan G.	1988-90
Porterfield, Carolyn	1977-79
Pounder, Jeff	1979-81
Prince, Keith	1986-88
Pruitt, Jane [Gatewood]	1974-76
Rayburn, Angie L.	1989-
Richerson, Toni	1977-79
Robbins, Pat	1976-78
Robinson, Charlene [Kelley]	1974-76
Rulon, Carol L.	1987-89
Sauer, Michelle	1987-89
Sawyer, Camille [Richardson]	1974-76
Segars, Jackie [Behrens]	1969-71
Shaver, Wendy	1978-80
Sherman, Eugenia [Brown]	1979-81
Sherouse, Marsha	1974-76
Sherouse, Neil	1974-76
Shoemake, Robert	1967-69
Shows, Pam [Williamson]	1978-80
Shull, C. Andrew	1987-89
Shuman, Peggy	1984-86
Siler, Jeanine [Jones]	1983-85
Simmon, Randy	1982-84
Stan, Elaine [Krol]	1965-67
Stillman, Jennie	1977-79
Stillman, Peter	1977-79
Stone, Susan V.	1989-
Strickland, Cindy	1987-89
Stroh, Jeanne Ellen	1983-85
Thomas, Calen	1987-89
Thomas, Erin L.	1987-89
Todd, Naomi [Khan]	1978-80
Tolliver, Cheryle D.	1988-90
Tomita, Louise [Kuramoto]	1968-70
Turner, Edwin	1972-74
Tyson, Susan	1985-87
Valentine, Scott G.	1988-90
Vessey, Susan	1977-79
Villar, Sandra E.	1988-90
Wagner, Olivia [Wakefield]	1984-86
Watkins, Elizabeth	1984-86
Westfall, Susan [Campbell]	1971-73
Whitaker, Carol [Adkins]	1974-76
Wiggs, Deborah	1984-86
Wilson, James	1970-72
Yeargan, Teresa	1984-86
Youree, Roddy	1985-87

Appendix 4

Statistics

Source: Field statistical reports of the Foreign Mission Board, SBC, on the Japan Mission. Reports are found in *Annual of the Southern Baptist Convention*, issues dated one year after statistical years indicated. Figures may vary from those in the main text taken from other sources.

Table A. Missionary Personnel

	1899	1909	1919	1929	1939	1949	1959	1969	1979	1989
Career	8	15	22	20	16	41	121	129	122	150
Men	4	8	9	7	7	17	49	56	55	71
Married women	4	7	8	7	6	17	48	56	55	70
Unmarried women			5	6	3	7	24	17	12	9
Associate								12	14	11
Journeymen								7	18	17
Special Project										2
TOTAL	8	15	22	20	16	41	121	148	154	180

Table B. Evangelism and Church Development

	1899	1909	1919	1929	1939	1949	1959	1969	1979	1989
Churches	1	10	24	17	25	26	73	141	180	242
Self-supporting				6	5	6	46	141	180	242
Preaching stations	9	11	33	12	10	10	129	108	75	87
National pastors	7	14	17	22	21	24	122	211	236	325
Ordained	1	6	11	15	10	16	39			
Unordained	6	8	6	7	11	8	83			
Baptisms	10	58	90	140	117	303	1,312	1,035	795	921
Church membership	75	504	1,084	2,515	2,776	2,686	12,419	21,260	25,485	31,654
Sun. school enrollment	80	617	1,527	2,375	1,682	5,721	18,017	23,567	24,328	24,735
WMU enrollment				217	222	350	1,534	3,382	4,657	4,100
Brotherhood enrollment								1,780	2,421	3,391

Table C. Other Ministries

	1899	1909	1919	1929	1939	1949	1959	1969	1979	1989
Kindergartens			4	6	6	9	60	74	84	86
Kindergarten enrollment			107	258	221	670	3,400	6,240	7,520	4,443
Sec. school enrollment			230	871	1,370	2,300	2,903	3,202	3,144	3,376
College enrollment				268	320	800	2,803	7,373	9,282	9,119
Seminary enrollment		15		8	3	30	50	33	53	103
Hospital beds							70	140	155	155
Hospital inpatients							2,174	1,920		2,313
Nursing school enrollment										45

List of Abbreviations

ABMU	American Baptist Missionary Union
ASBC	*Annual* [or *Proceedings*] *of the Southern Baptist Convention*, 1845-
BSU	Baptist Student Union
BTU	Baptist Training Union
BYPU	Baptist Young People's Union
BYU	Baptist Youth Fellowship
DSSC	Division of Starting and Strengthening Churches, JBM
EBD	Edwin B. Dozier
EC	Executive Committee (JBC or JBM)
ESB	*Encyclopedia of Southern Baptists*, 4 vols., 1958-82.
FMB	Foreign Mission Board, SBC, Richmond, Va.
FMBA	Foreign Mission Board Archives, Richmond, Va.
FMJ	*Foreign Mission Journal*, Richmond, Va., 1869-1916
HFF	*Home and Foreign Fields*, Nashville, Tenn., 1916-36
JBC	Japan Baptist Convention, Tokyo
JBM	Japan Baptist Mission, Tokyo
JCY	*Japan Christian Yearbook*, Yokohama and Tokyo, 1903-70
JCQ	*Japan Christian Quarterly*, Tokyo, 1926-
MM	Mission meeting (full meeting of JBM)
NBRS	*Nihon Baputesuto Remmei shi (1889-1959)* (History of the Japan Baptist Convention [1889-1959])
PBD	*Program Base Design*
SBC	Southern Baptist Convention
WMU	Woman's Missionary Union
YWA	Young Woman's Auxiliary

Bibliography

Unpublished papers are listed only if they are more than 10 pages in length or are cited in the notes of more than one chapter. Short articles in Foreign Mission Board periodicals have been omitted. The absence of a comma after a Japanese author's surname indicates that the name appears in the Japanese order (surname first) in the work cited. See preceding section for key to abbreviations used.

Adachi, Kinnosuke. "The Topknot Nine." *Outlook* 146 (2 June 1927): 250-52.
Adams, Theodore F. *Baptists Around the World.* Nashville: Broadman Press, 1967.
Advent Review and Sabbath Herald, 1902.
Ai no hi (Sun of love). Mito: Mito Baptist Church, 1984. Booklet.
Allen, Catherine B. *A Century to Celebrate: History of Woman's Missionary Union.* Birmingham: Woman's Missionary Union, 1987.
------. *The New Lottie Moon Story.* Nashville: Broadman Press, 1980.
American Baptist, 1850-72.
Annual [or *Proceedings*] *of the Southern Baptist Convention*, 1855-1989.
Annual reports, Japan Baptist Mission, 1892-1989. FMBA or JMB.
Asheville Citizen-Times, 1990.
Asiaweek, 1990.
ASBC. See *Annual of the Southern Baptist Convention*.

Baker, Robert A. *A Baptist Source Book.* Nashville: Broadman Press, 1966.
------. *The Southern Baptist Convention and Its People, 1607-1972.* Nashville: Broadman Press, 1974.
Baptist and Reflector, 1986.
Baptist Courier, 1943.
Baptist Family Magazine, 1858-60.
Baptist Magazine, 1876.
Baptist Missionary Magazine, 1859.
Baptist Missionary Society. Minutes, 1864. Baptist Missionary Society Archives, London. Issued in microfilm by SBC Historical Commission, Nashville.
Baputesuto (Baptist), 1950-89.
Barker, Dianne. "Summary: The Life of Floryne Miller." Typescript.
Barnes, William Wright. *The Southern Baptist Convention 1845-1953.* Nashville: Broadman Press, 1954.
Barnhart, Joe Edward. *The Southern Baptist Holy War.* Austin: Texas Monthly Press, 1986.

Beaver, R. Pierce. "The History of Mission Strategy." *Southwestern Journal of Theology* 12 (Spring 1970): 7-28.

Bennett, Albert Arnold. "Rev. Nathan Brown, D.D." *Japan Evangelist* 2 (1895): 317-21.

Bible Society Record, 1879-81.

Bollinger, Edward E. *The Cross and the Floating Dragon: The Gospel in Ryukyu*. Pasadena: William Carey Library, 1983.

Bouldin, George W. "Autobiography." Typescript, ca. 1960. George W. Bouldin Collection, SBC Historical Commission.

------. Papers. George W. Bouldin Collection, SBC Historical Commission, Nashville.

Boxer, C. R. *The Christian Century in Japan 1549-1650*. Berkeley: University of California Press, 1951.

Brown, E. W. *The Whole World Kin: A Pioneer Experience among remote tribes and other labors of Nathan Brown*. Philadelphia, 1890.

Brumbaugh, T. T. *Christ for All Japan*. New York: Friendship Press, 1947.

Business Week, 1990.

Cary, Frank. *History of Christianity in Japan*. Tokyo: Kyo Bun Kwan, 1959. Reprint of "Historical Section" in *Japan Christian Yearbook, 1959*.

Cary, Otis. *A History of Christianity in Japan: Roman Catholic, Greek Orthodox, and Protestant Missions*. 2 vols. 1909. Reprint (2 vol. in 1). Tokyo: Charles E. Tuttle Co., 1976.

Cauthen, Baker J., and Others. *Advance: A History of Southern Baptist Foreign Missions*. Nashville: Broadman Press, 1970.

Chicago Daily News, 1971.

Clark, W. Thorburn. *Outriders for the King*. Nashville: Broadman Press, 1931.

Clarke, W. Harvey. *Boys' School for Fukuoka, Japan*. Richmond: Foreign Mission Board, n.d. Pamphlet.

Clarke, Mrs. W. Harvey. *Girls' School Kumamoto Japan*. Richmond: Foreign Mission Board, 1912. Pamphlet.

Clayton, John Powell. "Crawford Howell Toy of Virginia." *Baptist Quarterly* 24 (1971): 53-56.

Clement, A. S. "The Baptist Missionary Society in Japan." *Baptist Quarterly* 26 (Apr. 1975): 68-73.

Clement, Ernest W. *A Handbook of Modern Japan*. Chicago: A. C. McClurg & Co., 1910.

Cole, Leone. *Sentenced to Life: 50 Years of Missionary Life in Japan*. Huntington Beach, Cal.: National Design Associates, 1987.

Commission, 1856-61, 1938-90.

Copeland, E. Luther. "The Crisis of Protestant Missions to Japan 1889-1900." Ph.D. diss. Yale University, 1949.

Correspondence files, Japan missionaries. FMBA; JBM.

Crawley, J. Winston. *Global Mission: A Story to Tell*. Nashville: Broadman Press, 1985.

------. *New Frontiers in an Old World*. Nashville: Convention Press, 1962.

Culpepper, Robert H. *God's Calling: A Missionary Autobiography*. Nashville: Broadman Press, 1981.

Davis, J. Merle. *Davis, Soldier Missionary: A Biography of Rev. Jerome D. Davis*. Boston: Pilgrim Press, 1916.

Dawson, L. O. "Pioneer of the Japan Mission, S.B.C." Typescript. EBD papers.

DeForest, Charlotte B. *The Woman and the Leaven in Japan*. West Medford, Mass.: Central Committee on the United Study of Foreign Missions, 1923.

Dozier, Charles Kelsey. Diaries, 1917-33. FMBA.

Dozier, Edwin B. *A Golden Milestone in Japan*. Nashville: Broadman Press, 1940.

------. "Japan Faces the Sunrise." In *Light for the Whole World: A Symposium*, by M. Theron Rankin and others. Nashville: Broadman Press, 1948.

------. *Japan's New Day*. Nashville: Broadman Press, 1949.

------. "Lantern Lights of Baptist Work in South-western Japan." Fukuoka: Japan Baptist Mission, 1935. Mimeographed.

------. "The Mission and the Convention: A Historical Survey." 1963. Mimeographed.

------. Notes, on Japan Baptist Mission and JBC history, 1857-1945. Typescript. JBM.

------. Papers. JBM.

------. "Report to the Foreign Mission Board of the Southern Baptist Convention." 12 Dec. 1946. Typescript.

------. "A Supplementary Report to the Foreign Mission Board." 10 May 1947. Typescript.

Dozier, Mary Ellen. Oral history interview on tape. FMBA.

Dozier, Maude B. "Baptist Woman's Work in Japan." Mimeographed.

------. *Charles Kelsey Dozier of Japan: A Builder of Schools*. Nashville: Broadman Press, 1953.

------. "Seinan Gakuin." Typescript. Seinan Gakuin, Fukuoka.

------. *Trials and Triumphs of W.M.U. Work in Japan*. Birmingham: W.M.U. Literature Dept., [1932]. Leaflet.

Drummond, Richard H. *A History of Christianity in Japan*. Grand Rapids: William B. Eerdmans, 1971.

------. "A Missionary 'Exodus' from Japan." *Christian Century*, 26 May 1965.

Ecumenical Missionary Conference. 2 vols. New York: American Tract Society, 1900.

Eden, Josephine. Book manuscript with letters of Lucile Clarke. Typescript. Portion in Seinan Jo Gakuin, Kitakyūshū.

Egasaki Kiyomi, ed. *Baputesuto senkyō hachijūnen no ayumi* (Eighty years of Baptist evangelism). Tokyo: Nihon Baputesuto Remmei, 1969.

Eighmy, John Lee. *Churches in Cultural Captivity: A History of the Social Attitudes of Southern Baptists*. Knoxville: University of Tennessee Press, 1987.

Emanuel, Bill. *I Enlisted for the Duration: An Autobiographical Story of 35 Years of Spiritual Adventure*. Privately printed in Japan, 1979.

Emanuel, Bill, and Rebekah Sue Emanuel. *A Call Comes Ringing*. Privately printed, 1955.

Encyclopædia Britannica, 1968 ed., 1970 ed.

Encyclopedia of Southern Baptists. 4 vols. Nashville: Broadman Press, 1958-82.

Endō, Akiko. *Ring in the New*. Nashville: Broadman Press, 1949.

Erickson, Lois Johnson. *The White Fields of Japan*. Richmond, Va.: Presbyterian Committee of Publication, 1923.

ESB. See *Encyclopedia of Southern Baptists*.

Estep, William R. *Baptists and Christian Unity*. Nashville: Broadman Press, 1966.

Evangelism Study Committee, JBM. *The Missionary and His Work*. Fukuoka, 1962.

Eyler, Marvin. "Research, Motivation, Training, and Mobilization." *Japan Christian Quarterly* 56 (Winter 1990):3-6.

Facts and Trends, 1978.

Farmer, Foy Johnson. *At the Gate of Asia*. Nashville: Sunday School Board, 1934.

------. *Hitherto: History of North Carolina Woman's Missionary Union*. Raleigh: WMU of North Carolina, 1952.

------. *Mrs. Maynard's House*. Nashville: Broadman Press, 1940.

Fletcher, Jesse C. *Baker James Cauthen: A Man for All Nations*. Nashville: Broadman Press, 1977.

FMJ. See *Foreign Mission Journal*.

Foreign Mission Board, SBC. Minutes, 1859-60, 1926.
------. Oral History Project. Taped interviews.
------. Press Releases, 1950-90.
Foreign Mission Journal, 1869-1916.
Foster, L. S. *Mississippi Baptist Preachers*. St. Louis, 1895.
Freeman (London), 1875-77.
Fukuoka ken hyakka jiten (Encyclopedia of Fukuoka Prefecture). 2 vols.

Gardner, E. Norfleet. *Journey to Japan*. Privately printed, 1952.
Garrett, James Leo, ed. *Baptist Relations with Other Christians*. Valley Forge: Judson Press, 1974.
Garrott, Dorothy. Oral history interview on tape. FMBA.
Garrott, W. Maxfield. Interview taped by Tom Masaki, 10 May 1971. JBM.
------. *Japan Advances*. Nashville: Convention Press, 1956.
------. "Jubilee in Japan." Typescript, 1940. FMBA.
General Conference Daily Bulletin, 1899.
Gill, Everett. *A. T. Robertson: A Biography*. New York: MacMillan Co., 1943.
Grant, Worth C. *Japan with Love*. Buchanan, Ga.: Baptist Missionary Service, n.d.
------. *A Work Begun*. Printed in Tokyo, n.d.
Greer, Genevieve, and Clara Selby Smith, comp. *Missionary Album*. Nashville: Broadman Press, 1954.
Grew, Joseph C. *Ten Years in Japan*. New York: Simon and Schuster, 1944.
Griffis, William Elliot. *A Maker of the New Orient: Samuel Robbins Brown*. New York: Fleming H. Revell Co., 1902.
------. *Matthew Calbraith Perry: A Typical American Naval Officer*. Boston, 1887.

Halvarson, Carl M. *Japan's New Baptists*. Nashville: Convention Press, 1956.
Hamrick, Delois. "Biographical Materials Concerning William Maxfield Garrott, Missionary to Japan." Project in Missionary Biography, Carver School of Missions and Social Work, 1958-59.
Hara, Matsuta, ed. *Rev. John Hansford Rowe: The Founder of Seinan Jo-Gakuin*. Kokura: Seinan Jo Gakuin, 1930.
------. In Memory of Rev. J. H. Rowe. Kokura: Seinan Jo Gakuin, 1939.
Harrington, C. K. "Baptist Work in Japan, the Past." In *Minutes of the Japan Mission of the American Baptist Foreign Mission Society, 1910*. Yokohama, 1910.
------. "Historical Sketch of the Theological School." In *Minutes of the American Baptist Missionary Union in Japan, 1893*. Yokohama, 1893.
Hawks, Francis L. *Narrative of the Expedition of an American Squadron to the China Seas and Japan*. . . . Washington, D.C.: Beverley Tucker, Senate Printer, 1856. Reprint. New York: AMS Press, Arno Press, 1967. Trade edition. New York: D. Appleton & Co., 1856.
Hepburn, James Curtis. Correspondence, 1862. Japan letters, Presbyterian Historical Society, Philadelphia.
HFF. See *Home and Foreign Fields*.
Hoare, James E. "Extraterritoriality in Japan, 1859-1899." In *Transactions of the Asiatic Society of Japan*. 3d ser., vol. 18 (1983): 71-98.
Hollaway, Ernest L., Jr. "Major Developments in Religious Education in the Japan Baptist Convention to 1961." D.R.E. diss. Southwestern Baptist Theological Seminary, 1965.
Holtom, Daniel Clarence. *Modern Japan and Shinto Nationalism*. Chicago: University of Chicago Press, 1947.
Home and Foreign Fields, 1916-36.

Howes, John F. "Japanese Christians and American Missionaries." In *Changing Japanese Attitudes Toward Modernization*. Edited by Marius B. Jansen. Princeton: Princeton University Press, 1965.

Howse, W. L. *East Asia Planning Manual*. Hong Kong, 1972.

Hunt, Alma. *History of Woman's Missionary Union*. Nashville: Convention Press, 1964.

Hurt, Billy Grey. "Crawford Howell Toy: Interpreter of the Old Testament." Ph.D. diss. Southern Baptist Theological Seminary, 1965.

Hyatt, Irwin T., Jr. *Our Ordered Lives Confess: Three Nineteenth-Century American Missionaries in East Shantung*. Cambridge: Harvard University Press, 1976.

Iglehart, Charles W. *A Century of Protestant Christianity in Japan*. Tokyo: Charles E. Tuttle Co., 1959.

Inoue Yoshimi et al., eds. *Seinan Jo Gakuin rokujūnen no ayumi* (Sixty-year history of Seinan Jo Gakuin). Kitakyūshū: Seinan Jo Gakuin, 1982.

Intercom, 1987.

Jabas News, 1959-89. Also called *Japan Baptist News* and *Mission News*. JBM in-house monthly, irregular in size and format.

Japan Christian Quarterly, 1903-90.

Japan Christian Yearbook. Yokohama and Tokyo, 1903-70.

"Japan Mission/Church Growth Study." Loose-leaf. Japan Baptist Mission, 1987.

Japan Times, 1969-88.

JCQ. See *Japan Christian Quarterly*.

JCY. See *Japan Christian Yearbook*.

Jennes, Joseph. *A History of the Catholic Church in Japan: From its Beginnings to the Early Meiji Era (1549-1873)*. Rev. ed. Tokyo: Oriens Institute for Religious Research, 1973.

Johnson, U. Alexis, with Jef Olivarius McAllister. *The Right Hand of Power*. Englewood Cliffs, N.J.: Prentice-Hall, 1984.

Katakozawa Chiyomatsu. "Nihon Baputesuto kyōkai no dendō hōshin" (Evangelistic strategy of the Japan Baptist church). *Kirisutokyō shigaku* 15 (1965): 17-24.

Kawai, Kazuo. *Japan's American Interlude*. Chicago: University of Chicago Press, 1960 (Midway reprint, 1979).

Keith, Billy. *Shinsei: New Life for Asia*. Tokyo: Jordan Press, 1963.

------. *What in the World is God Doing?* Nashville: Convention Press, 1973.

Kōhō Seinan Jo Gakuin, 1989.

King, C. W., and G. T. Lay. *The Claims of Japan and Malaysia upon Christendom*. New York, 1839.

Kirisutokyō nenkan (Christian yearbook), 1981-90.

Kodansha Encyclopedia of Japan. 9 vols. 1983.

Lancaster, Cecile E. "My Life on the Mission Field, 1920-1960." Typescript, 1967. FMBA.

Lash, Joseph P. *Helen and Teacher: The Story of Helen Keller and Anne Sullivan Macy*. New York: Delacorte Press/Seymour Lawrence, 1980.

Latourette, Kenneth Scott. *A History of the Expansion of Christianity*, 7 vols. New York: Harper & Brothers, 1937-45.

Lee, Edwin B. "Robert H. Pruyn in Japan, 1862-1865." *New York History* 66 (1985): 123-39.

Leonard, Bill J. *God's Last and Only Hope: The Fragmentation of the Southern Baptist Convention*. Grand Rapids: William B. Eerdmans, 1990.

Lindbergh, Anne Morrow. *North to the Orient*. New York: Harcourt, Brace and Co., 1935.

Love, J. F. *Southern Baptists and Their Far Eastern Missions*. Richmond: Foreign Mission Board, 1922.

MacArthur, Douglas. *A Soldier Speaks*. New York: Praeger, 1965.

McCollum, J. W. "A Historical Sketch of Southern Baptist Missions to Japan." In *Minutes of the Annual Conference of the American Baptist Missionary Union in Japan, 1899*. Yokohama, 1899.

McLemore, Richard Aubrey. *A History of Mississippi Baptists, 1780-1970*. Jackson: Mississippi Baptist Convention Board, 1971.

Mainichi Daily News, 1963.

Maizuru Yōchien, *Maizuru Yōchien rokujūnen no ayumi* (Sixty-year history of Maizuru Kindergarten). Fukuoka: Maizuru Yōchien, 1973.

Mason, Clara Arthur. *Etchings from Two Lands*. Boston, 1886.

Means, Frank K. *Advance to Bold Mission Thrust: A History of Southern Baptist Foreign Missions, 1970-1980*. Richmond, Va.: Foreign Mission Board, SBC, 1981.

------. "Japan Project of Office of Communications Anticipating Centennial of Japan Baptist Mission Work." Typescript. FMBA.

Mikushi Kazushi. "Itamashii omoide" (Painful recollections). 2 parts. *Seinan Gakuin daigaku kōhō*, 1974, nos. 27 and 28.

Miles, Fern Harrington. *Captive Community: Life in a Japanese Internment Camp, 1941-1945*. Jefferson City, Tenn.: Mossy Creek Press, 1987.

Mills, Ernest O. *Jottings from Japan*. Nashville: Broadman Press, 1949.

Minezaki Yasutada, ed. *Seinan Jo Gakuin sanjūnen shi* (Thirty-year history of Seinan Jo Gakuin). Kokura: Seinan Jo Gakuin, 1952.

Minutes of the [Annual Conference of the] American Baptist Missionary Union in Japan. Yokohama, 1890-1909.

Minutes of the Japan Mission of the American Baptist Foreign Mission Society, 1910. Yokohama, 1910.

"Mission Actions, 1963." Mimeographed, bound. JBM.

Missionary Album. Richmond: Foreign Mission Board, 1975, 1979. Supplements: 1976, 1980, 1981, 1982.

Mission Messenger (Georgia WMU). 1918.

Mizumachi Yoshio, ed. *A Memoir of C. K. Dozier*. Fukuoka: Seinan Gakuin, 1934.

Musto, David F. "America's Forgotten Drug War." *Reader's Digest* 136 (Apr. 1990): 147-50.

Moore, Marjorie E. *Japan's Southern Baptists: 60 Years of Missions*. Richmond: Foreign Mission Board, 1949.

Mueller, William A. *A History of Southern Baptist Theological Seminary*. Nashville: Broadman Press, 1959.

NBRS. See *Nihon Baputesuto Remmei shi*.

Neill, Stephen. *A History of Christian Missions*. Baltimore: Penguin Books, 1964.

Neve, Lloyd R. *Japan: God's Door to the Far East*. Minneapolis: Augsburg Publishing House, 1973.

Nevius, Helen S. Coan. *Our Life in China*. New York, 1876.

New Life. Occasional newspaper, Tokyo, 1963.

New Lifeline. Occasional newspaper, Tokyo, 1963.

"New Life Movement Scrapbook." 1963. JBM.

Newsweek, 1963.

New York Baptist Annual, 1898.

New York Times, 1860, 1990.

Nida, Eugene A. "My Pilgrimage in Mission." *International Bulletin of Missionary Research* 12 (1988): 62-65.

Nihon Baputesuto Remmei shi (1889-1959) (History of the Japan Baptist Convention [1889-1959]). Tokyo: Nihon Baputesuto Remmei, 1959.

Nihon Kirisutokyō rekishi daijiten (Dictionary of Japanese Christian history). Tokyo: Kyō Bun Kwan, 1988.

Nippon Times, 1952.

Nishikawa Shigenori, "The Daijōsai, the Constitution, and Christian Faith." *Japan Christian Quarterly* 56 (Summer 1990): 132-46.

Notehelfer, F. G. *American Samurai: Captain L. L. Janes and Japan.* Princeton, N.J.: Princeton University Press, 1985.

Operation Baptist Biography materials. SBC Historical Commission, Nashville.

"Operations Manual." Japan Baptist Mission, 1973.

Orangeburg (S.C.) Baptist Association. *Minutes*, 1892-97.

Orr, J. Edwin. *The Flaming Tongue.* 2d ed. Chicago: Moody Press, 1975.

Out of the Ashes: The Post War Decade in Japan. Japan Missionary Fellowship of the American Baptist Foreign Mission Society and the Woman's ABFMS, ca. 1956.

Parker, F. Calvin. "Baptist Missions in Japan, 1945-73: A Study in Relationships." *Japan Christian Quarterly* 40 (Winter 1974): 32-41.

------. "Ecumenism and the Evangelization of Japan." *Japan Missionary Bulletin*, Jan.-Feb. 1976, 19-24.

------. "Jonathan Goble, Missionary Extraordinary." In *Transactions of the Asiatic Society of Japan.* 3d ser., vol. 16 (1981): 77-107.

------. *Jonathan Goble of Japan: Marine, Missionary, Maverick.* Lanham, Md.: University Press of America, 1990.

Parker, P. *Journal of an Expedition from Singapore to Japan.* London, 1838.

PBD. See Program Base Design.

Pettigrew, George R. "John A. Brunson, D.D., the Man and the Preacher." *Baptist Courier*, 30 Dec. 1943, 9.

Phelan, Irving. *From Phelan's Note Book.* Privately printed, Peking, China, 1935.

Phillips, James M. *From the Rising of the Sun: Christians and Society in Contemporary Japan.* Maryknoll, N.Y.: Orbis Books, 1981.

Pieters, Albertus. *Mission Problems in Japan: Theoretical and Practical.* New York: Board of Publication, 1912.

Proceedings of the General Conference of Protestant Missionaries in Japan, 1900. Tokyo: Methodist Publishing House, 1901.

Proceedings of the Southern Baptist Convention. See Annual of the Southern Baptist Convention.

Program Base Design. Tokyo: Japan Mission, Foreign Mission Board, SBC, 1973, 1980.

Quarterly Review, 1990

Ramond, John S., comp. *Among Southern Baptists.* Vol. 1, 1936-37. Shreveport, La.; John S. Ramond, 1936.

Rankin, Jerry, et al. "Japan Mission/Church Growth Study Outside Evaluation Team Report." Japan Baptist Mission, 1988.

Reischauer, Edwin O. *My Life between Japan and America.* New York: Harper & Row, 1986.

Reischauer, Edwin O., and Albert M. Craig. *Japan: Tradition and Transformation.* Tokyo: Charles E. Tuttle Co., 1978.

Religious Herald, 1976.

Ritter, H. *A History of Protestant Missions in Japan*. Translated by George E. Albrecht. Tokyo, 1898.

Robertson, Archibald Thomas. *Life and Letters of John Albert Broadus*. Philadelphia: American Baptist Publication Society, 1901.

Roden, Donald T. *Schooldays in Imperial Japan: A Study in the Culture of a Student Elite*. Berkeley: University of California, 1901.

Royal Service, 1978.

Saitō Goki, ed. *Baputesuto no shinkō kokuhaku* (Baptist confessions of faith). Tokyo: Jordan Press, 1980.

------. "Life, Work, and Contributions of Edwin B. Dozier in Japan." Th.M. thesis. Southern Baptist Theological Seminary, 1971.

Sampey, John R. *Memoirs of John R. Sampey*. Nashville: Broadman Press, 1947.

Santee (S.C.) Baptist Association, *Minutes*, 1916-41.

Schneider, Bernardin. "Japan's Encounter with the Bible." *Japan Christian Quarterly* 48 (1982): 69-78.

Schwantes, Robert S. *Japanese and Americans*. New York: Harper & Brothers, 1955.

Seat, Keith, ed. "Jonathan Goble's Book." In *Transactions of the Asiatic Society of Japan*. 3d ser., vol. 16 (1981): 109-52.

Seinan Gakuin daigaku kōhō, 1989.

Seinan Gakuin nanajūnen shi (Seventy-year history of Seinan Gakuin). Fukuoka: Seinan Gakuin, 1986.

Seinan Gakuin shi shiryō (Seinan Gakuin historical materials). 2 vols. Fukuoka: Seinan Gakuin, 1980.

Seinan Jo Gakuin gojūnen shi 1922-1972 (Fifty-year history of Seinan Jo Gakuin, 1922-72). Kitakyūshū: Seinan Jo Gakuin, 1972.

Seinan News. Fukuoka, 1935.

Sissons, D. C. S. "James Murdoch (1856-1921)." In *Transactions of the Asiatic Society of Japan*. 4th ser., vol. 2 (1987): 1-57.

Smith, Anna Mae. *Adventuring with Rose*. Georgetown, Ky.: Georgetown College Press, 1964.

Smith, John Coventry. *From Colonialism to World Community*. Philadelphia: Geneva Press, 1982.

Smith, Lucy. Oral history interview on tape. FMBA.

Southern Baptist Foreign Missionaries. Richmond: Foreign Mission Board, 1936.

Southern Baptist Theological Seminary. *Catalogue, 1904-5*.

Southwestern News, 1988.

Spain, Rufus B. *At Ease in Zion: Social History of Southern Baptists 1865-1900*. Nashville: Vanderbilt University Press, 1967.

Spector, Ronald H. *Eagle Against the Sun: The American War with Japan*. New York: Free Press, 1985.

Supreme Commander for the Allied Powers. *Political Reorientation of Japan*. 2 vols. Washington: U.S. Government Printing Office, 1949.

Taylor, Charles E. *The Story of Yates the Missionary*. Nashville: Sunday School Board, 1898.

Taylor, George Braxton. *Virginia Baptist Ministers*. 6th ser., 1914-1934. Lynchburg, Va.: J. P. Bell Co., 1935.

Team Thrust Ministries. N.p., n.d.

Tenny, C. B. "Baptist Beginnings in Japan." *Japan Evangelist* 31 (June 1924): 9-18.

Thompson, James J. *Tried as by Fire: Southern Baptists and the Religious Controversies of the 1920s*. Macon, Ga.: Mercer University Press, 1982.

Thompson, R. Austin. "Historical Sketch of the South-West Japan Mission." In *Minutes of the Annual Conference of the Missionaries of the American Baptist Missionary Union in Japan, 1901*. Kobe, 1901.

Time, 1970.

Times (London), 1970.

Tobata Baptist Good Will Center. *Showers of Blessing 1929-1939*. Tobata, 1939.

Tokyo, 1977.

Torbet, Robert G. *Venture of Faith: The Story of the American Baptist Foreign Mission Society and the Woman's American Baptist Foreign Mission Society 1814-1954*. Philadelphia: Judson Press, 1955.

Tucker, Alice Johnson. "Rose of Three Countries." Typescript, 1966. FMBA.

Tucker, Ruth A. *From Jerusalem to Irian Jaya: A Biographical History of Christian Missions*. Grand Rapids: Zondervan Publishing House, Academie Books, 1983.

Tupper, H. A. *A Decade of Foreign Missions, 1880-1890*. Richmond, Va.: Foreign Mission Board, 1891.

------. *The Foreign Missions of the Southern Baptist Convention*. Philadelphia: American Baptist Publication Society; Richmond: Foreign Mission Board, SBC, 1880.

12th Baptist World Congress. Tokyo, 1970.

Ussery, Annie Wright. *The Story of Kathleen Mallory*. Nashville: Broadman Press, 1956.

Verbeck, Guido F. "History of Protestant Missions in Japan." In *Proceedings of the General Conference of Protestant Missionaries in Japan, 1900*. Tokyo: Methodist Publishing House, 1901. Reprinted from *Proceedings of the General Conference of the Protestant Missionaries of Japan, held at Osaka, Japan, April 1883*. Yokohama, 1883.

Wainright, S. H. *The Methodist Mission in Japan*. Nashville: Board of Missions, Methodist Episcopal Church, South, 1935.

Wall Street Journal, 1990

Walne, E. N. "The Japan Mission." In *Southern Baptist Foreign Missions*. Edited by T. Bronson Ray. Nashville: Sunday School Board, 1910.

Watkins, Elizabeth T. "How God Kept His Promises to a Teenager: The Autobiography of Elizabeth Taylor Watkins." N.d. Typescript. FMBA.

Wavelength, 1989-90.

Weatherspoon, J. B. *M. Theron Rankin: Apostle of Advance*. Nashville: Broadman Press, 1958.

Welsh Neck (S.C.) Baptist Association. *Minutes*, 1892-97.

Whaley, Charles L. "Development of a Pilot Program of Theological Education in Tokyo." D.Min. project report. Southern Baptist Theological Seminary, 1976.

Whaley, Lois. *Edwin Dozier of Japan: Man of the Way*. Birmingham, Ala.: Woman's Missionary Union, 1983.

Wheeler, W. Reginald. *The Crisis Decade: A History of the Foreign Missionary Work of the Presbyterian Church in the U.S.A. 1937-1947*. New York: The Board of Foreign Missions of the Presbyterian Church in the U.S.A., 1950.

Williams, Harold S. *Foreigners in Mikadoland*. Tokyo: Charles E. Tuttle Co., 1963.

Williams, S. Wells. "Narrative of a voyage of the ship Morrison." *Chinese Repository* 9 (1837): 209-29.

Willingham, Elizabeth Walton. *Life of Robert Josiah Willingham*. Nashville: Sunday School Board, 1917.

Wood, James E., Jr. "The Teaching of English as a Missionary Method." Th.D. diss. Southern Baptist Theological Seminary, 1957.

Wright, Morris J. "Survey and Growth Evaluation of the Japan Baptist Convention, 1950-1960." Mimeographed, 1961.

Wynd, William. *Seventy Years in Japan: A Saga of Northern Baptists*. Privately printed ca. 1943.

Yanaga, Chitoshi. *Japan Since Perry*. New York: McGraw-Hill Book Co., 1949.

Yomiuri (English-language newspaper), 1963.

Young, John M. L. *By Foot to China*. Tokyo: Radiopress, 1984.

Yuya Kiyoki. Taped interview by Tom Masaki. JBM.

Zen Nippon ni Kirisuto no hikari o (The light of Christ to all Japan). Tokyo: Nihon Baputesuto Remmei, 1980.

Index

About the Author

Franklin Calvin Parker was born in 1926 in Apopka, Florida. He was introduced to Japanese language and area studies in the World-War-II Army Specialized Training Program at Yale University. He graduated from Carson-Newman College (B.A. magna cum laude), Southwestern Baptist Theological Seminary (B.D.), and Southern Baptist Theological Seminary (Th.M.). From 1951 to 1989 he worked in Japan as a missionary of the Foreign Mission Board, Southern Baptist Convention. His assignments were varied: field evangelist, mission treasurer, research and design consultant, pastor, and seminary teacher. Parker also served as editor of the *Japan Christian Quarterly* and president of the Fellowship of Christian Missionaries in Japan. Prior to his retirement in 1989, he was a professor in the theology department of Seinan Gakuin University. Parker is the author of *Jonathan Goble of Japan: Marine, Missionary, Maverick.*